Sponsored Jointly By
The Greater Baltimore Committee, Inc., and
The Baltimore City Commission
on Historical and Architectural Presentation

Windsor Publications, Inc.
Woodland Hills, California

Previous page:
*This 1859 view of Baltimore Street looking
east from Calvert Street shows the wide variety of people
and vehicles along the city's main business thoroughfare*

ISBN 0-89781-009-0
Library of Congress Card Number: 80-50004
Windsor Publications, Woodland Hills, California 91365

Published 1980
Printed in the United States of America

First Edition

Baltimore

Baltimore
An Illustrated History

By Suzanne Ellery Greene

Contents

This page is dedicated
to all those who have participated
in the production of
BALTIMORE: AN ILLUSTRATED HISTORY

Chief Researcher & Illustrations Editor
DR. JEAN ARENDES WITTICH

Business Biography Writers
EVELYN DE GAST
LINDA JOHNS
CAROLYN SULLIVAN
NANCY WINTER

"The Surviving Past" Photographer
ALAIN JARAMILLO

Photo Researcher
ARLENE LAWSON

Windsor Publications Staff
DON L. SPRING, Editor-In-Chief
JUDITH ZAUNER, Editor
PAULA SCHOERNER, Business Biography Editor
CATHERINE WILLIS, Business Biography Editor
PHYLLIS RIFKIN, Assistant Editor
KAREN STORY, Assistant Editor
SHIRLEY LEUIN, Composing Editor
BERYL MYERS, Compositor
BARBARA NEIMAN, Compositor
LISA SHERER, Layout
MELINDA WADE, Layout
DEE COOPER, Production Supervisor
SANDY BELL, Production Artist
CONNIE BLAISDELL, Production Artist
PAT BRUCE, Production Artist
NANCY SCHMITT, Production Artist
JANET UYEDA, Production Artist
TOM ROBERTSON, Lithography

Special Thanks To
WILLIAM BOUCHER and DAGMAR MILLER
of The Greater Baltimore Committee,
and BARBARA A. HOFF of The Commission For Historic
and Architectural Preservation

This book was designed by
ALEX D'ANCA,
set in Benguiat and Optima types,
printed on 80lb. Mead Enamel
and bound by
WALSWORTH PUBLISHING CO.

Top:
A View of Gilmore's Holliday Street Theatre taken from an 1876 lithograph

Left:
A lithograph of the Pimlico Race Course taken from an 1875 drawing by Conrad Ludloff

Preface

When this book was proposed, I felt a sense of sheer excitement at the prospect of writing the first comprehensive history of Baltimore in many decades. Although more practical considerations like deadlines soon loomed large, the excitement has remained. With it grew a sense of frustration over all the material that had to be excluded because of the limitations of time and space. One major conclusion of this comparatively brief study is that many episodes mentioned here deserve more comprehensive treatment in the future. In the past decade, a group of local scholars has undertaken a wide-ranging investigation into Baltimore's past. I hope that this book will help stimulate interest in the numerous more detailed studies that will be published within the next few years.

I am greatly indebted to a large number of people who helped in the creation of this history: people who allowed me to use their unpublished manuscripts and who lent me photographs and rare books; scholars who read and critiqued various segments of the manuscript; members of museum and library staffs who went out of their way to aid the effort; and many others. Many individuals' names are listed in the bibliography and among the picture credits. To those names I add with gratitude: John Bereska, Muriel Berkeley, Andrew Carlson, Berkeley Cooley, Dean Esslinger, John Hankey, David Herman, Ronald Hoffman, Alain Jaramillo, James Kramer, Arlene Lawson, F. Pierce Linaweaver, Etta Lyles, Adelaide Mayo, Dagmar Miller, Avery Muller, Nancy Oppel, Edward C. Papenfuse, Constance Platt, Rosalie Russell, J. Brough Schamp, Pieter Van Slyck, Larry Sullivan, Lawrence Walko, and Helena Zinkham.

I cannot forego the real pleasure of thanking several other people individually. Catherine Grover, as both typist and critic, helped enormously. Gary Browne read the entire manuscript and served in the dual capacity of historian and editor. Don Spring, editor-in-chief of Windsor's series of urban histories, stuck with the effort and provided encouragement and support when needed. Jean Arendes Wittich, the chief picture researcher, often spent hours tracking down one rare picture. Her help has been absolutely essential. Without her, this book would be far less than it is. I want to thank my colleagues at Morgan State University and my friends who have understood my hectic schedule and the ways in which this history has impinged on day-to-day life. Finally, I dedicate this book with love to my daughter Jennifer.

Suzanne Ellery Greene
Baltimore, April 1980

A view of Baltimore as it looked in 1752. Originally a sketch made by early Baltimorean John Moale, it was later improved upon by several artists

Beginnings
1608-1773

I

Only one house stood on the land that would soon be Baltimore, when Maryland's colonial General Assembly passed the enabling act for the erection of a town on the north side of the Patapsco River. By 1773, when the annexation of eighty acres of Fells Point marked the pinnacle of a series of territorial additions, Baltimore had been transformed into a flourishing port city with a cosmopolitan population and a wide range of urban amenities. Despite the periodic flooding of the Jones Falls and the malarial marshes which had to be drained, many natural advantages boosted the growth of Baltimore Town. The safe and deep harbor facilitated shipping. Rapid streams from the northern and western hills provided abundant water power for milling. The fertile soil rendered the back country wealthy in agricultural produce. Fine forests which surrounded the town furnished timber for building material and fuel. Stone of good quality and mines rich with iron ore lay within easy hauling distance. The moderate climate spared the settlers the rigors of the harsh northern winters and the pestilences of the southern heat. Into this setting came several generations of pioneers who made a city out of the wilderness.

Captain John Smith recorded the first known description of the site of Baltimore Town in his journal of explorations of the Chesapeake Bay in 1608. Sailing up the bay from the mouth of the Patuxent River, he noted: "Thirtie leagues Northward is a river not inhabited, yet navigable; for the red clay resembling *bole Armoniack* we called it Bolus. At the end of the Bay where it is 6 or 7 myles in breadth, it divides it selfe into 4 branches, the best cometh Northwest from among the mountaines." His map shows the spot. The clumps of red clay along the river banks reminded Smith of the medicinal Armenian Bole used in Europe. By the time George Alsop drew his map in 1666, common

parlance had restored the Indian name Patapsco to the river that flowed into the Chesapeake Bay.

Most of the Indian place names along the western shore of the Chesapeake Bay came from the Algonquin dialect spoken by the Piscataway Indians who lived south of the site of Baltimore. It is agreed that Chesapeake meant "great shellfish bay." The meaning of Patapsco is uncertain, but the heaviest evidence points to a reference to the water's "penetrating a ledge of rock" as it flowed. Another opinion gives "back water," or "tide-water covered with froth" as the translation for Patapsco.

The place that became Baltimore had no permanent Indian settlements in the seventeenth century. The area did lie within the hunting grounds of the Susquehannocks whose villages were located further north, along the Susquehanna River, the "smooth-flowing stream." Game was abundant throughout Maryland and bears were especially plentiful on the site of Baltimore. The Susquehannocks ate their meat and used the hides, often whole, for clothing. They were tall and strong and presented an awesome picture attired in a bear skin with the neck hole cut below the animal's face. Susquehannock warriors were feared by the Piscataway and also the Eastern Shore Nanticokes on whom they made war, generally victoriously. Colonial settlers and the Susquehannocks experienced only minor conflicts until the Senecas began to push southward into Susquehannock territory. Squeezed between the attackers and the white settlers, the Susquehannocks sometimes fell upon the colonists.

Before the end of the 17th century, however, smallpox and tuberculosis, diseases new to America, had weakened the Susquehannocks so greatly that the few survivors, who moved to the area around Lancaster, Pennsylvania, became tributaries of the Senecas.

By 1700, only a few hundred Indians lived in any part of Maryland.

Baltimore County was established in 1659. At that time it stood on the frontier of Maryland, the proprietary colony of the Calvert family, granted by King Charles I to George Calvert, the first Lord of Baltimore, in 1632. Maryland's first settlers, who landed in the *Ark* and the *Dove* in 1634, had built their town, St. Mary's City, in southern Maryland at the junction of the Potomac River and the Chesapeake Bay.

At a time when many colonies and nations promulgated one official religion to which all citizens were supposed to adhere, Maryland had a Roman Catholic proprietor and passed the Toleration Act of 1649, which specifically allowed the practice of all Christian religions. Catholics, Protestants and Quakers all began to move to Baltimore County frontier area which included all of today's Harford and Carroll Counties and parts of Anne Arundel, Howard and Frederick Counties.

The General Assembly appointed county commissioners and people began to take out patents on the land. A few pioneering settlers came to the vicinity of the Patapsco River. In February, 1661, Charles Gorsuch, a Quaker, patented fifty acres at Whetstone Point, where Fort McHenry now stands. He agreed to pay the proprietor, Cecilius Calvert, son of Charles, 61 pounds per year for the use of the land. In June of the same year, David Jones hired Peter Carroll to survey 380 acres along the stream later named the Jones Falls in his honor. He built a house and is said to have been Baltimore's first settler. In 1663 Alexander Mountenay took up two hundred acres along Harford Run, where Central Avenue now lies, which he called "Mountenay's Neck." Later this same land was surveyed for William Fell. In 1668 Thomas Cole patented 550 acres that stretched from Harford Run on the east to what became Howard Street

on the west and Madison Street on the north. "Cole's Harbor" became "Todd's Range," when purchased by James Todd, and finally was sold to Charles and Daniel Carroll of Annapolis, who bought that land and more, totalling 1000 acres, in 1696. Also in 1668, "Timber Neck," lying between the current Howard, Paca and Eutaw Streets, was patented by John Howard. In 1706 Whetstone Point was made a port of entry by act of the legislature. Although a few ships loaded cargo there, it never grew into a town. In 1711, Charles Carroll sold 31 acres to Jonathan Hanson, who erected a mill, probably the first along the Jones Falls.

Life was very primitive in the country surrounding the future town of Baltimore. The best transportation was by water. A few narrow roads traversed the woods. A law of 1704 required that enough trees be cut down to widen the main roads to twenty feet and that roads be marked. The marking system consisted of cutting slashes in tree trunks: one vertical slash on trees beside a road leading to a church and three horizontal lines, two close together and one a bit higher, on roads leading to a county courthouse.

Courts were convened in every county. In 1715 the legislature authorized the Baltimore County court to hold sessions four times a year, on the first Tuesday of March, June, August and November. Court business must have been slight.

Little hard money circulated, either English or provincial silver. In trade with local Indians, some colonists used *peake* and *roanoke*, wampum made from shells. Most trade was conducted by barter or by using tobacco as currency.

In Baltimore County, most farmers rolled hogsheads of tobacco to either Joppa or Elkridge Landing for shipment and these towns grew, but slowly. Annapolis was the one city of wealth and

George Calvert, the first lord of Baltimore and first proprietor of Maryland, received the grant from King Charles I in 1632, almost a century before the establishment of Baltimore Town. Many generations of Calverts ruled the colony during the century and a half before independence. The coat of arms of the Calvert family provided the inspiration for Maryland's state flag

Left:
In his journal John Smith wrote the first known description of the site of Baltimore

Above:
In the exploration of the Chesapeake Bay and its tributaries in 1608, Captain John Smith sailed up "a river not inhabited, yet navigable," which he named the Bolus Flu. Indians who hunted in the region called it the Patapsco

status on the western shore of the Chesapeake Bay.

As more people settled along the Patapsco, the need for a town there became apparent. Thus in 1729, a group of leading citizens petitioned the legislature for the establishment of a town. The original plan called for the purchase of the land along the middle branch of the Patapsco belonging to John Moale, a merchant from Devonshire. Moale objected, because he believed that valuable iron ore was located there. Daniel and Charles Carroll then consented to the use of a portion of "Cole's Harbor" on the northwest branch of the river. The sole known resident was John Fleming, a tenant of the Carrolls', whose house stood near what is now the southeast corner of Charles and Lombard Streets.

According to the enabling legislation, sixty acres of land were to be divided into one-acre lots, to be bought in fee simple. The Carrolls would receive 40 shillings an acre in currency or tobacco at the rate of one penny per pound. The buyer of each lot would have to build a house of 400 square feet within 18 months or forfeit his land.

Commissioners were appointed to supervise the design of the town and the sale of lots. The act stated that these town commissioners were to hold their office for life and gave the group the power to fill vacancies as they occurred. The appointed commissioners were "gentlemen of consequence," including county justices of the peace and delegates to the General Assembly. Their names were specified in the act: Thomas Tolley, William Hamilton, William Buckner, Dr. George Walker, Richard Gist, Dr. George Buchanan, and William Hammond. The fathers of Gist and Hammond had apparently settled in Baltimore County in the late 1600s. Dr. Buchanan and Dr. Walker both practiced medicine.

County surveyor Philip Jones laid out the town. Three streets were built: Calvert Street; Forest Street, now Charles; and Long Street, which became Market, then Baltimore Street. Nine narrow alleys ran between the three streets. Lots were divided and numbered. On January 14, 1730, Charles Carroll, who, as owner of the property had first choice, selected Lot 49 at the corner of Calvert Street and the harbor basin. Philip Jones, with second choice, picked Lot 37, on the basin at the foot of Charles Street. Sixteen other men took up lots that first day, many along the waterfront. The process continued over the next few years with some of the claimants forfeiting their land because of failure to build within eighteen months. Ten years later, some of the forfeited lots were still in the hands of the commissioners. Baltimore was not an instant boom town. Its growth resulted rather from the ingenuity of its citizens and half a century of hard work.

Steiger's Meadows and Harrison's Marsh had separated Baltimore Town and the earlier settlement on the other side of the falls. In 1726, Richard Gist made a survey of the area for Edward Fell and reported three dwelling houses, several tobacco houses, an orchard, and a mill, Jonathan Hanson's, which stood by the Falls at the present Holliday Street. Edward Fell built a store. He found the area so favorable that he convinced his brother William, a carpenter, to leave Lancashire and join him. William arrived in 1730, and purchased "Copus Harbor," a 100-acre piece of land on Long Island Point. Here William built a house and a shipyard in the vicinity of Lancaster Street, establishing the industry that would bring prosperity and fame to the area later called Fells Point.

Settlers began to build on the land between Hanson's mill and Edward Fell's store, and in 1732 they petitioned the General Assembly to establish a town called Jones's Town. This was

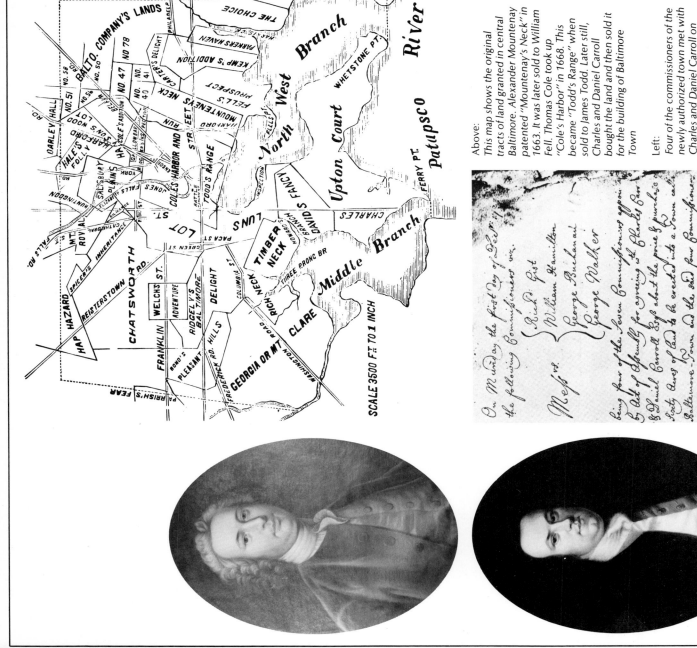

SCALE 3500 FT TO 1 INCH

Above:
This map shows the original
tracts of land granted in central
Baltimore. Alexander Mountenay
patented "Mountenay's Neck" in
1663. It was later sold to William
Fell. Thomas Cole took up
"Cole's Harbor" in 1668. This
became "Todd's Range" when
sold to James Todd. Later still,
Charles and Daniel Carroll
bought the land and then sold it
for the building of Baltimore
Town

Left:
Four of the commissioners of the
newly authorized town met with
Charles and Daniel Carroll on
December 1, 1729. They agreed
that the selling price for the land
would be 40 shillings an acre, or
tobacco at the rate of one penny
per pound

Above:
Charles Carroll of Annapolis and
Daniel Carroll, his brother,
agreed to sell part of their land to
be divided into lots for the
building of Baltimore Town

done in August and lifetime self-perpetuating commissioners were once again appointed to lay out the lots, which were to be sold subject to a ground rent. Like the first commissioners of Baltimore, these men were well established citizens and landowners. Major Thomas Sheridan had taken up land in the county in 1721. Captain Robert North, one of the original lot owners in Baltimore Town, commanded the ship *Content* in which he carried freight as early as 1723. Thomas Todd was the son and heir of Captain Thomas Todd who had purchased land in North Point in 1664. John Cockey (whose brother Thomas settled in the Limestone Valley on York Road and gave his name to Cockeysville) purchased land near the Patapsco in 1728. John Boring was a merchant whose father had bought land on Patapsco Neck in 1679.

The commissioners had Philip Jones lay out 10 acres into 20 lots along four streets. Three streets ran parallel with the Jones Falls, one alongside the water and the marsh. The only cross street, now Gay Street, was named Bridge Street after the citizens of the two towns built a bridge across the stream and marsh which divided them. A major civic undertaking for two eighteenth century villages, this bridge could bear the weight of carts and wagons as well as horses and men on foot. More than any other single factor, the bridge made the two towns one. A stipulation of the act of consolidation was that the bridge be public and be maintained by the county.

The merger of Baltimore Town and Jones's Town (also known as Old Town) officially took place on September 28, 1745 by an act that proclaimed "the same Towns, now called Baltimore and Jones's Town be incorporated into one entire town, and for the future be called and known by the name of Baltimore Town and by no other name."

Even before the merger, the small number of people who dwelt along both sides of the Jones Falls began to build the institutions and join in the physical development that would make Baltimore a leading American city in just a few decades.

The first institutional building project began with the vestry of St. Paul's Parish, who purchased Lot 19, the most elevated point of land in Baltimore Town, following an act of the Assembly passed in June, 1730, moving the seat of the parish to the new town from its former location eight miles east. After the return of Protestant monarchs to the British throne with the crowning of William and Mary, the Church of England had become established in Maryland in 1692. This meant that it was supported by tax money. Furthermore, at this time, the vestries were elected by all the voters in each parish. It is worth noting that the only other elected officials in the colony were the delegates to the lower house of the General Assembly.

The building project, directed by the rector, the Rev. William Tibbs, and his successor, the Rev. Joseph Hooper, continued until 1739, when the new church finally stood complete at Charles and Saratoga Streets. It was constructed with the first bricks manufactured in Baltimore — 100,000 of them — made by Charles Wells for 90 pounds. The early church must have been less than resplendent as William Tibbs complained in one of his reports that St. Paul's owned neither "Surplice, pulpit Cloth, Cushion, nor Plate for the Communion Service but Pewter." Time and money improved the situation. The growth of the parish also resulted in the opening of a school at St. Paul's under the supervision of the rector.

After St. Paul's was built, residents began to use brick to construct houses as well. Edward Fottrell, who came from Ireland and bought the land belonging to Jonathan Hanson and George Walker in 1741, built the first brick house in

Baltimore Town was divided into lots in 1730, and Jones's Town was divided in 1732. Charles Carroll, who had the first choice, selected lot 49. Philip Jones, with second choice, took lot 37. Richard Gist chose lot 48 across Calvert Street from Carroll's land. Captain Robert North selected lot 10. In Jones's Town, Edward Fell took up lot 4, William Fell lot 6, and Thomas Boone lot 5

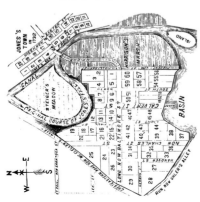

Above:
County surveyor Philip Jones laid out the town in 1730. Beginning at an oak tree located at the present corner of Charles and Camden Streets, he surveyed sixty acres and divided them into lots

Right:
The vestry of St. Paul's Church in 1731 purchased lot 19, the most elevated point of land. It took eight years to complete the town's first church, constructed with the first bricks manufactured locally

— OLD — ST — PAUL'S — CHURCH —
FIRST — CHURCH — ON — ST — PAUL'S — LANE.
FACING — PRESENT — LEXINGTON — ST — 1731.
ST — PAUL'S — PARISH — BALTIMORE.
ESTABLISHED : 1692 — AT —
BACK — RIVER.

town. It had freestone corners and was the first house stood at the location of the northwest corner of Calvert and Fayette Streets. Before Fottrell's arrival, all the houses and commercial structures were built of wood. This was the case in almost all colonial towns and resulted in one of the greatest common dangers: fire.

A number of fledgling towns were wiped out by fires that swept from building to building and could not be stopped. The wooden structures burned rapidly and fire equipment was almost non-existent. Baltimore's first attempt at dealing with this problem came in a 1747 regulation, promulgated by the commissioners, which stated that housekeepers would be subject to a 10 shilling fine if they did not "keep a ladder high enough to extend to the top of the roof of such house, or if their chimnies blazed out at top." If a fire did break out, all the townspeople grabbed a bucket and rushed to the burning structure. At night, two men led the way; one carrying a torch, the other blowing a fog horn. This system of fire protection left much to be desired. Baltimore pioneered an improvement when a group of volunteer firemen who had organized themselves into the Mechanical Company in 1763 six years later discovered a hand fire engine on board a Dutch ship that was anchored in the harbor. They bought the machine for 99 pounds (or $264) and named it the "Dutchman." The city could boast that it had a fire engine ten years before Boston and thirty years before Paris.

The other major problem faced by all colonial towns was filth. Early streets were unpaved, dusty on dry days and muddy on wet ones. Horses drew vehicles through the streets. Most animals roamed at will through the towns. Often hogs served as the only garbage collectors. Baltimore's first attempt to clean up the streets took the form of a law included in the act for the merger of Baltimore Town and Jones's Town. Section 11 required that, "None shall keep or raise any swine, geese, or sheep within the said town, unless they be inclosed within some lot or pen." A further sanitary regulation of 1751 revealed another problem: ". . . whereas several persons permit stinking fish, dead creatures or carron to lie on their Lotts or in the Streets near their Doors which are very offensive Nusances and contrary to act of Assembly the Commissioners therefore Order the Clerk to put up advertisements to inform such Persons that they are to remove them . . ."

The animals apparently continued to roam in and out of town. In 1746 the commissioners hired Captain Robert North to build a fence around the area that was formerly Jones Town. Then in 1748 the townsfolk generally took up a subscription to build a post and rail fence around all of Baltimore Town and to keep it in repair. Although many people said later that the fence was to keep out Indians, the subscription paper specifically referred to the prohibition on raising hogs or geese in town. Robert North, William Hammond, Thomas Chase, Richard Chase, Darby Lux, William Rogers and William Lyon all contributed 10 pounds while others joined them with smaller amounts. By 1750, the fence was complete. Two gates, one at the west end of Market Street and one at the upper part of Bridge Street, permitted vehicular entry. A smaller portal, at the top of Charles Street, near St. Paul's Church, opened for foot passengers. Protection against intruders, whether human or animal, apparently was of less concern to people than the cold winters. Within several years most of the fence had disappeared for use as kindling in local fireplaces. The town commissioners tried to prosecute the offenders but found that they had no legal authority to do so and therefore in November 1752 ordered the rest of the wood sold before it, too, disappeared.

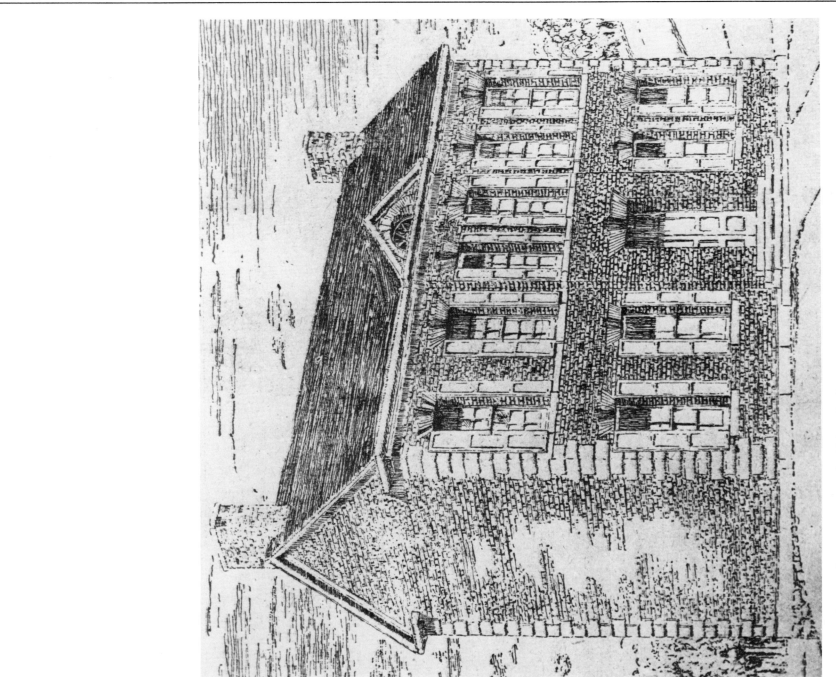

The first brick house with freestone corners, and the first which was two stories without a hip roof, was erected by Edward Fottrell on the hill close to where the Battle Monument now stands. It is said that Fottrell returned to his homeland, Ireland, before the Revolution, when his property was confiscated and sold to pay off a gambling debt

As the population grew, Baltimore Town could support a growing variety of industries and businesses. The success of Hanson's mill led to the establishment of other mills and soon bakeries. The manufacturing of bricks continued. In 1743, Captain Darby Lux opened the first tannery in town, on Exeter Street, and produced leather goods like harnesses, saddles, and buckets. In 1746 Dr. William Lyon and Mr. Brian Philpot joined as partners in the town's first drug store, located at Market and Calvert Streets.

In the late 1740s, Germans began to immigrate from Pennsylvania. The influx led to the opening of establishments for the spinning of wool and flax and the weaving of linens and wool, as well as the manufacture of leather goods. In 1748, two German brothers who moved to Baltimore Town from York, Leonard and Daniel Barnetz, erected the Town's first brewery, located at the southwest corner of Baltimore and Hanover Streets.

Most manufactured goods still were imported from England. The most common export was tobacco. Regular shipments of tobacco from Baltimore began in 1742. Farmers from throughout the area rolled their hogsheads of tobacco along the "rolling roads" to the port of Baltimore. By the year 1747 seven ships called at the harbor. In 1748, fifteen arrived, all bound for London. In 1750, residents built a tobacco inspection warehouse on the west side of Charles Street and began the construction of a public wharf. Individuals had been encouraged to build structures along the harbor by a section of the 1745 merger act which provided that "all Improvements of what kind soever, Either Wharves, Houses, or other Buildings, that have, or shall be made out of the Water, or where it usually flows, as an Encouragement to such improvers be forever deemed the Right, Title, and Inheritance of such Improver or Improvers, their Heirs and Assigns for ever." Most early

builders of wharves benefitted from this provision and added water territory to their holdings free of cost while at the same time increasing the town's capacity for trade.

Before beginning a chronicle of the phenomenal economic growth of the young town, it is worth pausing to look at Baltimore in 1752. A drawing and several documents from that year provide a good picture of the small town just before a major spurt of growth transformed Baltimore into a major city.

A boyhood drawing by John Moale, son of the man who declined to sell his land for the erection of the town, depicts each structure in the original Baltimore Town. The drawing does not include most of the former Jones Town or nearby settlements like Fells Point. In his sketch, John Moale showed twenty-five houses, four made of brick. St. Paul's, the only church, stands high on the hill. Two taverns, Payne's and Kaminsky's, hosted by William Rogers, lie closer to the harbor. The traditional gathering places for all colonial communities were the churches and taverns. It is fair to assume that Baltimore Town's two taverns and one church served that function here. Taverns especially provided a meeting place for people of high and low class, all religions, permanent residents and travellers bearing news. Of all the structures in Moale's picture, Kaminsky's Tavern stood the longest. The sketch also shows the Barnetz brothers' brewery, the tobacco inspection house, a barber shop and an insurance office.

Craftsmen generally ran their businesses from their houses. An early listing of the heads of household indicates the variety of services already available only 23 years after the founding of the town. This record of 1752 is considered one of the earliest census accounts put together in any American town. It tantalizes as much as it contributes but is, in any case, worth including. Thirty names appear, some with descriptions:

John Moale in 1752 made a drawing of Baltimore Town. This more recent version is based on his original sketch

This small wharf, Baltimore's first, was constructed at the foot of Calvert Street in 1750. The brig belonged to Nicholas Rogers

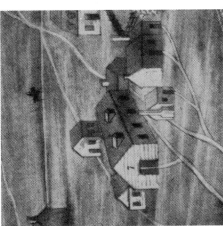

Baltimoreans built a tobacco inspection warehouse and paid an inspector to assure the consistent good quality of the town's first major export

"Capt. Lucas, Wm. Rogers, Nich. Rogers, Dr. Wm. Lyon, Thomas Harrison, Alex. Lawson, Bryan Philpot, Nick Ruxton Gay, James Cary (innkeeper), Parson Chase, Mr. Paine, Chris Carnan, Dame Hughes (the only midwife among English folk), Chs. Constable, Mr. Ferguson, Mr. Goldsmith, Mr. Jno. Moore, Mr. Sheppard (tailor), Bill Adams (barber), Geo. Strebeck (only wagoner, drove a single team), Jake Keeports (carpenter), Conrad Smith, Captain Dunlop, Jack Crosby (carpenter), Bob Lance (cooper), Philip Littig (whose wife was *accoucheuse* among the German population), John Wood, Hilt Stanwitch (laborer), Nancy Low, Mr. Gwinn."

People whose names do not appear in this census would include wives and children of the men listed, black slaves, and servants and convict slaves for life unless they were legally manumitted. Convict workers, often prisoners because of their political opposition to the English government or refugees from debtors' prison, had limited terms after which they became free. Many servants, under a 1638 law, worked for four years and then received 50 acres of land and a year's provision of corn. Slaves and servants frequently ran away. The advertisements for runaways printed in the Annapolis *Maryland Gazette*, the nearest newspaper, show that many such workers were not content with their lot and left to seek their fortunes elsewhere. No count of servants and slaves exists for Baltimore Town, but one such listing for the entire county in 1752 is presented by J. Thomas Scharf in his *Chronicles of Baltimore*. He enumerated: free whites, 11,345; white servants and convicts, 1,501; black and mulatto slaves, 4,143; free blacks and mulattos, 204. The population in town thus included a wide range

of people, many born in America and many immigrants of varied nationalities. The town's wealthier leaders shared English, Scottish and Irish backgrounds. Servants and convict workers came from those same countries. Slaves were of African ancestry. An increasing number of craftsmen and manufacturers were Germans, many of them recent immigrants from Pennsylvania.

By 1752 Baltimore Town was lucky enough to have a school, not as common an occurrence in towns south of Philadelphia as it was further north, especially in New England. Scharf wrote that the school was located at South and Water Streets and was kept by Mr. James Gardner. Either the demand for education was greater than Mr. Gardner could meet or something caused the need for a new teacher. In February and March 1752, the *Maryland Gazette* ran a notice: *"Wanted Person of a good sober Character, who understands Teaching English, Writing, and Arithmetic, and will undertake a School. Such a Person well recommended, will meet with very good Encouragement from the Inhabitants of Baltimore Town."* Any school in Baltimore during this period would have been limited to white children whose parents were able to pay tuition sufficient to support the teacher and maintain the building.

In 1752, Baltimore seemed little different from many small colonial towns with a church, a school, several taverns, and craft shops increasing as rapidly as the population could support them. The difference is that Baltimore grew into a city while hundreds of others remained small towns or faded into oblivion. The colonial towns that did succeed, like Philadelphia, New York, Boston and Baltimore, shared several characteristics. Their wealth was based on trade. All were situated on good natural harbors. All drew on productive hinterlands to which good access was estab-

Kaminsky's Tavern, one of the oldest meeting places in Baltimore

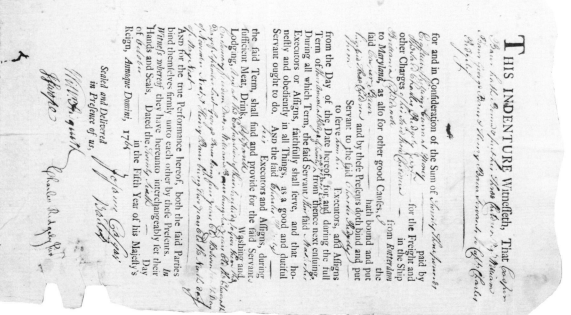

town as a whole. This mercantile leadership in Baltimore represented both descendants of early settlers and new immigrants. Some began with money, some with just a skill and an idea. The town and the surrounding countryside depended on each other for their growth. The hinterland produced the raw products which were either transformed into some saleable item or taken into town for shipment to another colony or to England. The countryside also provided a market for manufactured goods imported by the town's merchants and goods and services sold by its craftsmen and business people.

Baltimore's earliest trade, like that of much of Maryland, depended on tobacco. The real boom came because of the realization that another product, for which demand was even greater, could be shipped through Baltimore. That product was wheat, which was grown by farmers in Western Maryland and Pennsylvania. A Scotch-Irish Presbyterian who immigrated from Londonderry in 1745, Dr. John Stevenson, first recognized the potential. He and Captain Benjamin North joined forces and in 1758 shipped 1000 bushels of wheat to New York. Their small schooner, *Sharp Packet*, also carried one hogshead of tobacco, 15 barrels of flour, 16 barrels of bread, and one barrel of beeswax. A week after its return from the first voyage, the *Sharp Packet* sailed for Newport, Rhode Island with 900 bushels of wheat. William Lux, John Ridgely and others quickly joined in the profitable new export trade and Baltimore boomed. Soon ships sailed for the West Indies and Great Britain carrying wheat and locally milled flour and baked ship's bread. Mills sprung up rapidly, along both Jones's Falls and Gwynn's Falls, to meet the rising demand. Jonathan Hanson's original mill site, sold to Edward Fell, passed into the hands of William Moore and thence to Joseph Ellicott in partnership with

This documents the 1765 indenture by Casper Baur of his three children, ages two, four, and six, to Charles Ridgley. The children were indentured until they reached the age of twenty-one. Many parents sent their children to serve such apprenticeships so they could learn a marketable trade

lished early. And all enjoyed the leadership of a group of merchants and other citizens who recognized the potential and knew how to make it work, for their own profit as well as that of the

The Waterloo Inn, the first inn along the main road south from Baltimore, was a typical stage coach stop during the eighteenth century. It provided a respite from the very rough and dirty roads, as well as meals and lodging

John and Hugh Burgess. Joseph Ellicott returned to Pennsylvania but moved to the area again in 1772 and along with his brothers, John and Andrew, established the very successful Ellicott's Mills on the Patapsco River upstream from Baltimore.

The real secret to the success of the milling and shipping of grain and its products lay in the opening of roads between Baltimore and western Maryland and central and eastern Pennsylvania. The early roads made it easier and faster for the farmers to sell their grain through the port of Baltimore than through Philadelphia which was reached by a longer and more strenuous journey. From its earliest days, Baltimore was in communication with Annapolis and Philadelphia by the Great Eastern Road and the northern route of the post road used for inter-colonial mail. In 1745, citizens of Baltimore and York, Pennsylvania completed a wagon road connecting their two cities. In that same decade, roads were built from Baltimore to Reisterstown and on up to Gettysburg and Hanover, Pennsylvania. Later in the century a road was built going eastward, through Bel Air and Rising Sun in Maryland and Oxford, Pennsylvania. More and more farmers, many of them Germans, settled in the areas opened up by the new road system and shipped their products through Baltimore. Countryside and city prospered together.

Letters from contemporary residents and visitors written to friends and relatives attest to the success. After Governor Horatio Sharp visited Baltimore in February 1754 amid a great celebration of parades, a dance and fireworks, he reported to Lord Baltimore that the town "has the Appearance of the most increasing Town in the Province." William Otley wrote from Baltimore in 1761 to John Cook in Northumberland encouraging him to emigrate: " . . . this place is excellently situated for Trade . . . and

the Country about well adapted for Farming and Grasing, the Land in General Producing good Wheat and without Manure . . . and the demand for Wheat is Large, a good Quantity of Oats and Barley might be sold. Green peas might be Introduced for feeding Hogs Instead of Indian Corn which is the Bane of the Land . . ." Edward Cook, joining the effort to convince his brother to move to Baltimore, wrote that there were: "All sorts of Mechanicks . . . Masons, Brickmakers, Brick layers, Carpenters, Wheelwrights, Shoemakers, Barbers, Gardners, Sadlers, Watchmakers, Butchers . . . ," and that "Building is going fast on and [the town] cannot get workmen." He added that "Horses [are] dear, servants very scarce." Edward Cook noted some interesting figures: that seven years' service of a convict sold for 12-15 pounds and Negro slaves sold for 40-60 pounds, sometimes more. Compare to this a few consumer prices he recorded: wheat for 3 pence a bushel, beef and mutton for 2 to 3 pence a pound, and hay for 50 pence a ton.

William Eddis, the Royal Collector of the Port of Annapolis, wrote to friends in London ten years later in 1771: "This place, which is named Baltimore, in compliment to the Proprietary's family, is situated on the northern branch of the river Patapsco . . . Within these few years some scattered cottages were only to be found on this spot, occupied by obscure storekeepers, merely for the supply of the adjacent plantations. But the peculiar advantages it possesses, with respect to the trade of the frontier counties of Virginia, Pennsylvania, and Maryland, so strongly impressed the mind of Mr. John Stevenson, an Irish gentleman who had settled in the vicinity in a medical capacity, that he first conceived the important project of rendering this port the grand emporium of Maryland commerce . . . Persons of a commercial and enterprising spirit emigrated from all

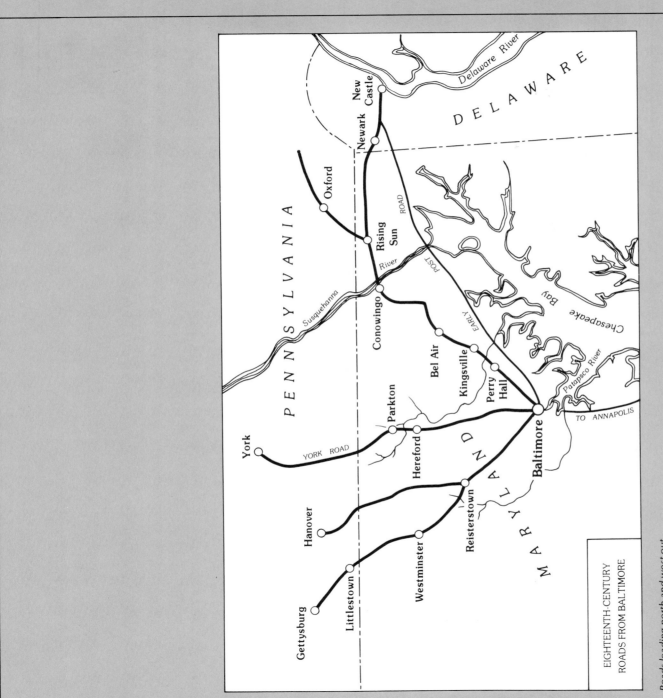

EIGHTEENTH-CENTURY
ROADS FROM BALTIMORE

*Roads leading north and west out
of Baltimore opened up a
hinterland rich in grain, which
local entrepreneurs began to buy
for export. The milling and
shipping of grain quickly became
the town's major source of
prosperity*

quarters to this new and promising scene of industry. Wharfs were constructed; elegant and convenient habitations were rapidly erected; marshes were drained; spacious fields were occupied for the purposes of general utility; and Baltimore became not only *the* most wealthy and populous town in the Province, but inferior to few on this Continent."

The town certainly did thrive, and not just because of the wheat trade. Baltimore also became a center of a growing iron industry. The area's first successful smelting enterprise, the Principio Company based in Cecil County, was founded in 1715 by a group of British iron-masters, merchants, and investors. The firm eventually bought 30,000 acres of land to supply wood for its furnaces and needed the labor of over 100 slaves. In 1731, a group of influential Marylanders, among them Daniel Dulany, the elder, Benjamin Tasker, Sr., Dr. Charles Carroll, Charles Carroll, Esq., and Daniel Carroll, established the Baltimore Ironworks Company. Ironworks expanded and the products exported through the ports of Baltimore and Fells Point proliferated.

Fells Point was laid off as a town in 1763, and divided into streets with English names like Thames and Shakespeare and alleys called Strawberry, Apple, Happy and Petticoat. Fells Point proved a formidable rival and major shipbuilding center. Following William Fell's example and determined to benefit from the combined advantages of the natural harbor and the nearby supplies of wood and iron, other men flocked to open more shipyards and to build wharves and warehouses. Benjamin Griffith, a shipwright from Cecil County, purchased a waterfront lot as did Captain Charles Ridgely. Samuel Purviance, who came from Ireland by way of Philadelphia, erected a distillery in Baltimore and bought a waterfront lot in Fells

Point. The shipbuilding industry and Fells Point prospered together and eventually made a major contribution to Baltimore's growth.

A group of new immigrants helped foster the shipbuilding industry. Many ship carpenters and mariners were among the Acadians who arrived in Baltimore in 1756. These French-speaking refugees from Nova Scotia left their homes in the Canadian maritime province when the British wrested control from the French. They were forcibly dispersed throughout the colonies. Longfellow wrote their tale in his narrative poem *Evangeline.*

The Acadians, having been forced to leave most of their possessions behind, arrived in Baltimore almost destitute. A public subscription was taken to provide aid. Some of the refugees were sheltered in private homes and a large number stayed at the two-story brick house abandoned by Edward Fottrell when he returned to Ireland. Eventually many of the Acadians settled along South Charles Street near Lombard in an area that Baltimoreans began to call French Town. Many built primitive cabins of mud and mortar, which they gradually replaced with frame houses.

Another group of refugees that swelled Baltimore's population in the mid-1750s came from Western Maryland following the defeat of British General Edward Braddock in the French and Indian War. Indian allies of the French pushed past Fort Cumberland and Fort Frederick to within 50 miles of the city, driving many fleeing settlers before them. Some Baltimoreans panicked fearing that they too would be subject to attack and boarded ships in the harbor, but the attack never materialized. Instead, Baltimore gained settlers who left the west or were prevented from moving westward and it grew accordingly as a market. The war effort occasioned a rather peculiar tax that remained in effect from 1756 to 1762. All bachelors 25 years

Priests who accompanied the refugees may have said mass in Baltimore for the first time

When the Acadians first arrived, many built primitive cabins of brick and mortar, which they replaced gradually with sturdier houses like this one

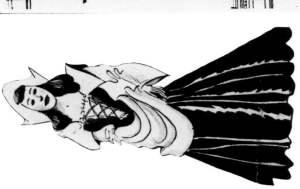

An Acadian woman in a costume which originated in Normandy

of age and over had to pay, 5 shillings a year if they had property worth 100-300 pounds, 20 shillings if worth over 300.

The growth in population spurred the increase of institutions and services that required the support of the greater number of residents. Churches, particularly, proliferated as various groups grew large enough to form a congregation and undertake a building project. In view of the large number of German immigrants, it is not surprising that they built the second church in town.

The first German Reformed congregation was founded around 1750. In 1756 they invited the Rev. John Christian Faber to become their pastor and began the building of a church just north of St. Paul's on Charles Street. The local Lutherans worshipped with them; then they built their own church in 1758 on Fish Street (now Saratoga Street). This congregation, the only Lutheran one until 1824, later built the church on Gay Street, the original Zion Lutheran Church, where services in German are still held. The church opened a school in 1769 where courses were taught in the German language.

When the Acadians arrived in Baltimore in 1756, the nearest Catholic priest resided 15 miles away at the Carrolls' Daughoregan Manor. They converted a room of Edward Fottrell's house into a chapel and the Rev. John Ashton came once a month to celebrate Mass for a congregation of 20 to 40 French and a few Irish Catholics. Around 1770, Baltimore Catholics determined to build a church on a lot at Charles and Saratoga donated by Charles Carroll. St. Peter's was not completed until 1783 because of financial difficulties and the intervention of the Revolutionary War.

In 1763, a group of Scotch-Irish Presbyterians, including Drs. John and Henry Stevenson, Robert Purviance, John Brown, Benjamin Griffith and William Spear, leased two lots at the corner of Fayette and Gay Streets and erected a small log meeting house. Several years later they purchased a lot at Fayette and North and built a larger structure.

Ministers of the fervently emotional evangelical Great Awakening conducted revival meetings in Baltimore. George Whitefield preached here in 1740. New denominations like Methodists and Baptists grew out of this movement away from Calvinist coldness and from the formality and corruption of the Church of England. Methodist leader Francis Asbury preached in Fells Point in 1772 and in the following year a group which included Richard Moale, Jesse Hollingsworth and George Wells built the first Methodist meeting house in Strawberry Alley in Fells Point. The Baptists also erected their first meeting house in 1773. It stood at Front and Fayette Streets. Quakers had lived in the area of Baltimore since its beginnings, but until 1781 their log meeting house stood outside the town limits on Harford Road.

Not only churches but large homes and a variety of public structures began to proliferate from the 1750s on, transforming Baltimore from a town to the city it had become on the eve of the Revolutionary War. In 1753, Baltimoreans, including John Stevenson, Richard Chase, John Moale, William and Nicholas Rogers, John Ridgely, Nicholas Ruxton Gay, William Lux and Brian Philpot, managed a lottery to raise money to build a public wharf. In 1754, great effort went into rebuilding after the Jones Falls flooded and washed away the bridge and most of the mills. The same year saw the erection of several famous mansions, among them Mount Clare by Charles Carroll the Barrister (a cousin of Charles Carroll of Carrollton) and Parnassus by Dr. Henry Stevenson (brother of John) along York Road. According to legend, this house was called "Stevenson's Folly" by townspeople jealous of

Bookplate of Charles Carroll, Barrister. From the library at Mt. Clare

Photograph of Mt. Clare painting on a chairback, probably done by John Findley, between 1800 and 1810. Begun in 1754, it is the only colonial house still standing in the area. It was the home of Charles Carroll, Barrister, and his wife, Margaret Tilghman

Charles Carroll, Barrister, a distant cousin of Charles Carroll of Carrollton, was a major investor in the Baltimore Iron Works and later a prominent leader in the protest against England. He served as one of Maryland's delegates to the Continental Congress and is credited with drawing up the Maryland Declaration of Rights and much of the state's first constitution. Painting by Charles Willson Peale

its elegance.

In 1769, Baltimoreans had cause to be thankful, when Dr. Henry Stevenson turned "Parnassus" into a smallpox hospital and began innoculating local citizens. Smallpox was one of the scourges of colonial settlements, capable of wiping out large numbers of people in one epidemic. Those who could, often fled rather than trust their fate to the as yet unproven vaccinations. In 1757, a smallpox epidemic in Annapolis had driven the members of the legislature to Baltimore to hold their sessions. In 1771, Dr. Stevenson advertised in *The Maryland Gazette* that: "he continued Innoculations the Year round after the most improved *American Manner*: his Patients are not at all confined to the House, nor disagreeably restrained in their Diet. Those who incline to put themselves under his Care, are requested not to alter their Way of living before they come to be innoculated, as a long Course of successful Practise has shown it hurtful instead of beneficial. Negroes are insured at five percent on their value." He noted further that twenty-two people who had been innoculated had recently been exposed to smallpox without contracting the disease.

Another edifice which served the city well was its first market, erected in 1763 with 3000 pounds raised by a lottery. An effort, in 1751, to raise funds by subscription had failed, so it was not until twelve years later that a majority of town commissioners, including William Lyon, Nicholas Gay, John Moale, and Archibald Buchanan, leased the land at the northwest corner of Baltimore and Gay Streets from Thomas Harrison and oversaw the construction of the two-story market house. Many colonial markets were built with a large hall on the second floor to be used for public meetings, dances, travelling shows and other entertainments. Baltimore followed this pattern. An ordinance of 1773 set the market days as Wednesday and Saturday from early morning till twelve noon.

One event that signaled the success of the town was the removal of the county seat from Joppa to Baltimore in 1768. When the move was announced, the townsfolk collected 900 pounds to pay for building the new courthouse. Court was held in the room over the market house until the new two-story brick building with a tall lookout and spire was erected high on Calvert Street, where the Battle Monument now stands. A whipping post, pillory and stocks stood in front of the courthouse and a jail was built a bit further out from town. The citizens of Joppa resented their town's loss in status and resisted Alexander Lawson's removal of the records with some violence. Despite that, Baltimore Town became the county seat.

The growth in population and status not withstanding, formal amusements remained scant until after the Revolution. Horse races were always popular and easy to arrange since they required neither a building nor special equipment. At least as early as 1745 fairs were held in Baltimore at which the main events were races. Once the market house had been constructed, indoor events could be planned. One William Johnson advertised in July, 1764; "For the Entertainment of the Curious, Will be Exhibited at the Market House in Baltimore Town, a Course of Experiments in that instructive and entertaining Branch of Natural Philosophy, called Electricity. To be accompanied with Lectures on the Nature and Property of the Electric Fire." This sort of spectacular lecture and also travelling exhibitions of oddities and freaks of nature provided a common form of entertainment during the colonial period.

The first known regular theatrical performance was produced by the British touring company of Lewis Hallam in a large warehouse at the corner of Baltimore and Frederick Streets.

Above Left:
Miniature of Henry Stevenson, M.D., 1721-1814. Born in Londonderry and educated at Oxford, he and his brother John arrived in Baltimore around 1745. He established a medical practice and introduced smallpox inoculation to Maryland

Left:
As the town grew, public buildings proliferated. Baltimoreans collected 900 pounds sterling to pay for a new courthouse when the county seat was moved from Joppa to their town in 1768. The courthouse stood high on Calvert Street, at the current location of Battle Monument

Above
Parnassus, the home begun by Dr. Henry Stevenson in 1763, stood near the northwest corner of what is now Eager Street and Greenmount Avenue. Often called "Stevenson's Folly" because of its size and pretentious appearance, the house was used as a smallpox inoculation hospital

Baltimore received the theatricals with such enthusiasm that the company constructed a small theater at the corner of King George's (now Lombard) Street and Albemarle. The repertory companies that toured the colonies produced standard British theatrical fare, plays by Shakespeare, Addison, Farquhar, Sheridan and others. Maryland never had the prohibitions against dramatic productions that the Puritan and Quaker colonies further north did and thus both Annapolis, quite early, and Baltimore later became centers of theatrical performance.

Colonial towns did not escape consumer fads and marketing ventures. Scharf in his *Chronicles* made the following notation for 1772: "In this year the first efforts were made in Baltimore to introduce the use of umbrellas as a defence from the sun and rain. They were then scouted as ridiculous effeminacy. On the other hand, the physicians recommended them to keep off vertigos, epilepsies, sore-eyes, fevers, etc. Finally, as the doctors were their chief patrons, they were generally adopted. They were of oiled linen, very coarse and clumsy, with rattan sticks, and were imported from India by way of England . . ."

In 1773 Baltimore grew both territorially and economically with the annexation of 80 acres of Fells Point. The unification of the two towns helped end their rivalry and joined their resources to the eventual profit of both. By the outbreak of the Revolution, Baltimore had become one of the colonies' foremost cities. Before beginning to trace the conflict which finally led to the War for Independence, it is worth pausing to look at Baltimore in 1773. The year was marked by "firsts" that signaled the continuing growth of the town.

In November 1773, the Assembly established the first Alms House and an adjoining Work House for Baltimore Town and County. Refugees from the frontier areas, widows and children, men without jobs and disabled persons had grown in number to the point where they were a burden on the town. The Alms House and Work House provided refuge for both white and black people who had nowhere else to go. The hope was always that temporary relief would allow the recipients of the public support to become self-sustaining soon again. The buildings were constructed on land bought from William Lux for 350 pounds (property values were going up), located on the square bounded by Howard, Eutaw, Biddle and Garden Streets.

The Assembly appointed a group of leading citizens as trustees: Charles Ridgely, William Lux, John Moale, William Smith, and Samuel Purviance of Baltimore Town, and Andrew Buchanan and Harry Dorsey Gough of the County. It is interesting to note the overlapping directorates that existed even before the Revolution.

A major first for Baltimore in 1773 was the establishment of the town's own newspaper, the *Maryland Journal and Baltimore Advertiser*. Publisher William Goddard brought out the first issue on Friday, August 20. The paper appeared weekly thereafter and provided Baltimore with a source of news and communication far preferable in terms of local matters to the copies of the *Maryland Gazette* previously imported from Annapolis. Goddard had printed the *Pennsylvania Chronicle* in Philadelphia from 1767 to 1773, when he was forced to cease publication because of his pro-Tory leanings. In Baltimore Goddard opened up shop on Market Street, set up his presses, and began producing his journal. The papers carried world and local news, features including kitchen helps and poetry, and a lot of advertising. Goddard travelled frequently and when he did, Mary Katherine Goddard, his sister, edited and published the newspaper. She later became the Postmistress of Baltimore, a job she held for 15

Umbrellas were introduced in Baltimore in 1772. Physicians recommended them to ward off vertigos, epilepsies, sore-eyes, fevers, and various other ailments

Baltimore's first post office on Front Street near Exeter typifies the small wooden structures built during the eighteenth century

When the Goddards arrived in Baltimore, they set up shop on Market Street, near South Lane

years.

Perusal of the early issues of the *Maryland Journal and Baltimore Advertiser* gives a good indication of what life was like just before the conflict with Britain. In the two decades since 1752, life had obviously become easier in terms of the availability of goods and services attainable locally. Benjamin Levy, for example, advertised that his store carried imported wines, spices, corks for bottles, tea, coffee, chocolate, buckets, pails, fine pickled salmon, Irish beef, rose blankets, English cloth, rugs, felt hats, silk, cloth umbrellas, and sundry other articles. Another shopkeeper, John Flanagan, advertised port wine from London, Lisbon wine, Malaga wine, West India and New England rum, tea, coffee, chocolate, allspice, ginger, raisins, sugar, indigo, cotton, soap, etc. Although weavers made cloth locally, Baltimore merchants continued to import cloth. In September 1773, Clark's Warehouse featured a newly arrived shipment of Yorkshire broadcloths which brought from 3 to 15 shillings a yard. Hugh Young was selling Irish linens for 10 pence to 3 shillings a yard.

Frequently the *Maryland Journal and Baltimore Advertiser* published lists of prices current in Baltimore. These included food products like wheat at 6 shillings 6 pence a bushel, corn at 2 shillings 9 pence a dozen, superfine flour at 20 shillings, West Indian rum at 3 shillings 6 pence a gallon, salt at 2 shillings a bushel, pork at 85 shillings a barrel, 100 feet of pine board for 7 shillings 6 pence, and cotton at 18 pence per pound.

Skilled craftsmen sold both services and products to the townspeople. Watchmaker Jacob Mohler maintained a shop on South Street. Christopher Hughes and Company, Goldsmiths and Jewelers, sold tea pots, flatware, buckles, rings, chains and combs in a shop at Market and Gay Streets. Francis Sanderson, a coppersmith, sold his own goods as well as

MARYLAND AND **BALTIMORE**

Containing the FRESHEST ADVICE.

Omne tulit punctum qui miscuit utile dulci. Hor.

(1) THE **MARYLAND JOURNAL,** AND THE **BALTIMORE ADVERTISER.**

both FOREIGN and DOMESTIC.

Libertas & natale solum, pulchrius aureola. Hor.

FRIDAY, AUGUST 20, 1773. [Vol. I.]

[AUGUST, M.DCC.LXXIII] [NUM. I.]

Opposite Page Left:
William Goddard came to Baltimore from Philadelphia in 1773 and published the town's first newspaper, the Maryland Journal and Baltimore Advertiser

Opposite Page Right:
Mary Katherine Goddard, William's sister and frequent editor of the newspaper, later served as Postmistress of Baltimore

Above:
The first issue of the Maryland Journal and Baltimore Advertiser, Baltimore's first newspaper, appeared on Friday, August 20, 1773

kettles, pots and pans imported from England. Although all these goods were available, they were fairly expensive, compared to the wages of a working man. At this time, a day laborer during the harvest earned 1 to 2 shillings a day. A regular farmhand earned 8 to 10 pounds a year. A teacher earned 15 to 30 pounds a year. (Twelve shillings equals one pound). Clearly only the elite could afford more than the necessities.

Many problems still plagued the young city. The streets remained unpaved and rather dirty. Fire continued as a major hazard although the Mechanical Company and its "Dutchman" offered more effective relief than had been available previously. The approximately ten doctors and Henry Stevenson's innoculating hospital couldn't remove the threat of fevers and epidemics which periodically swept through all cities, leaving many dead in their wake.

Crime troubled city residents even then. A September 1773 issue of Goddard's paper included this account of the robbery of a prominent Baltimore physician and druggist: "On Saturday night last, the house of Dr. John Boyd, of the Town, was broke open, and sundry goods taken away. The Thief or Thieves appear to have forced their Way through a Window, by first boring a Shutter with a Gimlet, and then introducing a small saw, with which an Hole was made large enough for the Admission of a Finger, by which the Key that secured the Window, was pushed out, and entrance obtained."

The list of stolen goods included clothing, surgical instruments and a pair of pistols. These apparently were sold around town as the article summarized: "Many of the Goods have not yet been recovered, but the Persons with whom they are lodged will, no Doubt, think it prudent, after this Notification, to return them to their Owner, without further inquiry, as they *now* *know them to be stolen goods.*" "Not only would

the holder of the goods know them to be stolen, but so would most of their neighbors who had read the article.

In 1773, Baltimore combined the characteristics of a colonial city and a small town. With a population of just under 6000, it was small enough that most people could still know each other. Certainly all the leading citizens and merchants and their families knew each other and probably most of the other residents as well. Although much smaller than the older cities like Philadelphia with 40,000 people and New York with 25,000, Baltimore offered a wide variety of goods and services to its inhabitants and was receiving widespread attention for its remarkable growth rate.

The town's population was quite cosmopolitan, including an increasing number of children and grandchildren of Baltimoreans, natives and immigrants with backgrounds in England, Scotland, Ireland, the west coast of Africa, Germany, and France. People spoke English or German, and a few spoke both. A wide variety of religious groups including Anglicans, Quakers, German Lutherans, followers of the German Reformed tradition, Roman Catholics, Presbyterians, Methodists, and Baptists, were represented. In 1773, Baltimore's first permanent Jewish residents settled. Benjamin Levy, the shopkeeper, and his wife Rachel and their son, Robert Morris Levy, who had been named for their good friend and future financeer of the Revolution, came from Philadelphia.

The war soon to come, with all its factionalization, would serve to lessen divisiveness based on religion and ethnicity. Baltimore would go into the Revolution with a cosmopolitan population typical of America's leading cities and a thriving economy based primarily on the success of the port. When the trauma of war ended, the city was ready to continue the pattern begun during its first forty-four years.

Before the Revolution, most luxury items were imported from England. These tea cannisters (right), for example, were imported by Charles Carroll, Barrister. The earthenware inkwell (lower right), made by Peter Perine, Jr., in 1793, typifies the simple, utilitarian manufacturing that went on locally both before and after the Revolution. By the 1790s, however, Baltimore was also producing finer objects like this coffeepot (below) made by John Walraven in his Gay Street shop

TO ALL BRAVE, HEALTHY, ABLE BODIED, AND WELL
DISPOSED YOUNG MEN,

IN THIS NEIGHBOURHOOD, WHO HAVE ANY INCLINATION TO JOIN THE TROOPS,

NOW RAISING UNDER

GENERAL WASHINGTON,

FOR THE DEFENCE OF THE

LIBERTIES AND INDEPENDENCE
OF THE UNITED STATES,

Against the hostile designs of foreign enemies,

TAKE NOTICE,

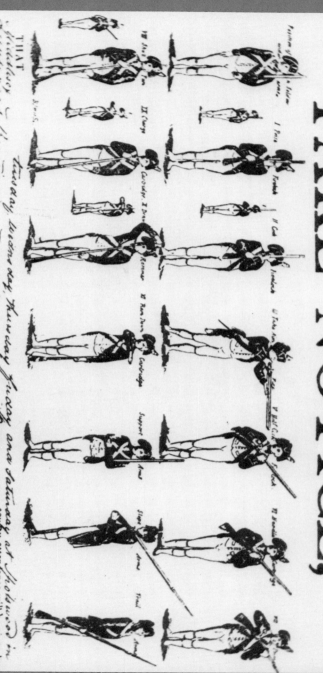

THAT such youth of spirit, as may be willing to enter into this HONOURABLE service, will have an opportunity of hearing and seeing in a more particular manner, the great advantages which these brave men will have, who shall embrace this opportunity of spending a few happy years in viewing the different parts of this beautiful continent, in the honourable and truly respectable character of a soldier, after which, he may, if he pleases return home to his friends, with his pockets FULL of money and his head COVERED with laurels.

GOD SAVE THE UNITED STATES.

War, Peace & War Again

1773-1814

II

The Revolutionary War resulted in independence from British rule and also a social and political transformation in the newly independent states. The conflict grew out of a combination of idealistic theories of the rights of the governed and specific interests of particular people living under British rule in North America. In Baltimore, as elsewhere, the decision to fight for independence rather than mere reform of the imperial system evolved through agonizing debate and the leadership of a fairly small group of men, many of whom had concrete stakes in the outcome.

In Baltimore, as in the colonies generally, the first widespread expression of discontent came in the wake of the French and Indian War which ended in 1763. The British chose the time when their troops were no longer needed for defense to commence programs of taxation to raise money to defray colonial expenses and regulation of trade and manufacturing to help bolster the troubled British economy. Colonists resented these intrusions, in part because of their effect on trade and manufacturing and in part because the regulations were new. Before Britain's warring with France and domestic economic and political problems prompted the interference, the colonies had been free, in reality if not in theory, to go their own way, largely unhampered by the mother country.

The post-1763 grievances generally exacerbated those already held by segments of the population of Baltimore and Maryland. A number of people were already dissatisfied with the enormous power held by the proprietor. The proprietors, Frederick Calvert, 1751-71, and his illegitimate son Henry Harford, 1771-76, and their governors, Horatio Sharpe, 1753-69, and Robert Eden, 1769-76, could exercise absolute veto power over the colonial assembly. This procedure was seldom necessary as the members of the Upper House of the legislature

received their appointment by the governor on the advice of the proprietor. Generally, these representatives came from the great landholding families. The most lucrative appointive governmental offices went to these same men. By the 1760s, the governor could distribute over 12,000 pounds a year in patronage positions. Kickbacks from these salaries were customary. The proprietor himself received an income of over 13,000 pounds from quit-rents, land offices, and trade duties. Especially during down cycles of the economy, this situation was hard for the many Marylanders who were not part of the proprietor's inner circle to accept.

In addition to money paid to the proprietor and his colonial officials, funds raised by a general tax went to support the Church of England. While many of the large landowners did belong to the Anglican Church, some were Catholics, Quakers, or members of other non-established churches. Many of the prosperous merchants of Baltimore Town were Scotch-Irish Presbyterians or Germans who belonged to the Reformed Church or the Lutheran Church. Most non-Anglicans resented being forced to support a church to which they did not belong. Furthermore, many Anglican clergymen not only failed to perform their duties but were known to be corrupt. One particularly notorious priest absented himself frequently to run a bawdy house in Philadelphia.

Roman Catholics held the additional grievance of having been disenfranchised and barred from public office and the practice of law since 1718. During the French and Indian War, Catholics had to pay double taxes. For a while, they were forbidden to construct churches and could say masses only in private homes. Unlike the very small number of Jews who faced similar political restrictions and the large number of blacks who faced even harsher restraints, the Roman Catholics numbered among their leaders some men of wealth and position, including Charles Carroll of Annapolis and, later, his son Charles Carroll of Carrollton.

To these and other existing grievances was added an economic crisis in the mid-1760s. This precipitated a dry run for the final battle which was joined a decade later. Economic events propelled Baltimore's merchants and those of other Maryland towns to undertake a protest, in which other troubled groups joined, against both proprietary rule and imperial regulation. By the 1760s, Baltimore's political leaders came predominantly from the merchant group. Even the owners of nearby large tracts of land were involved in commercial undertakings. Therefore, any events which affected mercantile interests in general had a particularly powerful impact on Baltimore Town.

A brief economic explanation must precede any comprehensible account of the political reaction. Maryland, like all the colonies, exported raw materials to England and imported manufactured goods and commodities, such as tea, not available locally. The most important cargoes loaded at the port of Baltimore and other Maryland docks included tobacco, grain, lumber and iron. Maryland currency and British pounds sterling were exchangeable at a rate that varied according to general economic stability and the import-export balance. When Maryland imported more than it exported, Maryland merchants owed British merchants and bankers the difference between the value of the imports and that of the exports. When Marylanders owed a lot of money to their British creditors and those creditors demanded payment, the exchange rate went against the Maryland currency and more Maryland money was required to satisfy the debt in pounds sterling. In 1764-65 tobacco prices sank. This meant that Americans received less money with which they could buy British manufactured goods. Many

merchants owed money on manufactured goods already received. British creditors demanded payments which American merchants could not meet. Britishers then withdrew credit or raised the interest rates charged to Americans. Baltimore merchant William Lux had his credit cut off in 1765. Charles Ridgely became involved in a long dispute over the amount of interest he owed. Merchants whose credit was cut off or limited could not import the goods they wanted and thus could not sell them here. Both merchants and the growers of exportable agricultural staples felt the squeeze.

This troubled economic situation prevailed when the British Parliament passed the Stamp Act in March, 1765. The Stamp Act levied the first direct, internal tax ever imposed on the colonies by Parliament. And it was a heavy tax: 3 shillings on every kind of legal paper such as contracts or wills; 2 pounds on school or college diplomas; 1-4 pounds for a liquor license; 10 pounds for a license to practice law; 1/2 pence a sheet on every copy (not issue) of a newspaper; 2 shillings an issue for each advertisement in a newspaper; 1 shilling per pack of playing cards; and so on. Furthermore, every document or sheet of paper subject to this duty had to bear a stamp sold by official distributors, whose jobs only added to the already high number of officials whose salaries colonists did not want to pay. Reaction in Baltimore, Annapolis and throughout the colonies came immediately. In Annapolis, a crowd chased the newly appointed stamp distributor, Zachariah Hood, from the colony and tore down his house. Maryland Attorney General Daniel Dulany wrote in the *Maryland Gazette* that Parliament should not tax Americans and suggested a peaceful boycott of English goods to remind England of the importance of the colonies to the imperial economy.

Baltimore merchants, like others through-

As a Catholic, Charles Carroll of Carrollton was barred from holding public office in colonial Maryland. He was a member of the local committees of Correspondence and Safety, a delegate to the Continental Congress, and a signer of the Declaration of Independence

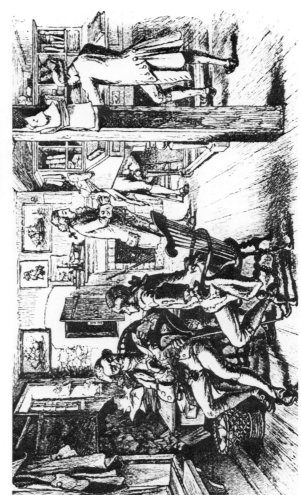

A typical day of business in a Baltimore mercantile establishment of the eighteenth century. Many of the city's Revolutionary leaders came from the merchant class

out the colonies, met to protest and in November 1765, implemented a program of non-importation of British goods. It must be noted that the poor exchange rate and the cutting off of credit had already reduced imports to the town. In February 1766, Baltimore merchants William Lux and Robert Adair organized the first Maryland chapter of the Sons of Liberty by converting the Mechanical Company, which since 1763 had been responsible not only for fire protection but also for policing, drilling, and mustering in Baltimore. Mechanical Company members came from the merchant and tradesman classes in Baltimore. This group provided the core of resistance both at this time and later. Lux and Annapolis radical leader Samuel Chase formed an alliance which proved powerful in the years to come. Sons of Liberty delegates from all counties assembled in Annapolis in early March to try to get officials to agree to transact business without using stamped paper. Protests like these finally resulted in the official repeal of the Stamp Act on March 18, 1766.

With repeal, the outbursts quieted, but the leaders particularly did not forget their wider-ranging grievances and were unwilling to let others forget or to allow their organization's collapse. Governor Robert Eden, after he took office in 1769, called the Baltimore Sons of Liberty the most "pronounced rebellious and mischievous organization in the province of Maryland." Yet things did quiet down for a while. Both wheat and tobacco rose in price. Exports increased, and that meant that imports also could increase and credit was easier to obtain. In the fall of 1766 an emission of currency in Maryland further eased the monetary situation by putting more currency in circulation. Baltimore's merchants did not forget, but prosperity assuaged their immediate distress. The contrast in the reaction to taxation by

Britain can be seen in Baltimore's response to the Townshend Acts of 1767, which imposed a tax on popular imports such as paper, glass, tea, and paint. At the behest of Philadelphia's merchants, Baltimoreans finally met in March, 1769. Leaders of the Sons of Liberty like William Lux, John Moale and Alexander Lawson won another non-importation agreement. This time, however, such a long list of exceptions were attached to the agreement that its impact was slight. In Baltimore, most merchants considered business too good to ruin for the sake of political protest. Because of the strength of protests elsewhere, Britain repealed all the duties except that on tea in April, 1770.

Another economic crisis preceded the final phase of the colonial rebellion which resulted in the outbreak of war and the declaration of independence. In 1771 and 1772 prices paid for American wheat, tobacco and corn began to decline. A general European depression in 1773 led English creditors to try to collect on all their American debts, just when the Americans did not have currency with which to pay. Economic chaos resulted. This led to the emergence in Maryland of a new political coalition whose quest for local economic stability resulted in their support for independence several years later. Leaders among the Baltimore merchants included William Lux, Charles Ridgely, and a newcomer to town, Samuel Purviance. Samuel Chase resurrected the Baltimore-Annapolis coalition around the leadership of Charles Carroll of Carrollton.

Several general points are crucial to understanding what went on in Baltimore in the 1770s. One is that by that decade the protest movement and the issues that moved its leaders had to be viewed as American, not local. Grievances about economic instability, the established church, and the corruption and wealth of colonial officials existed throughout

*Samuel Chase, son of the
Reverend Thomas Chase, rector
of Old St. Paul's, practiced law in
Annapolis during the years
immediately preceding the war.
In 1786 he returned to Baltimore
and ten years later was appointed
to the Supreme Court by
President George Washington*

the colonies. Certain groups in all the colonies sought a change in government in order to democratize political power, to bring the franchise or governmental control to groups who had been excluded because of property requirements or religious faith. Furthermore, throughout the years of conflict, an ideology had been put together which would find its ultimate expression in 1776 in the Declaration of Independence. Colonists from Massachusetts to Georgia read and talked about ideas of natural rights of all men, ideas that certain privileges and inequalities were wrong, theories of government that declared that all individuals had the right to choose their governors, the idea that people could be taxed only by representatives whom they had chosen. These theories went beyond specific complaints about taxes or the state of the economy and invoked a higher morality on the side of the rebellion. This mixture of economic strife and ideological protest took place throughout the colonies. The leaders, the decisions, the conflicts and the activities in Baltimore all formed a part of this national pattern.

Communication among the colonies played a vital role in forming the unity that was necessary for the ultimate victory. Baltimorean William Goddard, editor of the *Maryland Journal and Baltimore Advertiser*, made a major contribution to this communication when in 1774 he undertook the organization of a colonial postal system which would be free of the espionage practiced by royal postal officials. In Baltimore, the mails were collected and distributed at the *Journal* office by Postmistress Mary Katherine Goddard, William's sister. Communication among the revolutionary leaders meant that Baltimoreans could know and object to British policies not only in Maryland but throughout the colonies.

After Boston radicals dumped a boatload of taxed tea in their harbor in December 1773, the British closed the port of Boston until such time as the tea was paid for. Bostonians met and agreed to forego trade with Britain and passed a resolution urging other colonies to do the same. Sam Adams wrote to sympathizers throughout the colonies requesting support and aid. He wrote to William Lux in Baltimore, "As the very being of every colony, considered as a free people, depends upon the event, a thought so dishonorable to our brethren cannot be entertained as that this town will now be left to struggle alone. The town of Boston is now suffering the stroke of vengeance, in the common cause of America. I hope they will sustain the blow with a becoming fortitude, and that the efforts of this cruel act, intended to intimidate and subdue the spirits of all America, will by the joint efforts of all, be frustrated."

Baltimoreans met at the courthouse on May 25, 1774 and appointed a Committee of Correspondence to be in charge of inter-colonial communication. A second meeting held on May 31 resulted in a resolution to end trade with Britain and the West Indies. The group also called for a meeting in Annapolis of delegates from all Maryland and for a meeting of delegates from all the colonies in a general assembly. An enlarged Committee of Correspondence was appointed with Samuel Purviance as chairman. In June and July of 1774, Baltimoreans collected funds for the relief of Boston and Charlestown, Massachusetts and sent several vessels with gifts and provisions.

In June 1774 each county chose delegates to attend the general convention in Annapolis. Seven men represented Baltimore Town and County: Captain Charles Ridgely, Thomas Cockey Deye, Walter Tolley, Jr., Robert Alexander, William Lux, Samuel Purviance, and George Risteau. This Maryland Convention entered into general non-importation

Above:
William Buchanan, Baltimore merchant, served as commissary general of the Continental Army

Left:
John Smith with his brother-in-law, William Buchanan, established a shipping firm in Fells Point. He served as a member of the Committee of Correspondence and later as a state senator. His oldest son, Samuel Smith, became a well-known merchant, soldier, and statesman

agreements, made further collections for the relief of Boston, and appointed delegates to the all-colony First Continental Congress which would meet in Philadelphia in September. The convention chose Matthew Tilghman, Samuel Chase, William Paca and Robert Goldsborough. Although none of these men came from Baltimore, they represented the faction led by Charles Carroll of Carrollton which worked closely with the town's mercantile revolutionary leadership.

The Continental Congress recommended the appointment of committees in towns and counties throughout the colonies to enforce the non-importation agreements on which that general congress had also resolved. Baltimoreans assembled at the courthouse once again. All freeholders and others eligible to vote elected twenty-nine members to the town's Committee of Observation. The Committee predictably included Samuel Purviance who became chairman, William Lux who became deputy chairman, Robert Alexander, John Moale, William Buchanan, and Jeremiah Townley Chase. James Calhoun, who would later serve as first mayor of Baltimore, Mordecai Gist, William Spear, Dr. John Boyd, John Merryman and many others were also elected. Two Germans, Barnet Eichelberger and George Lindenberger, joined the predominantly Scotch-Irish and English merchants on the Committee of Observation.

One major effect the Revolution had on Baltimore was the integration of the German population into the political life of the town. Until this time, except for several members of the Mechanical Company and the Sons of Liberty, the Germans had formed a community apart from the English-speaking elite, valued for their skills, but not included in the power establishment and, for the most part, without the franchise. The pre-war protest marked the beginning of change in their position.

By the fall of 1774, violent incidents began to erupt throughout the colonies. The perpetrators and the opponents of violence reflected the division between radicals and conservatives within the protest movement. Although Maryland's leaders were generally cautious, the violent incidents were beginning to polarize the various factions.

The Maryland incident which received the most attention was the burning of the ship *Peggy Stewart* in October, 1774. The *Peggy Stewart* owned by James Dick and his son-in-law Anthony Stewart, arrived in Annapolis carrying seventeen chests of tea. In rampant violation of the anti-importation agreements (but well within the law), Stewart paid the duty on the tea preparatory to unloading it. The local committee suggested a general meeting of the citizenry to determine what action should be taken. Baltimoreans Charles Ridgely, Mordecai Gist, and John Deaver attended. The group decided to burn the tea and the vessel, which they did. The action represented a victory for the Annapolitan radical faction led by John Hall. Matthias Hammond, and Rezin Hammond. Charles Ridgely moved into the radical faction in his support of the burning. The more moderate Carroll-led group wanted to burn only the tea. From this time on, open splits between the conservatives, moderates, and radicals continued, with individuals frequently shifting sides. The moderates generally held the greater power and, except for isolated incidents, prevailed in Maryland throughout the Revolutionary period.

By the end of 1774, the Maryland Provincial Convention and local revolutionary groups clearly held control of the colony, despite the continuing nominal existence of the proprietary government. In December, the Convention undertook military preparations. All white males aged 15 to 60 were to be enrolled in companies, armed, equipped and drilled. A levy on the counties was to raise 10,000 pounds to furnish the militia with arms and ammunition. Baltimore County's share amounted to 930 pounds of which 72 pounds 7 shillings 6 pence was to come from Baltimore Town West and 26 pounds 12 shillings 6 pence from Baltimore Town East (Fells Point). These were the first of numerous similar levies. In January 1775 the Convention decreed that all who refused to support the militia would be considered "an enemy to America" and their names published in the *Maryland Gazette*. The first company raised in Baltimore called itself the "Baltimore Independent Cadets." Its captain was Mordecai Gist. By July 1775, three months after the fight at Lexington and Concord, seven companies were under arms in Baltimore. In the following year, two all-German companies were formed.

Clearly, confusion was a predominant characteristic of this period. A Continental Congress of delegates chosen by various revolutionary groups met in Philadelphia. The proprietary colonial government continued to exist in Maryland and to perform a host of routine functions, but the real power lay in the hands of a revolutionary convention and local committees of observation whose vast numbers precluded any centralized decision-making. Committee membership changed frequently. Militia companies springing up throughout the colony elected their own captains. On all levels, something had to be done.

During the spring of 1775, the Second Continental Congress began to organize its powers and lines of authority. One major step came in the appointment of George Washington as commander of the revolutionary forces. Washington passed through Baltimore en route to receive his command, spending the night at the Fountain Inn, Baltimore's most famous hostelry of the period. Even at that early date, an appearance by Washington drew out large cheering crowds.

During July 1775, the Maryland Provincial Convention began to bring some order locally. The Convention declared itself an official provisional government and adopted the "Articles of Association of the Freemen of Maryland" as its governing document. The Convention created a Committee of Safety to serve as its executive arm. This committee and its local branches were charged with the responsibility for military preparations and the administration of government. County Committees of Observation were to be elected to see that the orders of the Convention were enforced. In September, Baltimore County chose 37 members of its Committee of Observation as well as five new delegates to serve a one-year term in the Provincial Convention.

By the middle of 1775, the revolutionary leaders in Baltimore had established their positions. The men already mentioned as members of the various committees and as delegates to the Provincial Convention continued as political leaders for the duration of the war. Titles changed, the names of organizations changed, individuals differed on specific issues and on the extremity of measures to enforce loyalty, but the same men continued in power for the next decade.

From the middle of 1775 through 1776, several important developments took place. As fighting intensified, the army units became more tightly organized. In Maryland, during the summer of 1775, the Convention began to appoint battalion and field grade officers. At the session in December 1775-January 1776 the decision was made to appoint company officers as well. Many militiamen objected to the loss of the power to elect their captains. Service in the army already was a vehicle of upward mobility, politically if not economically. Because of their pressure and the necessity for loyal troops, the Convention finally granted the franchise to all militiamen.

Local committees began enforcing loyalty among the civilian population. In Baltimore, the Committee of Observation began a series of actions against people suspected of pro-British leanings. When merchant James Christie wrote in a letter to his brother that British troops should be kept in the colonies to maintain order, a guard was stationed at his house. He was then taken before the Convention for discipline and finally he was banished from Maryland.

Samuel Purviance led in the formation of the Whig Club, the aim of which was the expulsion of anyone not favoring the "American cause." "The Whig Club's activities were confined to the immediate area of Baltimore and did lead directly or indirectly to the departure not only of people loyal to England but also of those who took neither side in the war and those wrongly suspected of misdeeds. Dr. Henry Stevenson, founder of the inoculating hospital and brother of Dr. John Stevenson who sat on the Baltimore Committee of Observation, left Baltimore and joined the British Navy as a surgeon. He did not return until 1786, when passions had finally calmed. The Whig Club's most noted undertaking was the expulsion of editor William Goddard from the city for printing a controversial letter. It turned out later that Samuel Chase had planted the letter in order to publish a particularly strong rebuttal. The later safe return of Goddard could not undo the severe beating he received or the destruction of his offices and equipment. It is quite clear from this and other incidents that even the appearance of disloyalty to the patriot cause could be dangerous in Revolutionary Baltimore.

The Declaration of Independence was printed on page one of the *Maryland Journal and Baltimore Advertiser* of July 10, 1776. The official proclamation of independence took place at the courthouse on July 29. Baltimoreans illuminated the town that night and paraded through the streets bearing an effigy of King George III which they then burned.

Independence meant that all the states were obliged to write new constitutions. Maryland's Constitutional Convention met in August, 1776 and produced a rather interesting document. Each county sent four representatives to the Convention. Annapolis, as always, and Baltimore, in a tribute to its rising importance, were allowed to send two. Baltimore County sent radicals Charles Ridgely, Thomas Cockey Deye, John Stevenson and Peter Shepherd. Baltimore Town's delegates, Jeremiah Townley Chase and John Smith, as moderates were part of the political faction led by Charles Carroll of Carrollton. The moderates prevailed. The hottest issue was the franchise. Some radicals proposed universal manhood suffrage. The more conservative leaders of the state believed that only property owners had a stake in society sufficient to make likely their choice of capable rulers. The constitution of 1776 changed the property requirement for voting from 50 acres or 40 pounds sterling of visible property to 50 acres or 30 pounds current money or visible property. It established property requirements for officeholders: 500 pounds for members of the Lower House; 1000 pounds for members of the Upper House; and 5000 pounds for the governor. Of these, voters could elect directly only members of the Lower House. More than any other factor, this maintenance of control of the machinery of government by an economic elite rendered the Maryland Constitution a very conservative document.

Despite its conservatism, the Convention incorporated several democratic reforms into the document. It made the office of county sheriff elective, by a direct vote. It disestablished

Mordecai Gist, a merchant at the outbreak of the war, rose from captain of the Baltimore Independent Company to general in 1779. He was present at the surrender of British General Cornwallis at Yorktown

Fountain Inn, Baltimore's most famous hostelry during the Revolutionary period. George Washington and a great many other famous Baltimore visitors stayed here

John Merryman, whose ancestors had come to Baltimore County sometime before 1659, was a member of the Committee of Observation. He later served as President of the Second Branch of the City Council

the Church of England, which meant that no one church had greater privileges than all the others. It granted religious freedom to all Christians. (Jews remained disenfranchised, much as Catholics had been earlier.) It gave representation to Baltimore in allowing the town to join Annapolis in electing two delegates each to the Lower House. And, perhaps most surprisingly of all, the document placed no racial restrictions on the franchise with the result that free Negroes who met the property requirements, and a few did, could vote in Maryland until 1810 when a law limited voting and office-holding to white persons. On November 3, 1776, a Bill of Rights was accepted. On November 8 the Constitution was accepted. Elections took place. In March, the legislature elected Thomas Johnson Maryland's first governor and, the following day, the Committee of Safety officially surrendered its powers. Military victory was necessary to assure the permanence of the independent states, and that would follow after several years.

Articles in the *Maryland Journal and Baltimore Advertiser* reflect the wartime society in which Baltimoreans lived until British General Charles Cornwallis' surrender at Yorktown, Virginia in 1781. News from the battlefront and lists of the dead appeared prominently. When the state began confiscating Loyalists' property, advertisements for its sale appeared regularly. Pleas for enlistment, aid, provisions and equipment recurred frequently. Announcements of amusements such as fairs and theatrical performances disappeared during the Revolution. Such frivolities had been outlawed by the Congress so that energies and resources might be directed towards the war effort.

Maryland troops fought in New York, New Jersey, Pennsylvania, Virginia, the Carolinas and Georgia. The Maryland Line gained national fame as an effective fighting unit. Baltimore merchant and landowner John Eager Howard

was one of the best known field commanders. Another Baltimorean, James McHenry, received an appointment to General Washington's staff and later served as adviser to the French General Lafayette. Local militia units played the largest role in the defense of Baltimore, which luckily saw very little military action.

The first war scare hit Baltimore in March 1776 when the British sloop "Otter" approached, bringing some captured American ships with her. Baltimoreans feared a bombardment of the town. Captain Samuel Smith's company boarded the Maryland ship "Defense" under the command of Captain James Nicholson. Their surprise attack succeeded in chasing the "Otter" and recapturing the prizes. The incident hastened the completion of the city's defenses. Two hundred and fifty blacks were employed to erect a boom between Whetstone Point and the Lazaretto and to build batteries and mount guns. Beacons and signal stations were constructed along the banks of the Patapsco River and the Chesapeake Bay. Colonel Mordecai Gist took command of Fort Whetstone (later renamed Fort McHenry.)

The closest the fighting came to Baltimore occurred in August 1777, when the British fleet sailed up the Bay and anchored in the Elk River. Baltimore and Harford Counties summoned over 1000 militiamen. The British landed and began to march toward Joppa, but their goal was Philadelphia, not Baltimore.

The last scare took place in May 1779, when the British squadron entered the Chesapeake Bay and took possession of Portsmouth, Virginia. Baltimoreans, on full alert, removed records and portable valuables from town and waited. The British did not come, but sailed towards New York instead.

In the Revolution, as in most American wars, the army took in all able-bodied men and tended to level out some of the differences

By PERMISSION.

On THURSDAY EVENING, the Fifth of JULY, 1781,

MR. WALL,

From Annapolis, will present, at Mr. *Johnson's* Sail-Warehouse,
on Fell's-Point,

A new LECTURE on HEADS,
with Entertainments, viz.

AN EPILOGUE by Miss WALL, a Child of seven Years,

After the first Part of the LECTURE, she will sing an AIR, accompanied
by Mr. WALL, on the Mandolin.

An EPILOGUE on JEALOUSY,

After the second Part of the LECTURE, a SONG, by Miss WALL.

To which will be added,

A critical DISSERTATION on NOSES;

In which will be exhibited a *Roman-Nose*—a *Turning-up-Nose*,—a *Ruby-Nose*—
a *Blunt-Nose*—and Mother Gubbin's *Hook'd-Nose*, and *Chin.*

The whole to conclude with an EPILOGUE, addressed to *Everybody*, not
aim'd at *Anybody*, will be spoken by *Somebody*, in the Character of *Nobody.*

TICKETS at Three Dollars each.

To begin at Seven o'Clock.

No Persons to be admitted without Tickets, which may be had of Mr.
Lindsey, at the *Coffee-House*, on the Point.

BALTIMORE, *July* 4, 1781.

BALTIMORE: Printed by M. K. GODDARD.

between them. The need for brawn over-powered considerations of race, religion and class, at least to some extent. Baltimore's German companies have already been mentioned. Germans also served in English-speaking units. Nathaniel Levy, son of Baltimore's first Jewish residents, Benjamin and Rachel Levy, enlisted in the Baltimore cavalry and served under Lafayette. As enlistments slackened off around 1780, Maryland became the only southern state to recruit black soldiers. Before then, a number of black pilots sailed ships on the Chesapeake Bay and Maryland's rivers. It should be noted that many Maryland blacks supported the Loyalists because of Britain's promise of freedom to all slaves who served. Although some states further north matched this offer, Maryland never did. Financial encouragement was held out in a law of 1780 to lure all freemen, white and black, to enlist. Men who volunteered for three years service were to receive $200, fifty acres of land, and exemption from paying taxes while in uniform and for four years afterwards. A law of 1781 required the drafting of all able-bodied vagrants.

The army needed supplies and provisions almost as badly as it needed troops. Baltimore merchants sold grain and other necessities to the army and eventually made a good profit from those sales. Urgent situations called forth contributions without pay. Probably the greatest single outpouring of donations went to General Lafayette's forces as they moved towards Virginia for the final battles of 1781. In February, the army commandeered all wagons, carriages, teams of horses, drivers and vessels available in the Baltimore area to transport Lafayette's troops southward. Major James McHenry suggested that the French general seek the aid of local merchants. They established a procurement committee. Lafayette asked for loans of money and backed his request with a pledge of his personal fortune. Newcomers like Irish immigrant William Patterson and Jewish merchant Jacob Hart joined with merchants bearing such names as Rogers, Purviance, Carroll, Calhoun and McHenry in proffering money.

Before Lafayette's departure, Baltimoreans gave a grand ball in his honor. He took advantage of the occasion to extract one further contribution from the town's residents. An early historian wrote that when one elegantly attired lady observed that he looked sad, Lafayette replied that "I cannot enjoy the gayety of the scene while so many of the poor soldiers are in want of clothes." He gained his objective when, the next morning, the very ballroom became a clothing factory where many of Baltimore's most prominent women sewed uniforms for the French general who had charmed them all.

The Continental Congress met in Baltimore from December 1776 through February 1777. When Washington retreated across the Delaware River to Trenton, he left Philadelphia without defenses. The Congress, fearing an attack, moved to Baltimore and set up headquarters in a large inn built by a recent German immigrant, Jacob Fite, at the corner of Baltimore and Sharp Streets. The Congress elected two local ministers, Rev. Patrick Allison of the Presbyterian Church and Rev. William West of St. Paul's, to serve as chaplains. It appointed numerous Baltimoreans to perform functional and administrative jobs for the duration of the sojourn here. Many of the Congressmen objected to Baltimore's lack of paved streets and other amenities to which they had become accustomed in the well established city of Philadelphia. John Adams, however, wrote that he liked the town's spirited inhabitants. After two months, the Congress-men's own longing for Philadelphia and their hope to boost public morale led them to return

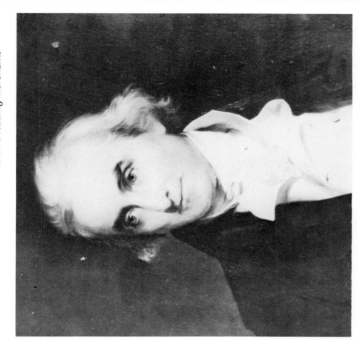

William Patterson, who arrived in Baltimore during the Revolution, lent his support to the war effort and soon became one of the town's leading merchants

Congress Hall where the Continental Congress met when the delegates fled from Philadelphia to Baltimore in December, 1776. Recently built by German immigrant, Jacob Fite, the inn stood at the corner of Baltimore and Sharp Streets

---

Baltimore, *Dec.* 31, 1776.

This Morning Congrefs received the following Letter from General WASHINGTON.

Head-Quarters, Newtown, 27th Dec. 1776.

SIR,

I HAVE the Pleasure of congratulating you upon the Succefs of an Enterprize, which I had formed againft a Detachment of the Enemy lying in Trenton, and which was executed Yesterday Morning.

The Evening of the 25th, I ordered the Troops intended for this Service, to parade back of M'Kenky's Ferry, that they might begin to pafs as foon as it grew dark, imagining we fhould be able to throw them all over, with the neceffary Artillery, by 12 o'Clock, and that we might eafily arrive at Trenton by five in the Morning, the Difrance being about nine Miles. But the Quantity of Ice, made that Night, impeded the Paffage of the Boats fo much, that it was three o'Clock before the Artillery could all be got over, and near four before the Troops took up their Line of March.

I formed my Detachment into two Divifions, one to march up the lower or River Road, the other by the upper or Pennington Road. As the Divifions had nearly the fame Diftance to march, I ordered each of them immediately upon forcing the out Guards, to pufh directly into the Town, that they might chrage the Enemy before they had Time to form. The upper Divifion arrived at the Enemy's advanced Poft exactly at 8 o'Clock, and in three Minutes after, I found, from the Fire on the lower Road, that that Divifion had alfo got up. The out Guards made but a fmall Oppofition, though, for their Numbers, they behaved very well, keeping up a conftant retreating Fire from behind Houfes.

We prefently faw their main Body formed, but, from their Motions, they feemed undetermined how to act. Being hard preffed by our Troops, who had already got Poffeffion of Part of their Artillery, they attempted to file off by a Road, on their Right, leading to Princeton ; but perceiving their Intention, I threw a Body of Troops in their Way, which immediately checked them. Finding, from our Dispofition, that they were furrounded, and they muft inevitably be cut to Pieces, if they made any further Refiftance, they agreed to lay down their Arms. The Number that fubmitted, in this Manner, was 23 Officers, and 886 Men. Col. Rohl, the commanding Officer, and feven others, were found wounded in the Town. I do not exactly know how many they had killed ; but I fancy not above twenty or thirty, as they never made any regular Stand. Our Lofs is very trifling indeed ; only two Officers and one or two Privates wounded.

I find that the Detachment of the Enemy confifted of the three Heffian Regiments of Landfpach, Kniphaufen, and Rohl, amounting to about 1500 Men, and a Troop of Britifh Light Horfe ; but immediately upon the Beginning of the Attack, all thofe who were not killed or taken, pufhed directly down the Road towards Burden Town. Thefe would likewife have fallen into our Hands, could my Plan have been completely carried into Execution. Gen. Ewing was to have croffed before Day at Trenton Ferry,

and taken Poffeffion of the Bridge leading out of Town ; but the Quantity of Ice was fo great, that though he did every Thing in his Power to effect it, he could not get over. This Difficulty alfo hindered Gen. Cadwallader from croffing, with the Pennfylvania Militia, from Briftol ; he got Part of his Foot over, but finding it impoffible to embark his Artillery, he was obliged to defift. I am fully confident, that could the Troops under Generals Ewing and Cadwallader have paffed the River, I fhould have been able, with their Affiftance, to have driven the Enemy from all their Pofts below Trenton ; but the Numbers I had with me being inferior to theirs below me, and a ftrong Battalion of Light Infantry being at Princeton, above me, I thought it moft prudent to return the fame Evening with the Prifoners, and the Artillery we had taken. We found no Stores of any Confequence in the Town.

In Juftice to the Officers and Men I muft add, that their Behaviour upon this Occafion reflects the higheft Honour upon them. The Difficulty of paffing the River, in a very fevere Night, and their March through a violent Storm of Snow and Hail, did not in the leaft abate their Ardour ; but when they came to the Charge, each feemed to vie with the other in preffing forward, and were I to give a Preference to any particular Corps, I fhould do great Injuftice to the others.

Colonel Baylor, my Firft Aid de Camp, will have the Honour of delivering this to you, and from him you may be made acquainted with many other Particulars ; his fpirited Behaviour, upon every Occafion, requires me to recommend him to your particular Notice.

I have the Honour to be,
with great Refpect, Sir,
your moft humble Servant,

G. *Wafhington.*

Inclofed I have fent you a particular Lift of the Prifoners, Artillery, and other Stores. RETURN of Prifoners taken at Trenton, the 26th December, 1776, by the Army under the Command of his Excellency General WASHINGTON.

Regiment of LANDSPATCH.

1 Lieutenant-Colonel, 1 Major, 1 Captain, 3 Lieutenant, 4 Enfigns, 36 Serjeants, 9 Drummers, 5 Muficians, 9 Officers Servants, 206 Rank and File.

Regiment of KNIPHAUSEN.

1 Major, 2 Captains, 3 Enfigns, 23 Serjeants, 6 Drummers, 6 Officers Servants, 258 Rank and File.

Regiment of ROHL.

1 Colonel, 1 Lieut. Colonel, 1 Major, 1 Captain, 2 Lieutenants, 1 Enfigns, 1 Surgeons Mates, 25 Serjeants, 8 Drummers, 4 Mufician, 9 Officers Servants, 244 Rank and File.

Regiment of ARTILLERY.

1 Lieutenant, 4 Serjeants, 1 Officer's Servant, 32 Rank and File.

TOTAL.——1 Colonel, 2 Lieutenant Colonels, 3 Majors, 4 Captains, 8 Lieutenant, 12 Enfigns, 2 Surgeons, 92 Serjeants, 20 Drummers, 9 Muficians, 25 Officers Servants, 740 Rank and File. 918 Prifoners.

6 double-fortified Brafs Three Pounders, with Carriages complete.

3 Ammunition Wagons.

As many Mufkets, Bayonets, Cartouch-Boxes, and Swords, as there are Prifoners.

12 Drums. 4 Colours.

Publifhed by Order of Congrefs,

Charles Thomfon, *Sec.*

General George Washington reported his first victory to the Continental Congress when it was meeting in Baltimore. Mary Katherine Goddard reprinted his letter in this broadside to that city.

The visiting Congressmen had noted the lack of amenities in Baltimore. Not all of them had been as perceptive as John Adams, who understood that the town's development had been cut off abruptly by the outbreak of the Revolution. The war effort precluded the large-scale use of money or manpower for local building. Once peace came, Baltimoreans could turn their attention to their unpaved streets, the housing shortage caused by the town's rapid wartime growth, and the massive financial and social disarrangements that had developed over the preceding decade.

Seeing contradictions appear in reports on Baltimore in the early 1780s. The local economy was confused at best. Wartime inflation had resulted in a distrust of paper money. The state of Maryland was bankrupt and could not pay its soldiers nor pay for internal improvements (public works). Individuals, who had not received their salaries as soldiers nor been paid for goods they sold to the army, could not pay their taxes. The sale of confiscated property, which was supposed to put cash into the state treasury, led primarily to lists of buyers owing Maryland for their new possessions. Debtors had no money to pay old or new debts. British ports remained closed to American traders. The severe winter of 1784-85 left the port of Baltimore iced in until March.

Despite all the confusion, Baltimore prospered. In 1782 its population had grown to approximately 8000. Grain exports had made Baltimore a boom town. In October 1783, American Revolutionary hero, General Nathaniel Greene wrote in his diary during a visit to the town: "Baltimore is a most thriving place. Trade flourishes and the spirit of building exceeds belief. Not less than three hundred houses are put up in a year. Ground rents is [sic] little short of what they are in London . . ."

The building boom extended to more than houses. Baltimore's first brick theater was erected on East Market Street, and that street was laid with cobblestones. A board of special commissioners was appointed by the legislature to oversee the construction and the paving of streets and the construction and repairing of bridges. The commission assessed landowners to pay the bill. The town commissioners put up street lights and established a permanent police force of three constables on duty during the day and fourteen watchmen at night. They levied a property tax to support them. The legislature appointed a board of port wardens to oversee harbor operations and the construction of new piers.

By 1784, the city had grown so large that Calvert Street had to be extended northward. The townsfolk saved their handsome courthouse, which stood at the top of Calvert Street, by taking up a subscription to pay for the underpinning of the building. The courthouse then stood twenty feet in the air and Calvert Street ran underneath. In that same year, the town built three new markets: Center Market, known as Marsh Market because it stood on the site of Harrison's Marsh; the Hanover Market at Hanover and Camden Streets for the convenience of the residents of Howard's Hill in the western part of town; and the original Broadway Market for the people of Fells Point.

The national government during the years 1781 to 1789 bore the title of the Confederation. The states were joined together only loosely and had no chief executive. Fear of creating a tyrannical government like the one they had just revolted against held Americans back from vesting any great power in a central government. This lack of any central authority made post-war reconstruction difficult. The economic problems that existed in Maryland plagued the other states as well. Both the Confederation and the state governments were bankrupt and in

Money for local improvements, like paving streets, was often raised by a lottery. This ticket was sold to raise funds for the paving of Howard Street in 1790

Warner and Hanna's map of Baltimore in 1801 shows the growth of the city in the two decades following the

Revolution. The outline of the original town is visible in the center, just north of the basin

debt to foreigners and American citizens alike. The states tried to collect taxes from citizens who had no money. Many soldiers still had not been paid or had been paid in worthless paper money. Many had had to borrow to get started again after the war. Since more money in circulation would make debts easier to pay off, debtors agitated for relief in the form of the issuance of paper money and also laws to stay foreclosures on mortgages. These same debtors were outraged that a few people were in a position to accumulate fortunes during this period. Men lucky enough to have hard cash speculated by buying up both the paper money and land confiscated from Loyalists at reduced prices. Local speculators included Jeremiah Townley Chase and Charles Ridgely. Creditors wanted debts paid off at full value. The financial conservatives feared the power of the masses. Even more importantly, they believed that economic stability was necessary if the new country was to succeed. Therefore, throughout the 1780s, a group of people who came to be called Federalists pressed for a stronger central government with a stringent sense of financial responsibility. Their opponents, who feared that a strong central government would become a dictatorship or a monarchy and who wanted economic relief for the ordinary people, soon were called anti-Federalists.

In Baltimore County, the demand for paper money led to control by anti-Federalists. Charles Ridgely, espousing the paper money position, became the political leader of the county. Thomas Cockey Deye, elected as an anti-Federalist legislator from Baltimore County, became Speaker of the House of Delegates for a brief time. The leaders of the radical Revolutionary faction tended to fall into the anti-Federalist camp. The moderate forces tended to lean towards the stability of a stronger government. Most of the merchants of Baltimore Town hoped for a stronger government which would foster trade and manufacturing as well as control the potential for violence that all recognized was possible because of the financial plight of many veterans and other debtors.

In 1787 a group of delegates from all the states met in Philadelphia to consider ways to revise and strengthen the Articles of Confederation. They ended by writing a new Federal Constitution which provided for a much stronger central government. The document, as it still stands, but without the amendments, was signed on September 17, 1787 and submitted to the states for ratification. The text appeared eight days later in the *Maryland Journal and Baltimore Advertiser* and touched off widespread local debate. Baltimore Town, Annapolis, and all the Maryland counties witnessed campaigns by candidates who wanted to be delegates to the state convention which would ratify or reject the new constitution. Baltimore Town sent two Federalists who favored the new Constitution, James McHenry and Dr. John Coulter, to the convention. The election was marred by frauds and violence on both sides. In Baltimore, where only 1,047 people were eligible to vote, 671 of those did not vote, and yet 1,050 votes were recorded. The Federalists won both in Baltimore Town as well as state-wide. The convention ratified the new Constitution, as did those of the other states, and the document stood as the basis for a new and stronger federal government. Baltimore celebrated ratification with a parade of some 3000 people. The procession terminated at Federal Hill, specially named for the occasion, where the marchers held a feast.

Federalist policies prevailed in the national government as it began to function under the presidency of George Washington. Secretary of

Baltimore about 1800, with the courthouse and the First Presbyterian Church in the foreground

The main city spring, located on Calvert Street near Saratoga Street. In the early 1800s the city landscaped the grounds and built the dome and a gatekeeper's house

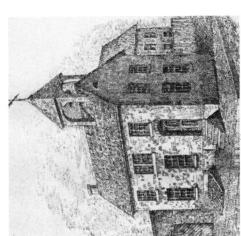

The old city watch located at the corner of Belvidere (now Guilford Avenue) and Orange Alley

the Treasury, Alexander Hamilton, successfully undertook a program to stabilize the economy and foster trade and industry. Baltimore benefitted from the national policies and Federalism received strong support. Baltimorean John Eager Howard, a Federalist, became governor of Maryland from 1788 to 1791. Federalist policies dominated the city and state.

Peace, stability, and prosperity brought a resumption of growth in the cultural life of Baltimore. Schools, libraries, and theaters sprang up during the post-Revolutionary years. The cultural expansion was not particularly systematic and was, for the most part, the result of the work of individuals and private institutions, not of the town's government.

Various religious groups and leaders worked at improving the town's educational offerings and made the most effective contributions. The Quaker Yearly Meeting voted in 1784 to support a school. In 1786 three local clergymen, Rev. John Carroll who would soon become America's first Roman Catholic bishop, Rev. William West of St. Paul's Episcopal Church, and Rev. Patrick Allison of the First Presbyterian Church, joined forces to establish a school to teach natural philosophy and classics and other higher level subjects. But by the end of 1787 the effort was abandoned. More successful schools were opened by the Zion Lutheran Church and the German Reformed Congregation. These taught German-speaking students in their own language.

By the first decade of the nineteenth century, several churches had organized schools which children could attend without paying the customary tuition. The Methodists began the Male Free School in the parsonage of a church on Light Street. St. Peter's Episcopal Church also operated a free school. The women of St. Paul's parish formed the "Benevolent Society of the City and County of Baltimore" to provide a free school for girls, especially orphans. Subjects included reading, writing, "cyphering," and needlework. The Society for the Abolition of Slavery and Protection of Free People of Color sponsored a school for black students. After the formation of the Sharp Street congregation of Negro Methodists, that church ran the school supported by a combination of tuition monies, donations from all the black churches, and gifts from Quakers and other abolitionists.

Several institutions of higher learning originated during the post-Revolutionary period. In 1791, Baltimore Roman Catholics established St. Mary's Seminary on Paca Street. In 1807 the College of Medicine of Maryland was opened, the first medical school in the state. From this partial listing, it is clear that a wide variety of individuals and institutions offered instruction in basic education and some fields of higher learning. Despite this, until the city's public school system was established in 1829, schooling was not available to more than a small percentage of students who could not pay their way.

The availability of books increased at about the same rate as that of schooling. While wealthy men had private libraries, circulating libraries to which readers subscribed made books available to far larger numbers of readers. Before the Revolution, Baltimoreans had to borrow books from a library in Annapolis. Then in December 1780, William Prichard advertised in the *Maryland Journal* that he was opening a bookstore and a circulating library of 1000 volumes. Four years later, William Murphy established a circulating library located on Market Street. The biggest library venture was another joint enterprise undertaken by three clergymen: Rev. John Carroll, Rev. Patrick Allison, and the new rector of St. Paul's, Rev. Joseph Bend, along with Dr. George Brown and several other wealthy citizens. In 1796 they

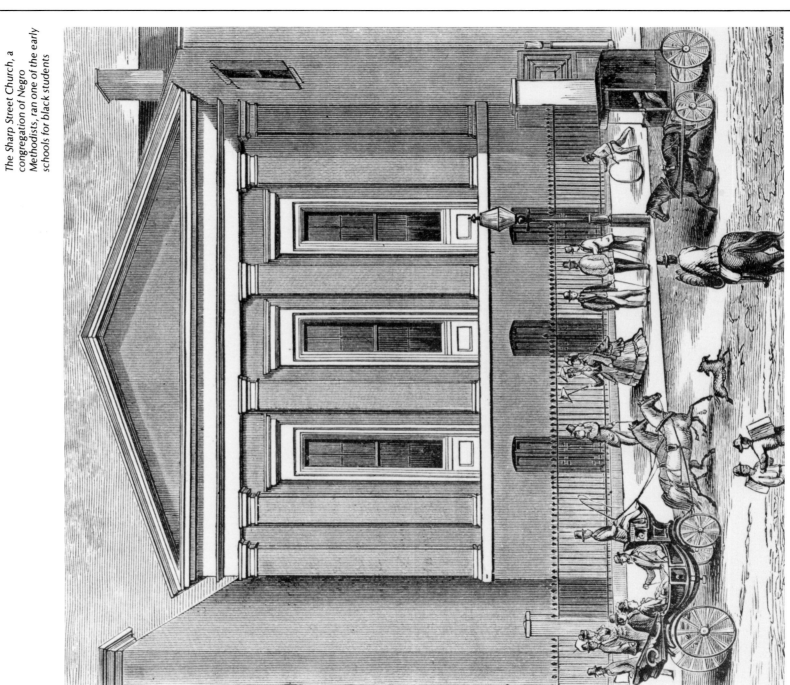

The Sharp Street Church, a congregation of Negro Methodists, ran one of the early schools for black students

incorporated the Baltimore Library Company. Members bought a share of stock in the library for $20 and thereafter paid $4 a year. The membership grew from 60 original subscribers to 300 by 1798. By 1809 the library had over 400 members and 7000 volumes. In 1799 the Society of Friends established a library by appropriating $100 for books and appointing a librarian.

Newspapers also increased in number. Baltimore's first daily newspaper, *The Baltimore Daily Repository*, appeared in 1791. Publisher Alexander Martin brought out the first issue of the *Baltimore American and Daily Advertiser* in 1799 from his shop in Fells Point. Unlike most early nineteenth century newspapers, the *Baltimore American* merged with other newspapers and has survived down to the present day. Most of the local papers that people read between the Revolution and the War of 1812 were short-lived. Most took clearly partisan political positions and were known to be strongly Federalist or strongly anti-Federalist. Their editors campaigned actively during elections and presented blunt opinions on major controversies. Objectivity was not even a goal for most editors.

Theaters, popular places of amusement in Baltimore before the Revolution, resumed operations as soon as peace permitted. In January 1782, the first brick theater in town opened on East Baltimore Street with a production of Shakespeare's *Richard III*. As was customary, a short farce, entitled *Miss In Her Teens*, preceded the program attraction. Box seat tickets sold for $1, seats in the pit (now orchestra) for 5 shillings and gallery seats for 9 pence.

In 1786, Lewis Hallam built the New Theater where his company performed. Seven years later, in 1793, William Godwin and Christopher Charles McGrath, managers of the Maryland Company, took over the building. Their opening

year program included *She Stoops to Conquer*, *The Beaux Stratagem*, *School for Scandal* plays: *Romeo and Juliet*, and at least three American by William Dunlap, and *A School for Soldiers* b by William Henry. Wignell and Reinagle, well-known producers, opened the Holliday Street Theater in 1794. Throughout this period, Baltimorean could see most of the popular British plays and some American ones as well. Baltimore was good "theater town."

Another art form that enjoyed widespread popular patronage was portraiture. Families o moderate means often commissioned minia tures, which were far less costly than the full sized portraits painted of wealthier subjects. Several Baltimore portrait painters achieved renown during the post-Revolutionary period Joshua Johnston, a black artist, produced portraits of many Baltimore merchants and their families, including the John Moales. Another portrait painter, Rembrandt Peale, achieved his greatest fame through the museum he opened on Holliday Street. In it he exhibited portraits of Revolutionary heroes and all sorts of artifacts: preserved birds, beasts, fish, Indian dresses and ornaments and, most notably, one of the mastadon skeletons that his father, Charles Willson Peale, had excavated near Newburg, New York in 1801. The famous architect Robert Carey Long designed the museum on Holliday Street, Baltimore's first. Lectures and the ever-popular flashy scientific experiments were presented several times a week. Band concerts and other performances were given on the intervening nights to draw an audience that paid an admission of 25 cents per adult and 12 1/2 cents per child.

The years after the Revolution saw a rebirth of a bright and widely varied social life in Baltimore. Horse-racing drew crowds of all classes. More elite patrons attended the meets

NEW THEATRE.

On Saturday, September 5, 1795.

Will be prefented a COMEDY, (never performed here,) called,

THE
CLANDESTINE MARRIAGE

Lord Ogleby,	Mr. Bates.
Sir John Melvil,	Mr. Green.
Sterling,	Mr. Morris. X
Lovewell,	Mr. Marshall. X
Canton,	Mr. Harwood.
Bruth,	Mr. Morton.
Serjeant Flower,	Mr. Francis
Traverfe,	Mr. Blissett,
Trueman,	Mr. Warrell,
Servant,	Mr. Darley junr.
Mrs. Heidelberg,	Mrs. Shaw.
Miss Sterling,	Mrs. Morris. X X X
Fanny,	Mrs. Marshall
Betty,	Mrs. Harvey.
Chambermaid,	Mrs. Francis.
Trufty,	Mrs. Bates.

To which will be added, a FARCE in two Acts, called,

THE SULTAN;
Or, A Peep into the Seraglio.

Soliman,	Mr. Morton.
Ofmyn,	Mr. Harwood.
Elmira,	Mifs Oldfield.
Ifmene, (with fongs,)	Mifs Broadhurft.
Roxalana,	Mrs. Oldmixon.

††† BOX, One Dollar—PIT, three fourths of a Dollar.

The Public are requefted *to take notice the doors of the Theatre, will open at a quarter before Six and Curtain rife at a quarter before Seven o'Clock precifely.*

Places for the Boxes to be taken at the Office in the front of the Theatre, on the days of performance from ten in the morning till three in the afternoon.

No admiffion without Tickets, which are to be had at the Office of the BALTIMORE TELEGRAPHE, at JAMES RICE's Book-Store, the corner of South and Market-ftreets, and at the OFFICE adjoining the THEATRE.

Ladies and Gentlemen are requefted to fend their fervants to keep places at a quarter before 6 o'Clock and direct them to withdraw, as foon as the company are feated, as they cannot on any account be permitted to remain.

No Tickets to be returned, nor any perfon admitted behind the fcenes, on any account whatever.

Vivat Respublica !

[BALTIMORE: PRINTED BY CLAYLAND, DOBBIN AND CO. MARKET-STREET.]

BALTIMORE THEATRE.
On MONDAY EVENING, April 13, 1812,
WILL BE PRESENTED THE COMEDY OF THE
Wheel of Fortune.

WRITTEN BY RICHARD CUMBERLAND, Esq.

Sir David Daw,	Mr. FRANCIS.
Governor Tempest,	Mr. WARREN.
Penruddock,	Mr. WOOD.
Woodville,	Mr. DOWNIE.
Sydenham,	Mr. CONE.
Henry Woodville	Mr. BARRETT.
Weazle,	Mr. BLISSETT.
Woodville's Servant,	Mr. HARRIS.
Officer,	Mr. LUCAS.
Jenkins,	Mr. DURANG.
Richard,	Mr. BRIERS.
Harry,	Mr. F. DURANG.
Mrs Woodville	Mrs. BARRETT.
Emily Tempest	Mrs. MASON,
Dame Duckley,	Mrs. SIMPSON,
Maid,	Miss PETIT.

After which will be prefented

(FOR THE THIRD AND LAST TIME) A CELEBRATED DRAMATIC ROMANCE, IN THREE ACTS, CALLED THE

LADY OF THE LAKE.

WRITTEN BY JOHN EDMUND EYRE.

(From the much admired Poem of that name, by *Walter Scott, Esq.*)

Performed at the Theatre Royal, Edinburgh, and the Philadelphia and Charleston Theatres, with the moft diftinguifhed fuccefs. with entire

NEW SCENERY, DRESSES AND DECORATIONS.

The Scenery defigned (exactly after the poem) by Mr. Robbins, and executed by him, affifted by H Warren and T. Reinagle. The Dreffes by Schroeder and assistants.

The Dances and Proceffions by Mr. Francis, affisted by Mr. Harris.

The Music by the celebrated Sanderson and Dr. Clarke, of Cambridge, and M. Pellesiere, the accompaniments by the latter.

SCENE FIRST DISCOVERS

LOCH KATRINE.

Several islands in perspective, scattered on the Lake, with a distant view of BEN VENUE and BEN-AN. A boat appears in the distance, which approaches swiftly, and Ellen alights from it.

Ellen,	Lady of the Lake,	Mrs. TWAITS.

INTERVIEW BETWEEN ELLEN AND FITZJAMES.

Fitzjames,	the Knight of Snowdoun	Mr. WOOD.

SCENE SECOND

THE BOWER.

Around the walls of this picturesque scene are hung *Battle-Axes, Targets, Broad words, Bows and Arrows;* several trophies of the fight and chase. *Irresistible Chorus;* "Huntsman rest, thy chace is done." The door is thrown open and Fitzjames enters conducted by Ellen. Chorus repeated, while the knight is regaled by Ellen and maids. The sounds of the *PIBROCH* (or gathering) are heard, which warn him to be gone. He views the approach of the clan of Roderick with concern from the window, takes his leave of Lady Margaret and the Minstrel, and presents Ellen with a ring.

Lady Margaret,	Mother of Roderick,	Mrs. BARRETT.
Allan Bane,	the Minstrel,	Mr. HARDINGE.

of the Hunt Club. The Baltimore Dancing Assembly attracted most of the town's upper class residents to its balls held at the Fountain Inn. Probably the most sensational social event of the entire period was the 1803 Christmas Eve marriage of Betsy Patterson to Jerome Bonaparte. Although Napoleon found the belle of Baltimore an unsuitable wife for his brother, annulled the marriage and summoned Jerome home to Europe, Betsy and her son, Jerome, stayed in town and Baltimoreans talked and wrote about the marriage for a long time afterwards.

Epidemics and fevers played havoc with life during this period, killing off large numbers of people with each recurrence. Many people moved to the country during the summer months in the belief that they could escape contagious diseases like yellow fever and influenza in the less densely populated areas.

Another preventive measure, generally unsuccessful, was the imposition of a quarantine against infected areas. A yellow fever epidemic in Philadelphia in 1793 evoked a quarantine on all vessels entering the port of Baltimore from that city. Any intercourse with Philadelphia was forbidden. Companies of the Maryland militia were stationed along the northern boundary of the state and at the major intersections of roads leading from Philadelphia. The militiamen turned away at gun point any traveller who might be carrying yellow fever. Despite the precautions the disease spread to Baltimore and recurred for a number of years. A hospital was opened on the site where the Johns Hopkins Hospital now stands to treat fever victims. The newspaper *The Federal Gazette* reported on one case where the doctor in treating a fever patient took 130 ounces of blood, gave 35 grains of mercury and rubbed in 12 ounces of mercurial ointment. In 1800, a Dr. J. J. Gireaud published his formula for the prevention and cure of

yellow fever: ipecac, rhubarb, columba, magnesia, kermes mineral, camphor, and nitre.

Despite the rather peculiar variety of treatments for yellow fever and other diseases as well, Baltimore's physicians undertook several projects that pointed the way towards the city's future leadership in medicine. In 1788, Dr. Charles Wiesenthal issued an appeal to the doctors of Maryland to put together a plan for the regulation of medical practices, to suppress quackery and restrict the profession to those who were qualified. As a result, a city Medical Society was organized and Wiesenthal elected president. Shortly thereafter, Maryland's doctors organized a State Medical Society. Local physicians conducted classes in their own homes and offices. Lectures predominated. In 1790, for example, the Medical Faculty announced the following lecture program: Andrew Wiesenthal (son of Charles) on Anatomy, George Brown on the Practice of Medicine, Lyde Goodwin on Surgery, S. S. Coale on Chemistry and Materia Medica, and George Buchanan on Midwifery. An attempt to teach anatomy by dissecting a cadaver failed. In 1788, when the city donated for research the body of Patrick Cassidy, an executed murderer, a mob snatched it away.

Permanent institutions began to appear in 1799 with the organization of the Medical and Chirurgical Faculty of the State of Maryland. Then in 1807 the College of Medicine of Maryland was incorporated. The college hired a faculty. Dr. John Beale Davidge erected an Anatomical Hall at Liberty and Saratoga Streets as a lecture and dissecting room. Once again the populace objected and showed it by tearing down the hall.

Along with their interest in teaching and regulating the practice of medicine, the town's doctors showed concern that medical care be available to the poor as well as the rich. Early in 1798, with the support of Baltimore's doctors,

The Maryland Hospital opened on the site now occupied by the Johns Hopkins Hospital to treat victims of yellow fever, a disease which plagued the city for many years

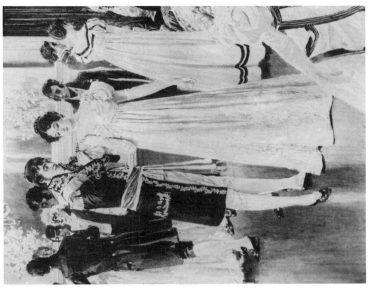

Betsy Patterson and Jerome Bonaparte at Grundy House, before Napoleon summoned his brother home to Europe

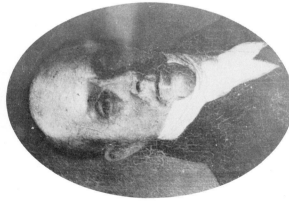

Dr. John Davidge first erected an Anatomical Hall at Liberty and Saratoga Streets in 1800 and offered courses in midwifery, surgery, and anatomy. The original hall was demolished by rioting citizens who objected to the dissection of corpses. Until a new medical school was built, lectures were held at the county alms house

the state legislature appropriated $8000 and later another $3000 for the construction of a City Hospital for the "sick and lunatics." A city council committee chose a site at Broadway and Monument Streets and the Baltimore General Dispensary opened there. The city and state augmented their responsibility for the poor in other ways. The poor laws became more specific. A law of 1793 allowed children of vagrants, of destitute persons and of convicted criminals to be apprenticed within Maryland. A law of 1799 provided for a payment of pensions to a limited number of persons in each county whose situation made the almshouse particularly unsuitable. Between the Revolution and the War of 1812, the almshouse provided shelter to an average of 230 people a year.

In 1793 a group of refugees who required an especially large amount of assistance arrived from Santo Domingo. Approximately fifteen hundred people who had opposed Toussaint L'Ouverture's rebellion against both slavery and French rule left when he won. One thousand whites and 500 blacks landed in 53 vessels, many of the refugees penniless. A benefit theater performance was given to raise money for their relief. A general subscription yielded $12,000 to help the destitute.

Churches grew along with the population of the city. Most denominations built either larger or additional churches during the years following the Revolution. In 1791 the Presbyterians erected a new larger church with two steeples on the lot of their old church on Fayette Street. When they installed an organ in 1811, a few families left the congregation in protest against the playing of music. The Baptists opened a second church in 1797, on Broadway near Pratt Street. In 1808 the Zion Lutheran congregation moved to its current location on North Gay Street.

The German Reformed Church experienced several crises during the 1770s and 1780s. The first resulted in a split in the congregation when one group tried to replace the original pastor, the Rev. John Christian Faber, with a new minister, Benedict Swope. The followers of Swope finally withdrew and built a Second Reformed Church on Conway Street at Sharp. In 1774, Mr. Swope was succeeded by the Rev. Philip Otterbein, a German who came to Baltimore from Lancaster, Pennsylvania. Otterbein's congregation in 1785 constructed the church which now bears his name and is the oldest in Baltimore. They built the two-foot thick walls with bricks discarded by ships which had used them for ballast. Otterbein led his congregation into the new Church of the United Brethren of which he was a founder. This denomination later merged with the Methodists.

The first German Reformed Church began a new building at Baltimore and Front Streets in 1785 with contributions collected from the membership. The following year, a flood of the Jones Falls swept away the walls before the new church was finished. In an early display of ecumenism, Mr. West of St. Paul's, Mr. Allison of the Presbyterian Church, and Mr. Kurtz of Zion Lutheran Church, all took up collections to aid in rebuilding the destroyed edifice. The church later rebuilt on a new site on Holliday Street further away from dangers of the Jones Falls.

Baltimore was the scene of major developments in both the Catholic and Methodist churches. Several events of national importance took place here shortly after the Revolution.

When the Revolution began, Maryland Catholics were still disenfranchised. The Constitution of 1776 removed the restrictions on their voting and holding office. For many years they had not been allowed to build public

Above:
Looking east across the Jones Falls in 1800. The wooden bridge along Baltimore Street was built in 1775. The large building is the First German Reformed Church which was bought by Christ Church (Episcopal) in 1796. The first Baptist Meeting House of 1773 is on the left

Far Left:
The new two-steeple First Presbyterian Church, on the northwest corner of the present Fayette Street and Guilford Avenue, was erected in 1791. When an organ was installed twenty years later, some families left the congregation in protest against the playing of music during worship

Left:
The first town clock was in the steeple of the new German Reformed Church

houses of worship. In the early 1770s Baltimore Catholics began construction of their first church, St. Peter's, and worshipped there before the building was finished. When the builder, John McNabb, went bankrupt, the principal creditor locked up the church. It was reopened during the war by a company of soldiers and remained in use. In 1784, the Rev. Charles Sewell became the first resident pastor. He was joined several years later by the Rev. John Carroll, cousin of Charles Carroll of Carrollton. John Carroll held an almost unique position in the combination of his elite family background and his priesthood. When the American Roman Catholic clergy met in 1789 and decided to request the establishment of an Episcopal see in this country, they also asked that John Carroll be bishop. He did become the first American Roman Catholic bishop, was consecrated in London in 1790, and returned to Baltimore where he served not only as head of the nation's Catholic hierarchy but as a local civic leader as well. St. Mary's Seminary opened in 1791. Fells Point Catholics formed a second congregation in 1792 and worshipped in private homes until St. Patrick's Church on Apple Alley was completed in 1796. In 1806 the cornerstone of the new cathedral was laid on land that had belonged to John Eager Howard, now the corner of Cathedral and Mulberry Streets. Two years later, John Carroll became the first American archbishop. It was appropriate and logical that the foremost city of Maryland, the only one of the original colonies granted to a Catholic proprietor should be the home of the first Catholic bishop and archbishop in the United States. Maryland's Catholics had been leaders in the revolutionary movement and now John Carroll from Baltimore led in the integration of Catholicism into the American religious mainstream.

Whereas Maryland's Catholics gained because of their association with the cause of independence, local Methodists frequently suffered because Methodism was often associated with the Tories. Although Francis Asbury favored the Americans, John Wesley spoke out against the Revolution. In addition, the known Methodist opposition to slavery led people to connect the denomination with the slave uprisings that took place during the Revolution. Despite all this, Baltimore, along with Philadelphia, was an acknowledged center of Methodism. After Baltimore Methodists built their second meeting house on Lovely Lane just south of Baltimore Street in 1774, Methodist preachers held several conferences in Baltimore culminating in the Christmas conference of 1784. At this meeting the American preachers voted to separate themselves from the Church of England and establish the Methodist Episcopal Church in America. This decision removed the taint of Toryism and also formally removed them from the jurisdiction of the new American Episcopal hierarchy. The Methodists chose Francis Asbury as their first American bishop at this same landmark conference.

The history of Methodists, Quakers, and American blacks is inextricably combined during this period. Methodists and Quakers had opposed slavery since before the Revolution. In Baltimore, both groups encouraged their members to free their slaves before and after the War for Independence. Quakers always stood in the vanguard of abolitionist activists, not only encouraging manumissions but donating substantial monies to schools for black students such as the African School opened on Sharp Street in 1793. The Baltimore Yearly Meeting several times enjoined individual members to educate Negroes.

Methodists, at a conference held in Baltimore in 1780, instructed their preachers to free their slaves and declared that Methodists should educate blacks and exert pressure for

Top left:
Archbishop John Carroll, cousin of Charles Carroll of Carrollton, was both America's first Roman Catholic bishop and an important civic leader in Baltimore

Left:
The Old Lovely Lane Methodist Church, where American preachers voted in 1784 to separate themselves from the Church of England and to establish the Methodist Episcopal Church in America

Top right:
The ordination of Francis Asbury as the first bishop of the Methodist Episcopal Church in America at the Lovely Lane Church, December 27, 1784. Asbury, who is kneeling, is surrounded by Thomas Koch, Thomas Vasey, Richard Whatcoat, and William Otterbein

Above:
St. Mary's Seminary, the Sulpician School founded in 1791, occupied the building on the right. When the college was established in 1805, the building on the left was constructed. The chapel, designed by Maximilian Godefroy, was dedicated in 1808. The tower, designed by Robert Cary Long, Jr., was not added until 1839

emancipation. Francis Asbury supported this. Methodists went a step further in establishing mixed congregations which sometimes heard black preachers. At the Christmas Conference of 1784, delegates passed a resolution declaring that slavery was "contrary to the Golden Law of God . . . as well as every principle of the Revolution." They declared that all Methodists should free their slaves. This proviso met strong opposition and was later revoked. Many manumissions did result, however.

Nationally as well as locally, the ideals proclaimed in the Declaration of Independence led many Americans to recognize the paradox of talking about the rights of all men, for which they claimed to have fought, and the continuation of the institution of slavery. In the northern states, the acknowledgement of the disparity was a major factor in the passage of laws abolishing slavery shortly after the Revolution. Although a number of Marylanders desired to do the same, the state legislature voted against abolition. It did, however, enact legislation making it easier for individuals to free their slaves.

In Baltimore in 1789 a group whose members included Samuel Chase, Luther Martin and Gerard Hopkins founded the Society for Promoting the Abolition of Slavery and the Relief of Poor Negroes unlawfully held in Bondage. Its several hundred members assisted runaways and free blacks and helped support the school on Sharp Street. Opposition eventually led to the disbanding of this group, but other societies followed. The combined activities of abolitionist societies and the legislation which eased the manumission process led to a significant growth in Baltimore's free black population. In 1800, 2,771 free blacks and 2,843 slaves lived in the city. By 1810, free blacks outnumbered slaves 3,973 to 3,713.

A large number of free blacks belonged to the Methodist Church. Methodist support for

abolition and the presence of black preachers in the integrated churches encouraged this membership. However, although many Methodist preachers supported abolitionism and integrated worship, many individual Methodists did not. As early as the 1780s, some white Methodists began segregating black worshippers in galleries so white members did not have to sit next to them. As the discrimination became overt, blacks began withdrawing from the mixed congregations. Baltimore with its growing free black population played a major role in the development of independent black churches and the leadership they required.

As early as the mid 1780s, blacks began withdrawing from the Strawberry Lane and Lovely Lane Methodist meeting houses. One group organized themselves into a prayer group and gave themselves the name of Bethel. Jacob Fortie, Caleb Hyland, Stephen Hill and other leaders helped build the group until it was large enough in 1797 to purchase an old building on Fish Street (now Saratoga) for use as a church. In that same year they drew up a formal letter of separation and soon joined with a group in Philadelphia to form the African Methodist Episcopal Church. While these developments were taking place, a Methodist church with a black congregation and a white pastor was formed and stayed within the Methodist Conference. The Sharp Street Methodist Church took over operation of the African School. Church and school prospered together. An outstanding black preacher from Sharp Street, Daniel Coker, moved to the Bethel A.M.E. Church and became its first ordained preacher in 1811. Coker had been born in Maryland to an English indentured serving woman and a black slave. He himself escaped slavery by running away to New York, where he met Francis Asbury and converted to Methodism. He returned to Maryland where he

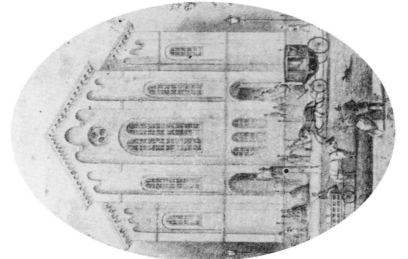
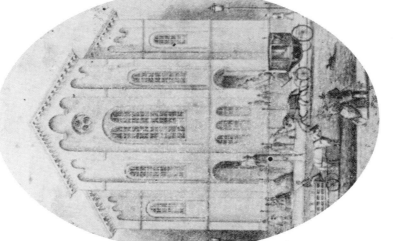

Top left:
The Bethel African Methodist Episcopal Church was formed by the first A.M.E. congregation in Baltimore

Top right:
Although increasing numbers of Baltimore's blacks became free each decade, slavery continued in the city and state until 1864. People were sometimes imprisoned in pens such as this one before a slave auction

Bottom right:
Many slaves ran away. Advertisements such as this one appeared frequently in the Baltimore Journal and Daily Advertiser and other local newspapers

remained hidden until he could raise the money to purchase his freedom. After rising to a position of prominence in Baltimore, he played a major role in the formal organization of the African Methodist Episcopal Church in 1816. The founding conference named Coker as first choice for bishop, but he declined and Richard Allen of Philadelphia was elected. The A. M. E. Church, which Baltimoreans had helped organize, has remained a major institution of the black community down to the present day.

Baltimore's Jewish community was by far the smallest minority group in town. The first United States census, in 1790, reported only six Jewish families, thirty-three individuals, living in Baltimore. By 1820 there were twenty-one Jewish families. One leader among these was Solomon Etting, who had opened a hardware store here in the early 1790s. In 1797 he and others petitioned the Maryland legislature for the right to vote and hold public office. Although Jews had participated in the patriot cause, the Maryland constitution of 1776 had limited suffrage to Christians and that restriction remained in force until 1826. Despite the limitation, Solomon Etting and his brother Reuben both were active Jeffersonians. In 1798 Reuben became captain of the Baltimore militia unit, the Independent Blues, and in 1801 President Thomas Jefferson appointed him federal marshal of Maryland, although he still could not vote. From the Ettings and others, it is clear that individual Jews were active in political and civic affairs. During this early period their numbers remained so small, however, that they had neither political clout nor enough men to form a synagogue or any other unifying institutions for the community.

During the post-Revolutionary period Baltimore's population remained heterogeneous. Residents spoke English, German, and some French. Several groups had become more fully integrated into politics and society because of the Revolution. Germans regularly were included in the economic and political power structure. Some Germans like Dr. Charles Wiesenthal began to move into positions of prominence based on their own individual skill and achievements. Catholics had gained full political rights. Bishop John Carroll, as a religious and civic leader, fostered Americanization of the Catholic church, cooperation with other local churches, and integration of individual Catholics into all phases of life in Baltimore. Other ethnic and religious groups did not gain such full inclusion after the Revolution. Jews, who joined in the economic and social life of Baltimore, were forbidden to vote or hold public office by the constitution of the state of Maryland. Baltimore's black population faced even greater hardships. Roughly half were slaves. Free blacks, although not entirely disenfranchised on the basis of race until 1810, faced growing discrimination by the white majority and were beginning to establish separate institutions to avoid that discrimination and to put some of the rights of leadership in their own hands.

Besides ethnic and religious groupings, Baltimore's population could be divided into two other major categories. Economically, a small group of wealthy men, many of whom by now could trace their families back several generations in Baltimore or the area nearby, stood above the ever growing numbers of craftsmen, mechanics, and shopkeepers who in turn outranked ordinary laborers. The Maryland constitution required the possession of a certain amount of property to enable a man to vote and an even larger amount of land or visible assets for a man to hold public office. This inequity and the problems of the economy in the immediate post-war period began to divide Baltimoreans into two political parties: the Federalists and the anti-Federalists who soon took on the name of

Above:
A formal presentation by Baltimore's black community to the city occasioned this sketch of the interior and congregation of Bethel

Left:
The Reverend Daniel Coker was the first ordained preacher at Bethel African Methodist Episcopal Church. Born in Maryland, he escaped slavery by running away to New York, where he met Francis Asbury and converted to Methodism. He was one of the leaders in the formation of the A.M.E. Church

their national leader and were called Jefferso-nians and later Republicans. Any account of Baltimore during the years between the Revolution and the War of 1812 must include consideration of these divisions. They were of central concern in the process of establishing an incorporated city government. The eventual reconciliation of the factions allowed the efficient functioning of the city that helped make possible the military victory during the War of 1812.

During the period of the Confederation, it will be recalled that most of Baltimore's leading merchants joined in the Federalist thrust for the new and stronger central government that they hoped would foster trade and manufacturing and sort out the financial chaos that had grown during the Revolution. In supporting the constitution, the Baltimoreans joined with the large land owners from the Eastern Shore and the area along the Potomac region who advocated Federalism as a bulwark against economic and social change. Once the economy had grown stable and Baltimore began to boom, it is not surprising that the alliance between the urban and rural politicians began to collapse. In fact, the two groups soon came into direct conflict.

The first big dispute centered on the location of the national capital. Baltimore, like many American cities, put in a bid to be chosen as the seat of the federal government. Merchants subscribed over 20,000 pounds in two weeks for public buildings. Baltimore's congressmen pushed their city. The Eastern Shore and Potomac leaders favored the site where Washington, D. C. is now located. After this time, Baltimore began to vie with the rural landed gentry for control of the state and to move out of the Federalist Party into the Jeffersonian camp.

The growth of Jeffersonianism took place throughout the nation, partly because Alex-ander Hamilton's economic policies had brought stability and partly because the anti-democratic excesses of the Federalists elicited immediate opposition. People feared the elitism of the Federalists and believed that it might lead to a monarchical government. Furthermore, many Americans believed that Federalist policies would lead us into another war. By the end of the eighteenth century, when fighting broke out between England and France following the French Revolution, the Federalists openly favored the British, because the United States had reopened trade with that country. Jeffersonians favored neutrality or took the side of our recent French allies. The fear of war led to the passage of the Alien and Sedition Acts. These controversial laws worked primarily against Jeffersonians. They extended from 5 to 14 years the time that aliens had to live in this country to be eligible for citizenship at a time when immigrants tended to vote for the Jeffersonian party. They outlawed all writing and speaking against the government or any of its policies. The first man convicted under this Sedition Act was a Jeffersonian newspaper editor from Vermont. Many similar arrests followed. The atmosphere became ever more repressive as the national elections of 1800 approached.

Baltimoreans clearly noticed the connec-tion between strong centralization of the federal government and loss of individual liberty. As early as the celebrations of President George Washington's birthday in 1795, even before the passage of the Alien and Sedition Acts, public speakers proclaimed different points of view. Everyone celebrated Washington's birthday with partying and drinking toasts. At the elegant Fountain Inn one patron offered a toast to "George Washington, the early, the uniform, the unshaken friend of his country." More typical was the toast offered at Winant's Tavern, where an obvious Jeffersonian volunteered, "The Congress of the United States. May they never be influenced by Despotic Council." At Evans' Tavern one man said, "George Washington. May he retain the Applause of a Free People." In the 1800 presidential election, Baltimore voted overwhelmingly for the victor Thomas Jefferson over Federalist John Adams.

Despite the widespread support of the national Jeffersonian party, Baltimoreans split on local issues, and the divisions tended to reflect people's economic status. The wealthy merchants fought to retain control against the opposition of those who wanted the power spread out among a wider range of citizens. The first big battle was fought over the issue of a charter of incorporation for Baltimore City.

Since the colonial period, Baltimore had been administered by commissioners appointed by the legislature. Residents could not elect local officials and had no legal control over them. During Baltimore's astonishingly rapid growth after the Revolution, when the town commissioners could not handle all the city's problems, special commissions and jobs proliferated. A commission on streets and bridges, a board of port wardens, and others shared the responsibility for running Baltimore. There was no central authority. Even such obvious undertakings as the building of a new market required a special act of the legislature. This system resulted in great inefficiencies.

In 1793, Baltimore's merchants began to work for a charter of incorporation which would allow the city to choose its own officials and set its own policies. The specific provisions would have consolidated power in the hands of the wealthy merchants. Under the proposed charter, citizens would vote only for a lower house of the city council. That group in turn would vote for an upper house, and the whole council would vote for mayor. This system of indirect elections was opposed by the artisans and shopkeepers who formed the majority in the Republican (Jeffersonian) Society, and by the Mechanics and Carpenters' Societies. Most of the working class residents of Fells Point also opposed the charter. They had the additional worry that one of the primary programs of the Baltimore merchants was the deepening of the harbor basin to allow big ships to dock there. Fells Point, with its deep harbor, had profited from the shallowness of the basin. Fells Point residents certainly did not want to be taxed to pay for the dredging of a competitive anchorage. All this opposition combined led the legislature to abandon the plan for several years.

The charter that was finally passed in 1796 was once again a product of the merchant aristocracy and served to centralize power in the hands of that group. Under the charter, Baltimore City was to be governed by a mayor and a two-house city council. The charter divided Baltimore into eight wards. Voters from each ward would vote annually for two members of the First Branch of the City Council. Every two years they would choose an elector. The board of eight electors would vote for mayor and the Second Branch of the City Council. (Direct election of the Second Branch began in 1808 and of the mayor in 1833.) Members of the First Branch had to be rated on the assessor's books at $1000 and members of the Second Branch at $2000. This system clearly concentrated power in the hands of the men of means.

Despite its undemocratic features, the charter increased enormously the efficiency in governing Baltimore by placing in local hands the authority over police powers, levying of taxes, surveying the city, locating and bounding streets, the preservation and deepening of the harbor (Fells Point residents were exempted from taxation for this purpose), and establishing markets and fire companies. For the first time in Baltimore, a locally chosen central government would be able to control and coordinate all these municipal functions.

The city was divided into wards which gave the advantage to the neighborhoods around the basin where the wealthier men lived. The outlying wards took in both a larger area and more people. The results of the first elections held in 1797 gave the overwhelming majority of offices to merchants and upper class gentlemen. Baltimore's first mayor, James Calhoun, was president of the Chesapeake Insurance Company, an elder of the First Presbyterian Church, and son-in-law of William Gist. Most of the councilmen were men of means. Revolutionary War leaders were elected to other major offices as well. Colonel John Eager Howard and Charles Ridgely of Hampton were chosen to be state senators. Since Howard was appointed to the U. S. Senate, David McMechan succeeded him in Annapolis.

As this elite group solidified its power, the opposition in Baltimore joined with allies throughout the state and began to press for universal suffrage, by which they meant giving the vote to all white men, 21 years or older, regardless of the amount of property they owned. This continued struggle did not affect the Jeffersonian alliance of either group within the city. In fact, the Federalists' national policies served only to strengthen Republicanism in Baltimore. An unsatisfactory treaty with England negotiated by John Jay drew opposition from residents of all ports. The Alien and Sedition Acts evoked a strong negative reaction from Baltimore's large numbers of emigrants from Germany, France and the French West Indies. Baltimoreans of Irish and Scottish backgrounds disliked the strong pro-British position of the Federalists. So, despite the feuding, Baltimore remained Republican.

One key factor in the endurance of the Republican sway in Baltimore was the enormous personal popularity of some of the men who became the city's political leaders. Men acceptable to both factions moved into positions of power and maintained party unity. Foremost among these stood General Samuel Smith. A wealthy merchant who cultivated and won over artisans and workers, he also maintained a staunch following among members of the militia. A significant lieutenant of Smith's was Edward Johnson, son of a Baltimore physician, and owner of a brewery in Old Town. Although his assessed value was $2,088 in 1798, he lived near his brewery and enjoyed close relations with many people in Old Town and Fells Point. Other Jeffersonian party leaders resembled Johnson in that their financial worth was considerable but they came from outside the old merchant elite. Among these were: Robert Steuart, a stonecutter; Adam Fonerden, a manufacturer of wool and cotton and president of the Mechanical Company; Joseph Biays, a shipjoiner; and Cumberland Dugan, a ropemaker and tanner. The political coalition oversaw the continuing growth of Baltimore that took place during the late eighteenth and early nineteenth centuries. It also successfully led the defense of the city the only time it ever faced foreign attack, during the War of 1812.

The causes of the War of 1812 have been debated since it was fought. Opponents said that a war fever had caught hold of a group of young Congressmen who used the war as an excuse for territorial aggrandizement and their own political advancement. Supporters of the war claimed that we had to fight England in order to reaffirm our rights as a truly independent nation. Certainly, most of the conflict that led up to the fighting took place because of the British failure to recognize American rights as neutrals while they were engaged in warfare against Napoleon.

Far Left:
Edward Johnson, a close political ally of Samuel Smith and mayor during the War of 1812, held office when the city began to illuminate the streets by gas. During his administration the city acquired the fire plugs of the Baltimore Water Company

Left:
General Samuel Smith, a military leader in the Revolution, was responsible for the defense of Baltimore during the War of 1812. A leading Jacksonian, Smith combined his martial skills, his political powers, and his personal popularity in this successful effort

Above:
Water piped through fire plugs greatly increased the efficiency of fire fighters such as these. The volunteer companies did continue to operate independently and often in competition with one another

Right:
James Calhoun, a native of Carlyle, Pennsylvania, was one of Baltimore's leading merchants at the time of the Revolution. His wife, Ann Gist, came from an old Baltimore family. He was a member of the Sons of Liberty and the Committee of Observation and later a Deputy to the Commissary General of the Continental Army. When Calhoun first became mayor, funds to run the city had to be raised by lottery until taxes were due

Because of their war with France, the British tried to stop American ships and to impress into service in their navy sailors whom they claimed to be British subjects. More importantly, British and French efforts combined resulted in practical strangulation of American trade. American ships were seized by England if they sailed first to the Continent without stopping in England first for inspection. They were seized by the French if they had any dealings with England, including stopping for inspection.

Discontent rose to war fever in June 1807, when the British ship, the *H.M.S. Leopard*, fired on the Baltimore-built sloop, the *Chesapeake*, whose captain had refused the British permission to board. The British, having gained entry by force, proceeded to impress four sailors. In Baltimore, local leaders formed a Committee of Correspondence headed by General Samuel Smith. War did not come then, however. President Thomas Jefferson, believing that the young nation was not strong enough to wage war against Britain, persuaded Congress in December 1807 to invoke an embargo on all trade. This had the effect of removing American ships from places where they could be shot at or boarded.

The Jeffersonian Embargo also inflicted huge damage on the American economy. Baltimore's exports sank from $7,601,300 in 1805 to $1,904,700 in 1808. Merchants tended to support the Embargo in hopes of gaining a permanent solution. Harder hit than the merchants, many of whom had substantial assets on which to fall back, were the farmers who had no market for their wheat. Even after the Embargo's repeal early in 1809, trade did not pick up to its former level.

The continuing conflict finally led to an American declaration of war against England on June 18, 1812. Ironically, the British government had repealed its orders in council on restrictions on neutral shipping two days before, but word of this had not yet reached the United States. By the time it did, the war had already begun. The war split the nation. Many Federalists continued to speak against the war down through its end in 1814.

In Baltimore, on June 20, 1812, Alexander Contee Hanson, editor of the Federalist newspaper, the *Federal Republican*, wrote a scathing article against the war: "Thou hast done a deed whereat valour will weep. Without funds, without taxes, without an army, navy or adequate fortifications — with one hundred and fifty millions of our property in the hands of the declared enemy, without any of his in our power, and with a vast commerce afloat, our rulers have promulgated a war against the clear and decided sentiment of a vast majority of the nation."

Two days later, a mob of 300 to 400 people armed with axes, hooks, ropes and other makeshift weapons gathered in front of the newspaper's offices at Gay and Second Streets. They threw the presses, type, and paper into the street and levelled the building. Hanson took refuge in the house of his partner, Jacob Wagner, on South Charles Street. On June 27 the *Federal Republican* reappeared with a lead editorial that condemned the police, the town and the mayor, Republican Edward Johnson, for conspiring to destroy Federalism with means as violent as those of the French Revolution. The mob verified his charges by attacking the house on South Charles Street. The following morning, Mayor Johnson and General John Stricker prevailed upon Hanson and the other Federalists inside the house to accept safe conduct to the jail where they could be protected. That night, the mob attacked the jail, killed Revolutionary General James Lignan, set one man on fire, and cut in two the nose of another. This series of events earned for Baltimore the nickname of

Mobtown. Local reaction was so extreme that Federalist candidates won the elections in the fall of 1812, among them Alexander Contee Hanson who was sent to Congress. After this unhappy episode, Baltimore settled down to conduct its own wartime effort with great success and unanimity.

When war broke out, Baltimoreans were convinced that the city would be subject to British attack. Naval and commercial vessels as well as government stores and local warehouses all offered tempting prizes. Furthermore, Baltimore was a center of privateering. Before the war ended, Baltimore sent out over sixty privateers that captured over 475 prizes. Privateers were commissioned by the government to sail the seas and seize the property of the enemy. They were unpaid, but kept the valuable prizes they captured and thus aided the war effort and their own fortunes at the same time. Captains like Thomas Boyle, who commanded the "Comet" and then the "Chasseur," and Joshua Barney, who commanded the "Rossie," struck fear in the hearts of the Englishmen they encountered.

Baltimoreans knew their city would not be easy to defend. The unfortified shores of the Chesapeake Bay allowed attack from almost every direction. Fort McHenry lay in a state of severe decay, without sufficient manpower or weapons. The federal government, with its very limited resources, could not spare much aid for the Chesapeake region while the main battles were being fought along the northern frontier. Baltimore's fate thus rested in the hands of its own citizens.

The military commander put in charge of the forces around Baltimore was General Samuel Smith. A fortunate choice, Smith had good contacts in Washington and the loyal support of both the Maryland militia and Baltimore's citizenry. The General began by rebuilding Fort McHenry, placing it under the command of Major George Armistead, and installing sixty large cannon. He set up a system of lookouts near the tip of North Point and a string of guard boats between North Point and the city. He put the militiamen from Baltimore City and County through rigorous training that made the citizen-soldiers ready for battle.

All these achievements were possible only because Baltimore gave Smith strong and unified support. A Committee of Public Safety appointed by Smith's old political ally Mayor Edward Johnson included Smith's business partner James A. Buchanan, and merchants William Patterson and Samuel Sterett. This committee provided the financial support which allowed the arming of all the local troops.

As the Napoleonic wars ended in Europe, large numbers of British troops were sent to the United States and the pace of the fighting increased. In August 1814 Vice-Admiral Sir Alexander Cochrane trapped Commodore Joshua Barney's flotilla in the Chesapeake and forced him to burn his gunboats to prevent their capture. Major General Robert Ross smashed the American militia at Bladensburg and moved on to Washington where he proceeded to burn most of the public buildings and the naval yard.

At this same time in Baltimore, an elective Committee of Vigilance and Safety took over the operations of the Committee of Public Safety. Although its members still came from the merchant class, it enjoyed a broad popular constituency and loyally supported General Smith.

While the British paused in the Patuxent River, Smith secured the harbor and then turned his energies to land defenses. The General requested the Committee of Vigilance and Safety to mobilize work brigades. On August 27 all free Negroes and whites exempt from military service were ordered to report to Hampstead

Left:
Francis Scott Key wrote the words to "The Star Spangled Banner," while aboard a British ship where he and Lieutenant Frederick Skinner had been sent to arrange the release of Dr. William Beanes, a prisoner. During the first day they could observe the battle, but when night fell they could only hope the Americans were holding out. As dawn came, they saw the flag still flying over the fort

Below:
This 1821 version of the sheet music was one of many of the popular "Star Spangled Banner."

Hill (now the site of Patterson Park). Slaves also helped build the defenses. Smith asked the Committee of Vigilance and Safety to borrow $100,000 from the city's banks to buy arms and supplies. The money, raised from banks and private lenders as well, was collected within two days.

By September 10, the defenses stretched from Fells Point across to the flat lands north of the city's eastern hills. Troops numbering 15,000 waited for the attack. General Smith ordered General John Stricker and his crack third brigade to the western end of Patapsco Neck. Early on Monday, September 12, when Stricker learned that British troops were landing, he placed his troops on the narrow strip of land between Back River and Bear Creek and sent riflemen ahead to harass the British. Two of these men, generally acknowledged to be Daniel Wells and Henry McComas, shot and killed the British General Ross. That evening, after holding the British back for many hours, Stricker led his men back to Hampstead Hill.

On Tuesday morning, September 13, the British began their bombardment of Fort McHenry, and the troops that had come ashore at North Point began to march towards the fortifications on Hampstead Hill. They tried to go around the American left flank, but the defense there held. Smith then ordered a rearrangement of the American troops that would enable them to stop any direct attack on Hampstead Hill with a cross fire. The British saw this maneuver and retreated when night provided a cover. While the British troops were withdrawing from North Point, the American soldiers at Fort McHenry and other locations in the harbor repulsed the British effort there. Before British General Cochrane left the area, he released some American civilians, among them Francis Scott Key who had watched the battle at Fort McHenry and written the words to "The Star-Spangled Banner."

Shortly after the Battle of Baltimore and another American victory at Plattsburg, the British gave up demands for territorial concessions from the United States. Finally, both sides perceived that the underlying cause of the war, the war between Britain and France, had disappeared with the defeat of Napoleon, and a peace treaty was signed.

Baltimore from the end of the Revolution through 1814 experienced two major victories. One was its military triumph at the end of the War of 1812. The other was its ascendancy as a major port. The town's population and economy boomed during the turn of the century decades, placing Baltimore in the ranks of the largest and most prosperous of American cities.

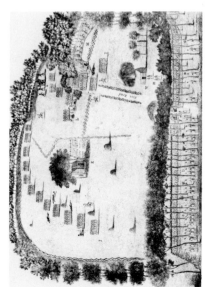

Left:
On September 12, General Samuel Smith ordered General John Stricker and his crack third brigade to the narrow western end of Patapsco Neck, where the Americans held the British back for many hours. The action is capsuled in this picture. Note the portrayal of the death of General Ross in the upper right corner

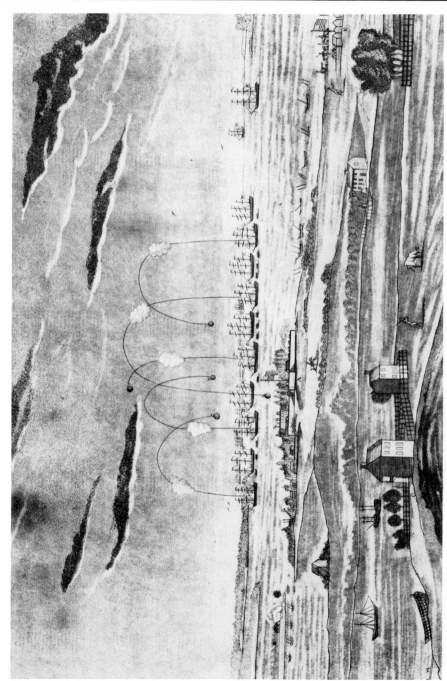

Above:
This view from the observatory on Federal Hill, September 13, 1814, shows the British fleet bombarding Fort McHenry during that morning

Left:
The death on September 12, 1814 of British General Robert Ross at the hands of Baltimore soldiers, generally acknowledged to be Henry McComas and Daniel Wells, was a severe blow to the British troops who had landed at North Point

The battle monument, designed by Maximilian Godefroy, was erected in 1814-1815 to commemorate the defense of Baltimore. It was unusual in that it honored all who gave their lives, regardless of rank. This drawing was made by William Goodacre, Jr., around 1825, when Monument Square was already a prestigious residential area

A City Divided
1814-1865

III

In Baltimore, a brief but marvelous boom followed the conclusion of the War of 1812. Peace brought prosperity and growth to the port city on the Chesapeake. The fast clipper ships returned to peacetime trade. Steam-powered industries, which had begun to develop before the war, expanded swiftly. Demand for labor drew immigrants from other American cities and from Europe. New buildings rose up. Streets were extended into former countryside. Soon the city added thirteen square miles of territory from surrounding county lands. Institutional growth accompanied the enormous population increase, although not always rapidly enough to meet the needs of all Baltimore's citizens.

Then in 1819, boom gave way to bust. Economic uncertainty hastened a transformation that was already underway locally and throughout the United States. New groups began to demand power in an increasingly factionalized society. The growth and change occurred so rapidly and the dislocations were so pronounced that confusion and conflict often resulted. All this was evident in the life of the city during the decades that followed the War of 1812.

The single fact that stands out above all others is population growth. In 1810, 35,583 people lived in Baltimore. By 1820, newcomers from other cities and from Europe made that number grow to 62,738, by 1840 to 102,054 and by 1860 to 212,418. They met the labor need of the new industries.

People immigrated from American cities further north and from Europe. Increasing numbers of free blacks became industrial workers. Roads, canals and railroads connecting Baltimore with points west, south and north employed thousands of other workers. And all of these people provided an additional market for goods and services. New housing was construct-

ed. Roads were extended into new areas. Master craftsmen and their journeymen produced consumer goods in such volume that they soon hired more helpers and began to call themselves manufacturers.

Baltimore's population quickly spilled over the city limits and by 1818 approximately twelve thousand people lived in the precincts of Baltimore County contiguous to the city. These "precincters" enjoyed the benefits of proximity to the city and its facilities without having to pay the considerably higher urban taxes. City officials wanted to bring these people and their tax resources under Baltimore's jurisdiction. Discussions of the question centered around coordinated planning as well as tax revenues. Many of the precincters preferred the low level of services in the county to the higher taxes of the city.

Although the precincters' protests stalled the process for several years, the state legislature in 1818 passed an annexation bill, adding thirteen square miles of county land to Baltimore City. The final decision was a political one. A Federalist-controlled legislature took the Republican precincters out of the county in the hope that Federalists would then dominate there and added them to the already heavily Republican city without changing its representation in Annapolis. The city sent two delegates and each county sent four to the state legislature. There city Republicans attempted to gain two additional delegates, but that amendment failed to pass the Federalist legislature. So, in 1818, the city gained thirteen square miles, twelve thousand people and the benefit of their taxes, but had proportionally lower representation in the House of Delegates.

Many newcomers worked in manufacturing establishments that proliferated with the introduction of steam power for production and processing. Textile manufacturers pioneered the use of steam power before the War of 1812. Many of the textile factories were located outside the city. The owners generally provided living accommodations and sometimes garden plots for their workers. Early operations remained relatively small. In 1814, for example, Robert and Alexander McKim opened the Baltimore Steam Works Factory within the city limits. By 1820 they employed seven men, twelve women, and fifty girls aged eight to thirteen. In 1829 Charles Crook, Jr. opened the Baltimore City Cotton Factory with 200 employees. A few master weavers organized a cottage industry that employed men and women working at home. By 1829, over 100 master weavers engaged in this hiring procedure.

Other industries also converted to steam. Charles Gwinn opened the first steam powered flour mill directly on the wharves in 1813. Flour milling expanded rapidly after that. Baltimore exported wheat and flour in increasing quantities to South America and elsewhere. Several Baltimoreans opened sugar and copper refineries. Industrialization increased the demand for iron ore and coal. Baltimore imported these from western Maryland and the Susquehanna Valley.

Population growth necessitated the increase of various services of the city. In the early 19th century, many services and utilities represented a cooperative effort between private individuals and the city government. For example, fire protection was provided by the volunteer companies until the 1850s, but they were regulated by city ordinance. The Baltimore Water Company, incorporated in 1805 to increase the supply of water in the city, was formed by a group of investors including James Buchanan, Jonathan Ellicott, Solomon Etting, John Hollings, John McKim, and James Mosher. Although it was a private enterprise, the

company was granted free use of Baltimore's streets and city protection for its property and facilities.

Baltimore pioneered in the field of street lighting when the City Council in 1816 authorized the establishment of the Baltimore Gas Light Company and contracted with its board of directors to install and maintain a system of street lights throughout the city. Although the network was not completed for many decades, Baltimore was the first American city to illuminate its streets with hydrogen gas instead of oil. Rembrandt Peale had introduced gas lighting to the city when he installed a system in his museum earlier in 1816. It created a sensation at the time. An account in the *Federal Gazette and Daily Advertiser* written by its editor William Gwynn publicized the experiment: "Yesterday evening, for the first time, the citizens who attended at Baltimore Museum were gratified by seeing one of the Rooms lighted by means of Carburetted Hydrogen Gas. The effect produced by the beautiful and most brilliant light far exceeds the most sanguine expectations of those who had not before witnessed an illumination by similar means." Soon Gwynn joined with Peale to persuade merchant William Lorman, who served as the company's first president, architect Robert Cary Long, and banker James Mosher to form the Baltimore Gas Light Company. On February 7, 1817, the first street lamp was lighted at the corner of Baltimore and Holliday Streets.

Other municipal services besides utilities expanded as the population did. One of the most difficult tasks facing the city was poor relief. The rapid economic changes and large numbers of newcomers strained an already difficult situation to the point where, in 1818, Baltimore created a poor relief board known as the Managers of the Poor. The mayor appointed one board member from each ward. These members

This view of Baltimore from
Federal Hill, painted in 1831 by
William J. Bennett, shows the
active port that was crucial for
the city's existence, and the rural
rolling hills that surrounded the
central business and residential
area

had the authority to determine who needed aid from their own ward and to commit the indigent sick and crippled to the almshouse. The almshouse was administered by another group of appointees called the Trustees of the Poor. Public help never sufficed, and much of the burden fell on private charities, religious institutions, ethnic organizations, and individuals. The depression which began in 1819 worsened the situation even further.

In 1819 the nation's economy lurched into a decline that startled many because it followed what had seemed like strong prosperity. Actually, over-expansion, speculation, and mismanagement of funds by officials of the Second Bank of the United States were the roots of the disaster. In those days of convertible paper money, the U. S. Bank tried to improve its own condition by calling in gold and silver specie from state banks. This led to a severe shortage of specie in Baltimore as well as throughout the nation. The local situation was complicated by the fact that many bank officials had used the institution's funds for private speculative ventures. When the crash came, many businessmen faced financial hardship or failure. They included many of the city's leading merchants like politician and general Samuel Smith, former mayor James Calhoun, and James A. Buchanan who was president of the Baltimore branch of the national bank. Because many of these same businessmen were implicated in the scandals they faced both bankruptcy and the loss of the dominant position in politics that they had enjoyed for so long.

Baltimore also suffered stagnation in its maritime trade. Investment capital, always comparatively scarce in Baltimore, was even harder to come by during the depressed 1820s. Furthermore, men who possessed cash turned to industrial investments. These included former merchants as well as those with new fortunes

made during the War of 1812. Buyers in the back country, who were also hit by the depression, began buying in New York City which could sell imported goods at lower prices because it lay closer to the British port of Liverpool. The port of New York grew at the expense of Baltimore. The worst blow came in 1825 when the opening of the Erie Canal gave New York City direct access to an enormous hinterland. After that, New York's volume of trade increased to a point where neither Baltimore nor Philadelphia could ever catch up again.

Such economic reverses meant hard times for Baltimore's workers. The lot of the nineteenth century laboring man was not a particularly enviable one. He commonly worked six days a week, fourteen hours a day during the summer and sixteen during the winter. Wages ranged between $1 and $2 a day. An unskilled laborer did well to bring home $1 per day.

Desperate for work, new immigrants often accepted even less. Construction and some other jobs were seasonal, with the result that the majority of unskilled workers could not earn more than $200 in a year. November through February marked the low point in employment and the peak of reliance on charity for food, clothing and wood. This scarcity of jobs and low wage scale sometimes led to bitter competition among native whites, the growing number of free black workers and immigrants. Everyone felt the tensions.

These strains were visibly reflected in politics, where change and redefinition marked the decades of the 1820s and 1830s. In Baltimore and the nation new leaders pushed innovations. Andrew Jackson's election to the presidency in 1828 was hailed by his supporters as a victory for the common man. Actually, the election signaled changes that had already begun throughout the country. More democratic suffrage requirements, officeholding by men

Below:
Volunteer companies provided
the city's fire protection until
1858, when the municipal fire
department was organized. Here
a company is shown fighting the
burning of the Front Street
Theatre in 1838

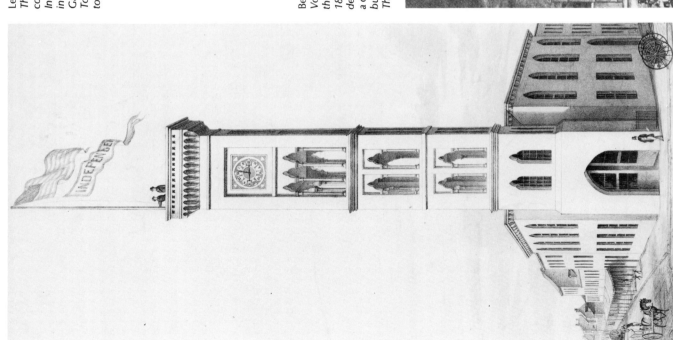

Left:
The only surviving volunteer
company firehouse, that of the
Independent Fire Company built
in 1819, stands at the corner of
Gay and Ensor Streets in Old
Town. The Venetian-Gothic bell
tower was added in 1853.

Left:
After the depression of 1819, the
city, needing a larger almshouse,
purchased "Calverton," which
was located on Franklintown
Road near Edmondson Avenue.
The two wings were added
before this engraving was made
in 1824 by Joseph Cone

from groups other than the old elite, and the growth of institutional services that benefitted ordinary people were taking place in Baltimore and elsewhere as part of a gradual change rather than a sudden revolution.

In Baltimore, the old political elite group dominated by General Samuel Smith had drawn its leadership largely from the mercantile class. The mayors who held office from 1808 to 1820, Edward Johnson and George Stiles, came from this faction. In 1818 a new suffrage law increased the eligible voters from all property-holding white males to all taxpaying white males. In 1819 Baltimore banks resulted in a decline in popularity of many of the politically active men who were thought to be involved in irresponsible financial dealings. In 1820 John Montgomery, leader of a new rival faction, defeated Edward Johnson's try for reelection.

Montgomery had come to Baltimore by way of Pennsylvania and Harford County, from which he had served as a Republican Congressman from 1807 to 1811. His subsequent tenure as Attorney General of Maryland and Delegate from Baltimore City gave him broad publicity. The appeal of his statewide connections, which led voters to hope he could effect economic improvement, and the disrepute of the old political leadership contributed to his victory. Much of his support came from Ward 4 where many of the textile workers lived and from the rapidly growing southern and western sides of the city where trade provided new jobs and led to the growth of new industries using raw materials from the hinterland.

In 1822, Edward Johnson recaptured the mayoralty. The bulk of his support came from the older established business area just north of the harbor basin and from the part of the city east of the Jones Falls which drew much of its income from maritime trade. But his return was brief.

John Montgomery recaptured the mayor's office in 1824. In this same year John Quincy Adams, representing the National Republican faction, defeated Democratic-Republican Andrew Jackson's first try for the presidency. Despite Sam Smith's alliance with Jackson on a national level, many of the new voters in Baltimore gave their support to Montgomery or to a third candidate for mayor, Jacob Small. The latter was a carpenter and building contractor who opposed the property taxes which were particularly hard on small property owners like tradesmen, craftmen and journeymen. Although the small property owners supported Jacob Small, the victory went to Montgomery.

Recognizing the growing need for urban services and the increasing voting power of the mass of ordinary people, Montgomery inaugurated a program of deficit spending to pay for all the new undertakings. Montgomery's administration pushed authorization of a new public school system for the City of Baltimore by the state legislature in 1826.

One of the major reforms of the Jacksonian era, public education was developed in many cities during this period. Democrats believed that all people should have access to an education. Elitists believed that public school systems should be established to teach the proper values to pupils who might otherwise fall prey to demogogic rhetoric. In 1827 the City Council approved Baltimore's public school system. Two years later, four small elementary schools began holding classes in houses rented by the city for use until proper schools could be constructed. The eastern and western sections of town each received one male school and one female school. Only white children could attend. In 1830, 3 percent of all white school-aged children took advantage of the new school system. By 1840 a high school, the original

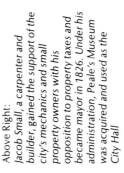

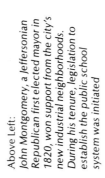

Above Left:
John Montgomery, a Jeffersonian Republican first elected mayor in 1820, won support from the city's new industrial neighborhoods. During his tenure, legislation to establish the public school system was initiated

Left:
Isaac McKim, son of "Quaker John" McKim, who endowed the free school for poor children, was a successful shipping merchant and aide-de-camp to General Samuel Smith during the War of 1812. He was active in the Protective Society of Maryland, a merchant group organized to aid free blacks

Above Right:
Jacob Small, a carpenter and builder, gained the support of the city's mechanics and small property owners with his opposition to property taxes and became mayor in 1826. Under his administration, Peale's Museum was acquired and used as the City Hall

Baltimore City College, had extended the education available. In that year, 7 percent of all eligible children attended. High schools for female students opened in the eastern and western section of the city in 1844 and 1845. A "Floating School" on a large sailing ship was added to the public school system in 1857.

Schools, students and teachers in the system increased gradually until 1860 when 23 percent of those eligible (over 14,000) were taught by more than 300 teachers. Education was available but not compulsory. Children whose families needed income from their work generally could not take advantage of the new public schools. Most students came from middle-class families.

Democratic forces in Baltimore made themselves felt not only in programs like the school system but increasingly at the ballot box as well. In the mayoralty elections held in October 1826, the Smith group joined with the middle class property owners and mechanics in support of their candidate, Jacob Small. The combination succeeded and the electors, chosen for that purpose, made Small mayor of Baltimore.

In 1827, Samuel Smith organized a group of Baltimoreans to work in Andrew Jackson's 1828 presidential campaign. The Smith Jacksonians and Small's faction split before the Baltimore mayoral election of 1828. For that campaign, Jacob Small realigned himself with Montgomery's faction and gained much of the Irish Catholic and German vote which he used against the Scotch-Irish Presbyterian and Quaker supporters of the Smith faction. Small won reelection in 1830.

By 1831 taxes had risen so high that a group of 85 large property owners persuaded the legislature to limit Baltimore's taxing power. Small resigned and was succeeded by William Steuart, a stone cutter and builder.

retained his seat in the United States Senate and his powerful position as chairman of the Senate Finance Committee. Chief dispenser of federal patronage in Maryland, Smith arranged the appointment of James H. McCulloh as Collector of the Port of Baltimore, the most remunerative federal office in Maryland, and multitudes of lesser officials. Locally, the Smith faction gained by shifting its emphasis away from the ethnic considerations that Small and Steuart had been stressing. In 1832 Jesse Hunt, the Smith candidate for mayor, successfully used economic issues and identified himself with the city's working men. By that time, Smith had introduced the Jacksonian style political machine which required party fidelity in both national and local elections in exchange for patronage and other benefits of power. The tactics succeeded and Jesse Hunt became mayor. The Jacksonian party reigned in Baltimore.

Despite the political confusion, the final years of the 1820s saw the success of several major pioneering economic ventures in Baltimore. The Canton Company, probably the first planned industrial and residential community in the nation, was chartered in 1828. Columbus O'Donnell, son of the sea captain who had brought the first cargo from China and owner of three miles of waterfront land directly east of Fells Point, joined with William Patterson, William Gwynn and other local investors to develop the new community. The charter gave the corporation the right to improve land belonging to the company "by laying out streets etc., in the vicinity of Baltimore, on or near navigable water, and erecting and constructing wharves, slips, workshops, factories, stores, dwellings, and such other buildings and improvements as may be deemed necessary ornamental and convenient." O'Donnell and Patterson were instrumental in bringing Pete

To help make up for the city's lack of a public school system before 1829, Isaac McKim donated funds from his father's estate for a free school that was built in 1822. The building is still standing at Baltimore and Aisquith Streets

Cooper from New York to Baltimore to invest in this endeavor. He established an ironworks at the foot of Clinton Street.

An even more important event of 1828 was the laying of the first stone of the Baltimore and Ohio Railroad. Baltimore businessmen viewed with alarm the advantage that the Erie Canal gave New York. Instead of trying to duplicate that, the Baltimoreans were willing to risk building the first commercial railroad and hope for its success. In February 1827 a group of twenty-five merchants and other civic leaders met at George Brown's house and determined to build a two-track railroad from Baltimore all the way to the Ohio River. This would yield large amounts of trade between Baltimore and points west.

The planners agreed to raise money by the sale of stock. Although the city bought some stock, control of the B&O remained in private hands. Directors included: Philip Evans Thomas, president; George Brown, treasurer; his father, investment banker Alexander Brown; Charles Carroll of Carrollton; William Patterson; Robert Oliver; future Jacksonian Congressman Isaac McKim; William Lorman; Solomon Etting; and future mayor William Steuart.

On July 4, 1828, Charles Carroll of Carrollton, by then a national hero as the last surviving signer of the Declaration of Independence, turned over the first spadeful of earth for the laying of the first stone. On May 24, 1830 the B&O began regular service between Baltimore City and Ellicott's Mills, 26 miles away. Passenger fare was $.75 per ride.

Peter Cooper believed that the success of the Canton Company depended on the B&O Railroad. When the B&O directors said that they thought a steam engine could not manage the curves on the tracks, Cooper set out to disprove them. Working with scrap iron and borrowed wheels, and using gun barrels as boiler tubes, he built the Tom Thumb, the first successful steam locomotive. During the summer of 1830, Cooper took the directors of the B&O on a 13 mile run in the unbelievably fast time of 57 minutes. Shortly thereafter, the famous grey horse beat the Tom Thumb in a race of one or two miles along tracks just west of Baltimore, but only because the engine's fan belt slipped. Convinced by the Tom Thumb's performance, the B&O directors announced in January 1831 a contest offering $4,000 for the best engine. The York, built by Davis and Gartner, won. It burned anthracite coal and carried 15 tons at 15 miles per hour.

The steam engine succeeded and the B&O boosted Baltimore's economy and prestige. Tracks reached Frederick by 1831, Harper's Ferry by 1834, Cumberland by 1842, and finally Wheeling on the Ohio River in 1853. Benjamin Latrobe, chief engineer of the B&O, personally explored the route through the Appalachian Mountains. He built the Thomas Viaduct at Relay which still supports trains.

But even the success of the B&O could not solve Baltimore's economic problems. The cycles of apparent prosperity were actually inflation, and financial panics and depression continued. National banking policy still produced local havoc. President Andrew Jackson believed that the Bank of the United States had too much power and he was determined to destroy it. In 1833 he withdrew the government's deposits from that bank and put them in favored state banks around the country. The fallout from the destruction of the national bank included many local bank failures, a scarcity of money and widespread unemployment.

The Bank of Maryland collapsed in March 1834, and failures of numerous smaller banks and savings institutions followed. In April, Baltimore lawyer and former Jackson supporter Reverdy Johnson became chairman of the Whig Party,

Many of Baltimore's leading merchants and bankers participated in the founding of the B&O. (From left to right) Alexander Brown, his son George Brown, Solomon Etting, and Philip E. Thomas, the railroad's first president, were among them

Baltimoreans pioneered in the building of the first major American railroad, the Baltimore and Ohio. In 1827 a group of local merchants and civic leaders met at George Brown's house and made the decision to build the two-track railroad from Baltimore to the Ohio River

newly organized in Maryland to protect Jackson's economic policies. Johnson served on the board of directors of the Bank of Maryland.

Another group protested economic losses in a somewhat different fashion. Many small depositors found that their savings had disappeared during the bank failures. By February 1835, their protests had become violent. Fires were set at the Athenaeum and the Maryland Academy of Fine Arts. In April, mobs attacked the houses of trustees in whose hands the affairs of the Bank of Maryland had been placed. Reverdy Johnson's house on Monument Square was a primary target of the mob. On the first night, a small group broke a few windows. On the second night, a larger crowd came but dispersed after a speech by Mayor Jesse Hunt. The following night the crowd attacked with bats and stones the armed guards stationed around the house. Then they moved on to John Glenn's house, where they gained access, and proceeded to break up all the furniture and woodwork. The next night, they succeeded in bypassing the guards at Reverdy Johnson's house. They made a bonfire in the street of his furniture and his extensive law library. They raided the wine cellars of Johnson, Glenn, and others, and hawked fine wines at low prices to all takers. Eighty-three year old General Samuel Smith was asked to take charge and called for an assemblage of armed citizens. The fire companies joined the effort. Mayor Jesse Hunt resigned. Guards took up stations throughout the city and finally order was restored. In a special election, Samuel Smith became mayor, a post to which he was reelected in 1836. The voters turned once again to the hero of the Battle of Baltimore of 1814 because they could find no one else to bring peace.

Violence was not limited to isolated riots. Turbulence frequently accompanied labor protests that punctuated the 1830s. Many of the worst incidents occurred during protests by railroad workers. In 1829, riots among B&O workers left one man dead and several wounded. Two years later, a contractor building one section of the B&O absconded, leaving his workers unpaid. Two or three hundred workers attacked the rails and other company property with pick-axes, hammers, and sledges. Instead of winning their wages, many were arrested. In 1834 a group of B&O railroad workers attacked a contractor and several of his assistants. After they killed three of them, the militia moved in and arrested 300 workers. Frequently the workers involved in incidents like these were immigrants whom employers paid the lowest possible wages. They were so desperate for work and for income that they were forced to accept pay far below what native Americans considered enough to live on. Any delay in wages generally meant no food for the workers' families.

Low pay and the insecurity of the job market led to bitter competition among individual workers and between native white Americans, immigrants and black workers, both slave and free. Employers often replaced native workers with the more easily exploitable immigrants. Resentments grew stronger when employment was scarce. Some white workers, both native and foreign-born, wanted the best positions reserved for them with black labor excluded.

Frederick Douglass, later a leading aboli-tionist, worked as a ship's carpenter in Baltimore. A slave, he was hired out to the owner of the shipyard, a Mr. Gardner. In his autobiography, he described an incident that happened to him as labor competition grew bitter:

Until a very little while after I went there, white and black ship-carpenters worked side by side and no one seemed to see any impropriety in it. All hands seemed to be very well satisfied. Many of the black carpenters were freemen.

Many industries, like the Avalon
Nail and Iron Works shown here,
were built along the Baltimore
and Ohio tracks west of
Baltimore. Homes along the road
on the right housed two families

Things seemed to be going on very well. All at once, the white carpenters knocked off, and said they would not work with free colored workmen. Their reason for this, as alleged, was, that if free colored carpenters were encouraged, they would soon take the trade into their own hands, and poor white men would be thrown out of employment . . . My fellow-apprentices soon began to feel it degrading to them to work with me . . . They commenced making my condition as hard as they could . . . They at length combined, and came upon me, armed with sticks, stones, and heavy handspikes . . . the one behind ran up with the handspike, and struck me a heavy blow upon the head. It stunned me. I fell, and with this they all fell to beating me.

After receiving more blows, Frederick Douglass managed to escape to his home. His master took him to see a lawyer to inquire what could be done about the incident. The lawyer replied that no recourse could be had unless a white man would testify. No black man's testimony was acceptable in court. No white man would dare testify against another white on behalf of a black man. So the case was dropped.

In light of the riots, labor violence, and individual attacks, Hezekiah Niles' comment in his nationally famous *Register* of September 5, 1835 is not surprising: *"Society seems everywhere unhinged,* and the demon of blood and slaughter has been let loose upon us!" All the conflict and danger led many to seek safety and protection within a limited, identifiable community.

Factionalization of society as a whole led to a greater cohesion within various groups themselves. Ethnic communities particularly developed a wide range of supportive and social organizations. The city's largest pre-Civil War ethnic groups, the German (including German Jews), the Irish, and blacks (both free and slave), all experienced a growth of institutions within their own community and a consciousness of group identity.

Germans had been coming into Baltimore since long before the Revolution. The descendants of some of those early immigrants held positions of political, social and economic leadership after the War of 1812. Mayor Jacob Small and a Jacksonian leader of the 1830s, William Frick, were of German descent as was a hero of 1814, General John Stricker. Their identity as individuals and as Baltimoreans far outweighed their German background in people's minds. The old German community had integrated into the mainstream of the city's life. But the arrival of many new immigrants, especially during the 1840s and 1850s, revitalized a sense of community among the Germans. Churches served as focal points for the city's ethnic communities. The German churches reflected the Americanization process in their addition of the English language. At the Reformed Church, in the midst of a public controversy, Dr. Michael Diffenderffer and thirty-five other members petitioned to have the sermon preached in English every Sunday afternoon. The Rev. Lewis Mayer delivered the first English sermon in September, 1818. The system of dual services continued until 1827 when the congregation dropped German altogether. Not until 1845 was another German Reformed church founded because a new wave of immigrants preferred services in their native tongue. The Zion Lutheran Church, which held German services, remained the only church of that denomination until the first English-speaking Lutheran congregation was formed in 1823. They worshipped in a schoolhouse on south Howard Street until 1826 when their

Above:
The collapse of the Bank of
Maryland in 1834 and
subsequent failures occasioned
much popular criticism of the
directors who were held guilty of
irresponsible financial practices.
This satire by Jack Downing was
published in 1834

Right:
Reverdy Johnson, a lawyer and
former supporter of Andrew
Jackson, organized the Whig
Party in Maryland to protest the
president's economic policies

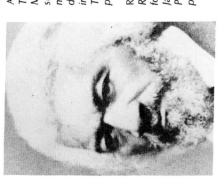

Above:
Frederick Douglas, an editor of
the abolitionist newspaper North
Star, lived seven years of his
childhood, from 1825 to 1832, on
Aliceanna Street in Fells Point.
He returned later, still a slave, to
work in a local shipyard, but in
1838 escaped, riding the train
north to find freedom in
New York

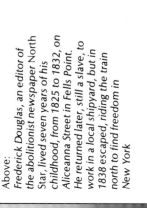

church was built.

Four additional English Lutheran congregations were formed in Baltimore before the Civil War. Non-Germans began joining these very Americanized churches. The Roman Catholic Church had always resisted attempts to establish a separate German-speaking congregation. The large immigration of the mid-nineteenth century included Redemptorist priests who worked in the German Catholic community. With some help from missionary societies in Germany, Austria, and France (King Ludwig I of Bavaria is said to have contributed $4000), the congregation built St. Alphonsus Church at Park Avenue and Saratoga Street. St. James at Aisquith and Eager Streets, formerly an Irish parish, became German. Before the Civil War, two more churches were opened to serve Baltimore's six thousand German Catholics.

All the German churches had schools. In the Catholic schools, many of the teachers were members of religious orders: Redemptorists, Christian Brothers, or Sisters of Notre Dame. The Zion Lutheran Church school, in existence since 1769, experienced a major revival from the efforts of liberal Pastor Heinrich Scheib. When Scheib came to Zion in 1835, he found the school in such a state of deterioration that he determined to establish a new German-English school. It opened in 1836 with 71 pupils. A secular school, only loosely affiliated with the church, the Scheib School attracted students of varied backgrounds. Just before the Civil War, over 400 pupils attended grades kindergarten through seven. The school lasted for sixty years. The St. Johannes German Reformed congregation brought several famous teachers to its school, among them Valentin Scheer and Friedrich Knapp.

Friedrich Knapp, one of the participants in the liberal revolution which failed in 1848 in Germany, arrived in Baltimore in 1850 and found

employment as a tutor and bookkeeper in the house of William A. Marburg. In 1851 he became principal of the school at St. Johannes Church. Then in 1853 he opened his own school, known as Knapp's Institute, which grew in reputation so much that by the time of the Civil War over 700 pupils were enrolled. Knapp's Institute survived long enough for H. L. Mencken to attend during the 1880s. Mencken's description of Knapp survives in an essay entitled "Caves of Learning."

Mencken wrote of his principal:

He was a Suabian who had come to Baltimore in 1850, and he still wore, nearly forty years afterward, the classical uniform of a German schoolmaster — a long-tailed coat of black alpaca, a boiled shirt with somewhat fringey cuffs, and a white lawn necktie. The front of his coat was dusty with chalk, and his hands were so caked with it that he had to blow it off every time he took snuff. He was of small stature but large diameter, and wore closely-clipped mutton-chop whiskers. His hands had the curious softness so often observed in pedagogues, barbers, and Y.M.C.A. secretaries. This impressed itself on me the first time he noticed me wiggling a loose milk-tooth with my tongue, and called me up to have it out. He watched for such manifestations sharply, and pulled, I should say, an average of six teeth a week. It was etiquette in the school for boys to bear this barbarity in silence. The girls could yell, but not the boys. Both, however, were free to howl under the bastinado, which was naturally applied to the girls much more lightly and less often than to the boys.

Gradually, the German church and private schools died out, but not until the end of the 19th century when they lost a large share of their pupils to the German-English public schools that opened in 1879.

The immigration of the first half of the 19th century enlarged the German population so greatly that by 1860 roughly one-fourth of Baltimore's population claimed German descent. Although a clear differentiation between the old wealthy merchants and the new immigrants existed, the older group banded together to aid the newcomers, especially those in greatest need. The German Society, founded in 1783, was reorganized in 1817 in response to the terrible conditions aboard the ship *Juffrow Johanna* which carried 300 immigrant redemptionists. The latter were people whose labor for a specified number of years would be sold by the agent in exchange for their passage. The cold and hunger that the group suffered were so severe that General John Stricker led a movement to find a means to regulate the redemption system. Lawyers William Frick, David Hoffman and Charles Mayer joined him as did many merchants including Lewis Brantz, Benjamin Cohen, Jacob Cohen, Michael Diffenderffer, Jesse Eichelberger, Samuel Etting, Philip Sadtler and Lawrence Thomson. They chose Christian Mayer president of the German Society, which was now reconstituted specifically for the purpose of "the protection and assistance of poor emigrants from Germany and Switzerland and of their descendents."

Led by such prosperous and influential men, the German Society secured rapid gains. In 1818 they won legislation regulating the redemption system for German and Swiss workers. Under the new law, no immigrant was to serve longer than four years; those under 21 had to attend school at least two months a year; and no one could be held on board ship longer than 30 days. The German Society took cases of mistreatment of redemptioners to court. Their charitable work was so extensive that an 1832 law granted a

Pastor Heinrich Scheib of the Zion Lutheran Church founded a school that lasted for sixty years

portion of the $1.50 head tax collected for each immigrant to the Society for such purposes.

A law of 1841 required that a German interpreter be available in all Baltimore courts. In 1845 the German Society established the so-called "Intelligence Bureau," really a free employment agency for German immigrants. In 1846 the bureau located positions for 3500 applicants.

The huge immigration of the 1840s led to the establishment of a wide variety of clubs. The Germania Club, a literary and social club, had the most elite membership. Another club, the Concordia, became famous for its musical and dramatic presentations as well as its lectures and social gatherings. Singing clubs included Liederkranz, Harmonie, Arion, and the Germania Mannerchor. In 1849 a *Sozial-demokratische Turnverein* opened in Baltimore. It combined gymnastic activities with lectures on political and literary topics. The membership tended to be working-class and freethinkers. They frequently met opposition from the German clergy, except for the liberal Pastor Scheib of the Zion Church.

The German community supported numerous newspapers, including several that survived into the Twentieth century. *Der Deutsche Correspondent* founded in 1841 by Friedrich Raine, when he was 19 years of age, became a daily in 1848. It supported the Democratic Party from its early years until World War I. The *Baltimore Wecker*, founded by writer and poet Carl Heinrich Schnauffer in 1851, was the voice of the liberal refugees from the 1848 revolution. The *Wecker* was the only Republican Party newspaper in Baltimore during the Civil War.

The German Jews formed a very special but integral part of the pre-Civil War German community. Like the Protestant and Catholic Germans, Jews in Baltimore counted merchants and political activists among their number. The census of 1820 listed only 21 Jewish families in Baltimore. Although they had been participants in both the Revolution and the War of 1812, Jews could not vote or hold public office under Maryland law, which required a profession of Christian faith, even for jurors. In 1818 a legislator from Washington County, Thomas Kennedy, introduced a bill, finally passed in 1826, which changed that situation. Popularly called the "Jew Bill," the legislation stated that "... every citizen ... professing the Jewish Religion and ... hereafter appointed to any office of public trust under the State of Maryland shall in addition to the oath required by the Constitution and laws of the State or of the United States, make and subscribe a declaration of his belief in the future state of rewards and punishments, in the stead of the declaration now required by the Consitution and form of government of this State."

Shortly after the passage of the new law, Baltimore businessmen Jacob Cohen and Solomon Etting were elected to the First Branch of the City Council.

Most Jews who immigrated to Baltimore before the Civil War came from Bavaria, where many German Jews lived and where they faced the greatest discrimination. Most of the Jews, like other Germans, arrived on the ships that carried Maryland tobacco to Germany on the return trip. By 1840 about 500 Jews had settled in Baltimore, many in the vicinity of Lombard Street between Lloyd Street in the west and the Jones Falls in the east. A number of Jews worked as peddlers when they first arrived. One of them was Moses Hutzler who emigrated from Bavaria in 1836. His three sons founded the department store which still exists.

Not until after the passage of the Jew Bill did members of the community establish a formal

religious organization. The Baltimore Hebrew Congregation was incorporated in 1830. At first, members worshipped in a rented room above a grocery store at Bond and Fleet Streets. Their first rabbi, Abraham Rice, came to Baltimore from Bavaria in 1840. Five years later the congregation built the first synagogue in Maryland, the Lloyd Street Synagogue. Designed by Robert Cary Long, Jr., this building is the third oldest surviving synagogue in the United States.

Several thousand German Jews came in the 1840s and early 1850s, and the community added three more synagogues before the Civil War: the Eden Street Synagogue, Har Sinai and Oheb Shalom. The congregations held the same sorts of debates that their Christian counterparts did over Anglicization of language and Americaniza-tion of practices.

Synagogues conducted schools. The first regular Hebrew school opened at the Lloyd

The Baltimore Hebrew Congregation invited Rabbi Abraham Rice from Bavaria to serve as the Jewish community's first rabbi

Friedrich Raine founded the Deutsche Correspondent, one of many newspapers which served Baltimore's German community

Church which seated 1600 people.

The Democratic delegates returned to Baltimore in 1835, met in the First Presbyterian Church and nominated Martin Van Buren, who followed Jackson into the presidency. In 1840, the party returned to nominate Van Buren for a second term. While the Democrats held their sessions in the Music Hall, the Whig Party rented the Canton Race Track, offered free hard cider, and invited Baltimore citizens to hear Henry Clay, Daniel Webster and others praise their candidate, William Henry Harrison, who won the election the following November.

In 1844 both the Whigs and the Democrats met in Baltimore. The Whigs assembled at the Universalist Church and chose Henry Clay to carry their party banner. When the Democrats met at the Odd Fellows Hall, the contest was between John Tyler who had proposed that the United States annex Texas and Van Buren who opposed the acquisition. A deadlock between the two finally resulted in the nomination of a dark horse, James K. Polk, who became president.

Only the Democrats came to Baltimore in 1848 when they met in the Universalist Church and nominated Lewis Cass of Michigan. This convention established the first national committee, which consisted of one member from each state and was charged with the job of running the campaign. Their techniques must not have been perfected as the Whig candidate, General Zachary Taylor, took the victory.

The Democrats returned to Baltimore in 1852 when five thousand assembled at the Maryland Institute and labored through 49 ballots. The result was a rather obscure figure, Franklin Pierce of New Hampshire. Later the Whigs also came to the Maryland Institute, and in 53 ballots, chose Mexican War hero General Winfield Scott, whom Pierce defeated.

In 1856, only the nativist third party, the

American Party, convened in Baltimore where they nominated Millard Fillmore. The local strength of the Know-Nothings, the name generally used by the nativists, may have been responsible for the major parties' choices of other locations for their conventions.

In 1860 Baltimore more than made up for its lack of conventions in 1856. The year before the Civil War broke out, the Constitutional Union Party and two groups of Democrats brought their troubles to the city. By 1860 slavery was the dominant question in the country. Passions ran high, and many already believed that civil war was unavoidable. A group of men, mainly from border states, formed a Constitutional Union Party whose primary purpose was to remove the slavery question from national politics. Sam Houston, headquartered at Eutaw House, and John Bell of Tennessee, working from Barnum's Hotel, vied for the nomination. The party delegates, meeting in the First Presbyterian Church, chose Bell. Baltimorean John Pendleton Kennedy was a leading local supporter of this party that hoped for compromise but lost.

The Democratic Party divided so severely that its first convention, held in Charleston adjourned without agreement on a candidate. The delegates reconvened in Baltimore's Front Street Theater on June 18, 1860. Unionists and secessionists faced each other for a second time. Sen. Stephen Douglas of Illinois, who proposed "popular sovereignty," whereby each state and territory would be allowed to decide for itself whether or not to have slavery, ran his campaign from Reverdy Johnson's house. The secessionists, who wanted the Democratic Party to endorse slavery without reservation, operated out of Robert Gilmor's house. Because both men resided on Courthouse Square, the area became the scene of rival speeches and bands, and crowds alternately cheering and booing. When the pro-Southern delegates found that they

Thomas Kennedy introduced the legislation which finally granted the franchise for Jews in 1826

The Schutzen (shooting club) located on West Baltimore Street was a popular recreational spot for many of Baltimore's Germans

Street Synagogue in 1848. Joseph Sachs, a native of Bavaria, taught the classes. At the same time, Samuel Gump conducted a school at the Eden Street Synagogue. When Jonas Goldsmith, a graduate of the University of Wurzburg, replaced Gump, so many students attended that the school had to hire five teachers. In the 1850s, Mrs. Solomon Carvalho organized the first free school, a Sunday school which offered instruction in Hebrew, German and English.

While Jews participated in the numerous German charitable groups, they also organized some of their own, among them the Society for Educating Poor and Orphan Hebrew Children, and the Hebrew Ladies Sewing Society which made clothes for the poor. Social groups included the Young Men's Literary Society, the Mendelsohn Literary Society, the Y.M.H.A., and the Harmony Circle which held balls.

Thousands of people came from Ireland to Baltimore during the first half of the nineteenth century. By the Civil War, over 15,000 people born in Ireland lived in the city, as did innumerable children and grandchildren of earlier immigrants. The potato famine of the 1840s forced a massive emigration by a people facing death by starvation and disease. The desperate situation in Ireland drove thousands of people onto the ships headed for America. Most were rural people who arrived with little or no money and without urban skills. Many had to take the lowest paying unskilled jobs, especially the seasonal construction work. Some had contracted to work for years in exchange for their passage and could not accept higher paying jobs until the specified years had passed.

Of all the pre-Civil War immigrant groups, the Irish bore the harshest fate. A Baltimorean recorded in a journal the arrival of the immigrant ship *Hampden* just arrived, freighted with human misery and death. Six of her passengers died at a month.

sea, and there are about 60 more on board, languishing with fever and destitution." Those that did survive the trip often faced prejudice because of their poverty, their lack of education, and sometimes because of their Catholic religion.

An older Irish community in Baltimore joined together to help the newcomers. Even before the potato famine the Irish had faced the difficulties experienced by most immigrants. In 1803 Baltimoreans of Irish ancestry organized the Hibernian Society to provide financial, social, medical and moral assistance to newcomers. The society chose Dr. John Campbell White its first president and Thomas McElderry vice-president. In 1815 John O'Donnell, the sea captain who had participated in building Canton, assumed the presidency. In 1818, John Oliver was elected head of the group.

The Hibernian Society counted some of Baltimore's most prestigious business and civic leaders among its membership: John McKim, Robert Oliver, William Patterson, John Pendleton Kennedy, and J. H. B. Latrobe who was general counsel of the B&O and founder of the Maryland Institute. Though most of these early leaders were Scotch-Irish Protestants, their Hibernian Society continued to provide aid as the immigrants became predominantly Catholic.

The Hibernian Society offered assistance in various forms. Sometimes it made cash payments to families in need. In 1838, for example, the society donated between $.50 and $20 to 105 families. In 1852 it gave money to 700 families. The funds came from membership dues and from the head tax paid by steamship companies. A portion of that tax was divided between the Hibernian Society and the German Society for their charitable work. For several years after 1852 the Hibernian Society operated an employment agency that placed at least 25 men and women

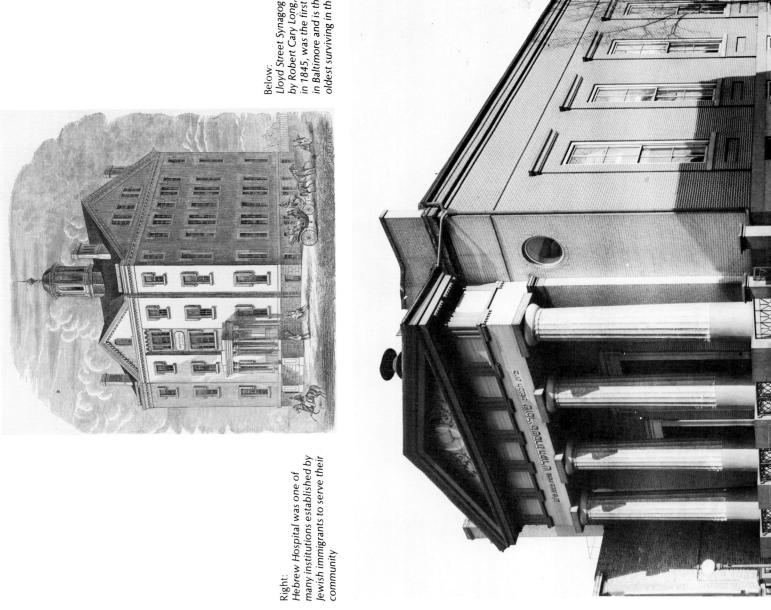

Right:
Hebrew Hospital was one of many institutions established by Jewish immigrants to serve their community

Below:
Lloyd Street Synagogue, designed by Robert Cary Long, Jr., and built in 1845, was the first synagogue in Baltimore and is the third oldest surviving in the nation

The Irish immigrants coming to Baltimore arrived in a city with a long Catholic tradition. The first two archbishops, the Rev. John Carroll and the Rev. Leonard Neale, came from old Maryland Irish Catholic families. The parish churches played an especially important role in the lives of people uprooted from their familiar villages and thrust into an unfamiliar and impersonal city. Many of the newcomers settled around St. Patrick's Church on Broadway and St. John's Church at Valley and Eager Streets. So many of Baltimore's Irish lived in the vicinity of the present City Jail that the area was known for a while as "Old Limerick." It should be noted that Baltimore was not a ghettoized city. Irish and German immigrants and blacks lived in all wards of the city. Often the Irish and the blacks shared alley housing behind the homes of the more prosperous residents.

Although extensive poverty meant that many Irish children had to go to work, several schools served the community. St. Patrick's School, the oldest parochial school in Baltimore, opened in 1815. In 1824, John Oliver bequeathed $20,000 to the Hibernian Society for the establishment of a free school for the poor children of Baltimore. He specified in his will that preference be given to those with at least one Irish parent and that no distinction be made because of sex or religion. It is estimated that before it closed its doors in 1891 the teachers of the Oliver Hibernian Free School educated 12,000 pupils. The Christian Brothers opened a free school at the St. Vincent de Paul Church and also ran the St. Peter the Apostle School and the Cathedral School for boys at Calvert Hall.

One unique fact about Baltimore's ethnic history is that the city was home to the nation's largest free black community of the antebellum period. Baltimore combined the population characteristics of a typical northern city and a typical southern city in its large numbers of both European immigrants and Afro-Americans.

The widely diverse black community in Baltimore was a mixture of slaves and free men and women. Urban slavery differed from plantation slavery in that cities offered a measure of freedom unknown in rural areas where slaves generally could not leave the property of their owner. In the cities, most slaves worked either as house servants or in some industrial or skilled trade. Some slaves hired themselves out, that is, found a job, received wages, and paid part of their wages to their master. With the remaining income, they provided for their own lodging, sustenance and amusement. The line between slavery and freedom blurred under such conditions.

An increasing percentage of Baltimore's black population became free from 1800 until 1864, when slavery ended in Maryland. In 1810, the census registered 3,713 slaves and 3,973 free blacks. By 1860, over 90 percent of the total 27,898 were free. Men and women worked in a wide range of occupations and received commensurately varying incomes.

The majority of blacks held unskilled jobs in homes, restaurants, and factories and on the docks and railroads. A substantial number of black men worked as draymen and wagoners and women as washers and ironers. A significant proportion of blacks worked in the skilled trades as blacksmiths, butchers, carpenters, cigar-makers, coopers, milliners, shoemakers, tailors, and so on. Until the middle of the nineteenth century, blacks dominated the barbering and caulking trades and also the catering business in town. A few blacks owned small commercial establishments such as confectioneries, drug stores, groceries and tobacco shops. One black doctor, Lewis Wells, reportedly worked in Baltimore before the Civil War. Blacks as well as whites taught in schools for both children and adults. Black clergymen were prominent as

John Oliver, a local merchant, bequeathed $20,000 to the Baltimore Hibernian Society for the establishment of a free school for poor students

Benjamin Henry Latrobe, who designed the new cathedral, also served as architect of the United States Capitol

The sale of lottery tickets like this one helped pay for the new cathedral, seat of the first American Roman Catholic bishop

community leaders.

Blacks, like immigrants, resided throughout the city, often sharing alley blocks with Irish and other immigrants. During the 1830s, 40s and 50s, most slaves and house servants lived in the north central part of Baltimore near the homes of the most prosperous whites. Laborers and wagoners tended to live in the central district near railroad stations, docks and shipyards. Many free blacks and slaves who hired themselves out lived south of center city, the less prosperous in wooden shacks that gave the appearance of a shantytown. The general condition of free blacks deteriorated over these decades as white workers pushed many blacks out of skilled and semi-skilled jobs. For example, many men who had labored as draymen or stevedores were forced into jobs as domestics or porters and received commensurately lower pay. In 1858, whites rioted in an attempt to drive blacks from jobs in several shipyards. As the violence continued, some free men left Baltimore to seek work in other cities.

Churches played as important a role in the black community as they did in the immigrant ethnic communities. The Methodist and A.M.E. churches established earlier continued to prosper, especially Sharp Street and Bethel A.M.E. In 1824, William Levington, the third black man ordained as an Episcopal priest in the United States, founded St. James Church. From 1824 to 1827 the congregation worshipped in an upper room on the corner of Park Avenue and Marion Street. In 1827 the Bishop of Maryland, James Kemp, consecrated a church at Saratoga and North Streets. The congregation moved several times again before settling at its current location on Arlington Street.

The other major black church founded before the Civil War began as a mission. Then in 1850 the Madison Avenue Presbyterian Church bought a building at Madison and Park from the Baptists. Much later, the congregation moved to

Madison Avenue and Bloom Street. One minister who served at Madison Avenue, Hiram R. Revels, was elected to the United States Senate from Mississippi where he lived after the Civil War.

The churches provided much of the schooling available to blacks in Baltimore. Most churches conducted Sunday schools where rudiments of reading, writing and arithmetic were taught. The Sharp Street congregation had maintained a school since the late eighteenth century. Daniel Coker, who left Sharp Street to join the independent Bethel A.M.E. Church, directed an African School which in 1812 instructed 17 students, and 150 in 1820. Some of the pupils came from as far away as Washington, D.C.

After 1820, when Coker left for Liberia, William Watkins, a former student, took over many of the students. Known as the Watkins Academy, his school lasted for 25 years. In the 1820s, several new day schools opened for black pupils. St. James Episcopal Church operated both a day school and a Sunday school. A school for black Catholic girls, St. Frances Academy, opened in 1828 under the direction of Father James Joubert and several nuns who belonged to the Oblate Sisters of Providence, Sister Elizabeth Lange who came from Cuba, Sister Elizabeth Balas who was a refugee from Santo Domingo, and Sister Rosina Bogue. English, French, religion, arithmetic, sewing, and embroidery and other subjects were taught to both day and boarding students.

Late in the 1820s, a Negro master from Fells Point, William Lively, was put in charge of the Sharp Street school. He renamed it the Union Seminary and introduced a liberal arts curriculum that included English, French, and Latin. He taught classes for both day and evening students and also conducted a free sabbath school for children on Sunday mornings and for adult women on Sunday afternoons.

A ticket from the Washington Monument Lottery

Support for the schools came from the black churches, students' tuition money, and donations from interested white groups, especially Quakers, and individuals. Baltimore did not maintain public schools for black students, although both Boston and Philadelphia did. Ironically, black residents of Baltimore still had to pay the school tax. At least one petition against this by black taxpayers was turned down as were all efforts to convince the city to open public schools for black pupils.

However, needy people among the Negro population did receive aid from city facilities such as the almshouse where black residents were in approximate proportion to their numbers in the population as a whole. As with immigrant groups, this help did not suffice and blacks formed numerous mutual aid and benefit societies. Baltimore's blacks sought and won exceptions to the statewide prohibitions on meetings and on the establishment of societies by Negroes. In 1835, a committee of Negro ministers reported more than thirty benevolent institutions, among them the African Friendship Benevolent Society for Social Relief, associations of caulkers, coachmen, and mechanics, and many church organizations. Like the other ethnic communities in the increasingly factionalized nineteenth century society, blacks were turning inward to meet many of their needs.

In 1860 over 35 percent of Baltimore's total population had been born in Germany or Ireland or were Afro-Americans. This group of Baltimoreans provided much of the labor that went into the important building of new industries and the construction of port and transportation facilities that accompanied industrialization. With the exception of the Germans, whose leaders came primarily from the older, well established segment of the population, these large ethnic groups did not

hold much political or economic power during the antebellum period.

The slums that grew because of the immigrants' poverty and the industries that spewed pollution into the air made the downtown area an undesirable place to live. Those people who could afford it began to move out of the central city business district to establish residential enclaves which were designed to provide a pleasant environment. Most notable among these was Mt. Vernon Square.

Mt. Vernon Square was constructed on land which George Eager purchased from Lord Baltimore in 1688. The estate passed on to his son John and then to John's daughter Ruth, who married Cornelius Howard. Their eldest son, John Eager Howard, donated part of what was known as Howard's Woods for the construction of the Washington Monument which began in 1815. Only the house of Nicholas Hitzelberger, foreman of the stonecutters and later keeper of the monument, stood nearby until 1829. Where the Peabody Institute now stands was the Bevan and Sons marble yard where workers cut and prepared the stone brought from the Ridgely quarries in Baltimore County.

In 1829, Charles Howard, youngest son of John Eager Howard, built a house on the future site of the Mt. Vernon Place Methodist Church. Howard's friends ridiculed his choice of location, saying that he might have to sell his home as a beer garden because his father allowed the public to visit the site of the monument and to hold military exercises and public meetings on the estate. Visitors picnicked by the monument. And, it is said, a site northwest of the monument served as a dueling ground.

When John Eager Howard died in 1827, the land, known as the Belvidere estate, was distributed among his heirs. They contributed the land for the park, laid out in the shape of a Greek cross, in 1831. The surrounding space was divided into lots and sold. By the 1850s, Mt. Vernon Place and Washington Place, the squares to the north and south of the monument, became the social center of Baltimore.

The rapid population growth spurred concern for planning the physical development of the city. During the decades preceding the Civil War, the government and several individual Baltimoreans made provision for maintaining open spaces within the ever more crowded city. Only a few houses had been built near the Washington Monument in 1839 when two builders, James and Samuel Canby, proposed a large-scale development of middle-class housing on the western outskirts of the city. They bought a 30-acre tract and offered a square of ground in the middle to the city as a public park. Franklin Square became the first of many similar small squares, followed by Lafayette, Harlem Park, Perkins Spring, Johnson, Madison and Collington. Landscaped boulevards such as Eutaw Place, Park Avenue and North Broadway were planned to serve the same purpose. The row houses for which Baltimore has become so famous soon lined the squares and boulevards where they offered an attractive alternative to downtown living.

The early suburbs were made viable by the beginning of an omnibus service in 1844. Within the first decade, Washington Square, Fells Point, Canton, Towsontown, Ashland Square, and Franklin Square all could be reached by omnibus. Their popularity increased after 1859 when the horsedrawn trolleys of the Baltimore City Passenger Railway Company began to link the new residential neighborhoods to the central business district. These nineteenth century suburbanites became Baltimore's first regular commuters.

Awareness of creating a pleasant environ-ment also led to the establishment in 1860 of a Public Park Commission. Using tax money paid on the gross receipts of the street railway company, the Park Commission purchased the 500-acre estate Druid Hill from Lloyd Nicholas Rogers and began landscaping according to the plan of Howard Daniels, a landscape gardener and engineer. Daniels planned the park to provide picturesque views, wooded pathways and formal promenades, lakes for swans and boats, and a grand formal entrance at the gate at Madison Avenue. The official opening of Druid Hill Park took place on October 19, 1860. Several thousand of Baltimore's public school children marched in the parade. A military display, band music, a dedication address by Mayor Thomas Swann, the firing of a gun for each state and territory and a final salvo for the park all marked the occasion.

When Druid Hill Park was planned in the western section of town, the city purchased 29 acres in East Baltimore to add to Patterson Park. Most of the planned improvements had to be put off until after the Civil War when a lake, music pavilion, and 19 more acres of land were added.

Parks built for the use of all the citizens were symbolic of a broadening of life in Baltimore. During the antebellum period the government and individuals both established many institutions with the wide variety of membership and purposes possible only in a large city with its diverse population. Facilities for education and entertainment received widespread support for all segments of the population.

In addition to the schools already discussed, numerous institutions and societies came into existence. In 1822 the Apprentice's Library was formed with the purpose of making books available to young people wanting to better themselves. In 1823 a number of Baltimoreans joined together to sponsor the construction of

Below:
In 1848 the land adjacent to the monument was still countryside, as shown by August Köllner in this lithograph. The wide street on the right is Pennsylvania Avenue

Bottom:
Lotteries were a popular way of raising money for all sorts of civic and charitable projects. Here the blindfolded boy on the platform is drawing a winning number

an Athenaeum, whose rooms would be used for meetings and lectures for many years to come. The cornerstone was laid in 1824 at the site at the corner of St. Paul and Lexington Streets. In 1825 two other important and enduring institutions were incorporated: The Maryland Academy of Science and the Maryland Institute for the Promotion of the Mechanical Arts, now known simply as the Maryland Institute.

In 1829, the "New Theatre and Circus" opened on Front Street with a performance of a musical farce, "The Spoiled Child." Announcements advertised the price of seats: boxes 50¢, pit 25¢, colored gallery 25¢. Three thousand spectators attended the first night. During that same year, a group of Baltimoreans formed a temperance society to combat the evil influence of liquor on the town's citizens.

In 1839, a new subscription library appeared: the Mercantile Library Company. Initiation cost only $2, a sum much more readily payable than the old Baltimore Library Company's $50 fee. Several facilities came together nine years later in 1848 when the new Baltimore Athenaeum opened. Built with $40,000 raised by contributions, the building housed the merged Baltimore and Mercantile Library Companies and the Maryland Historical Society which a group of local citizens had organized in 1844. John Spear Smith, son of General Samuel Smith, served as the latter's first president.

One notable fact about the institutions established during this period is that many have survived to the present day. The educational and cultural institutions especially received sufficient support from the expanding city's private sector to allow them to prosper. Several important educational institutions opened their doors during this period. In 1846, Professor Evert Marsh Topping, whose unorthodox methods of teaching Latin had created great controversy at

Princeton, opened a school on Garden Street and began teaching Latin to sixth grade students. After Topping's death, George Gibson Carey took over what became known as the Carey School and later as the Boys' Latin School.

In 1848 the School Sisters of Notre Dame began their work in Baltimore when they established a school for boarding and day students. In 1873 the academy purchased 64 acres from David Perine and Joseph Reynolds and began construction of the campus on North Charles Street. The College of Notre Dame of Maryland graduated its first class with an A.B. degree in 1899.

Loyola College opened in September, 1852 with 58 young men enrolled. The president, the Rev. John Early, S.J., and eight Jesuits comprised the faculty. After two and a half years of holding classes in two rented houses on Holliday Street, the college moved to its new home on Calvert at Madison, the current location of Center Stage, where the college remained until 1922 when it moved to Charles Street and Cold Spring Lane while the high school remained downtown. In the year 1857, George Peabody donated $300,000 to the city to establish an institute. His philanthropy and the Peabody Institute will be discussed later.

No account of the antebellum period would be complete without some mention of the "great happenings" of those years. From time to time a famous visitor or a major event drew enormous crowds. Rich and poor, members of all ethnic groups, turned out to mark certain grand occasions.

In late summer, 1824, the Revolutionary War hero, French General Lafayette, made a return visit to Baltimore. A delegation met his ship at the Delaware line and sailed with him to Fort McHenry where the formal welcome took place. Four ships fully dressed with flags and streamers sailed into the harbor to greet the

Baltimore's Washington Monument, the first in the nation, was paid for by funds raised by a lottery conducted in 1816. When it was first built the monument stood in the country and was a popular spot for picnickers. By the middle of the century, the squares surrounding the monument had become the city's most fashionable residential area

This view of the Washington Monument in 1850 shows the fashionable houses that had been built on Mt. Vernon Place and Washington Place

Omnibuses, like the one in the foreground, began service in Baltimore in 1844. This 1859 view of Baltimore Street looking east from Calvert Street shows the wide variety of people and vehicles along the city's main business thoroughfare.

Horse-drawn trolleys such as this one shown in front of the Holliday Street Theatre began to link new suburban neighborhoods to the central business district after 1859

General and his son Washington Lafayette and Secretary of State John Quincy Adams. The crowd of dignitaries included Samuel Smith, John Eager Howard, Charles Carroll, and Maryland Governor Samuel Stevens. A later chronicler described the reunion with Revolutionary War comrades: "The scene was one of the most impressive and heart-touching that was ever witnessed. All were convulsed into tears, but they were tears of joy and gratulation." The welcome in town was even more elaborate. Special arches, paintings and crowds lined the route. After the mayor welcomed him, Lafayette reminisced: "It is under the auspices of Baltimore patriotism, by the generosity of the merchants, by the zeal of the ladies of this city, at a critical period when not a day was to be lost, that I have been enabled in 1781 to begin a campaign, the fortunate issue of which has still enhanced the value of the service then rendered to our cause." All this endeared him even more to the city whose parades and celebrations continued for several days until Lafayette's departure.

Several years later, a crowd of 20,000 turned out to mourn John Adams and Thomas Jefferson who died on the same day, July 4, 1826, exactly fifty years after the signing of the Declaration of Independence. On the morning of July 20, the tolling of bells announced the commencement of ceremonies. Businesses closed. The Battle Monument was draped with black shrouds. A funeral procession marched northward through the city to Howard's Park, turned through the Belvedere gate at the north and into the woods to a natural amphitheater where 20,000 people heard Methodist Bishop Joshua Soule deliver the eulogy.

The newer generation of politicians drew smaller crowds than did the Revolutionary heroes. Baltimoreans welcomed Andrew Jackson in March, 1825 with a ball at Barnum's Hotel, a military presentation of colors, an open public reception and an evening at the theater. When Henry Clay came to town in May, 1828, the ship *Patuxent* carried a crowd down the river to greet him. Like Jackson, he held hours of open reception for all who chose to visit him. Clay, however, declined formal festivities like dinners and theater parties so commonly arranged for visiting dignitaries.

Henry Clay and Andrew Jackson both came to Baltimore in 1833. Clay typically received citizens individually but declined the invitation to a public dinner. On the other hand, Jackson's visit this time drew enormous crowds. Most people turned out not so much to see President Jackson as to catch a glimpse of the man with whom he met: Chief Black Hawk. The year before, Black Hawk had led the Sauk and Fox tribes in rebellion against Jackson's policy of removing all Indians from land east of the Mississippi River. Even in defeat, the chief defied Jackson magnificently at the conclusion of the hostilities, "I am a man and you are nothing more." The government imprisoned Black Hawk for several weeks and then took him on tour of the eastern cities to impress him with their strength. Two of his sons and several other prisoners accompanied him. Crowds expected to see a savage but discovered instead a patriarch, standing tall in a red-collared blue coat, wearing bright ear decorations and carrying the "medicine" skin of a sparrow hawk at his side. The press of people was so great that Jackson and Black Hawk had to move to Fort McHenry to carry on their discussions.

A less happy but very enthusiastic crowd assembled in Monument Square on May 23, 1846 to support the American annexation of Texas and the war that followed. Reverdy Johnson, General Sam Houston, and William Yancey, a member of Congress from Alabama, all addressed the Baltimore audience. The city contributed a unit of soldiers known as "Baltimore's Own" and three other companies which left the city on June 4 under the command of Col. William H. Watson. They fought at the battle of Monterrey and in other engagements until their term of service expired in May, 1847. Other Maryland companies fought throughout the war. The, Baltimore *Sun*, founded by Arunah S. Abell in 1837, did some extraordinary reporting of the Mexican War. Using relays of horses and riders the newspaper often brought stories before the official messengers did. In the spring of 1847 the *Sun* telegraphed to President James K. Polk word of the fall of Vera Cruz. Samuel F. B. Morse's first telegraph message had been sent from Washington to Baltimore only three years earlier.

A different sort of crowd assembled to welcome the Swedish singer, Jenny Lind, on December 8, 1850. Several thousand people waited at the depot and at Barnum's Hotel to catch a glimpse of the young woman who was taking America by storm. The great demand for tickets for her performances at the Front Street Theater led to an auction. Although the price had originally been set at $3, the first choice ticket sold for $100, and the sales finally averaged out at $7 a seat. Spectators were allowed to sit on the stage. On the night of the last concert, theater officials charged 12½¢ for the right even to bid in the ticket auction. Even this financial chicanery did not deter people's quest to hear the famous "Swedish Nightingale."

In 1851, a foreign political leader, the exiled Hungarian patriot Louis Kossuth, drew cheering crowds who identified his struggle for national liberty with America's own. Kossuth had led the Magyars in 1848 and 1849 in their losing struggle against Austrian domination. Ice and snow notwithstanding, Baltimoreans paraded in his honor.

An assemblage of a rather macabre nature occurred in April, 1859 when 30,000 spectators turned out to witness the execution of four convicted murderers. The event marked the culmination of a legal drama. Three of the four convicted were young men of respectable parentage. Influential friends had tried to convince Governor Thomas Hicks to intervene. Twice he delayed the execution but finally he declined to lessen the sentence. Some called the execution a tragedy, others a victory for the impartiality of the law.

One uniquely American festivity is the political nominating convention. Baltimore was a popular convention city from the 1830s through 1860. Good transportation facilities made the city easily accessible. Baltimore lay close to Washington, D. C., the practical residence of many of the leading delegates. Furthermore, in this border city neither the worst aspects of slavery nor too many abolitionists were visible. For all these reasons, Baltimore frequently witnessed parades of the politically famous and nominations of winners and losers throughout the antebellum period.

In 1831, in September, the Anti-Masonic Party met at the Athenaeum and nominated Baltimore lawyer, William Wirt, for president. The Anti-Masons, the first party to hold a nominating convention, made the secrecy of Masonry its primary concern, but were drawn into the anti-Jacksonian camp because Andrew Jackson was himself a Mason. The other anti-Jackson group, the National Republicans, also met in the Baltimore Athenaeum in December and chose Henry Clay to oppose Jackson's bid for reelection. The following May, the Democrats gave Baltimore a clean sweep of the convention trade when they assembled in the city to confirm Jackson's renomination and chose Martin Van Buren as his running mate. This group spilled over into the Universalist

Baltimore was a popular site for presidential nominating conventions in the decades before the Civil War. In 1840 while the Democrats convened in the Music Hall, the Whig Party rented the Canton Race Track, offered free hard cider, and invited Baltimoreans to hear Henry Clay and Daniel Webster praise their party's candidate, William Henry Harrison

could not carry the convention, they withdrew, reconvened at the Maryland Institute Hall and nominated John C. Breckinridge of Kentucky. This left the regular Democrats free to nominate Stephen Douglas. The only candidate not nominated in Baltimore in 1860 was Abraham Lincoln. Changing their name to the Union Party, the Republicans did come to this border state city in 1864 when Lincoln was renominated at the site of the 1860 Democratic cleavage, the Front Street Theater.

Baltimore's local politics was as confused as national politics was during the decades that preceded the Civil War. Confusion, disorder, and violence characterized the last antebellum generation. But through it all, there was a beneficial trend towards greater centralization of city services, facilities, and powers. This movement continued in the hands of whichever party or faction held power. Democrats, Whigs, and, later, Know-Nothings vied for control. Regardless of which group was in power, they presided over the construction of new public buildings, the extension of city streets, increasing governmental control of services and utilities, and a continuing drive for greater municipal authority and autonomy.

After the termination of Samuel Smith's mayoralty in 1838, a succession of Whigs and Democrats held the office, none for very many years. From 1838 to 1854, Baltimore had eight different mayors. In chronological order these were: Sheppard C. Leakin, Samuel Brady, Solomon Hillen, Jr., James O. Law, Jacob G. Davies, Elijah Stansbury, John Hanson Thomas Jerome, and John Smith Hollins.

Following the riots of 1835 and the panic of 1837, the city faced huge administrative problems. For one thing, its tax collection procedures were unreliable. In its most prosperous year, 1836, Baltimore collected just over half of the total $295,000 levied. To remedy

this situation the state legislature authorized the city to confiscate the property of delinquent taxpayers in 1841. For another example, before 1834, street repairs could be made only when every resident in the affected area agreed and paid two-thirds of the cost in advance. In 183- the requirement was changed to approval by only two-thirds of the residents. And in 1836 the power of street extensions within the city was transferred from the state to the city. Only under Mayor Samuel Brady, in 1841, did Baltimore begin appointing street commissioners with the power to initiate both construction and repairs.

Other municipal services, especially police and fire protection, were equally far from the professional calibre modern urbanites expect. In Baltimore, the daytime police remained separate from the night watch. Politicians appointed the policemen, only one-third of whom earned salaries. The other two-thirds' income came from fines collected for violations of city ordinances. Fire protection continued in the hands of the volunteer companies that were also undisguised political organizations. In order to stop the fights over which company would put out a given fire, the City Council in 1842 divided Baltimore into three fire districts and appointed over each a Chief Marshal with absolute authority in his area.

In politics, the transformation to Jacksonian style machines took place in all groups. Political parties offered steamboat rides, picnics, dances, free food and free liquor to their followers. One of the more gala events occurred in 1844 when the Democrats invited thirty thousand Baltimoreans to a picnic in Gibson's Woods and distributed free hard cider to all. On election days, the party faithful distributed circulars, transported voters to the polls, and sometimes even provided lodging for potential voters. They also fought for their

Some Baltimoreans considered visiting conventioneers from the West a bit rowdy

candidates, and election days were marked by much violence.

A common practice was "cooping," the rounding up of drunks, strangers, and anyone else who looked like an easy victim for the purpose of marching them from precinct to precinct to vote as ordered. The writer Edgar Allen Poe, who lived in Baltimore during part of this period, was probably the most famous person cooped during the city's electoral contests. Poe, who was the grandson of Baltimore's Revolutionary Deputy Commissary General, David Poe, died here in the Washington College Hospital in 1849, shortly after being cooped during the October elections.

One major cleavage was at least partially resolved before the end of the 1830s. The Democrats had remained split between the old Jacksonians like General Samuel Smith and his son John Spear Smith, longtime Baltimore merchants whose family connections played a role in their political ascendancy, and newer leaders like William Frick whose position was based on service to the party. By the mid-1830s, leading Democrats like Benjamin Chew Howard, John Eager Howard's son, were beginning to recognize the need for cohesion within the party. The appointment of Frick to the lucrative position as Collector of the Port of Baltimore symbolized the rise of the new faction. Frick reigned as the Democratic boss in Baltimore in the late 1830s.

A big gain for Baltimore City came in the Reform Act passed by the legislature in 1837. This gave Baltimore representation in the State Senate equal to that of each county and representation in the House of Delegates equal to that of the largest county. Continuing efforts by reformers to reduce the state budget and to modernize Maryland's constitution finally succeeded in 1851. The new order shifted apportionment in such a way that Baltimore and the populous counties of Western Maryland held the power. It also separated Baltimore City and County, making each an independent political unit. This constitution remained in effect until 1864.

By 1850 the Whigs were a dying party. Their last national effort came in the unsuccessful presidential bid of General Winfield Scott against Franklin Pierce in 1852. Their demise and the corruption within the ranks of the local Democrats led one former Jacksonian, later converted to the Whigs, to withdraw from politics. John Pendleton Kennedy declared, "Nothing can be more contemptible than the state of politics and management in Maryland. We have not a man in public office above mediocrity, and the whole machinery of our politics is moved by the smallest, narrowest, most ignorant and corrupt men in the State." Many men apparently agreed with Kennedy. The state was ripe for a new party. The first was a short-lived Temperance Party that swept Baltimore in 1853 and sent ten delegates to Annapolis. These men and their colleagues failed to gain prohibition of alcoholic beverages, and the party quickly declined in favor of a second new party, one promulgating a platform that more completely aroused people's ardor and loyalty.

The Know-Nothing Party began as a secret society whose members received instructions to say that they "knew nothing" if asked about the organization. Strongly nativist, the Know-Nothings served as a focal point for all the confusion and discontent resulting from the rapid industrialization, low salaries and poor working conditions, the massive immigration of the 1840s and 1850s, and the increasing violence and crime, all of which frightened people and seemed uncontrollable.

One group of victims were native American workers, whose wages and standard of living

Local politics had declined to such a low level in the 1850s that John Pendleton Kennedy declared that "We have not a man in public office above mediocrity"

were depressed because of competition, particularly from immigrants whose dire need forced them to accept long hours and little pay. The natives began looking back to what they believed to be better times. They talked about the heroes of the Revolution. Their contemporary program emphasized immigration restriction. They considered the Catholic Church to be an anti-American foreign power and talked about prohibiting Catholics and immigrants from holding public office. These fears resulted in irrational violence by followers of the new society that brought condemnation to the group.

In addition to their xenophobia, the Know-Nothings criticized corruption in politics and the growing national agitation over slavery, which they feared as destructive to national unity. In Maryland, their strong anti-sectional position attracted support from men who did not want to divide the Union over the question of slavery. Educated upper-class men like John Pendleton Kennedy and Anthony Kennedy, Henry Winter Davis, and Thomas Swann became Know-Nothing Party leaders and gave the group a respectability it did not possess elsewhere. Baltimore became a Know-Nothing stronghold in the late 1850s.

The Baltimore Know-Nothings ended their secrecy in 1854 when they announced Samuel Hinks as their candidate for mayor only two weeks before the election. Most campaigning was conducted inside the Know-Nothing lodges. To the astonishment of all and the consternation of some, Hinks won. The next year, Know-Nothings won all ten of Baltimore's seats in the House of Delegates. In the state at large they elected four of six Congressmen, 54 of 74 Delegates, and 8 of the 11 State Senate seats that were open.

In 1856, Baltimore elected a second Know-Nothing mayor, Thomas Swann, a former

president of the B&O, and Maryland gave its majority vote to the Know-Nothing candidate for president, Millard Fillmore, who ran on the American Party ticket. Maryland was the only state that supported Fillmore. In 1857, Marylanders chose a Know-Nothing governor, Thomas Hicks, and in 1858, Mayor Swann won a second term and his party carried 29 of 30 City Council contests.

These elections were so marred with fraud and violence that Baltimore once again was referred to as "Mobtown." Clubs succeeded the volunteer fire companies as centers of political activity. Democratic party clubs like the Bloody Eights, Pluckers, Double Pumps, and Butt Enders physically fought the Know-Nothing Plug Uglies, Rip Raps, Gladiators, Stay Lates, Screw Bolts, Black Snakes and Tigers.

On election day, both Democrats and Know-Nothings used scare tactics against the opposition. Know-Nothings, for example, displayed pools of bloody water obtained from local butchers known as "blood tubs" to scare immigrants coming to vote for the Democratic candidate. In 1856 approximately 15 people died in the election day violence. In 1857 a Know-Nothing policeman was killed on election day. In that same year, the first ward Rip Raps greeted voters with a cannon. Both parties increased their votes by cooping strangers and drunks and then marching them from one polling place to the next under pain of injury or death if they did not vote the right way. Voting was not done in secret as people deposited large ballots, coded to their party's color, in a box in full view of everyone else present.

Despite the fraud and violence that soon discredited the Know-Nothings, the two men who served as mayors of Baltimore proved beneficial to the city and its development. They were efficient managers and did much to centralize the operations of the city govern-

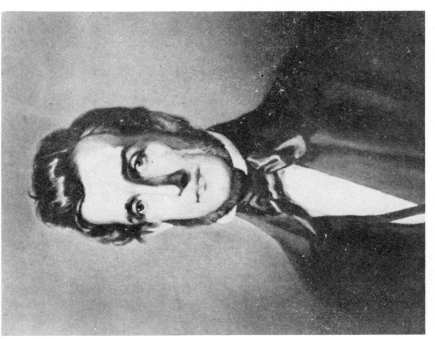

Much to everyone's surprise, the Know-Nothing Party candidate, Samuel Hinks, won the mayoralty election in 1854

Well-educated citizens so objected to corruption within the existing political parties, that many, including John Pendleton Kennedy and his brother Anthony, pictured here, joined the Know-Nothing Party

ment. In 1854, after the Baltimore Water Company refused to extend its services into areas with new housing, Samuel Hinks directed the purchase of the facility and organized the municipal Water Department.

Over the years from 1853 to 1857, the city government consolidated the day police and the night watch and organized four police districts under one city marshal. Policemen, about 350 of them, received their appointments from the mayor, often as a reward for political service.

In 1857, Mayor Thomas Swann created the office of city comptroller. One result was increased efficiency in the collection of taxes. In 1858, Swann replaced the volunteers with a salaried municipal Fire Department, administered by a Fire Board appointed by the mayor. In 1859 the Swann administration granted the franchise for the Baltimore City Passenger Railway Company. Within a few months, Baltimore had 22 miles of tracks and 65 passenger cars. All these measures, and many similar ones, aided in the ongoing expansion of Baltimore.

Despite the effective measures of Hinks and Swann, the bigotry, corruption and violence of the Know-Nothings soon led to organized opposition. In August 1857 the *Baltimore American* called for a town meeting to discuss the problems of corruption and disorder. This meeting and the Know-Nothing victory in 1858 resulted in the creation of the City Reform Association by old elite Baltimoreans, often Democrats. Statewide, the Know-Nothings were declining. In October 1859, Democrats regained control of the Senate and House of Delegates. This legislature, responding to a request by the Baltimore reformers, took control of the city police away from the mayor and put it in the hands of the state government. They also voided the results of the 1859 election on grounds of fraud and unseated Baltimore's Know-Nothing

delegates.

In the mayoral election of October 1860 reform candidate George William Brown, a member of the Baltimore banking family, defeated Know-Nothing Samuel Hindes in a landslide. Reformers also gained control of the City Council. Sadly, the reformers had little opportunity for real reform as the Civil War broke out a few months later. As war approached, many former Know-Nothing leaders moved into the Unionist camp to try to deal with the crisis.

On the eve of the Civil War, Baltimore was truly a city divided. Half northern, half southern, Baltimore's heritage included abolitionism and slavery, old southern families and recent immigrants, industries and remnants of a landed aristocracy. About sixty percent of Baltimore's trade was with the north. At the same time, Baltimore was considered the southern city with the most manufacturing. In 1860, roughly one-fourth of Baltimore's population had been born in Europe, a bit less than in many northern cities, a bit more than in most southern cities.

Twelve percent of all Baltimoreans were black, most of them free. Northern cities had only small black populations. Southern cities repressed free blacks, fearing the growing number of uprisings and escapes. As 1861 began some Baltimoreans supported Lincoln while others talked of secession. Most stood in between those extremes. When war broke out Baltimoreans fought for both North and South. Families, friends and business partners split. Baltimore was a city divided during the Civil War.

The conflict had been a long time coming. Post-Revolutionary abolitionism resulted in free states in the North and slave states in the South. In Baltimore, slave owners and abolitionists lived side by side. Late in the eighteenth century, a Baltimore chapter of the Maryland Society for Promoting the Abolition of Slavery wa

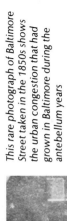

Thomas Swann became Baltimore's second Know-Nothing mayor in 1856. He later served as Maryland's Unionist governor during the Civil War

This rare photograph of Baltimore Street taken in the 1850s shows the urban congestion that had grown in Baltimore during the antebellum years

established. The membership, although heavily Quaker, included many prominent Baltimoreans like Philip Rogers, Dr. George Buchanan, Samuel Sterett, and Alexander McKim.

During the 1820s, an abolitionist of national renown, Benjamin Lundy, lived in Baltimore and published the nation's only exclusively anti-slavery newspaper, *The Genius of Universal Emancipation*. His printer, Daniel Raymond, ran for the City Council in 1826 but was defeated. In 1829 and 1830, William Lloyd Garrison came to Baltimore to work as Lundy's co-editor. Garrison, for the first time, lived where slavery existed and the experience led him to take a more extreme anti-slavery position. An article Garrison wrote against Francis Todd, the owner of a slave ship, resulted in a libel suit. Garrison was convicted, was unable or unwilling to pay the $5000 fine and instead spent several months in the Baltimore jail. After his release, Garrison moved to Boston and on January 1, 1831 issued the first edition of his own famous anti-slavery newspaper, *The Liberator*. Although Lundy remained a gradualist, even that position was becoming unpopular in Baltimore and he moved the *Genius* to Washington, D. C.

After 1830, the few abolitionists left in town were shunned by much of the community. A small abolitionist paper, The *Saturday Visitor*, was viewed as an outrage by most citizens. Baltimore's most vocal abolitionist of the 1840s and 1850s, William Gunnison, had to close his mercantile establishment in 1851 because the local bankers refused to do business with him. Undeterred, he campaigned for the Republican Party in 1860, when only 1087 Baltimoreans voted for Lincoln. During that election, the few Republicans that dared campaign had eggs and bricks thrown at them. The one Republican newspaper in town, the *Baltimore Wecker*, voice of the German liberals, was the target of mob attack a few months later.

As abolitionism became suspect and as popular fear of the increasing number of free blacks grew, more and more Baltimoreans became involved in the movement to "colonize" free blacks in Africa. The American Colonization Society began in 1816. In 1831 a group of Baltimore businessmen founded the Maryland State Colonization Society "to promote and execute a plan to colonize (*with their own consent*) the free people of color in our country, either in Africa or such other place as Congress shall deem most expedient . . . Many prominent Baltimoreans, including Solomon Etting, John Eager Howard, John B. Latrobe, and Luke Tiernan, actively supported the effort to send people to the Society's colony at Cape Palmas, known as Maryland in Liberia. Benjamin Lundy and other former abolitionist leaders became active once abolitionism was impossible in Baltimore. Despite heavy propaganda and expenditures, no more than 1,250 people were convinced to make the move. Most free blacks agreed with the resolution passed at a meeting of black Baltimoreans in 1831: "that we consider the land in which we were born and in which we have been bred our only true and appropriate home . . ."

By 1860, most Baltimoreans were less interested either in destroying or in maintaining slavery than they were in the question of whether there would be war. Republicans were feared, because they were considered radicals. In the election, John C. Breckinridge of Kentucky, the nominee of the southern Democrats, carried Baltimore, as did the reform Democratic candidate for mayor, George W. Brown. The year 1860 saw a realignment in Maryland politics because of the desire to avoid war, the fear of Republicans and also free blacks and the collapse of the Know-Nothings. Many former Know-Nothings, consistent with their earlier position, became Unionists. The

Right:
Reform candidate George William Brown won the mayoralty in 1860 as the public showed its increasing dissatisfaction with continuing political corruption and violence

Below:
This view of the harbor, c. 1850, shows different vessels engaged in Baltimore's already established shipping trade

Democratic Party revived its strength in Baltimore and throughout the state. Democrats tended to favor states' rights, including the South's right to secede. Unionists, including the slaveholders among them, opposed secession and also, before the fighting broke out, generally opposed war.

The year 1861 was destined to be an agonizing one for Baltimore. The city was

suspect in the North because of the pro-Southern leanings of some of its residents. As the year progressed, Baltimore fell into increasingly greater disrepute in the North. The first blot on Baltimore's reputation came from what was probably a non-event. When Abraham Lincoln left Springfield, Illinois early in February to go to Washington for his inauguration, the detective Allan Pinkerton warned him that there was a plot to kill him when he passed through Baltimore. Lincoln was due to pass through the Monumental City around noon on February 23. Because an ordinance forbade railroad engines from traversing the city, Lincoln was to ride from the Calvert Street Station of the North Central Railroad to the Camden Street Station of the B&O in a horse-drawn carriage. Pinkerton asserted that a group of assassins would approach the carriage and kill the president-elect. This would then be the signal for Southern sympathizers to seize Washington, D. C.

Lincoln resisted cancelling engagements at Philadelphia and Harrisburg but was finally convinced to leave Harrisburg early in order to traverse Baltimore under cover of darkness. Taking a Philadelphia, Wilmington and Baltimore train, he arrived at the President Street Station at 3:30 A.M. A team of horses pulled his sleeping car silently through the streets of Baltimore. The group departed from Camden Station at 4:15 A.M. The next day, when crowds lined the streets to see the new president, he was already in Washington. Baltimoreans generally were offended. Later, Pinkerton was accused of inventing the plot to gain publicity for his detective agency. No proof has ever been found that the plot really existed.

April 1861 was marked by violence in Baltimore. One week after the first shots of the Civil War were fired at Fort Sumter on April 12, the first deaths of the war occurred in Baltimore. On April 19, the Massachusetts Sixth Regiment

Opposite:
John Work Garrett, president of the B&O during the Civil War, was a staunch supporter of the Union and offered the government the services of his railroad

Above:
En route to his inauguration, Abraham Lincoln traversed Baltimore in the middle of the night and arrived in Washington just after dawn the following morning. He had been warned of possible danger from the city's Southern sympathizers

arrived in Baltimore on its way to Washington, D. C. Many residents objected to their transit and barricaded the streets between the President Street Station and the Camden Station where they were expected to march. Although Mayor George Brown walked at the head of the line of soldiers and Police Marshal Kane at the rear, bystanders began throwing rocks. Soon somebody fired a shot. The riot was on and, before it ended, four soldiers and twelve Marylanders lay dead, the first casualties of the war.

On the following day, a mob attacked the Wecker office, because of the newspaper's Republican stance, and destroyed the press of Sinai, a German-Jewish monthly edited by Dr. David Einhorn, an abolitionist. When word came that additional troops might be headed for Baltimore some of the authorities, fearing further violence, burned all the railroad bridges north of the city. Mayor Brown and Maryland Governor Thomas Hicks met with Lincoln and requested that no further troops be sent through Baltimore. Lincoln agreed, and temporarily troops going south bypassed the riot-torn city. Calm returned slowly and pro-Union sentiment began to reassert itself.

Then on May 13, Union General Benjamin Butler and one thousand troops arrived in the city. When Baltimoreans awoke the following morning, they found the unit encamped on Federal Hill, setting up weapons designed to ensure Baltimore's loyalty to the Union. General Butler issued a series of proclamations, among them that his troops would enforce the law, that armed men were not to assemble, that arms and ammunition headed south to aid the Confederates would be seized, and that no one was to display Confederate flags or banners. After this time, federal troops began to pass through Baltimore again.

Once it was clear that there was to be war, pro-Union sentiment began to assert itself more strongly. By the spring of 1861, the Know-Nothing and Constitutional Union parties had collapsed and the Democrats were split between unionists and secessionists. On May 23, 1861 a convention met in Baltimore to organize the new Maryland party. Brant Mayer became chairman. The new Maryland party opposed secession, endorsed the federal government's right to use force to preserve the Union, and supported Lincoln's war policies. At a special election held in June, Marylanders chose members of the

Opposite:
Police Marshal George P. Kane joined Mayor George Brown in escorting the Massachusetts regiment. Despite their escort, bystanders began the attack

Below:
Rifles like this, with bayonets attached, were carried by the Massachusetts soldiers

Above:
The first deaths of the Civil War occurred in Baltimore on April 19, 1861, when local citizens rioted against the Massachusetts Sixth Regiment which was passing through the city on its way to Washington, D.C.

Left:
Baltimoreans awoke the morning of May 14, 1861, to find Northern General Benjamin Butler and 1500 troops encamped on Federal Hill to assure the city's loyalty to the Union

Unionist Party to fill all six of the state's Congressional seats. In August, the party convened in Baltimore and nominated Augustus W. Bradford to oppose the States Rights Party candidate, Benjamin C. Howard, for governor.

Before the November victory of Bradford and the Unionist candidates for the State Senate and House of Delegates, there was some fear that pro-Southern forces in Annapolis would try to get Maryland to secede and join the Confederacy. The Union would not tolerate a Confederate state between the northern states and its capitol. Operating under Lincoln's suspension of the writ of *habeas corpus*, federal forces took into custody a large number of Marylanders who were merely suspected of harboring pro-Southern sentiments. The most important case was the arrest of John Merryman of Cockeysville, who was imprisoned in Fort McHenry for seven weeks before his release was secured, probably with the help of Chief Justice Roger B. Taney. The inventor and builder of railroad cars, Ross Winans, who was a member of the House of Delegates and favored secession also served time in Fort McHenry. Police Marshal George P. Kane was imprisoned there too and the federal government took over the city's police force. Many other Baltimore officials, including Mayor George Brown, and Delegates Severn Teackle Wallis and Henry M. Warfield spent time in prison. Once the elections of November 1861 put Unionists in power in the state government, Northern fears that Maryland would fall into the hands of secessionists subsided and the repression grew less harsh. Gradually the federal authorities released the civilians and Fort McHenry housed predominantly military prisoners through most of the war.

The Union Army maintained an active presence in Baltimore throughout the war. Well-equipped military establishments stood on Federal Hill, which by the end of 1861 held fifty heavy cannon, and at Fort Marshall just east of Patterson Park. Army encampments appeared in Druid Hill and Carroll Parks, in Lafayette Square, near the McKim mansion, and on the grounds of the Maryland Agricultural Society around the present corner of Charles and 27th Streets. The Army brought Confederate prisoners taken at Antietam and Gettysburg to Baltimore. By 1863, Fort McHenry housed 680 southern prisoners and the Baltimore City Jail an additional 700. Pro-Confederate Baltimoreans sent clothing, food, blankets, and money to the prisoners.

The federal government confiscated the estate of General George H. Steuart, Confederate States Army, and turned it into Jarvis Hospital. Located near Mt. Clare Station, the hospital was protected by a nearby ridge. Other large hospitals were located in Patterson Park, in the National Hotel near Camden Station, and in the Union Dock on Pratt Street.

Although the situation eased somewhat after 1861, pro-Confederate Baltimoreans felt repressed by the federal occupation. Display of Confederate banners was forbidden. The most famous pro-Confederate newspaper, *The South*, and eight others were suppressed. Organizations and clubs run by Southern sympathizers were closed. The occupying army wanted to ensure that northern soldiers' lives were not endangered because of pro-Confederate activity in Baltimore.

Baltimore men joined the armies of both the North and the South. No exact figures are available. One estimate is that thirty thousand people left Baltimore during the Civil War, some to fight, some to live where there was less danger of war. From Maryland as a whole, roughly sixty-three thousand men, including nine thousand blacks, served in the Union forces and twenty thousand fought for the Confederacy. Very little military action took place in the

Far Left:
John Merryman's detention at Fort McHenry became a cause célèbre. Many of the area's leading citizens were arrested because of their suspected or certain confederate sympathies

Left:
Severn Teackle Wallis, a Baltimore member of the House of Delegates, spent time in prison

Major General Benjamin Butler commanded Union troops stationed at Fort Federal Hill

vicinity of Baltimore. Fighting near Frederick in July 1864 and the Union defeat at Monocacy made Baltimore fear that the Confederates would next attack Baltimore. Women and children fled the city. Businesses loaded their money and valuables onto ships in the harbor. The attack did not come, however, because the Southern troops headed towards Washington.

Military action took place within the current city limits only during the raids of Confederate General Bradley T. Johnson and Major Harry Gilmor. Just before the Battle of Monocacy, General Johnson's cavalry brigade and the Baltimore Light Artillery received orders to cut off Baltimore and Washington from the north and then release over fifteen thousand southern prisoners detained at Point Lookout, Maryland. Johnson's men rode from Frederick through Westminster and on to Randallstown, Reisterstown and Cockeysville. Following the Northern Central Railroad tracks, they destroyed bridges, ripped out track, and pulled down telegraph wires. Then they rode into Towson and south along Charles Street to burn the summer home of Maryland Governor Augustus Bradford, located where the Elkridge Club now stands. Next they rode west to the Northern Central Relay House by Lake Roland, destroyed more railroad equipment, and pushed on through Owings Mills towards Washington, destroying B&O property along the way.

The arrival of northern reinforcements forced abandonment of plans to free the Point Lookout prisoners and to attack Washington. Before the Confederates turned south from Cockeysville, Johnson ordered Major Harry Gilmor of Baltimore County to take the 135 men of the First and Second Maryland Cavalry to raid the Philadelphia, Wilmington and Baltimore Railroad. They rode through Texas and Timonium and on along the Dulany Valley. In

Kingsville they burned the farmhouse of Ishmael Day who refused to lower the United States flag at their command. Then, at Magnolia, they captured and destroyed two trains and took five Union officers prisoner. They returned south along the Philadelphia Pike. At Towson, they encountered a group of Union cavalrymen whom they chased down York Road as far as Govans. Then they rode west through Riderwood and the Green Spring Valley, turned south down Reisterstown Road, cut across to Randallstown and rejoined General Johnson at Poolesville.

The major political development of 1864 was the passage of a new constitution for the state of Maryland. More than a year after Lincoln's Emancipation Proclamation went into effect in rebellion areas, Marylanders voted to hold a convention to write a new constitution. The document, which passed by a narrow margin in October, ended slavery in Maryland, set up a system of test oaths and voter registration, and reapportioned the state in such a way that Baltimore increased its representation in the legislature. Democrats opposed the constitution and argued against Unionists using dire predictions about the future of blacks without slavery as a means of control. The constitution went into effect on November 1, 1864, and the war continued.

On April 9, 1865, General Robert E. Lee surrendered the Army of Northern Virginia to General Ulysses S. Grant at Appomattox Court House in Virginia. The remaining Confederate forces surrendered within a few days. Finally, the war had ended. On the night of April 14, John Wilkes Booth assassinated Abraham Lincoln as he watched a performance at Ford's Theater in Washington. Most Baltimoreans mourned their dead president. Then, like the nation as a whole, they began the long, slow, and painful process of reunification.

This early photograph shows
troops marching through the city

Camp Carroll was one of the
many installations that the Union
Army maintained throughout the
Civil War

This lithograph portrays Baltimore's celebration of the passage of the Fifteenth Amendment, which enfranchised the nation's slaves, and depicts scenes from black history and heroes of the struggle for emancipation as well as the local festivities

Reconciliation & Growth

1865-1917

IV

The tragic Civil War left a nation and a city divided. On June 6, 1865, Baltimore Army paraded through town, then marched to the new Druid Hill Park where they stacked their weapons and heard Governor Augustus Bradford thank them and welcome them home. A month and a half earlier, in the wake of Lincoln's assassination, the City Council had passed a resolution against allowing ex-Confederates to return to the city. Despite the resolution, Confederate veterans slowly came home, too, and soon violent clashes broke out between the two groups of former soldiers. Some Baltimoreans formed societies to aid the devastated South, among them the Baltimore Agricultural Aid Society, the Southern Relief Association and the Ladies' Depository.

Ultra-Unionist John Lee Chapman was mayor and was reelected in 1866. Thomas Swann, the former mayor of Baltimore and also a Unionist, was governor. A required oath of *past* loyalty limited the franchise to Marylanders who had remained loyal to the Union. But change was brewing. The conservative Unionists were moving closer to a coalition with the Democrats, many of whom had been pro-Southern. This new coalition opposed the voter registry law and its required oath, Negro suffrage, and the Radical Republicans in Congress. The Democrats accused the Unionists of supporting Negro equality. The Unionists countered by calling the Democrats traitors, because so many had favored the Confederacy.

In 1866 Baltimore, along with Southern Maryland and the Eastern Shore, returned the Democratic Party to power in Annapolis. In April, 1867 the Unionists became Republican Unionists, and in May they held the first racially integrated political convention in Maryland. They adopted a position in favor of universal manhood suffrage, which meant enfranchising black men. The Democrats' popularity had returned so quickly that the Republicans needed all the votes they could get. Also in May, 1867 a convention controlled by Democrats produced a new state constitution to replace that of 1864. When it was adopted in September, the test oaths disappeared and control of the state returned completely into the hands of the Democratic Party. Reconstruction had ended in Maryland. In October 1867 Democrat Robert T. Banks was elected Mayor of Baltimore. In November Democrat Oden Bowie replaced Thomas Swann as governor. Swann and Montgomery Blair, both former Unionist leaders, joined the Democratic Party. The Democratic Party acknowledged Maryland's return to the fold when it held the 1872 convention here. Horace Greeley won the nomination but lost the general election to Ulysses S. Grant.

The one irony of Maryland's Reconstruction is that, although it ended a decade before Northern troops withdrew from the last Southern states, Negroes began to vote three years after the Democrats regained power and, unlike what happened further South, they never lost that right. The Democratic Maryland legislature itself revised the registration laws after it became obvious that the 15th Amendment which enfranchised Negroes, would pass. On April 8, 1870, Elijah Quigley of Towson voted in an election for county commissioners. Blacks in Baltimore City voted in the municipal elections in October. Reconstruction had ended quickly, but not as finally as it did in the former Confederacy.

All the accommodations to political realities did not mean that the wartime bitterness had passed. Indeed, as long as the men who fought in the armies and their contemporaries remained politically active they were always associated with the side they had served. The

Baltimoreans lay the cornerstone for the new City Hall in 1867. In the aftermath of the war, the city began to look to its future

immediate hostilities did disappear though, and reminiscences of local writers who grew up in Baltimore in the 1880s and 90s show a very different city than the suspicious, war-torn, town of the 1860s.

Henry L. Mencken spent his childhood, as well as most of his adult years, in a house on Hollins Street, one of the newer squares that had been built following the success of Mt. Vernon Square. Looking back many years later, he wrote:

The city into which I was born in 1880 had a reputation all over for what the English, in their real-estate advertising, are fond of calling the amenities. So far as I have been able to discover by a labored search of contemporary travel-books, no literary tourist, however waspish he may have been about Washington, Niagara Falls, the prairies of the West, or even Boston and New York, ever gave Baltimore a bad notice. They all agreed, often with lubricious gloats and gurgles, (a) that its indigenous victualry was unsurpassed in the Republic, (b) that its native . . . females of all ages up to thirty-five were of incomparable pulchritude, and as amiable as they were lovely, and (c) that its home-life was spacious, charming, full of creature comforts, and highly conducive to the facile and orderly propagation of the species.

There was some truth in all these articles, but not, I regret to have to add, too much. Perhaps the one that came closest to meeting scientific tests was the first. Baltimore lay very near the immense protein factory of Chesapeake Bay, and out of the bay it ate divinely.

Mencken proceeds to wax eloquent on the subject of crabs, terrapin, and luncheons at the Rennert Hotel. Truthful to the core, he also

Above:
In the Baltimore of Mencken's childhood, wagons still banged over cobblestone streets. Here Franklin Street has been torn up and the cobblestones have been laid along the sidewalks

Left:
This circus parade was clearly a grand event, drawing a large and varied crowd

Public parks enjoyed great popularity and wide use in the nineteenth and early twentieth centuries. The boat lake in Druid Hill Park was a Sunday afternoon favorite

described the summertime stench around Back Basin and the Inner Harbor where the sewage drained, the noisy streets where delivery wagons still banged over cobblestones, and the epidemics of typhoid, malaria and smallpox which killed many, especially children living in overcrowded slum neighborhoods.

On the lighter side, he wrote of grass growing to such heights in the cobblestone streets that carters allowed their horses to graze there. He also recorded that:

On the steep hill making eastward from the Washington Monument, in the very heart of Baltimore, some comedian once sowed wheat, and it kept on coming up for years thereafter. Every spring the Baltimore newspapers would report on the prospects of the crop, and visitors to the city were taken to see it.

Another local newspaperman, Meredith Janvier, wrote of attending Barnum's Greatest Show on Earth in the mid-1880s when circuses showed out on Belair Road, of riding for three cents the horse-drawn phaetons in Druid Hill Park, and of minstrel shows that played at the Academy of Music and at Ford's, Holliday Street and Front Street theaters. Janvier remembered seeing Blind Tom, a Negro musician, at Ford's Theater, and the composer and performer James Bland at the Holliday Street Theater. He remembered the opening in 1890 of the New Lyceum Theater where Edwin Booth, Otis Skinner and William S. Hart all performed. Helena Modjeska played Camille and Lady MacBeth there. Janvier saw Buffalo Bill's Wild West Show at the baseball park in the middle 1880s. Annie Oakley, who grew up in Cambridge, Maryland, was travelling with the show. When the show arrived, Druid Hill Park had recently acquired its first sea lion. The seal conveniently escaped just in time to be

Above:
Sheep grazed in Druid Hill Park
until the mid-twentieth century

Left:
Spectators in their own carriages
lined the edge of the Pimlico
Race Track where the first
running of the Preakness took
place in 1873

Bicycles built for one and for two
gained wide popularity at the
end of the nineteenth century

recaptured by cowboy Buck Taylor and his lasso. Janvier, like Mencken, wrote about what he ate and drank:

On the corner of Charles and Mulberry Streets, opposite Reese's grocery, was the apothecary shop of Dr. Adam Gosman, a fine old character with a long grey beard. He invented a gingerale and manufactured it for years in a small way in the rear of his store. His men could be seen at work through a doorway in the wall. Just here on Mulberry Street was Carrington's Dairy, where milk and ice-cream were sold. Delicious claret and port ices I got here on hot summer days. Dr. Gosman also had a small "single-cylinder" soda fountain, where the knowing one could get a glass of his famous "tonic" flavor. It must have consisted for the most part of a fine old rum and the uninitiated fellow who drank it on an empty stomach walked off sideways. This "tonic," I understand, was always a great favorite with the clergy and the few drys who existed in those days.

A wide variety of sporting activities gained in popularity in the latter days of the nineteenth century. Pimlico Race Course opened in 1870 and drew large crowds from Baltimore and out of town. The first running of the Preakness took place during the spring meeting of 1873. The new sport of lacrosse was acquiring fans, and in 1879 the first interclub lacrosse game was played in Baltimore. New York's Ravenswood Lacrosse Club defeated the Baltimore Athletic Club 3 to 1. By the 1890s, the newest craze was cycling, and several thousand cyclists belonged to at least eight bicycling clubs in town.

Major league baseball came to Baltimore in 1872 when the billboard firm A. T. Houck and Brother bought a franchise in the National Association and built a new club, the Lord

Baltimores (known simply as the Lords), and a new stadium, Newington Park. Both the team and the league disappeared in 1875. A variety of Baltimore teams played non-league games until 1883, when the American Association Brooklyn Athletics moved here and became the Baltimore Orioles. Since that time a team called the Orioles has almost always played ball in this city. They belonged to the American Association, the Eastern League, the International League and finally the American League. In the days of segregated sports, Baltimore fielded teams in a Negro league beginning in 1887, when a new Lord Baltimores team began to play in Oriole Park. After 1920 the famous Black Sox played for a decade followed by the Elites just before World War II.

One grand event of the period signaled a new civic spirit and enthusiasm which had been lacking for many years before the Civil War — Baltimore's Sesquicentennial celebration in 1880. evoked sentiment and enthusiasm of an enormous magnitude and served as a focal point around which the city's diverse population could unite. Two thousand vehicles and thirty thousand persons marched in the parade. The city raised ten elaborately decorated arches. Virtually all public and private buildings were decorated. By the year of this sesquicentennial outburst the scars of division and warfare were healing and Baltimore began to prepare to enter the twentieth century.

Turn of the century Baltimore was a city of contrasts. While wealthy merchants donated fortunes to build civic and cultural institutions, many people lived in filthy, over-crowded, disease-ridden slums and worked twelve or fourteen hours a day. Political machines organized the city's voters and drew wide support. Reformers fought them for control of both offices and policy-making. The happy memories of Mencken and Janvier show onl

Top Left:
Apothecaries and other shopkeepers were selling nationally merchandised products by the late nineteenth century

Above:
A group of women posed in 1893 by the pagoda in Patterson Park

Left:
George Peabody's gift establishing the Peabody Institute provided for "a library, a course of lectures, an academy of music, a gallery of art, and prizes to encourage private and public school students"

one part of the very complex new urban world that grew at the end of the nineteenth century.

One very important facet of late nineteenth century urban life was the establishment of many major cultural, educational, and civic institutions that have benefitted the city ever since. Throughout the nation, before and primarily after the Civil War, men who had accumulated fortunes in business and industry gave large portions of their wealth, not to charity, but rather to create schools, museums, libraries and hospitals which would serve all who came to them. The creations of these philanthropists still provide the cultural base in many American cities. Baltimore's philanthropists included George Peabody, William Walters and his son Henry, Enoch Pratt, and Johns Hopkins.

George Peabody, whose gift of $1,240,000 established the Peabody Institute, was born in Danvers, Massachusetts in 1795. Because his parents were poor, he was apprenticed to a storekeeper at age eleven. In his middle teens, he journeyed to Georgetown to work with a merchant uncle there. At nineteen, Peabody formed a partnership with Elisha Riggs in a wholesale dry-goods business which they moved to Baltimore in 1815. The firm occupied "Old Congress Hall" at Baltimore and Liberty Streets. By 1830, when Peabody became the senior partner, it was one of the largest mercantile establishments in the nation. Peabody, like so many nineteenth century magnates, maintained a frugal existence. He lived in rented quarters, would not hire a cab, and carried a lunch of bread and cheese in his briefcase. Although several stories of shattered romances are told, Peabody never married.

While living in Baltimore, he mastered the principles of banking, and later he formed George Peabody and Company in London. In 1836 he moved to England. By 1850 he was beginning to distribute his fortune. Peabody

sponsored a pioneering slum clearance proje? that grew at the end of the nineteenth century. in London and later an educational fun? designed to help rebuild the shattered Sout? and extend educational opportunities t? ex-slaves and their children.

To Baltimore, Peabody gave the Institute providing for "a library, a course of lectures, a? academy of music, a gallery of art, and prizes t? encourage private and public school pupils." Although the cornerstone was laid in 1859 an? the original white marble wing completed i? 1861, the dedication had to wait until 1866 whe? Peabody returned to attend the ceremonies in city once again at peace.

William Thompson Walters was born in 182? in Pottsville, Pennsylvania, studied civil an? mining engineering in Philadelphia, and came t? Baltimore in 1841. He entered the produc? commission business and became a controllin? director of the Baltimore and Susquehann? Railroad. In partnership with Charles Harvey h? sold foreign and domestic liquors. As hi? business shifted southward to Virginia and th? Carolinas, Walters discovered the need for a fa? freight line to carry perishable souther? produce to the northern urban markets. H? began consolidating small railroad lines, ? process which led eventually to the building o? the Atlantic Coast Line Railroad and Walter? fortune.

Because he sympathized with the Sout? Walters chose to leave occupied Baltimore i? 1861. For the duration of the war he lived in Par? where he got to know contemporary Frenc? artists like Corot, Millet, Delacroix, Daumie? and the sculptor Antoine Louis Barye. H? purchased many of their works as well as ? collection of Oriental ceramics. On returnin? home, he displayed his collection in a gallery ? his house on Mt. Vernon Place. Walters opene? it to the public on selected days.

Henry Walters, William's son, shared h?

Far Left:
William Walters began collecting paintings and sculpture when he was living in exile in Paris during the Civil War

Left:
William Walters' son, Henry, added to the painting and sculpture collection, built the original museum, and bequeathed both to the city of Baltimore

For the city's sesquicentennial celebration in 1880 Baltimore raised ten of these elaborate arches, decorated virtually all the buildings, and held a parade in which 30,000 persons marched

father's business acumen and his love of art. He doubled the fortune he inherited and was reputed to have been the wealthiest man south of the Mason-Dixon line. He is said to have spent $1,000,000 a year on art works from 1891, when William Walters died, until his own death forty years later. He built the original museum which still stands at the corner of Mt. Vernon Place and Center Street. Henry bequeathed his entire collection, the gallery, and a maintenance fund of $2,000,000 to the city of Baltimore.

Enoch Pratt was born in North Middeborough, Massachusetts in 1808. His father, Isaac Pratt, originally a farmer, moved into the wholesale hardware business. Enoch attended the local academy and then worked as a clerk in a wholesale hardware store in Boston. In 1831, at 22 years of age, Pratt arrived in Baltimore and organized a company which sold nails, horse shoes and mule shoes. Pratt abandoned the Puritanism of his ancestors and joined the Unitarian Church which some New Englanders living in Baltimore had built. For many years he served as treasurer of that church, often paying its debts out of his own pocket. In 1848 he erected his home at Park Avenue and Monument Street, the building which is now owned by the Maryland Historical Society. Pratt supported the Union cause in the Civil War and rejoiced publicly when General Butler occupied Federal Hill.

As Pratt's profits from the hardware business grew, he diversified, gained control of the Maryland Steamship Company, became a vice-president of the Philadelphia, Wilmington and Baltimore Railroad, and invested in banking and fire insurance. Pratt, like Peabody, was reputed to be something of a miser. Baltimoreans jested about his habit of picking up nails from the street. One legend has it that a tramp, seeing the poorly dressed Pratt walking towards his own house, called out, "There's no use going

in there, Brother. You'll not get a damned cent." Pratt's good works around Baltimore belied his reputation. He provided financial support for the Maryland School for the Deaf and Dumb in Frederick and for Cheltenham, a reform school for young Negro boys. He bestowed $2,000,000 on his friend Dr. Moses Sheppard for a hospital for the mentally handicapped. Pratt kept his best known gift, the Free Library, a secret until excavation for the main building had already begun. Then he offered the city the library plus $833,333 provided the city give $50,000 annually to support and maintain the library. Pratt himself selected the nine original trustees and stated in a letter to them that the books were "for all, rich and poor, without distinction of race or color who, when properly accredited, can take out the books, if they will handle them carefully and return them." On January 5, 1886 the central library opened its doors and 28,000 books to the public. Four branches opened the same year.

The founder of Baltimore's internationally best known institution, Johns Hopkins, was the only native Marylander of the four major philanthropists. Born in 1795, Johns Hopkins grew up on a large farm in Anne Arundel County, where the family performed all their own labor after his Quaker father freed their slaves. It is said that Hopkins always valued education especially highly, since he had had so little time for it. At age 18, he came to Baltimore to work with his Uncle Gerard, a commission merchant and grocer. Johns Hopkins got in trouble with both his uncle and the Quaker community during the 1819 depression when he began allowing customers to pay their bills in whiskey. He left his uncle, opened his own wholesale provision company, and bottled whiskey sold under the label "Hopkins Best."

Hopkins later invested in the development of the port and the B&O Railroad, of which he was the largest single stockholder at the time of

Opposite Page:
Enoch Pratt kept his library gift a secret until the excavation for the main building began

Left:
The original main building of the Enoch Pratt Free Library opened at the corner of Cathedral and Mulberry Streets in 1886

Johns Hopkins made detailed plans before his death for the hospital and university which he endowed

Below:
Johns Hopkins left his estate Clifton to be the site of the university he endowed. The trustees chose to build downtown, and Clifton later became a park

his death. Hopkins supported B&O president John Garrett during the Civil War and even contributed $50,000 to furnish transportation facilities to the Union. As Hopkins accumulated his fortune, he moved into banking and became the leading financier in town.

Johns Hopkins, like his friend George Peabody, never married. The traditional explanation is that he was in love with his cousin Elizabeth and that his Uncle Gerard forbade the marriage. When Hopkins made his will he left one million dollars to various relatives and local charities. He divided the rest of his eight million dollar estate to provide for the founding of the hospital and university which bear his name. Before his death, he made detailed plans and chose his trustees. He bequeathed his Clifton estate to the university. He purchased the grounds of the Old Maryland Hospital on Broadway and oversaw the early planning of the hospital. His will specified that the hospital should constitute part of the university's medical school and that there should be full cooperation between the two institutions. The will also specified that only the interest should be used to pay for the buildings. The capital itself was not to be touched.

Hopkins died in his sleep on December 24, 1873. The university trustees convened. After consulting the presidents of Harvard, Yale, Michigan and Cornell, they invited Daniel Coit Gilman to become president. Gilman accepted and began to recruit a faculty. Proven scholars such as English mathematician James Joseph Sylvester and classicist Basil L. Gildersleeve committed themselves to teach at the new university, where studies were to follow the German practice.

Johns Hopkins became the first American institution to grant a Ph.D. for accomplishment in research work. The university, situated near Mt. Vernon Square, not at Clifton, grew by 1900

to nine buildings. By 1901 when Gilman retired, 143 faculty members and 651 students constituted the community. In that same year, William H. Buckler, Francis M. Jencks, R. Bren... Keyser, Samuel Keyser, J. LeRoy White an... William Wyman gave to the university the 17... acres of land on Charles Street where "Homewood", built by Charles Carroll, stoo... Clifton was sold to the city and the money from the sale used to erect the new buildings. Dr. Ir... Remsen, the university's first professor o... chemistry and known for his work on sacchari... succeeded Gilman and presided over the mov... to Homewood.

The hospital opened in 1889 in fourteen buildings on the East Baltimore site that John Hopkins had selected. As the hospital neare... completion, financial difficulties of the B&C Railroad led to a shrinkage in the university' income from that stock. The university ha... already attracted prominent professors for th... future medical school with promises that i... would be modelled after the best European ones. By 1890, other institutions were beginning to try to lure these professors elsewhere.

A group of local women came to the rescue. Mary Garrett, who had inherited a large fortune from her father John, the president of the B&O joined Martha Carey Thomas, who had earned ... Ph.D. at the University of Zurich, and severa... other girlhood friends, and women's activist Mary Gwinn and Elizabeth King. In 1890 the established the Women's Fund Committee an... by 1892 had raised the necessary $500,000, much of it coming from the gifts of Mary Garrett. The... offered the money to the university on the conditions that women be admitted to the medical school on the same terms as men, tha... it be a graduate school, and that prospectiv... students be required to have a knowledge o... physics, chemistry, biology, French and German.

The medical school finally opened in 1893

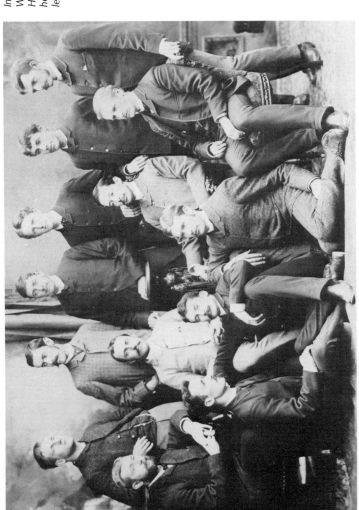

In 1885, future president Woodrow Wilson sang in the Hopkins Glee Club pictured here. Wilson is second from the left in the back row

The original biological laboratory of Hopkins' downtown campus stood at Eutaw and Little Ross Streets

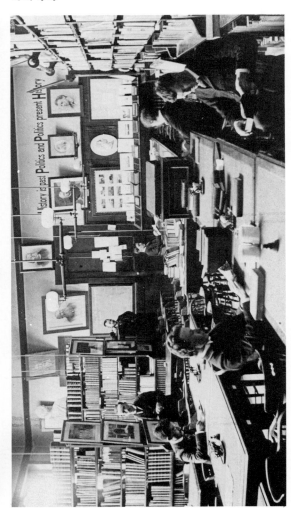

In Hopkins Hall on Little Ross Street, the seminary of History and Politics looked like this around the year 1890

Its high standards and stringent admission criteria made it a model for the nation. Dr. William Osler, the hospital's first Physician-in-Chief, is reported to have joked to Dr. William Welch, first dean of the medical school, "Welch, we were lucky to get in as professors, for I am sure that neither you nor I could ever get in as students."

The magnitude of the growth of educational institutions at the turn-of-the-century period is quite remarkable. Not only did the four philanthropists give to Baltimore the nationally renowned facilities of the Peabody Institute, the Walters Gallery, the Pratt Library and the Johns Hopkins University and Hospital, but many other colleges and schools first opened their doors in these decades. In fact, most of the city's centers of higher learning originated late in the 19th century.

In 1865 when the General Assembly in Annapolis authorized a statewide public school system, it also established the Maryland State Normal School. At the time of its formal opening in the old Red Man's Hall on North Paca Street in January 1866, eleven women students had enrolled. H. A. Newell was principal. By the end of the first year 48 students attended. In 1872 the Normal School moved to larger quarters at Charles and Franklin Streets. By 1876 when the school moved to its third location at Carrollton and Lafayette Streets, the student body had grown to 206. In 1915 the State Normal School moved to its current location on York Road north of the city where it now exists as Towson State University.

The first normal school to train black teachers formally opened in December 1867 in a renovated Friends' Meeting House at Saratoga and Courtland Streets. Privately supported, this school received added funds in 1871 when the trustees of Nelson Wells' estate contributed the entire remaining capital to the school after the

opening of the Negro public schools. The normal school eventually evolved into the present-day Bowie State College located in Anne Arundel County. It was not until 1900 that the Baltimore Board of School Commissioners established a Colored Training School to prepare Negro teachers. This public institution was renamed the Fannie Jackson Coppin Normal School in 1926 in honor of a former slave who bought her freedom and became the first American black woman to earn a college degree. The institution became the Coppin State Teachers' College in 1950 and, when it broadened its curriculum, the Coppin State College in 1963.

In 1867 a second Negro college was chartered: the Centenary Biblical Institute, which is now Morgan State University. Centenary was established by the Methodist Conferences of Baltimore, Washington, Wilmington and Delaware. The school held classes at the Sharp Street Church until the building on East Saratoga Street was completed in 1872. The Rev. J. Emory Round served as first president of the school, whose primary function was to train young men as Methodist ministers.

By 1880, the student body of 125 had outgrown the Saratoga Street building. When this was discussed at the Methodist Conference Dr. and Mrs. John F. Goucher offered to donate a lot at Fulton and Edmondson Avenues along with $5000 towards a building on the condition that Negro Methodists raise the additional money needed. In this way the building would open free of any mortgage. Hundreds of small donations from the black Methodist churches poured in, and in 1881 an $18,000 building was dedicated.

In 1890, Dr. Lyttleton F. Morgan, former chairman of the Board of Trustees, donated a large sum of money which enabled the school to offer general collegiate courses, and the

Opposite Page:
In the 1880s, Dr. John F. Goucher, shown here, and his wife Mary donated land and funds to Methodist Colleges that were established in Baltimore for both black and female students

Left:
A group of local women founded a college preparatory school, Bryn Mawr, for girls in 1885. The same group raised money for the Hopkins Medical School and donated it on the condition that women students be admitted on the same terms as men. This group included (left to right) Martha Carey Thomas, Mary Mackall Gwinn, Mary Elizabeth Garrett (seated), Julia Rebecca Rogers (on floor), and Elizabeth Tabor King

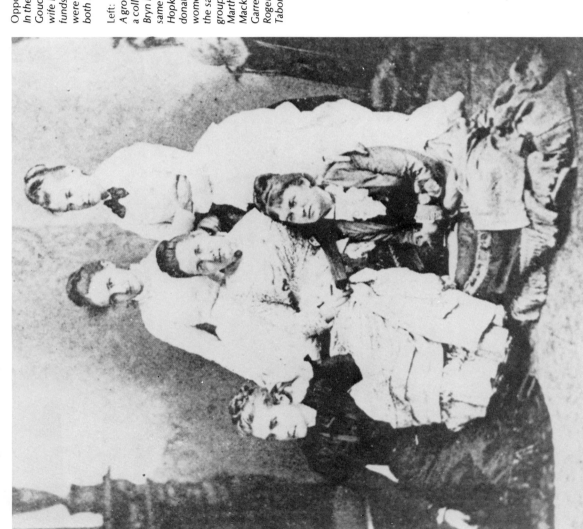

The first campus of Goucher College on St. Paul Street remained in use until the move to Towson was completed in the 1950s

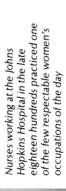

Nurses working at the Johns Hopkins Hospital in the late eighteen hundreds practiced one of the few respectable women's occupations of the day

institution became Morgan College. At the end of World War I, Morgan purchased its current property on Hillen Road. In 1939 the school affiliated with the state college system.

The Methodist Conference of Baltimore sponsored another local college, one for female students. The Women's College of Baltimore, incorporated in 1885, opened three years later under the leadership of its first president, William H. Hopkins. In 1890, the Rev. John F. Goucher, donor for a second time of a site and main building for a Baltimore college, became president. In a period when women were forbidden admission to most major men's universities, including Johns Hopkins' undergraduate school, Goucher College, as the school became known in 1910, offered an academic program in an urban location to young women from Baltimore and out of town. Goucher was one of a number of women's colleges established throughout the country which played an enormously important role in offering professional and academic training and creating a large and significant group of educated women.

A Roman Catholic college for women, Mount Saint Agnes, increased the availability of education for women in Baltimore. It opened in 1890 in conjunction with St. Mary's School, which had been established in 1867 by the Sisters of Mercy. The Mount Washington Seminary, later the Mount Washington Country School for Boys, opened on the same campus in 1899. A different sort of school, St. Mary's Industrial School, was established in 1866 by Archbishop Martin John Spalding for boys without homes and boys who were sent there by the courts. Babe Ruth was surely the most famous alumnus of that Catholic institution which served the community until 1950.

Most of Baltimore's leading private schools also opened during this period. They met a variety of needs not served by the city's public school system which, following the Civil War, provided a less than excellent education. The schools were overcrowded and understaffed. Teachers got jobs because of political connections, not ability or training. All the private schools benefitted from the philanthropy typical of the era.

McDonogh School, originally a "farm school for worthy boys" which was to provide sound academic offerings as well, opened in 1873, the gift of John McDonogh. In 1884 the group of women who later raised the money for the Hopkins Medical School pushed for the establishment of an institution to prepare girls to attend good universities. Bryn Mawr School was the result. Previously, only the Quakers offered high level academic subjects to girls in Baltimore. Now, Martha Carey Thomas, who served as the first dean of Bryn Mawr College outside Philadelphia, Mary Garrett and the others led the way and the new school opened in 1885. Less than a decade later, in 1894, another girls' institution, the Roland Park Country School, began offering instruction. Until 1908, it benefitted from the sponsorship of the Roland Park Company, then in the process of developing the new suburb.

Another Baltimore woman activist, Mrs. Francis Carey King, led in the founding of the Country School for Boys of Baltimore City in 1897. It was located at Homewood until it moved to Roland Park in 1911. The purpose of the school, which received strong support from Daniel Coit Gilman, for whom the school was renamed in 1910, was to provide the educational offerings and activities of boarding schools which most of Baltimore's upper class boys had attended previously. In the same year that Gilman opened, a small school, later called the Calvert School, began teaching fifteen pupils in a room over a drugstore at Madison Street and

Opposite Page:
This picture of Morgan's fourth year class in 1923 shows a formality characteristic in all schools during the pre-World War II period

In the late nineteenth century, only a small percentage of the students in the city's public school system managed to graduate from the elite high schools such as Baltimore City College (below) and Eastern Female High School (right)

Park Avenue. Its goal was to provide excellence in primary education. The school, now located on Tuscany Road, pioneered in home instruction courses used both for bedridden children and Americans living abroad. The last of Baltimore's leading private schools established during this period, the Park School, opened in 1912 in a house near Druid Hill Park. Like the other schools, Park moved away from the center city, first to Liberty Heights Avenue and then in 1959 to its current location on Old Court Road.

The establishment of the new schools, although some offered a free education to a small number of select students, benefitted primarily the well-to-do residents of Baltimore. In this period of great contrasts, people of fairly substantial means were not only acquiring wide opportunities for entertainment and education but were engaged in the process of moving into newly burgeoning suburbs with their open spaces and new homes.

First horse car lines and then electrified trolleys allowed people to commute downtown from even more distant locations. Fashionable town houses were built north of the business district along streets like Madison Avenue and McCulloch Street, on Eutaw Place, in Bolton Hill. East, south and west of town, smaller row houses soon lined the streets and boulevards. The development of these moderately priced homes and the growth of neighborhood building and loan associations allowed many middle and working class residents to become home owners. Baltimore consistently has enjoyed one of the highest rates of home ownership among major American cities.

More rapid public transportation led to the development of suburbs as urban residents sought to combine the benefits of spaciousness with the conveniences of city living. During the 1870s and 1880s such diverse areas as Arlington, Catonsville, Highlandtown, Huntingdon, Mt.

Washington, Peabody Heights, and Pimlico began to grow. Old mill towns like Hampden and Woodberry along the Jones Falls were connected to central Baltimore by the street railway lines.

The suburban belt, located in the county, grew rapidly during the latter part of the nineteenth century. As more and more belt residents became commuters, annexation once again became an issue. Under Maryland's constitution of 1867, residents of the area to be annexed had to vote their approval. Several times the belt's populace chose to remain in the county with its inferior services and lower taxes. The eastern segment of the belt, Canton and Highlandtown, strongly opposed the city's regulations of slaughterhouses, many of which were located there, and also the blue laws which would close the beer gardens and other drinking establishments on Sundays.

By 1888, however, the belt's problems were becoming unmanageable. The population was increasing rapidly. The county failed to provide adequate water and sewer facilities and this lack threatened the public health. Police and fire protection were meager. The county government reaped large revenues from the suburbanites of the belt but favored the rural areas when money had to be spent. When the annexation question was put on the ballot in 1888, the western, northern, and eastern districts of the belt voted separately. The northern and western districts chose to join with the city, while Highlandtown and Canton opted for continued freedom from urban restrictions. Baltimore City thus gained about 23 square miles of land and 38,000 people.

The acquisition of so much new land apparently inspired schemes both for development and for protection of open spaces. The city purchased additional land for public parks. In the southwest, Baltimore bought the land of a

Above:
The construction of moderately priced row houses and the growth of neighborhood building and loan associations created a high rate of home ownership among Baltimoreans

Left:
Baltimore gained twenty-three square miles of land in 1888 and more than fifty additional square miles in 1918

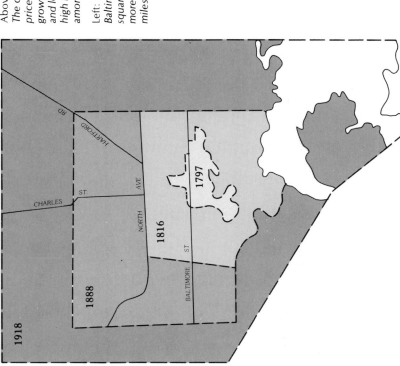

1918

1888

1816

1797

CHARLES ST.

HARTFORD RD.

NORTH AVE.

BALTIMORE ST.

German Schuetzen (shooting) park and landscaped Carroll Park there. Mount Clare, the home of Charles Carroll, the Barrister, which was located in the new park, was renovated. At the same time, the city purchased Johns Hopkins' estate, Clifton, to be converted into a park for residents of the northeast.

A major suburban innovation came in the 1890s in the form of Roland Park, which was privately developed and planned first by George E. Kessler and then Frederick Law Olmsted, Jr. and John C. Olmsted. One goal of the planners was to preserve the natural beauty of the landscape. The streets curved with the contours of the land. Large and comfortable family houses were built and a trolley car line opened. Restrictive covenants designed to preserve the residential nature of the area prohibited stables and other unhealthy use of the land. Business development was limited. The restrictions went much further, however, and effectively prevented both Jews and blacks from buying property in Roland Park for many years.

Once Roland Park was completed, Frederick Law Olmsted, Jr., whose father had planned Central Park in New York, formulated a plan for a system of parks throughout the city. At the behest of reformers like Theodore Marburg of the Municipal Art Society, whose primary interest lay in beautifying the city and making it a healthful place to live, Olmsted introduced a scheme for maintaining as green areas all the valleys along Jones Falls, Herring Run, Gwynn's Falls, and parts of the shoreline of the Patapsco.

Parks and suburbs were only part of the expansion that permeated Baltimore's life during the end of the nineteenth century. The real basis of the prosperity that allowed beautification and pleasant living was the income produced by commerce and industry. Baltimore's commerce had been hurt when the Civil War ended much of the trade between the city and the South. Once peace returned, however, Baltimore investors began to pour capital into the rebuilding of the devastated region. By 1900 an estimated $100,000,000 had been invested by Baltimoreans in southern railroads, street cars, cotton mills, coal, iron and phosphate mines, lumber tracts and municipalities. Prominent firms like Alex Brown and Company, Wilson, Colston and Company, and Middendorf, Oliver and Company profited in these undertakings. While bringing raw materials out of the South, Baltimore gained further by selling many manufactured goods there, among them dry goods, notions, provisions and groceries, liquors, clothing, boots and shoes, hats, toys, and articles of the jobbing trade. The city was frequently called the "gateway to the South."

Baltimore was also nicknamed "The Liverpool of America," reflecting the size of its foreign trade. In 1870, Baltimore's $33,000,000 worth of foreign trade ranked fifth in the nation. By 1900, the city ranked third nationally with $130,000,000 in foreign trade. Baltimore was one of the chief outlets for raw materials: grain and grain products, cotton, and leaf tobacco. Imports from Latin America were especially important and included coffee, sugar, tropical fruits, copper and other metals, and Peruvian guano. The inauguration of direct steamship service between Baltimore and Bremen in 1868 augmented the already strong connections between the two cities.

Baltimore possessed all the prerequisites for the large-scale industrial development that had begun before the Civil War. The city was served by excellent rail and shipping facilities, had a supply of raw materials available at a low cost, potential markets, a supply of capital, and a ready labor force. Furthermore, the city's government actively supported industrialization. For example, in 1877 the City Council appointed a

Top Left:
Baltimore's industries expanded rapidly at the end of the nineteenth century. Hats, clothing, boots, and shoes were among the city's major exports. Shown here is an advertisement of Armstrong, Cator and Company

Top Right:
Bromo Seltzer had its home office and laboratories in Baltimore

Above:
The port was a major factor in the city's economic success. In 1870, the approximate date of this picture, Baltimore's foreign trade ranked fifth in the nation. By 1900 the city ranked third

commission to consider ways and means to encourage industrial development. Ferdinand C. Latrobe, who was mayor at that time, gave enthusiastic support.

Between 1870 and 1900, the number of industries established in Baltimore trebled and the capital invested increased six-fold. This was typical of the national pattern. Locally, growth came in widely diversified areas such as men's clothing, foundries and machine shops, straw hats, copper, and steel, especially steel rails made at Sparrows Point by the Maryland Steel Company. Boot and shoe making were important as was the manufacture of fertilizers. Slaughtering and meatpacking increased on the outskirts of town. Canning of fruits and vegetables and especially oysters benefitted from new techniques. By 1870 over one hundred packing houses were located in Baltimore. Cotton mills along the Jones Falls in towns like Woodberry became part of the city in 1888. Nationally-known rye whiskey was distilled here.

Baltimore's industries expanded to the south and east, along the waterfront and the tracks of the B&O and what was to become the Pennsylvania Railroad. The industrial center shifted from the Jones Falls Valley to new areas like Canton, Highlandtown, Locust Point and Curtis Bay. A subsidiary of the Maryland Steel Company built Sparrows Point, complete with housing for everyone from executives to unskilled workers, with a separate village for black workers on the other side of Humphrey's Creek.

Near the end of the nineteenth century, industries began to consolidate, both to acquire capital for mechanization and to end the competitive price wars that bankrupted many firms. In some cases the consolidation was a local affair as it was when sixteen breweries formed the Maryland Brewing Company and the street

car lines joined in the United Railways and Electric Company. In other cases, local companies were absorbed by national conglomerates, as were many local canneries by the American Can Company and the Maryland Steel Company by Bethlehem Steel.

The increased use of ever more highly sophisticated machinery led to the replacement of skilled by unskilled workers. While mechanization meant lower prices for consumers, it also meant lower wages for workers. Many of the unskilled positions were held by women and children who might earn as little as $.40 a day. In 1885 the average male unskilled worker earned $1.25 a day, and skilled workers $1.75 to $3.00 a day. An average-sized row house rented for about $78 a year. The average work day lasted 10 to 12 hours. Many women and children worked in East Baltimore's sweatshops which produced over half the men's clothing manufactured here. The canneries also employed large numbers of women and children. Workers employed in hazardous jobs often were fired if faulty machinery injured them severely enough to prevent them from doing their work.

Various labor unions organized to press for better wages and hours, an end to blacklisting union members, abolition of child labor, and laws requiring compulsory education and workmen's compensation. The Knights of Labor formed their first local assembly in Baltimore in 1878. Eight years later, 16 local assemblies claimed twenty-five thousand members. On Labor Day, 1886, seventeen thousand marched in the parade. Locally and throughout the nation, the Knights of Labor was superseded by the craft-oriented unions that formed the American Federation of Labor. Members tended to be in the skilled trades. Because their skills were not easily replaced and because their relatively high wages allowed the accumulation of a strike fund, the strike became an important

Labor unions worked hard to improve wages and working conditions. But in 1890, the year of the Labor Day parade, their impact remained limited

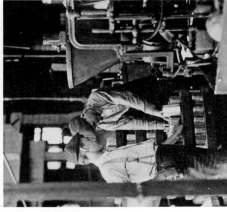

Top:
Better lit than many, this garment factory shows the crowded conditions in which the women worked, often earning less than a dollar a day

Above:
Children often worked at hazardous jobs such as this one in a local cannery

weapon in the hands of these craft unions. The Baltimore Federation of Labor, which affiliated with the AFL in 1889, consisted of a wide variety of craft unions. Despite a setback during the depression years 1893 to 1897 when almost half the industrial workers in the city were unemployed, approximately twenty thousand members belonged to 65 or 70 different trade unions in Baltimore in 1900.

Nearly two hundred strikes involving thirty thousand workers occurred between 1881 and 1900. Many were violent affairs. Sometimes workers lost their jobs. Other times they achieved limited gains. Before World War I, the few concrete gains were limited to strong union or to measures supported by middle-class Progressive reformers. For example, the Federation of Labor won for municipal employees a 9-hour work day in 1892 and an 8-hour day six years later. But this was rare. In 1886, the building trades union achieved a reduction of their working hours from 10 to 9 per day. In 1892, clothing workers won a 10-hour day, reduced from 15 or more, but did not succeed in improving conditions in their overcrowded, unsafe sweatshops. The first law requiring city inspection and licensing of sweatshops was passed in 1902 and strengthened in 1914. The first workmen's compensation law was passed in 1902. By 1914, only a third of the labor force worked more than 60 hours a week.

An interesting sidelight on local labor developments were the policies developed by John Garrett of the B&O. After defeating the worst strike in the railroad's history in 1877, he offered several benefits to his workers: pension plan, a burial society, accident insurance paid for by the employees, and payments to widows. The company established savings accounts and a system of home loans for its workers. The whole plan served as a model for companies trying to rationalize some progressive scheme of

DUESTE OF ABOVE, PASSING REVIEWING STAND OFFHILL, SENSOR HALL SAND...

Baltimore and Ohio workers
benefitted from welfare policies
developed by railroad president
John Garrett after a strike in 1877

management-labor relations.

Child labor laws were supported strongly by many segments of society not involved in the labor movement as a whole. A series of laws culminated in the 1902 enactment of a compulsory education law for children 8 to 12 and a 1906 law which forbade children under 12 from being employed in any gainful occupation. Ten years later, children under 16 were prohibited from working except in the canning industry and domestic service.

World War I strengthened the status of labor organizations when the government agreed to grant unions the right to organize and bargain collectively in exchange for a promise not to strike. Wartime demands led to higher wages. Many of the gains were not permanent, however. Peacetime brought renewed resistance to labor organization that was halted only by the Wagner Act of 1935.

In Baltimore, industrial development, working conditions and labor organization followed the national pattern. The depression of 1893, however, ended the boom in Baltimore. At the time many local companies were bought up by larger corporations headquartered elsewhere, many of the new owners began to purchase in other cities things once supplied by

local manufacturers. Consequently Baltimore's industrial position relative to other cities declined. Baltimore ranked 8th nationally in total manufacturing in 1880 and 11th in 1914. Despite this decline, however, the city's absolute production grew as did its income and its population.

Immigration into Baltimore after the Civil War brought a wide variety of newcomers to live and work in the city. Ex-Confederates from Virginia arrived, as did farmers from Lancaster County. Black farm workers from Southern Maryland came seeking better opportunities in the urban economy. Europeans came from an increasing number of countries.

In 1860 and 1870, most of the immigrants still came from Germany or Ireland. Diversification began slowly as Bohemians, Scandinavians, Italians and Poles began to arrive. By 1880 more than one thousand Bohemians lived in Baltimore. Ten years later, more than four thousand Russians, mostly Jews, had settled on the eastern side of the city. By 1900, over ten thousand Russians outnumbered the more than two thousand people born in Poland and Italy and the country now called Czechoslovakia. In the early part of the twentieth century, Lithuanians, Greeks, and smaller numbers from other countries moved to Baltimore. From 1920 until 1960 foreign immigrants came only in small numbers. Changes in the immigration laws resulted in the increases seen in the census reports of 1960 and 1970.

Until 1920 Germans continued to be the largest foreign-born group in Baltimore. Over thirty thousand German-born residents were counted in each census from 1860 through 1910. They maintained and augmented the wide range of institutions they had established earlier. German-English public schools, the Turnverein, social and musical clubs, and churches all flourished. As many Germans began to move

Above:
Delivering newspapers was popular work for children because they could earn money and attend school at the same time. This substation stood on Bank Street around the year 1910

Despite the gains by organized labor and reformers, enormous gaps in life-style remained between the upper class and the working class. Evergreen House (opposite page) on North Charles Street, was purchased by the Garrett family in 1878. Alley houses such as these (left) provided homes for a large segment of Baltimore workers

Mt. Vernon Place and Charles Street, one of Baltimore's elite neighborhoods, shown here during the blizzard of 1899

around Lexington and Lombard Streets, and then after 1895 turned northward. By 1910, all the German-Jewish synagogues were located in an area bounded by North Avenue, Bolton, Lanvale and McCulloch Streets. Many Germans, both Christians and Jews, participated in early labor organizations and often transmitted ideas on reform and class struggle from Europe. More and more Germans moved into political offices and professional and management jobs throughout the city.

Like the Germans, the Irish continued to solidify their position. They had a strong ally in James Cardinal Gibbons, who had been born in 1834 of Irish parents living on Gay Street in the heart of Old Town. Ordained in 1861, made bishop of Baltimore in 1877, and invested as cardinal in 1886, he rose to a position of eminence in Baltimore and played an active role in civic and social reform throughout his career. Other members of the Irish community rose to power through the political machines that characterized municipal politics in the latter part of the nineteenth century. The Irish population had increasingly dispersed throughout the city as large numbers of second and third generation Irish-Americans moved into better jobs and middle class status.

The newcomers who arrived in the late nineteenth and early twentieth centuries faced many of the same problems that had greeted the Germans and Irish of the previous generation. Most landed with little or no money and without the ability to read, write or speak English. Most had no jobs or could obtain only menial ones. They generally received the lowest pay and lived in the worst housing. They faced prejudice and discrimination from both native Americans and earlier immigrant groups.

Bohemians began arriving in Baltimore at the end of the Civil War and settled first in Fells Point, then further uptown along Barnes and

outward from the center city, their institutions followed them. A Schuetzen park was opened on Harford Road. The Redemptorists built churches on Belair and Hillen Roads. German Jews tended to move westward across town in the 1880s to the area west of Greene Street

*Most immigrant ships docked at
Piers 8 and 9 at Locust Point*

Abbott Streets near Broadway, then still further north along Collington Avenue near the Northeast Market. Many Bohemians migrated to escape the exploitation of the Austrian Empire, of which they were a subject people, and especially to avoid service in the Austrian army. By 1870, over 700 Bohemians had settled in Baltimore. They appealed to the Redemptorist priests at St. Michael's, a German church, to help them establish their own parish. St. Wenceslaus Parish was formed in 1872 and placed under the charge of the Rev. Valentine Vacula, the first Bohemian priest to come to Baltimore.

St. Wenceslaus parochial school opened in 1880 and offered morning sessions in Czech and afternoon sessions in English. Not until 1910 did English become the primary language in both sessions. The parish grew, and in 1914 Cardinal Gibbons was present at the laying of the cornerstone for the present Romanesque church on Ashland Avenue. Two additional churches served the Czech community: the Mount Tabor Bohemian Methodist Church and the Moravian Presbyterian Church whose pastor, the Rev. Frank Novak, played a leading role in sectarian activities as well as church affairs.

Many early Bohemian settlers worked as tailors. Others did piecework at home. Although most Czechs did not earn high wages, they tended to be thrifty and rapidly adopted the Baltimore practice of buying their own homes. In 1900, twenty men met at Joseph Klecka's Tavern on Ashland Avenue and formed the Slavic Savings and Loan Association, the first of many similar institutions that made it possible for a high percentage of Bohemians to buy homes. August Klecka, one of Joseph's sons, in 1915 was the first Bohemian elected to the City Council.

Another community leader, Col. Wenceslaus Shimek, had arrived in Baltimore at the age of 15, just after the end of the Civil War. Seven

years later he opened a barrel-organ factory on President Street. Shimek served as president of the Bohemian Building Association. He started a Czech-language newspaper, the *Telegraf*, which, after 1929, was edited by the Rev. Frank Novak and published by August Klecka. Shimek was a politician, too. He often went to meet the boats and greet newcomers, helping them find a place to stay and a job.

The Sokol was almost as important as the church in the Bohemian community. The Sokol, which means falcon, served originally as an organization to train members to fight for Czechoslovakian independence. In this country, the Sokols resembled the German Turnverein, which emphasized athletics and physical conditioning and fostered an interest in major issues of the day. Baltimore's Sokol was formed in 1872. Members met on Frederick Street near Fells Point until 1902 when the group accepted an offer to use Shimek's Hall on North Broadway.

When an independent Czechoslovak state was created after World War I, local Bohemians and Slovaks joined in the celebrations and for years afterwards held parades and festivities on October 28, the Czechoslovak independence day. Before and during World War II, the community strongly opposed Hitler and his takeover of Czechoslovakia. After the war, many residents began to move away from the neighborhood around Collington Avenue, and people of Czechoslovak descent are now widely dispersed throughout the city.

Early Polish immigrants in Baltimore settled in Fells Point where about ten families lived in 1870. From then until 1920, Poles came in large numbers to escape the economic hardship that resulted from the partitioning of Poland by Germany, Austria and Russia. Many were peasants driven from their small farms by hunger and desperation. Although a lucky 25 percent knew German, most spoke no English. The new

Above:
On arrival, newcomers had to
wait to be processed by
immigration and health officials.
This photograph of an immigrant
pen at Locust Point was taken
early in the twentieth century

Left:
B&O trains came directly onto
the piers to meet immigrants
leaving Baltimore for points west

arrivals often worked on the railroads and in the shipyards, for construction companies and clothing manufacturers and in the steel mills.

The first Polish Catholic church, St. Stanislaus, was organized in 1880 when members of the community invited Father Peter Koncz to come to Baltimore. The church now stands at Ann and Aliceanna Streets in Fells Point. As the community continued to grow and move northward towards Eastern Avenue, a second church, Holy Rosary, was built on South Chester Street in 1886. In the early 1900s, the Polish community spread eastward towards Canton where St. Casimir's Church was built. Significant numbers of Poles settled in Locust Point and Curtis Bay, where St. Aloysius Church was founded. All the parish churches conducted schools.

Because the immigrants were extremely poor, the home buying process was often stretched out over several generations. Immigrants frequently lived in crowded conditions where both sanitation and health were poor. Families were large, and many women went to work, often in canneries, to make ends meet. Like the Germans and the Bohemians, Poles began to found building and loan societies, twenty of them by 1914, and to buy homes.

Numerous other institutions were created by the Polish community. The Polish Home has provided facilities for various social, educational, and recreational groups. The Polish National Alliance opened Baltimore's first library of books and other materials in Polish. The Polish Falcons began as a gymnastic club similar to the Turnverein and the Sokols, but the organization never played the major role in the Polish community that the others did among Germans and Bohemians. A newspaper, the *Jednosc-Polonia*, was published for many years. It had been preceded by other newspapers dating from 1891.

Perhaps because of their harsher economic struggles, Baltimore's Poles were comparatively slow in gaining political representation. The first Polish city councilman, a grocer named Edward Novak, won election in 1923 when roughly 11,000 Poles lived within Baltimore.

Polish people maintained an interest in the land of their birth, or their parents' birth. Before America's entry into World War I, several hundred men from Baltimore joined a Polish legion attached to the British army. Poles celebrated their nation's unification after World War I, and later opposed Hitler's invasion. Since the easing of immigration restrictions, Poles have once again begun to arrive in Baltimore. Although many people of Polish descent have spread throughout the city and county, especially to the east and northeast out Belair Road, centers of Polish settlement are still visible in East Baltimore and Locust Point, especially near the churches.

The most enduring ethnic community in a physical sense is Little Italy. In the 1870s and 1880s, Italians began to settle in this area around the President Street Station, often renting rooms from earlier German, Irish and Jewish immigrants. Driven from Italy by droughts and pervasive poverty, few spoke any English. Italian men worked on the railroad and as vendors of fruits and vegetables. Some were skilled barbers, masons, and tailors. Italian women tried to remain in the home instead of working in nearby industries. As families were able to buy their own homes, women often supplemented the family's income by taking in boarders.

The most pressing desire of the new community was to build a church in its midst. Archbishop Gibbons in 1880 appointed Father Joseph Andrei, a native of Turin, to build St. Leo's Church. Religious festivals became major events. The two largest were celebrated to

Left:
Immigrants often held festivals where they wore traditional clothes and enjoyed food, music, and dancing. This picture shows a Czech folk festival held in 1938

Above:
James Cardinal Gibbons, shown here at Mt. Royal Station later in his life, grew up in Baltimore's Irish community. He provided support for the many successive groups of newcomers as they arrived in the city

honor St. Anthony and St. Gabriel. St. Anthony's fete on June 13 began in 1904. When the great Baltimore fire had threatened Little Italy earlier that year, a group of residents had prayed to St. Anthony. The flames stopped at the Jones Falls and Little Italy was saved. The St. Gabriel's procession began soon after the canonization of the saint from Abruzzi in 1920. The festival bore special meaning because many Baltimore Italian families had their roots in the vicinity of Abruzzi. The church provided an institutional center for the community. As the Germans, Irish and Jews began to move away from the area around Exeter and Stiles Streets, Italians remained. By 1920 the neighborhood was almost exclusively Italian, a characteristic it has maintained to the present day.

As the Italian community became better established and people had time to save some money, prosperity increased. Men who had worked for Irish contractors began their own companies. Many worked in politically connected jobs in departments like public works and sanitation. Others opened the now famous restaurants. Others stayed in school and became professionals. As community resources increased, a lodge of the Order of the Sons of Italy was founded in 1913 to aid new arrivals.

Italians gained political power relatively early compared to many immigrant groups. The community's first political leader, Vincent Palmisano, was elected to the Maryland House of Delegates in 1914, to the Baltimore City Council the following year, and to the United States Congress in 1926. A second powerful man succeeded Palmisano as Little Italy's best known Baltimorean. Thomas D'Alesandro succeeded Palmisano as a Delegate in 1926, then went to Congress in 1938 when he defeated Palmisano, and was elected Mayor of Baltimore in 1947. His son, Thomas D'Alesandro III, was elected mayor in 1967. Since 1960, Italian immigration has increased again, and in 1970 more people born in Italy, almost 13,000, lived in Baltimore than in any previous census year.

Lithuanians came to Baltimore in smaller, yet significant numbers, beginning in the 1880s. Many left their homeland because of the efforts of the Russian government to force assimilation of Lithuanians by forbidding the teaching of the Lithuanian language in the schools and forcing Lithuanian men into service in the Russian army.

Early immigrants settled in East Baltimore, where many worked in the garment industry. They organized the St. John the Baptist Church, whose congregation worshipped in the old Lloyd Street Synagogue building from 1889 until 1905, when they moved to a new church at Paca and Saratoga Streets. The Lithuanians gradually moved westward across the city until the center of the community was located around South Paca, South Greene, West Lombard and Hollins Streets. Around 1900, fraternal organizations and beneficial societies joined in purchasing a hall on West Barre Street to use for community functions. The new Lithuanian Hall was built in 1921 at Hollins and Parkin Streets. St. Alphonsus Church on West Saratoga Street now serves part of the Lithuanian community. Over two thousand persons born in Lithuania have lived in Baltimore every census year since 1920, when they were first counted separately from Russians. Like other groups, the total has increased since 1960.

Most of Baltimore's Greeks arrived after the turn of the century. They settled along Eastern Avenue, in an area which still remains the center of the Greek community with its shops, restaurants, coffee houses and one of the churches, St. Nicholas, located on South Ponca Street. The first Greek Orthodox church in Baltimore, "Evangelismos," the Annunciation, began in 1908 when the congregation purchased a building at Homewood Avenue and Chase

The Italian community produced prominent political leaders who won local and later national offices

Vincent Palmisano (above) won the nomination and the subsequent election to the city council. Eleven years later he was elected to the United States Congress. Thomas D'Alesandro, Jr. (left) defeated Palmisano in the Congressional election of 1938. He became mayor of Baltimore in 1947

Street. In 1936 the congregation bought and renovated the current building at Maryland Avenue and Preston Street. As Greeks followed East Baltimore's other immigrants in their northeastward path out from the city, they built a third church, St. Demetrios, on Cub Hill Road. As early as 1912 a school to teach the Greek language and religion opened. Children attended three times a week after their regular classes.

The Greek community has never been large enough to be a major force in urban politics. Political leaders like Peter Angelos and Paul Sarbanes have risen to prominence by appealing to the broader community. Although they are the last large group to immigrate to Baltimore, Greeks live in widely dispersed neighborhoods. They are joined more by a common heritage and church than by geographic unity.

By far the largest group of newcomers, other than Germans who outnumbered all other immigrant peoples before and after the Civil War, were the Russian Jews who began arriving in Baltimore during the 1880s. By 1900, over ten thousand Russians lived in the city and by 1910 almost twenty-five thousand. Most fled from persecution in Russia and nearby countries like Poland and Lithuania which were subject to Russian domination.

As the German Jews moved westward towards Eutaw Place, Eastern Europeans began to move into East Baltimore. Most were Orthodox and established their own synagogues, often using the buildings vacated by the German congregations. The vast majority of Eastern European Jews worked in the sweatshops, later garment factories of East Baltimore. Many of the owners were German Jews. The workers tended to be active in labor organizations. The largest, the International Ladies Garment Workers Union, formed a local chapter in 1909, the fourth in the nation. But despite their union activity,

poverty pervaded the community.

At first, tensions grew between the older, Americanized German Jews, who had fought difficult battles to overcome prejudice and discrimination, and the new immigrants who spoke Yiddish, insisted on Orthodox observances, and frequently preferred to remain within their own closed community. Slowly, however, people began to bridge the gap. Henrietta Szold, the daughter of Rabbi Benjamin Szold, in 1889 organized the Russian Night School to teach English and American history to people who worked all day. Several thousand studied here. The Szold School, as it was known, became a model for night schools in many other cities.

A wide variety of charitable work among the new immigrants was supported by the more established segment of the community. In the first decade of the twentieth century, the German-Jewish charities united to form the Federated Jewish Charities. Jacob Hollander served as the first president. The Russian organizations joined in the United Hebrew Charities. Finally in 1921 these two merged into the Associated Jewish Charities. Jewish philanthropy was a well-established tradition and benefitted the immigrant community as well as the city as a whole. Over the years, settlement houses, like the Maccabean House, free schools, an orphanage, Sinai Hospital which was founded in 1866, and other institutions received strong support.

Time worked to overcome some of the differences. As years passed the newcomers moved into positions of political and economic power. In 1903, two Eastern Europeans, William Weissager, a Latvian, and Joseph Seidenman, a Russian, won election to the City Council. A Lithuanian immigrant of 1882, Jacob Epstein, began as a peddler and then opened a store and then a large mail order business. By

Immigrant children often worked as vendors, sometimes in lieu of going to school

1910 he employed over 1000 workers and did over a million dollars worth of business a month. Epstein shared his good fortune with the Jewish community and with Baltimore as a whole. When the Museum of Art was first incorporated in 1914, he was among the original trustees.

At the end of World War I, the Eastern European Jews were beginning their move out of East Baltimore, first to Park Heights Avenue and then further north to Forest Park. New institutions which served the entire Jewish community came into existence. Baltimore Hebrew College opened in 1919. The *Jewish Times*, the newest of several papers, began publication. Recently, a new group of Eastern European Jews have been arriving in Baltimore, where the larger community is now in a position to provide significant aid for the resettlement process.

Certain settlement patterns characterized all of the various immigrant groups that came to Baltimore during the nineteenth and the early twentieth century. Most individuals arrived poor and without a skilled trade or knowledge of the English language. The majority began their new life in communities where they could use their own language. As soon as possible, they built a church or synagogue where services were conducted in their native tongue. Then each group established institutions to meet the needs of the newcomers: aid societies, schools, fraternal organizations, newspapers, building and loan associations, and so on. Such similar responses stemmed from similar needs and conditions. Moreover, the government did not yet operate in that sphere to any significant degree.

Over time, each generation of newcomers and their children learned English and began to ascend the socio-economic ladder. Participation in the city's political system generally accompanied this success. Gradually, people moved away from their original communities into new neighborhoods further from the central city. Often they built new houses of worship. Eventually the need for immigrant aid societies declined, and those that survived either changed their programs or became primarily fraternal organizations. Today, most foreign-language newspapers have disappeared.

These cycles of immigrant experience typify those of the nation. But Baltimore is somewhat unique in the nation in the combination of these sizeable immigrant groups with a larger antebellum black population which post-war migration increased. Before the Civil War, the city's blacks created community institutions, much like those of the German and Irish immigrants. After the war, however, the Negro community had not become as fully integrated into the life of the city as the pre-war immigrants had. Therefore, although they were one of the earliest minority groups, blacks continued to face the same deprivations and prejudices experienced by the newer immigrant groups and some additional disabilities imposed on them because of their race by both law and custom. In 1870, the year that they began to vote again, almost forty thousand blacks lived in Baltimore and represented 15 percent of the total population.

After the Civil War ended, large numbers of blacks from rural areas, especially southern Maryland, moved to Baltimore seeking work and better lives than they had known as slaves. Like immigrants, most were uneducated and had little or no money. Most worked at menial jobs. "Pigtown" in southwest Baltimore, where many rural migrants settled first, became a slum, at least as dirty and unhealthy as any immigrant settlement. Blacks, however, because of racial discrimination and the heritage of the disabilities of slavery, were less able to combat their problems than were many immigrant groups,

A Lithuanian Jewish immigrant who began as a peddler, Jacob Epstein later opened a store and developed a very successful mail order business. As he shared his good fortune with his adopted city, he became one of Baltimore's most prominent philanthropists

Henrietta Szold, daughter of Rabbi Benjamin Szold, organized a night school to teach the English language and American history to immigrants who worked all day. Her school became a model that was copied in cities throughout the country

whose members were less recognizable visually. Despite their numbers, blacks held very little economic or political power. Every gain came slowly and with great effort.

The public school system provides an example of the difficulties the black community faced. Before 1867, blacks had to pay public school taxes but could not attend. When the City Council voted to open public schools for Negro students, the city took over the 16 schools run by the Baltimore Association for the Moral and Educational Advancement of Colored People. Within a year, all the black teachers were fired and whites hired in their place. Only money collected from black taxpayers was assigned to these schools. After several years, the city began to contribute additional funds to the black schools, which were, frequently in buildings abandoned when new schools for white students were constructed. When continuing efforts to convince the city to rehire black teachers failed, the Rev. Harvey Johnson of the Union Baptist Church led a group of Baptist ministers in forming the Brotherhood of Liberty in 1885. One major concern was education. They succeeded in winning an ordinance in 1887 allowing the hiring of black teachers in new colored schools, and two years later Colored Primary School #9 opened with twelve black teachers.

In 1896, Dr. John Marcus Cargill, a Negro physician and member of the City Council, introduced an ordinance calling for the gradual replacement of white teachers by blacks in all the colored schools. The process was not completed until 1907. In all areas, the black schools lagged behind the white schools. No colored high school was opened until 1882 when the future Douglass High School first opened, housed with the Colored Grammar School in the old City Hall on Holliday Street. The first teachers' training school for blacks did not open until 1900.

Black churchmen continued to play a major role in community affairs. The history of the Afro-American newspaper illustrates this. In 1892, three small newspapers were in circulation in Baltimore's black community. The Rev. William Alexander, pastor of the Sharon Baptist Church, had organized a provision store and started printing a newspaper called the Afro-American to advertise his business. John H. Murphy was publishing the Sunday School Helper. The Rev. George F. Bragg, rector of St. James Episcopal Church from 1891 to 1940, published the church-related Ledger. Murphy bought Alexander's paper. Then in 1907 Murphy and Bragg merged their papers and called their publication the Afro-American Ledger. As the enterprise grew, editions for other cities were published.

Another important institution of the black community, Provident Hospital, originated in 1894 in a small building on Orchard Street. Because white hospitals often gave different treatment to Negro patients, two black physicians in the city, Dr. John Marcus Cargill and Dr. William T. Carr, with their own money established a hospital to be run by black physicians, primarily for patients of their own race, although patients of other races were never excluded.

The single most difficult problem faced by blacks was unemployment. Often fired in favor of white workers, almost always paid less, most Negroes were unable to build the financial base that the immigrants gradually did. One black Baltimorean pioneered in this area. Isaac Myers, born in Baltimore in 1835, stands out as an entrepreneur and labor leader. When Civil War veterans returned and immigrants arrived after 1865, many blacks were driven out of skilled jobs they had held for years. In view of this, Myers, who had been apprenticed as a ship caulker at

Above:
Booker T. Washington, shown here addressing a Baltimore audience, encouraged the development of black-owned businesses to provide a stable economic base for the community

Opposite Page:
The Reverend George Bragg, rector of St. James Episcopal Church from 1891 to 1940, provided religious, intellectual, and social leadership within Baltimore's black community

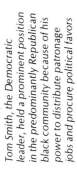

This group of ministers and lawyers worked for the improvement of education for Negro children and for the hiring of black teachers. Included in this group are: Harry S. Cummings (front row center), W. Ashby Hawkins (second row center), Warner T. McGuinn (third row, third from left), and the Reverend Harvey Johnson (back row center). The picture was taken in front of Johnson's house on Druid Hill Avenue

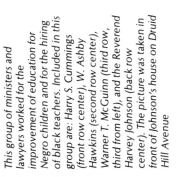

Tom Smith, the Democratic leader, held a prominent position in the predominantly Republican black community because of his power to distribute patronage jobs and procure political favors

the age of 16, decided to found a black-owned shipyard which would employ black workers. He solicited funds from merchants and the black churches and sold shares of stock for $5. The Chesapeake Marine Railway and Dry Dock Company opened in 1868.

Myers also organized a Colored Caulkers Trade Union Society, one of the first Negro labor organizations. The shipyard operated until 1879 when it went out of business primarily because the wooden clippers were being replaced by steel-hulled ships. Another problem, ironically, was that other shipyard owners were paying lower wages to their white workers. By the time Myers' company went out of existence, the union had forced the white caulkers' union to accept blacks into their ranks.

Blacks in Baltimore had one advantage not possessed by most Negro residents in cities of former slave states. They voted. In northern cities, where blacks also had the franchise, their numbers were so small that they wielded little power. In Baltimore, blacks had both numbers and the franchise. Most Negroes voted for the Republican Party until the time of the New Deal. This was true in Baltimore and throughout the country. Several early 20th century attempts by the Democratic party to disenfranchise blacks in Maryland failed when reform Democrats, white Republicans, and many immigrants joined blacks in their opposition to measures like grandfather clauses.

Beginning in 1890, black Republicans won seats on the City Council almost every election until 1931. Harry S. Cummings represented a predominantly black ward for fifteen years between 1890 and 1917 when he died. When first elected, Cummings, who grew up in Baltimore and was one of the first two blacks to graduate from the University of Maryland Law School, received favorable newspaper comments because of his educational and professio-

nal background. Dr. John Marcus Cargill and Hiram Watty, a teamster and party regular, were the other black councilmen before World War I. As one of many councilmen, none possessed much power. Their greatest achievements lay in improving the colored schools and funneling some jobs into the black community. A few black Democrats also distributed patronage jobs. Most prominent among them was Tom Smith who, although he never held public office, wielded considerable power.

In the early 20th century, a system of rigid racial segregation grew up in the deep South. In Baltimore, some facilities and institutions were segregated while others were not. Schools, railroad cars, hotels, restaurants, and many stores were segregated. Streetcars were not. City Council ordinances of 1910, 1911 and 1913 requiring segregated housing were defeated when local black lawyers like W. Ashby Hawkins and Warner T. McGuinn tested their constitutionality in court.

By the outbreak of World War I, a small black middle class had moved into houses along Eutaw Place, Druid Hill Avenue, Madison Avenue and Mosher Street, formerly occupied by German Jews who by then were moving further out from the city. That relatively small group of lawyers, doctors, ministers, and teachers all worked to provide the best services and institutions possible in the society. The vast majority of blacks lived in poor conditions, received low wages, and had little or no opportunity to gain a good education. While the immigrants became more thoroughly assimilated, most Negroes were forced to remain in a segregated world.

Late nineteenth century politics was marked by the growth of political machines that dominated most of the nation's cities. Generally, they based their strength on the voting power of immigrants and their descendants to whose

Below Left:
Harry Sythe Cummings, a Republican, was the first black man elected to the Baltimore City Council in 1890

Center:
Hiram Watty, a Republican, served several terms on the city council before World War I

Below Right:
Isaac Myers, an entrepreneur and labor leader, organized one of the nation's first Negro unions

Bottom:
Myers founded the Chesapeake Marine Railway and Dry Dock Company in 1868. He employed black workers who were faced with an increasing discrimination in employment when the abolition of slavery put them in competition with free white workers

needs the leaders catered. Members of the machine hierarchy, often immigrants or first generation Americans, generally met new arrivals at the docks. They helped the newcomers find lodging and a job. The machine often provided emergency food, coal, and even medical care. In exchange, the beneficiaries of these services voted their friends into office.

Baltimore had a machine, but with a difference. Its first boss, Isaac Freeman Rasin, grew up on Maryland's Eastern Shore, the son of an old Maryland, Protestant family that was listed in the Social Register. Local supporters of his Democratic machine reflected Baltimore's unique political situation as a city whose heritage was half northern and half southern.

Baltimore's foreign born population was proportionately smaller than that of most northern, industrial cities. Alone, the foreign born and their children could not have dominated the city's politics. Baltimore had, however, a strong source of Democratic party strength in its southern sympathizers and others who considered the Republican party of the 1870s to be the party of Reconstruction and Negro equality. When these two Democratic groups joined forces, they made their party dominant in Baltimore.

Rasin worked his way up through the Democratic party hierarchy, representing the 7th ward on the city's executive committee and later becoming Clerk of the Court of Common Pleas, a lucrative job which he held from 1867 to 1884. In 1870, Rasin met Arthur Pue Gorman, Maryland's future United States Senator, and the two formed an alliance between city and county political groups which lasted until Gorman's death in 1906 and Rasin's in 1907. When the system was perfected, Rasin controlled the city and Gorman the state, and they cooperated with each other.

Rasin consolidated his power in the city when his candidate for mayor, Joshua Vansant, won in 1871 as did his candidate for governor, William Pinkney Whyte. The double victory gave Rasin control over many patronage jobs, the essence of machine power. Like all bosses, he also distributed city contracts, received campaign contributions from contractors, and placed his people in jobs with their companies. Rasin's powers included choosing the Democratic nominee for mayor. In addition to Vansant, at various times he backed Mayor Ferdinand C. Latrobe, whom he also opposed on occasion; George P. Kane, the former Police Marshal; James Hodges; Robert Davidson; Thomas G. Hayes; and Robert McLane, the last Rasin mayor. He made his former ally, William Pinkney Whyte, mayor of Baltimore in 1881 in order to get him out of state politics.

Like most machines, Rasin's faced opposition from groups who called themselves reformers and who accused the politicos of all sorts of corrupt practices. As early as 1873 in Baltimore, Republicans and some independent Democrats founded a Citizen's Reform party which accused the organization Democrats of fraudulent voter registration, stuffing ballot boxes, and irregularities in the awarding of city contracts, which invariably went to friends of Rasin.

Rasin's most effective response to the reformers was the nomination of respectable individuals for mayor. Ferdinand C. Latrobe, for example, who held office for 13 years between 1875 and 1895, was the son of the general counsel for the B & O. He worked hard for the city and was not a spoilsman. Rasin gave his mayors a free hand to make policies for the city except where they affected the machine. The boss kept a check on the mayors by retaining control of the City Council.

A serious challenge to Rasin came in 1885 when Charles J. Bonaparte and John Cowan led

The choice of competent mayors like Ferdinand C. Latrobe helped Rasin maintain his influence

Rasin consolidated his power in 1871 when his candidate, Joshua Vansant, won the election for mayor

Isaac Freeman Rasin, Baltimore's most powerful Democratic boss, dominated the city's politics from the 1870s until his death in 1907

in the formation of the Reform League. Bonaparte, who was the grandson of Betsy Patterson and Jerome Bonaparte, at that time was a successful lawyer and well-known local reformer. After his friend and fellow reformer Theodore Roosevelt became president, Bonaparte served as his Secretary of the Navy and later Attorney General. John Cowan had already fought the machine for the principle of non-partisan judges. As president of the B & O, he naturally favored any opponent of Gorman's, because the Senator favored the Pennsylvania Railroad over his. These leaders were typical of Progressive reformers in cities throughout the United States. They came from prosperous families, were well educated, and sought to change the system by replacing men they considered crooked and poorly trained with ones they deemed honest and competent.

The reformers' first big victory, one of their few complete ones, came in 1895 when a Republican candidate for mayor, Alcaeus Hooper, won the election. Hooper was supported by Republicans, white and black, and reform Democrats. During the campaign, Hooper had attacked not only the corruption of the machine but also slum conditions in Baltimore, the lack of food inspectors, gross mismanagement of city departments, especially the school system, and the Policy, a lottery run by the machine.

The reformers were aided by Charles H. Grasty whose *Baltimore Evening News* had been exposing problems it attributed to the political leadership; the high prices and poor service of the Consolidated Gas Company; the telephone monopoly; the streetcars; the system of paving streets where contracts were awarded to machine supporters; slums, where there was inefficient garbage removal and building regulation; and the Policy, which lured precious nickels from people who earned few of them.

Once in office, Hooper began personal inspections of schools, streets, and sewers. One January night in 1896 he was on the streets after midnight checking on the cleaning crews. Hooper's major contribution was the replacement of some incompetent officials and the institution of more business-like administrative policies.

Hooper was followed in 1897 by a second Republican mayor, William T. Malster. The most important reform during his term was a new city charter. The new charter provided several major changes. School reform stood out, especially the provision requiring merit appointment for teachers, for whom the sole qualifications previously had been good political connections. A Board of Estimates, consisting of the mayor, comptroller, president of the Second Branch of the bicameral City Council, and two others, was created to draft the budget, set limits on expenditures, and grant franchises. A Board of Awards was established to award contracts, taking that power away from the City Council. With these boards that were limited in membership, responsibility for both good and bad deeds was easy to assign.

The success of the reformer-Republican alliance brought several responses from the organization Democrats. One was a series of attempts to disenfranchise blacks because their vote was so heavily Republican. Democratic campaigns became openly racist. In Annapolis, Democrats passed three separate constitutional amendments in 1904, 1908, and 1910 designed to disenfranchise Negroes and thus make a Republican majority impossible. All failed because of strong opposition from all Republicans, reform Democrats, and many Baltimore machine Democrats, including Rasin, who feared that literacy tests, property requirements, and grandfather clauses might disenfranchise immigrants as well as blacks.

Charles J. Bonaparte, grandson of Betsy Patterson and Jerome Bonaparte, was one of the local reform leaders who challenged Rasin and his machine

Republican mayors Alcaeus Hooper (above) and William Malster (left) defeated the machine in 1895 and 1897

A second response by the Democrats was the nomination of a known reformer, Thomas G. Hayes, to run for mayor in 1899. He won and then appointed the president of the Reform League president of the Board of School Commissioners. He also chose able and trained men as city engineer, building inspector, water engineer and health commissioner. Several state laws passed during his administration effected major reform in Baltimore City. A building inspection act brought the beginning of the end of the sweatshops. A primary election law for the city removed the nomination machinery from the party caucus and gave it to the voting public.

Hayes accumulated enough personal power that Rasin dumped him in 1903 in favor of Robert McLane, who did, however, promise continued "good government." Both Hayes and McLane supported the undertaking of a project to build a sewage system for the city where raw waste still drained in open gutters. Both also supported the Olmsted plan for city beautification. On February 2, 1904 the Board of Estimates approved a loan for sewers, schools, street paving, fire houses, and parks. The commitment was made just in time, because on Sunday, February 7, a fire broke out in the Hurst Drygoods Company on Liberty Street.

Inside the warehouse, smoldering cotton exploded, spewing debris over the neighborhood. A half dozen buildings were soon blazing as a southwest wind spread the fire across German Street. Before the fire stopped, 140 acres in the heart of the downtown business district, the area of the original Baltimore Town, had been consumed. The fire did not cross the Jones Falls, thereby sparing the residents of Little Italy the destruction of their homes. Miraculously, no one was killed. Estimated damage from the great fire was set at $125,000,000 with approximately two thousand buildings destroyed.

174

Mayor McLane appointed an Emergency Committee headed by a Progressive, William Keyser, to advise him on the best plan to deal with the burned-out area and a subsequent Burnt District Commission which carried out the first group's recommendations. Keyser's committee, which included many members of the Municipal Art Society, determined to use the tragedy as an opportunity to institute improvements long needed. They suggested the widening of streets to accommodate increased traffic. Although the property owners, whose lots would be smaller, protested, all but Baltimore Street were rebuilt with extra footage and smooth paving.

Sewer connections were installed under the new streets in anticipation of a complete system which followed soon. Seven years and $20,000,000 later, the system described by a visiting engineer as "the most modern and progressive engineering feat in the world" was completed. In May, 1904 Baltimore's voters approved a $6,000,000 loan for modernization of the harbor. The reconstruction of buildings was managed on an individual basis with no attempt at coordination of design and style. Wide-scale planning of that sort lay two generations in the future.

Mayor Robert McLane's suicide in June, 1904 made E. Clay Timanus mayor. Timanus, a Republican businessman and president of the Second Branch of the City Council, chose prominent reformers George Gaither and William Cabell Bruce as advisors. The new mayor called a General Public Improvements Conference in December. Neighborhoods, business groups, charitable agencies and planners all sent delegates. The program the group produced had the support not only of reformers but also of Rasin and his rising lieutenant, John J. "Sonny" Mahon. Under Timanus and J. Barry Mahool, who was elected mayor in 1907, sewers, parks,

The Great Fire of 1904
demolished 140 acres in the
heart of the downtown business
district

Above:
Though the B&O building was
gutted by the flames, the offices
of Alexander Brown and
Company survived

Left:
Guards patrolled the area to
prevent looting

school facilities, paving, fire equipment and the city's water supply all improved. The changes meant better public health and safety and also the creation of jobs.

Two important political events occurred in 1907: the death of I. Freeman Rasin and the election of Mayor J. Barry Mahool. Rasin's demise left the way open for a new leader at the top of the machine. Mahool's victory was the last for Baltimore's Progressives.

Sonny Mahon, the only politician in the city with practical knowledge of each ward and a strong following in each, moved to the pinnacle of the political hierarchy. Born of Irish immigrant parents who ran a boarding house on South Frederick Street, Mahon as a boy had thrown bricks at the 6th Massachusetts Regiment as it marched through Baltimore in 1861. By 1870 he was the youngest of the Democratic ward heelers. His 9th ward waterfront gang helped him gain control. In 1878 he served his first of eleven terms on the city council.

Mahon could never concentrate his power to the extent that Rasin had. He always had to share it with others. By 1911, News cartoonist McKee Barkley drew Mahon as king of a political "Royal Family," which included two street cleaning contractors, John S. "Frank" Kelly and Danny Loden, and Robert "Paving Bob" Padgett who owned a contracting business. Mahon, Kelly and Loden were all Irish. Padgett was of recent English stock. Irish Americans dominated Baltimore's politics even though they were greatly outnumbered by Germans and native Americans. Mahon, like Rasin, worked closely with the business community and also adopted a conciliatory approach towards reformers. Even more than Rasin, he capitalized on the needs of the new immigrants, whose numbers were expanding rapidly at this time. Mahon maintained his power until his death in the late 1920s.

In the same year Rasin died, 1907, the last progressive mayor of Baltimore, J. Barry Mahool took office. He believed in "good government" (by reformers), regulation of corporations, women's suffrage, and social reform. Mahool's government, like those of his recent predecessors, operated efficiently under the influence of a number of well-trained and responsible high officials. It compared favorably with those of many large cities. In 1910, the state legislature passed a bill creating a public service commission to regulate utilities. A pure food law was also passed in 1910 allowed regulation of slaughtering and food processing.

Women's suffrage had been an issue in Baltimore long before Mahool espoused the cause. In 1894, Etta Maddox, the city's first female lawyer, and her sister, Emma Maddox Funck, led in the creation of the Baltimore Women's Suffrage Association. The group had 160 members in 1905. The following year, the organization sponsored the annual convention of the National American Suffrage Association. Susan B. Anthony, Jane Addams, Clara Barton, Julia Ward Howe, and Carrie Chapman Catt all came to Baltimore. Local activists included Mary Garrett and Elizabeth King Ellicott. Elizabeth Ellicott formed the Equal Suffrage League in 1908. In the following year, both local units took a stand for complete suffrage. Both Mahool and Mahon endorsed their stand.

All the suffragists were involved in the general reform movement and campaigned for clean water and streets, pure food and milk, playgrounds, and better schools. Mrs. Benjamin Corkran formed the first Baltimore Chapter of the National Consumers League. Elizabeth King organized the Maryland Federation of Women's Clubs. These groups and the Arundell Good Government Club, another women's group, all supported a wide range of progressive reforms. Social reform was a major component of

Opposite Page:
*Mayors E. Clay Timanus (far left)
and J. Barry Mahool (left) oversaw
construction of major
improvements including sewers,
parks, school facilities and roads*

Top:
*Officials toured the sewer system
built under the new streets*

Left:
*Sonny Mahon (right) took over
control of the Democratic
machine in 1907. He is shown
here with his lieutenant, Frank
Kelly, apparently studying their
racing forms*

Above:
*Etta Maddox, Baltimore's first
female lawyer, was a leader in
the formation of the Baltimore
Women's Suffrage Association
in 1894*

progressive programs in cities throughout the nation. In addition to achievements already mentioned in labor legislation, housing regulation, sanitation and health, several other notable programs were instituted before World War I. Under the leadership of Eliza Ridgely, Children's Playground Association was established. Robert Garrett organized a Public Athletic League. Most reformers including Mayor Mahool supported their efforts and by 1908 the city had opened 28 park and school yard playgrounds with supervised programs.

Proponents of public health programs supported the establishment of public baths, where people whose houses had no running water could bathe and wash clothes. Henry Walters contributed the money for the city's first three public baths. These were followed by additional baths, portable showers, and swimming pools. In 1909, another public health proposal finally became a reality. A hospital for infectious diseases was opened on the grounds of Bay View, the city's poor house.

The progressives' efforts at reforming the process of government were all aimed at bringing about concrete reforms such as those achieved in Baltimore in the late nineteenth and early twentieth century. The last great effort of the local reformers before the outbreak of World War I was a new charter designed to increase still further the efficient operation of the city government. Although the charter was rejected in 1910 by the state legislature, its provisions all became law during the post-World War I years. In 1918 Baltimore won home rule and a merit system was instituted for civil service jobs. In 1922 the City Council was revamped. The unwieldy bicameral body was replaced in 1923 by a single chamber whose members were to be elected from six districts instead of 28 wards. Eventually the Boards of Estimates and Awards were combined.

As the election of 1911 approached, Mahool made it clear that he was not satisfied with the number of patronage positions that Mahool had allotted him. Sonny and all the ward bosses threw heavy support to the Democratic candidate, James H. Preston. Preston's victory and subsequent two-term administration, which lasted until 1919, gave more power to the machine than it had enjoyed since 1895. City contracting became political again, and a big campaign to pave cobblestone streets and cover open sewers resulted in lucrative contracts and lots of jobs.

The Jones Falls was covered over by the Fallsway, thus in one stroke ending the danger of flooding and creating a new expressway. The sanitary sewer system was completed. The Baltimore Symphony Orchestra and the Municipal Band were established, both supported by the city. Parks were improved and extended. The personnel had changed with the return to power of the machine, but most of the improvements instituted by the reformers remained and often were extended. Ironically, just after the city's political power reverted to the machine, the national Democratic Party convened here, in 1912, and nominated Woodrow Wilson, the last of the progressive presidents.

From 1914 to 1917 people's attention turned more and more to events in Europe. As the war there continued and the war at sea worsened, the American's position evolved from neutrality to involvement. Although it is too arbitrary a date, April 6, 1917, the day of our declaration of war on the Central Powers, is generally given as the end of the progressive period. Energies, both national and local, turned away from domestic reform to the pursuit of the war effort. When the war ended, life was different. Clearly, World War I marked the end of one era and the beginning of a new one.

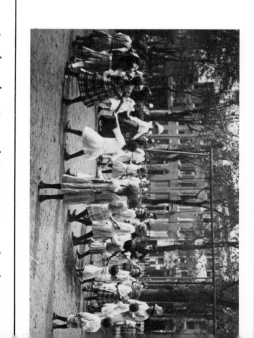

Opposite Page:
Reformers like Eliza Ridgely pressed for the establishment of playgrounds and supervised recreational programs. This one on Calvert Street was one of twenty-eight opened by 1908

Left:
Reformers and public health workers supported the establishment of public baths, where people whose homes had no running water could bathe and wash clothes

Above:
The public baths enjoyed wide use for many years. These girls were photographed around 1920

Left:
The opening of public swimming pools followed the successful establishment of the public baths. The Gwynns Falls Swimming Pool was a popular place for outings such as this one

World War I aroused a fierce patriotism in many Americans. Baltimoreans turned out in large numbers to see this parade along Mt. Royal Avenue

National Crises & Urban Renaissance
1917-1980

V

On April 6, 1917, the United States declared war on Germany. President Woodrow Wilson, former student and lecturer at Johns Hopkins, had gone before Congress four days earlier and asked for the vote to "make the world safe for democracy." He plunged America into the conflict which he knew "would overturn the world we had known." He told Frank Cobb, editor of the New York *World*, that the end of our neutrality would mean: "that we should lose our heads with the rest and stop weighing right and wrong . . . that the majority of people in this hemisphere would go war-mad, quit thinking and devote their energies to destruction."

He predicted that later we would "attempt to reconstruct a peacetime civilization with war standards." In all his predictions, he was sadly correct. Our entry came at the crucial moment, however, for Great Britain had less than a two-month's supply of grain on hand and the German blockade at sea was succeeding in preventing new foodstuffs from reaching that island nation. American ships made the difference.

When war first broke out in Europe in 1914, most Americans believed that it would not affect their lives. But as time passed, more and more Americans, Baltimoreans among them, grew less and less neutral. Involvement came for a wide variety of reasons. All groups strongly asserted their American patriotism. Many individuals, like President Wilson, felt an affinity for the country whose language and culture formed the bases of our own. These people, many of whom traced one or another of their ancestors to England, believed that British civilization must be preserved.

Other people took sides with the Entente nations against the Central Powers for different reasons. American Jews observed anti-Semitism growing in Germany and Austria during the war and therefore opposed the governments guilty of it. Furthermore, if the British drove the Ottoman Turks out of the Holy Lands, there was the possibility of the establishment of a Jewish homeland in the Palestine, a hope the British government promised to support in the Balfour Declaration. Italian Americans supported Italy, which was allied with the British and French, and they knew that a German-Austrian victory might lead to their subjugation of Italy. And, finally, Americans with roots in central Europe, like Polish Americans and Bohemian Americans, sided with the British in the hope that their homelands would gain independence from imperial domination if Germany and Austria were defeated.

Other people in Baltimore and throughout the nation favored Germany or at least wanted to maintain neutrality during the early part of the war. German Americans, of course, did not want to wage war against the nation where many of their relatives and friends still lived and whose language many continued to speak. Many Irish Americans opposed helping England which was then engaged in trying to prevent Irish independence. And, of course, some people opposed war out of principle. Pacifists, especially Quakers, believed that all war was wrong. A significant number of progressives and some socialists believed that the war would take the national attention, energy, and resources away from reforms that were needed to better living conditions in American cities and asserted that the Europeans should be left to solve their problems without our intervention.

Intervene we did, however, and the effects of war were felt rapidly in Baltimore and throughout the nation. Baltimore's sixty-one thousand eligible men hastened to register for the draft. Many German Americans enlisted quickly to prove their loyalty before it could be questioned. City Councilman Harry Cummings wrote to Governor Emerson C. Harrington on behalf of the states' Negroes: "... we are willing and ready to defend our State and Nation. We know but one country and one flag." Before the fighting ended, over sixteen thousand Baltimoreans served in the American armed forces. The 313th Infantry "Baltimore's Own" and the 115th Infantry commanded by Colonel Milton A. Reckord fought with General John J. Pershing's Expeditionary Force in France.

The war effort involved the community. Along with soldiers, the government needed money. Liberty Bonds were sold and Baltimore's quota was set at $25 million. Everyone bought them. School children collected pennies until they had enough. The *Sun* reported that by April 16, Baltimore's German American community had purchased bonds worth $500,000. Promotion gimmicks included a Liberty Bond Balloon in which rides were given to any purchaser of a $1000 bond.

Baltimoreans also feared sabotage and took various precautions. Guards were posted around munitions plants and by railroad bridges. Loch Raven Dam and the Montebello filtration plant were patrolled to prevent the enemy from poisoning the city's water supply.

Shortages occurred quickly. Sugar and cheese became scarce early, and a near panic developed when Baltimore ran out of potatoes. The cessation of trade with Germany cut off equipment for medical and scientific laboratories. Before long, most foodstuffs and consumer goods were in short supply and what was available rose in price. Wages increased, too, but prices went up faster. The disparity created hardship throughout much of Baltimore, particularly as coal and food prices accelerated abruptly. Children began to gather coal along the railroad tracks where it had fallen from trains. A child was killed while doing this. Despite the hardships, Baltimoreans rallied to support the cause. Rallying was almost mandatory because those who did not were viewed with disdain or hatred by their neighbors who believed that nonconformity and treason were the same thing. The federal government's Committee on Public Information made visible patriotism seem obligatory. Most people, however, did their part with enthusiasm. Baltimoreans planted liberty gardens in window boxes, school playgrounds, city parks, and vacant lots as well as in their own backyards. Dr. John Goucher plowed up the front lawn of his estate, Altodale, and the college students helped plant and harvest 256 bushels of potatoes.

Women made bandages for the Red Cross and the wartime economy accelerated social change. Baltimore's industry boomed, supplying the necessities of war. While local industries expanded their output, some of their employees were leaving to join the army. Suddenly women were welcomed in jobs previously closed to them. They worked on assembly lines and drove streetcars. Women's working became an act of patriotism rather than one of economic necessity. Blacks, too, found jobs from which they had been excluded suddenly opening up to them. Industrial positions and wartime wages drew both blacks and whites from rural areas into the city. During the decade from 1910 to 1920, Baltimore's population increased by over 175,000. Public facilities were strained and housing was hard to find. All resources were directed towards the war effort, not civilian comfort.

The war touched everyone, but, as a group, Baltimore's German Americans were probably affected the most. In 1914 many German Americans throughout the country had sided with the Central Powers and had spoken out against Britain's propaganda here. They wanted the United States to remain neutral. German language newspapers openly supported

Far Left:
The Baltimore American promoted sugarless Tuesdays to help preserve the scarce commodity

Left:
Goucher students joined the war effort by farming a large liberty garden on the front lawn of Altodale, home of Dr. John Goucher

After Baltimore's women said goodbye to the soldiers, a variety of jobs were left vacant and many women joined the work force

184

neutrality. German Americans sent aid to German civilians. Then the situation changed. When the war at sea, especially the attacks by German submarines, led to the breaking of diplomatic relations, the *Deutsch Correspondent* warned Baltimore's German Americans in February 1917 that: "It is not yet a crime to defend Germany's position, but it is unpatriotic and, above all, unwise." Several days later the newspaper cautioned readers: "Be calm! Keep your tongue! Keep wisely silent! Remember your oath of allegiance! Keep in mind that while Germany is the land of your fathers, this is the land of our children and children's children."

After war was declared, German Americans in Baltimore joined the war effort, enlisting for service in the army and buying war bonds as soon as they were sold. Many applied quickly for naturalization so they would not be classified as enemy aliens. Others went to court to have their names Americanized. Despite the clear pro-American stance of the vast majority of the German community, suspicions and hostile feelings grew. Although Mayor James Preston forestalled any massive detentions, a few people defended the United States by attacking individual Germans. Accusations and humiliations abounded. H. L. Mencken, whose anti-war writings led to suspicions that he was a spy, responded with verbal scorn and sent to the authorities long, elaborate, anonymous accusations against him.

The year 1918 marked the end of many German-American institutions, including the *Deutsch Correspondent*. Although groups like the singing clubs and the Turnverein reappeared in the mid-1920s, the strength of the community was never as great as it had been before the war. A new bi-weekly newspaper, the *Baltimore Correspondent*, came into circulation after peace returned, but the German-language schools were closed forever. In an early symbolic gesture, the City Council changed the name of German Street, where many German shopkeepers' businesses had once been located, to Redwood Street, in honor of George Buchanan Redwood, the first Maryland officer to die in France.

By October, 1918, when the Allied forces drove through the German lines, the German high command urged the chancellor to propose an armistice on the basis of Woodrow Wilson's Fourteen Points. On November 9 Kaiser Wilhelm abdicated, and two days later Americans received the happy news that an armistice had been arranged. The brutal war had finally come to an end.

Although the war had ended, it was several years before there was much peace at home. Severe post-war dislocations continued the hardships for many people. One immediate effect of the peace was economic confusion. Returning veterans found many industries laying off workers who had been hired to produce war material. White and black rural migrants were laid off. Sometimes veterans got their jobs back, but often there were no jobs.

Wartime had brought union recognition and gains in wages and working conditions for many workers. Peacetime brought strikes to maintain these gains. Workers struck the B & O and Western Maryland Railroads and the Maryland Drydock Company. Longshoremen struck; mill workers in Hampden and Woodberry struck; and some Baltimoreans, accustomed during the war to blaming all troubles on foreign espionage, held Russian Communism responsible. They feared a Bolshevik revolution would take place in the United States similar to the Russian Revolution of 1917.

Housing had become scarce during the war as thousands moved into Baltimore to work in the war industries. Returning veterans found

Colonel Milton Reckord leads the homecoming of the 115th Infantry in 1919

homes were even harder to locate. Overcrowding grew even more severe. The scarcity of homes and the poverty that resulted from the unemployment of many war workers resulted in visible slums by 1920. Blacks, who were not allowed to live in many neighborhoods and who were often the last hired and first fired, suffered most.

Rivalries for jobs and housing intensified prejudices that had existed before the war. Wartime fears and experiences predisposed men to violent and summary actions. The time was ripe for the rise of groups like the Ku Klux Klan. The Klan was active in Baltimore in the early 1920s. All their enemies were here: Catholics, immigrants, Jews, Negroes, and union members, whom the Klan viewed as Communists. Although Governor Ritchie denied them the use of the 5th Regiment Armory, masked Klansmen paraded in Baltimore in 1922. The *Catholic Review*, under the direction of

Archbishop Michael Curley, led the opposition to them and ran a series of articles linking Catholics and American patriotism. The *Jewish Times* stressed Jewish contributions to the city and patriotism during World War I. Eventually the city passed an antimasking ordinance. Revelations of scandals within the Klan contributed to its decline. The Klan never became as dominant a force in Baltimore as it did in other cities, and a gradual return of prosperity resulted in a distinct decline in the limited popularity that the group did enjoy here.

The housing shortage, deteriorating living conditions in the central city, and the rapid population increase stimulated the momentum of the movement to the suburbs already in progress before the war. As the peacetime economy picked up in the early 1920s, more people could afford the move. Baltimore's last major annexation of county land occurred in 1918 and brought large open tracts within the city limits. By vote of the state legislature, 46.5 square miles of Baltimore County and 5.4 square miles of Anne Arundel County filled out the city. Further annexations were forbidden by a constitutional amendment passed after World War II.

Suburban communities developed rapidly in the annexed area and contiguous land beyond. Working-class commuter suburbs like Dundalk in the east and Brooklyn in the south opened up green spaces and the new life-style to blue-collar workers. Upper-class Baltimoreans continued to move northward. The Roland Park Company first offered lots in Guilford for sale in 1913. Guilford proved so popular that in 1924 the company bought Homeland, the estate of David Perine, which the city had considered purchasing for park land two years before.

Institutions follow people, but the intervention of the Depression and World War II slowed the process in this case. After the end of the Second World War, a number of the city's leading churches were built along North Charles Street.

Planning for the Episcopal Cathedral of the Incarnation took several decades. The structure as it now stands was finally completed in 1947. The Episcopal Church of the Redeemer, which began as a small country chapel used by the Perines and a few neighboring families, grew to be the largest parish in the state. Architect Pietro Belluschi of the Massachusetts Institute of Technology designed a new, larger church building in the 1950s to compliment the older Gothic chapel. The Roman Catholic Cathedral of Mary Our Queen is located on Charles Street, two blocks south of the Church of the Redeemer. The Cathedral, also built in the 1950s in a neo-Gothic style, stands on land donated by the Baltimore dry-goods merchant, Thomas J. O'Neill. The legend is that he decided to make the gift when his store survived the great fire of

1904. The Grace Methodist congregation, a union of three older churches, began worshipping at Charles Street and Northern Parkway in 1951. The Brown Memorial Presbyterian Church of Bolton Hill did not move, but opened a second church on North Charles Street in 1961.

After World War I, German and Eastern European Jews moved to the northwest suburbs. Like blacks, Baltimore's Jews in the 1920s faced restrictive housing covenants which excluded them from many neighborhoods. The northwest was open, however. By the 1950s, the major religious congregations had begun building new synagogues. The Baltimore Hebrew Congregation, Har Sinai, Oheb Shalom and many others, with histories going back to East Baltimore during the mid-1800s now stand along Park Heights Avenue, both inside and beyond the city limits.

As the immediate post-war dislocations subsided, the country slipped into the period historians have dubbed the "Roaring Twenties." Prosperity and rebellious assertion of new freedoms characterized the period. An economic boom supported the social and intellectual rebellion.

Baltimore's 1920s boom, like that of the rest of the nation, was based on demands for consumer products that had not been available during the war as well as new items like radios and automobiles. The construction industry boomed. Baltimore businessmen reflected the nation-wide mania of boosterism and promoted their city. Both of Baltimore's mayors during the period, Republican William F. Broening and Democrat Howard W. Jackson, joined with them. They attracted new industries to the city. Glenn L. Martin Aircraft came. American Sugar built a processing plant. Western Electric opened a plant for manufacturing telephone equipment. Bethlehem Steel added a $100,000,000 expansion at Sparrows Point. In the

Right:
The new Roman Catholic Cathedral of Mary Our Queen, built on North Charles Street in the 1950s, is two hundred and seventy feet long. Its stone towers stand one hundred and twenty-eight feet high

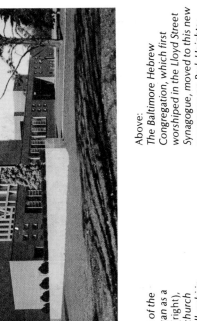

Above:
The Baltimore Hebrew Congregation, which first worshiped in the Lloyd Street Synagogue, moved to this new synagogue on Park Heights Avenue at the city line in the 1950s

Center:
The Episcopal Church of the Redeemer, which began as a small country chapel (right), added the new main church designed by Pietro Belluschi in the 1950s

Above:
Dry-goods merchant Thomas O'Neill left his fortune to the archdiocese of Baltimore to build the new cathedral

six years following 1920, Baltimore's volume of foreign trade rose from seventh in the nation to third. The boosters were succeeding magnificently.

The city's building program reflected its prosperity. The Baltimore Museum of Art opened next to the Hopkins campus. A new municipal office building and fire and police department headquarters appeared around War Memorial Plaza. The city built a wading pool in Carroll Park, a swimming pool in Riverside Park, and two swimming pools in Druid Hill Park, one for whites and one for blacks. For all the new commuters, the city constructed new roads and extended existing ones like Charles Street Avenue, Walther Avenue, the Alameda, and Loch Raven Boulevard out into the developing suburbs. Automobile ownership caused a new problem for the city: traffic congestion. Everyone discussed it, but little was done.

Throughout the boom, politics continued as usual. Sonny Mahon and Frank "Slot Machine" Kelly, vied for power within the Democratic Party. In 1919, Kelly's candidate, George William Weems, defeated James Preston for the Democratic mayoral nomination. In the general election, Mahon's forces sat by and let the Republican candidate, William Broening, win. His party won nine City Council seats as well. Two of these men, Warner T. McGuinn and William L. Fitzgerald were black. Democrats resumed their use of Reconstruction politics and charged that Republican Mayor Broening was a threat to Baltimore's system of white supremacy, even though he had allowed the Ku Klux Klan to parade as evidence of his support for segregation.

Kelly and Mahon scrambled to register new Democratic voters to enlarge their own camps. They had a substantial pool of potential voters to fight over. Rural white migrants voted Democratic as did most foreign immigrants

except for a large minority of Germans and some Jews who registered as Republicans. By 1923, about 75 percent of Baltimore's voters were Democrats.

The election of 1923 showed the results of a temporary truce between Mahon and Kelly that had been orchestrated by Governor Ritchie two years before. Kelly allowed Mahon's candidate, Howard Jackson, to run for mayor with the understanding that the other city offices and patronage jobs would be divided evenly. Jackson defeated the incumbent Broening in a landslide. For the first time the City Council was chosen in that year from six districts which elected three councilmen each. The Democrats had gerrymandered most of the Republicans into the 4th District, containing heavy proportions of blacks and Jews. Much to the surprise of everyone, only one Republican, Daniel Ellison, a Lithuanian Jewish immigrant, won a seat in the City Council. The two black candidates were defeated by white Democrats, although by the next election, those two seats reverted to black Republicans.

Clearly, neither Jackson, nor Mahon, nor Kelly possessed the kind of city-wide control that the pre-war Rasin machine had exercised. The mid-twenties saw even greater dispersion of power with the rise of William Curran, who in 1923 helped the Kelly faction gain control of the City Council. In 1927, the Democrats nominated Curran for mayor. William Broening, with Mahon's help, defeated Curran and carried nine city councilmen into office as well. Frank Kelly and Sonny Mahon both died in 1928 leaving control of the Democratic Party in the hands of Governor Albert Ritchie and William Curran. Curran, a criminal lawyer, was the last city-wide leader. He maintained his influence until he died in 1954. Under Curran, several district leaders acquired considerable influence, among them Richard Coggins and Patrick O'Malley in the

Left:
William Curran is generally considered to have been the last Democratic boss of Baltimore city. Since his death in 1954, political power has been divided among various district leaders

Below:
The United Railways buses parked by the Johns Hopkins campus ran along Charles Street carrying commuters from the popular new northern suburbs to the central business district

Above:
Automobile ownership caused a new problem for Baltimore: traffic congestion

Left:
This filling station which opened in 1911 is said to have been the first in Baltimore. It was located on the corner of St. Paul and Lexington Streets

third district and James H. (Jack) Pollack in the fourth district.

In 1931 Curran and Ritchie conceded to popular demand and allowed vote-getter Howard Jackson to run for mayor, provided he accept Curran men for City Council president and comptroller on his ticket. A group of reformers, working with some independent ward bosses, managed to elect their own candidate, E. Lester Muller, as City Council President. Jackson did win the mayoralty and became Baltimore's only four-term mayor, remaining in office until 1943.

One archenemy of Jackson's was Marie Bauernschmidt. A reform leader who campaigned for years to rid the city school system of graft and politics of corruption, she found Jackson particularly objectionable because of his periodic bouts with demon rum. She challenged him to "take the cure" or resign from office. Jackson's drinking helped him politically in some parts of town, especially during Prohibition.

The 18th Amendment, originally proposed as a wartime conservation measure, became effective in 1919 when the Volstead Act provided enforcement procedures and funding. Throughout the dry years, Baltimore was known as a "wet" town. Several breweries continued to produce the real thing under the guise of near-beer. Distilled liquor arrived regularly through the ports of both Baltimore and Annapolis and was manufactured locally as well. Speakeasies proliferated as the laxity of prosecution became apparent. The city government under Ritchie, a national leader of the wets, never appropriated money for enforcement of Prohibition. In fact, Ritchie's attorney general ruled that the local police did not have the right to make arrests under the Volstead Act. Federal agents did occasionally conduct raids in Baltimore, but frequently they were met by hostile crowds and violent opposition against which local police officials declined to provide aid.

Drinking in spite of Prohibition was one of many forms of rebellion during the "Roaring Twenties." Although roots of the rebellion stretched back into the late nineteenth century, it was nurtured in the wartime spirit of "eat, drink, and be merry for tomorrow we may die." Many people, particularly members of the younger generation who had served overseas, began to question old values, to look for new meanings, and to experiment with new life-styles. This breaking out and innovation, often accompanied by a rejection of traditions was opposed particularly by those members of the older generation who felt that their whole way of life and moral system were being threatened. People who already felt threatened by immigrants, strikes and Communists, tended also to react with fear to cocktail parties, new fashions, new trends in music and theater, and the new life-styles of women. Despite the opposition, rebellion flourished in the prosperity of the 1920s.

New forms of music, especially jazz, and theatrical presentations with themes of realism, rebellion, and explicit sex drew large crowds. Baltimore both before and after World War I was a good theater town. Leading actors and musicians performed before large audiences in the city's numerous theaters. A gradual transition from vaudeville and live theater to movies took place during the early decades of the twentieth century.

At the turn of the century, at least eight theaters were thriving in Baltimore. The two leading playhouses were the Holliday Street Theater, housed in the 1872 structure which survived until 1927 when it was razed to make way for War Memorial Plaza, and Ford's Grand Opera House, which opened in 1871 with a

It appears that Baltimoreans expected liquor to be available, but more expensive, after the Volstead Act went into effect

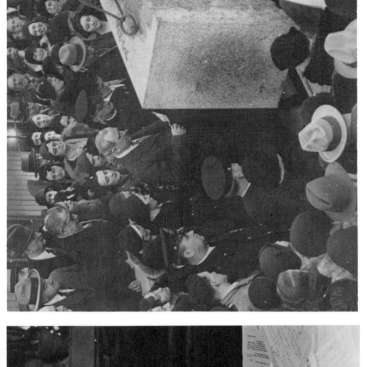

Howard Jackson, one of Baltimore's most popular mayors and the masterful leader during the depression of the 1930s, makes a speech at the laying of the cornerstone of the new Enoch Pratt Free Library central building which opened in 1933

Marie Bauernschmidt, a reformer and an archenemy of Jackson's, was unfortunately noted for leading many unsuccessful campaigns against him

performance of *As You Like It* and closed ninety-three years later with *A Funny Thing Happened on the Way to the Forum*. For many years a family business, Ford's Theater brought stars like George M. Cohan, Edwin Booth, Helen Hayes, Maurice Evans, and Tallulah Bankhead to Baltimore. When movies were new, Ford's screened big features like D. W. Griffith's *Birth of a Nation* in 1915 and Cecil B. DeMille's *Ten Commandments* in 1925. Under the ownership of Morris A. Mechanic, Ford's remained beyond World War II the only legitimate theater in town.

At the turn of the century, vaudeville reigned as the national entertainment. Admission usually ranged from 25 to 50 cents. Some shows were rough and ready; others were billed for the whole family. James Kernan, who donated the land for the hospital for crippled children, made his fortune from the Monumental Theater, where some of Baltimore's more daring acts were presented. Women dancers wore tightly laced corsets, but raw flesh was taboo. Hawaiian style hula dancers provided the most naked entertainment. With his profits from the Monumental, Kernan opened the Maryland Theater for "refined" vaudeville. He censored the acts himself to make sure nothing would offend the ladies and children in his audiences. Ethel Barrymore and Lillian Russell appeared, and Al Jolson debuted in Kernan's Theater. Variety shows included jugglers, bicyclists, acrobats and animals. In the winter, when cool temperature modified the odor, acts featuring horses and elephants were popular. The Maryland led the way in incorporating movies into its live shows, a practice the theater began in 1904. Finally, it became exclusively a movie theater before it was torn down in 1951. Most of the old vaudeville theaters became movie theaters and then either closed or burned down.

One rather unique theater, the Lyceum, shows the transition well. Built in the 1890s in the fashionable neighborhood of 1200 North Charles Street, the stage originally featured amateur performances. A little bar and smoking room were located beneath the lobby. The first few rows of spectators sat on comfortable sofas. John Albaugh, who operated a vaudeville syndicate, purchased the theater and brought in stars like George Arliss, Blanche Bates, and George Fawcett. During the Great War, the Lyceum offered a mixture of road shows, musicals, vaudeville, and films. In the early twenties, when legitimate theater drew smaller crowds, offerings like *White Cargo* and *Seduction* brought audiences seeking the sensational. The police gave the theater good publicity when they arrested some of the performers and charged them with indecent exposure. The next show, *Getting Gertie's Garter*, was a sellout. In 1925, the Lyceum burned down.

As filmmaking technology improved, movies proliferated and drew even larger crowds. By 1920, Baltimore's biggest movie houses, the New, the Hippodrome, and the Victoria, each averaged thirty thousand spectators weekly. The Hippodrome featured big band concerts as well. The Municipal Band and the Colored Municipal Band played summertime concerts in the city's parks. With all the merrymaking, many people forgot the fear that had characterized the immediate post-war period.

Baltimore's segregated society led to the growth of a separate black entertainment district. Pennsylvania Avenue emerged as the center of black culture in the 1920s. The spirit of the Harlem Renaissance came to Baltimore, and "the Avenue" flourished. The Douglas Theater built by the black-owned Douglas Amusement Company, dominated the 1300 block of Pennsylvania Avenue. Later known as the Royal, the theater throughout the years between the

In the 1920s, elaborately decorated movie theatres like the New drew an average of 30,000 spectators weekly

wars featured the big-name musicians like Eubie Blake, Count Basie, Cab Calloway, and Duke Ellington. After World War II, Ella Fitzgerald, Nat "King" Cole, Dizzy Gillespie, and Billie Holiday all performed at the Royal, and later the Supremes, the Platters, and James Brown. Live performances lasted until 1965 at the Royal, when it went the way of the city's other old vaudeville theaters and became exclusively a movie house. Five years later it was bulldozed to make space for a new school.

During the heyday of the Royal Theater a cluster of clubs, where big name entertainers also appeared, opened along the Avenue. Gamby's, the Ritz, the Comedy Club, owned by Isaiah Dixon, and the Casino Club, where owner Willie Adams introduced Redd Foxx, all drew crowds. Some of the performers stayed at the Casino Club. Others made their quarters at the black-owned Penn Hotel, whose guests included Ethel Waters and Pearl Bailey as well as the band leaders.

Pennsylvania Avenue meant more than theaters. Movie houses were there. A YMCA was located nearby. Businesses that catered to blacks opened stores along the Avenue. As Negro customers found themselves unwelcome in many of the big downtown stores, they turned more and more to the Avenue shops. From the 1930s through the 1950s, the Pennsylvania Avenue Merchants Association sponsored an Easter Parade. While whites paraded their Easter finery around Mt. Vernon Square, Negroes showed theirs along the Avenue.

A major institution, Douglass High School, moved in 1925 to new quarters just west of Pennsylvania Avenue at Calhoun and Baker Streets. Almost all of Baltimore's middle class Negroes sent their children to Douglass, which was noted for its high academic standards. In the 1920s fully one-third of its graduates went on to college or normal school. Douglass' more

famous alumni include band leader Cab Calloway, civil rights activists Clarence Mitchell Jr. and his wife, the former Juanita Jackson, and Supreme Court Justice Thurgood Marshall.

Although some black Baltimoreans clearly shared in the prosperity and revelry of the twenties, many did not. Discrimination in hiring and lack of educational background left many in poverty. Overcrowded and unhealthful living conditions were one result of that. Tuberculosis especially plagued Baltimore's Negro community. The city's health officials dubbed as "Lung Block" the square bounded by Pennsylvania Avenue, Druid Hill Avenue, Biddle and Preston Streets because so many cases of tuberculosis occurred there.

But progressivism was not completely dead. Medical officials and social workers still labored in Negro and white slums. City-wide charity organizations carried an increasing share of the burden previously borne by ethnic and religious societies. Reformers like Elisabeth Gilman, the daughter of Johns Hopkins' first president, a social worker who became a socialist, fought to keep people's consciences aroused. The reform impulse remained, but it was no longer as dominant as it had been before the war to save the world for democracy had been fought and won and left the world still unperfected. Social activists were no longer society's celebrities.

Popular heroes of the twenties and thirties tended to be either outstanding individual achievers or outspoken rebels. Baltimore provided its share of national heroes. H. L. Mencken, who never really left, and F. Scott Fitzgerald, who came to Baltimore during the 1920s, drew the attention of the nation's literati to the city on the Patapsco. Babe Ruth, even after he played for the Yankees, and Roy Campanella who played for the Baltimore Elites gave the city fame among sports fans.

The joyous days of the twenties provided a

Left:
Supreme Court Justice Thurgood Marshall is one among many nationally famous alumni of Douglass High School

Below:
Big names like Al Jolson (left) and Cab Calloway (right) performed on Pennsylvania Avenue in its heyday

Left:
Douglass High School, noted for its high academic standards when Baltimore's public schools remained segregated, sent an unusually high number of graduates on to college or normal school

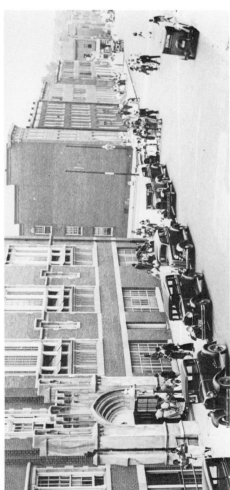

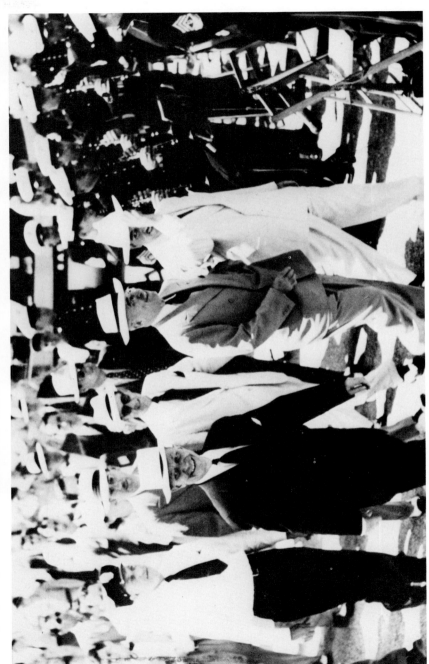

Right:
Pitcher Dave McNally and Brooks Robinson cheer the winning of the 1966 World Series

Below:
President Harry S. Truman joined Governor Preston Lane (left) and Mayor Thomas D'Alesandro (right) at the dedication of Friendship Airport in June 1950

1929. Housing construction fell off after the post-war shortage was satiated. Farmers faced the consequences of their wartime expansion once a recovered Europe no longer purchased so much American food. Such poor agricultural markets and also the devastations of the boll weevil drove many farmers and agricultural workers into cities like Baltimore in search of employment.

Just as some segments of the economy had wound down before the crash, others continued to operate at a fairly high level after 1929. A states and cities faced grave difficulties, but the specific problems varied somewhat from place to place. During the period immediately following the stock market crash, Baltimore fared better than some other cities.

Unemployment spread more slowly in Baltimore because of the city's diversified economy. The numbers of jobless people rose gradually here. Towns that were dependent on one major industry often felt a more sudden shock wave. Furthermore, only a few big banks in Baltimore failed. The Baltimore Trust Company was the first to close its doors in September, 1930. Most of the big banks in town did not fail. They were managed by conservative bankers not given to the speculative policies of their more adventuresome colleagues. Because of this, most Baltimore depositors did not see their lifetime savings wiped out. One other advantage Baltimore possessed was its large number of home owners. In an era when many mortgages were paid off in five years, a large number of people owned their homes clear of debt and therefore did not face losing them in foreclosure proceedings.

All these factors notwithstanding, Baltimore soon began to feel the effects of the national slowdown. Men and women began to face layoffs or salary cuts. Unemployment ran higher among the city's blacks, who were often the first

needed respite between World War I and the difficult years of the Depression and World War II which followed. Although the date of the great crash, October 24, 1929, generally marks the beginning of the crisis, in reality the transition from prosperity to depression was somewhat less abrupt. Throughout the nation, several sectors of the economy were in trouble before

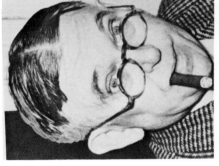

Henry L. Mencken, who lived most of his life on Hollins Street, brought renown to the city of his birth as one of the leading pundits of his time

George Herman Ruth first played baseball at St. Mary's Industrial School. Jack Dunn, owner of the Orioles, gave the Babe his first major league job, and the Baltimore boy became a national hero

Opposite:
Novelist F. Scott Fitzgerald, pictured here in his World War I uniform, lived in Baltimore during the 1920s, for some time occupying an apartment overlooking the campus of the Johns Hopkins University on North Charles Street

Roy Campanella, who played in the Negro League for the Baltimore Elites, was one of many players who moved into the major leagues when they desegregated after World War II

fired. Women workers faced layoffs from employers who felt they should not take jobs away from men. This was true sometimes even when the women were responsible for the support of their family. Blacks and women may have lost their jobs first, but everybody was threatened. By January 1931, roughly 42,000 Baltimoreans, or one-eighth of the total work force were unemployed. In September 1931, Baltimore's labor unions reported that 31 percent of their members were unemployed and 27 percent could find only part-time work. President Herbert Hoover's Commission for Unemployment set Baltimore's rate at 19.2 percent in 1931. People were suffering.

The men in charge in 1930, while this situation was developing, were known humanitarians. Maryland's Governor Albert C. Ritchie began his career as a progressive. A popular politician, he held his office from 1920 to 1935. Baltimore Mayor William Broening was known for siding with the "little guys" and working for safety rules in industry and other such protective measures. In particular, Ritchie was loathe to accept funds from the federal government. Maryland was one of only eight states that turned down the first federal monies offered.

In 1930 no state agency existed to handle unemployment or relief problems. The Board of State Aid and Charities served primarily to give advice to private charities and to make inspections. In May, 1930, Mayor Broening established a Commission on Employment Stabilization and in December a Municipal Free Employment Service. Neither agency could handle the large numbers of unemployed. There simply were not enough jobs to go around.

Private charities did their best to provide relief. In Baltimore, 80 percent of the relief cases were handled by the Family Welfare Association. Additional help came from the Bureau of Catholic Charities, the Jewish Social Service

Bureau, the Salvation Army, and smaller groups. In 1930, the city reluctantly granted $8900 to the Family Welfare Association and $3900 to the Jewish Social Service Bureau when those organizations ran out of funds.

Police Commissioner Charles Gaither announced that the department would assume a role in providing relief and asked for donations of money and gifts in kind. By February, 1931, the Police Department had provided fuel and food for 7500 families and had fed 6600 persons at local station houses. That same month, the Baltimore Association of Commerce organized a Citizens' Emergency Relief Committee. W. Frank Roberts served as its chairman. Mayor Broening contributed $50,000 from the city's contingency fund. By April the businessmen had raised $350,000. The Sunpapers sponsored Self-Denial Day on March 27, 1931. Boxes appeared all over town. Baltimore's citizens were asked to deny themselves something they wanted and contribute the money for distribution among the needy. The 1931 Community Chest drive raised $2 million for relief in Baltimore. The Citizens' Emergency Relief Committee total rose to $650,000. Ritchie contributed $125,000, four days proceeds from the racetrack, for relief in Baltimore. But none of this was enough.

As the May, 1931 mayoral election approached, Howard Jackson campaigned promising that the municipal government would do all it could to bring relief and employment. He won. And the situation continued to get worse. In September, 3800 families in Baltimore received aid from the Citizens' Emergency Relief Committee. Five months later, 14,100 families requested relief. By March, 1932, the committee needed $50,000 a week. That month, Jackson contributed $100,000 from the city's contingency funds. Other money was raised by bonds which Ritchie had reluctantly agreed to issue. By January, 1933, 20 percent of all Baltimore's

workers were unemployed. Over 20,000 families were on relief. Finally, in March, Ritchie applied to the Reconstruction Finance Corporation for a loan to bring some federal money into the state.

Governor Ritchie's slowness, similar to President Hoover's, to experiment with new methods of government financing to meet the crisis, contributed to his election defeat in 1934. Jackson's people did not support Ritchie. The Republican candidate, Harry W. Nice, carried Baltimore and the state.

Howard Jackson soon realized that the situation he found when he took office in 1931 needed more than temporary relief. He led Baltimore into the New Deal, and he set out to run the city like a business. The logo he imprinted on his stationery bespoke his approach to his office: "Be courteous, efficient, and economical."

Jackson launched Baltimore on a plan of business-like management of municipal government, efficient relief projects, and useful public works. Accepting funds from Washington on one hand, he initiated a successful drive to collect local taxes on the other. When other cities faced large defaults in 1933 and 1934, Jackson collected 85 percent and 94 percent, respectively, of all monies owed. Such efficiency enabled him to reduce assessments and lower the tax rate from $2.54 to $2.34. Jackson did reduce salaries paid to municipal workers: those who earned more than $1000 received a five percent cut, and those whose salaries were over $1200 lost 10 percent. He decreased his own salary by 20 percent. But unlike many other cities, Baltimore's employees received checks every payday and the city maintained a good credit rating. That proved beneficial in attracting federal money, especially for programs that required matching funds.

Jackson won national acclaim for his

administration of Baltimore. His insistence on efficient management of all programs and appointment of competent people to run them were crucial to Baltimore's survival. Judge Thomas Waxter directed the Baltimore Welfare Department which handled all federal, state and municipal funds for general public assistance. Waxter was highly praised. Dr. Huntingdon Williams, who directed the city's Health Department, twice won awards for the most efficient health program in the nation.

Jackson insisted that all New Deal projects have long-term usefulness as well as providing employment for hungry people. City officials worked with representatives of the Civil Works Administration, the Works Progress Administration, the Public Works Administration and other agencies to plan the projects. The Maryland director of the Public Works Administration, Abel Wolman, a sanitary engineer from Johns Hopkins, was especially helpful. The list of projects is impressive. Jackson built a new wing for the Art Museum and the new Enoch Pratt Free Library. Collections at both places were catalogued. Additions were made to several city hospitals and to Morgan College.

New Deal funds constructed the Mount Pleasant Park and Golf Course, a second tunnel from Loch Raven Reservoir to Montebello, and the new Prettyboy Reservoir. New schools and playgrounds opened. Existing schools were repaired and beautified. Baltimore gained wider roads and the viaducts on Howard and Orleans Streets. Late in the New Deal the city's first public housing, the Edgar Allen Poe Homes, opened in East Baltimore.

With all these successes, it is not surprising that Howard Jackson won reelection in 1935 and 1939. In 1935 he defeated Willie Curran's man in the primary and in the general election won easily over both Republican Blanchard Randall, Jr. and Socialist Elisabeth Gilman. Jackson

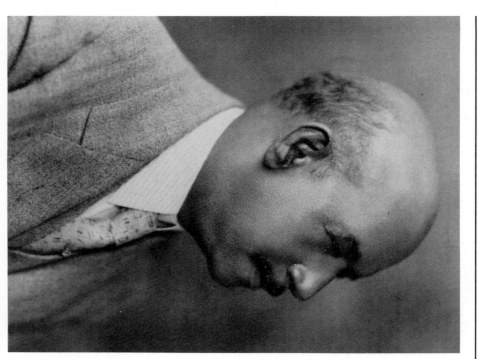

entered the gubernatorial primaries in 1938 but lost the nomination to Herbert O'Conor, an ally of Curran's. O'Conor defeated Nice for the governorship. The following year, Jackson defeated the Curran-O'Conor candidate for the mayoral nomination and then went on to beat a popular new Republican, Theodore Roosevelt McKeldin, to win his fourth and last term as mayor.

Despite Mayor Jackson's efficiency, life remained exceedingly difficult for a great many people during the 1930s. Soup lines continued to feed many hungry people. Others scraped by without enough food, without decent homes, and without opportunities for education.

Throughout the nation, different groups protested the system under which these conditions persisted through the decade. But although Socialists and other protest parties fielded candidates in many elections, most voters chose to work within the existing system. Somehow, President Franklin Roosevelt inspired confidence that everything would come out all right.

The New Deal marked a watershed in the American's political history. Before Roosevelt was president, the usual national majority was Republican. Since the New Deal, it has been Democratic. Baltimore was already a heavily Democratic city, but national changes were reflected in local politics. The most dramatic change occurred as black voters switched their allegiance from the party of Lincoln to the party of the New Deal. Former Republican City Councilman William Fitzgerald's move to the Democratic Party and his work as a W.P.A. official typified the transformation. As in so many similar cases, Roosevelt's economic policies precipitated the move.

An interesting black protest group was formed in Baltimore in 1931, at a time when many civil rights organizations were stagnating. Their techniques and goals prefigured the broader civil rights movement of the 1960s. The Young People's Forum was organized by a group of well-educated, younger members of some of Baltimore's leading black families. Juanita Jackson served as president of the group. Her mother, Lillie Mae Carroll Jackson, an experienced civil rights activist, was an advisor. Members met at the Bethel A.M.E. Church and other churches. They invited speakers chosen "to promote youth consciousness," among them Walter White of the National Association for the Advancement of Colored People, athlete Jesse Owens, diplomat Ralph Bunche, birth control advocate Margaret Sanger, and

Opposite:
City Councilman William
Fitzgerald moved into the
Democratic Party to support the
New Deal

Right:
As the depression made
economic difficulties even
harsher, black Baltimoreans
protested discrimination in
employment

Below:
Free entertainment like this
baseball game in 1931 drew
crowds during the depression
years

newspaperman Gerald Johnson. In an effort to change policies that hurt the black community economically, the Young People's Forum sponsored "buy where you can work" drives. Their boycotts and picketing of Pennsylvania Avenue stores, including the A&P, resulted in the hiring of black clerks. The group also helped register blacks to vote.

All the protests and all the New Deal programs continued on through the 1930s, and none of them ended the Depression. British economist John Maynard Keynes had figured out the solution: spending. But no one, in or out of the New Deal, imagined the magnitude of spending that would be necessary to put America's millions back to work and start the economic cycle upward again. What really ended the Great Depression was World War II. Millions of men were taken out of the civilian work force and paid by the Army. Millions more were hired to produce war material which the soldiers of all nations destroyed almost as fast as it came out of the factories. Prosperity returned, but with it came the agonies of war.

Three days after the bombs fell on Pearl Harbor, Mayor Jackson organized a Civil Defense Committee, headquartered at City Hall and chaired by Baltimore's Highways Engineer, George A. Carter. A crash program to train instructors was put together. During the Christmas holidays 1,100 teachers qualified as civil defense instructors and then taught others. Within six months ten thousand persons had been trained. Before the war ended, over twenty-five thousand Baltimoreans participated in some form of civil defense activity. Air raid wardens, auxiliary police and firemen, a medical corps, messengers, demolition and clearance crews all received training. Over four hundred people were trained to work in decontamination squads in case of gas attacks. Warning centers staffed by volunteer women telephone operators were set up to operate 24 hours a day. The media ran a campaign to teach people how to react in case of a bombing. Practice blackouts allowed familiarization with some of the procedures.

As thousands of Baltimoreans left to join the Armed Forces, and student pilots practiced in the sky beyond Mt. Washington, Governor O'Conor authorized a state guard, known as the Minute Men, to give local protection in case of local sabotage. Despite this precaution, fears of local enemies were not as great as they had been during World War 1. Although a small percentage of Baltimore's German Americans had joined the pro-Nazi Bund during the thirties, many more had been outspoken in their condemnation of Hitler and their loyalty to the United States. East coast Germans faced little of the paranoia that sent west coast Japanese Americans to detention camps. Some German groups were placed under surveillance, and a number did not survive the war, but the irrational hatred of all things German that had characterized the First World War did not reappear.

Baltimore, as it had in so many wars, served as a major military supply center. Men, food, and supplies moved rapidly through the port. Two local industries, shipbuilding and aircraft, and their suppliers were especially important. As early as the fall of 1941 the Bethlehem-Fairchild Shipyards received contracts to build 62 ships. Before the war was over, the company had hired forty-seven thousand workers to construct 384 Liberty ships, 94 Victory ships, and 30 LSTs. The Maryland Drydock Company hired twelve thousand new employees to work on conversion and repair orders received before Pearl Harbor. At the same time, Glenn L. Martin Aircraft was backlogged with orders worth $743 million and hired six thousand people to work on them. This rate of production continued throughout the

Above:
Air-raid sirens were installed throughout the city for use in blackout drills during the war

Left:
The Duke and Duchess of Windsor visited Baltimore in 1941. A large crowd, curiosity seekers among them, turned out to greet the former Wallis Warfield Simpson who once lived in the city

Right:
The war abroad changed the appearance of the streets of Baltimore. Here several men inspect sandbags installed by local civil defense officials

Center:
Sailors with loaded duffel bags march past the Richmond Market

war.

Thousands of men, women and children poured into Baltimore from rural Maryland, Appalachia and points south to work in the war industries. Women and blacks were hired in jobs previously closed to them. The burgeoning population placed a burden on all city services: schools, health, sanitation, transportation. Ten thousand new housing units were needed. Military needs, of course, took priority.

Everyday life in Baltimore quickly reflected those military priorities. Sugar shortages hit early. Waitresses in restaurants asked "how many?" if a person ordered sugar with coffee and often refused to give more than two cubes. The *Sun* reported in April 1942 that tea was getting scarce and so were lawn mowers. Tires were rationed. Price ceilings were established for tires, retreads, sugar, electrical appliances and much more, so people had a fair chance at purchasing the limited supplies that were available. Favorite soft drinks were unobtainable at the end of each month as that month's quota ran out. Rubber heels were more expensive. Razor blade production was curtailed. People carried old tubes to the drugstore to get refills of toothpaste and shaving cream. Home heating oil deliveries were limited. The Baltimore Transit Company's ridership grew by leaps and bounds as more and more people saved their cars and gasoline for special uses.

Despite a great degree of unity in national politics and widespread support of the war effort, local political rivalries continued as usual. Baltimore elected a new mayor in 1943. Howard Jackson ran for an unprecedented fifth term. The Democratic Party alliances had fallen apart, however, and Curran's forces once again opposed Jackson. Curran and O'Conor had also split in a patronage dispute. The result of the Democratic disunity was a victory for Republican candidate Theodore Roosevelt McKeldin, who served as mayor through the final years of the war and the first years of the peace.

Baltimoreans followed the war in Europe and in the Pacific on the radio and in newspaper reports. They watched eagerly as the tide of battle turned slowly in 1943 and 1944. They cheered the June 6, 1944 landing in Normandy and the Allied arrival in Paris on August 25. The mourned the death of President Roosevelt on April 12, 1945, and less than a month later, on May 7, rejoiced at the unconditional surrender of Germany. They watched the new president, Harry Truman, and read of the results of his first major decision as the atomic bombs fell on Hiroshima and Nagasaki, and were glad and relieved when Japan also finally surrendered on September 2. The long war was over.

Once again Baltimore began the transition from a wartime to a peacetime society. Veterans returned, war industries ceased production, and some workers lost their jobs. By October, 1945 approximately thirty-nine thousand persons had been laid off; but several factors cushioned the shock. Industries quickly reconverted to meet the large demand for consumer goods. Government programs for veterans, especially the G. I. Bill, funneled many veterans out of the labor market. Returning soldiers hastened to take advantage of the opportunity for higher education. The Johns Hopkins freshman class in 1946 enrolled half teenagers and half veterans. By the academic year 1948-49, 70 percent of all Hopkins undergraduates were ex-servicemen. While these people studied, industry reconverted. The government supervised this and other processes more than it did after World War I. Consequently, socio-economic dislocations were fewer.

Almost immediately, however, a cold war replaced the past conflict as the absorbing international concern. One domestic result of the rivalry between the United States and Russia

Before the war's end, the workers at the Bethlehem-Fairchild Shipyards built over 500 ships. Here the Liberty Ship Patrick Henry readies to set sail

Below:
Rationing cards regulated the amount of many scarce commodities people could purchase. Here, precious sugar is being weighed carefully

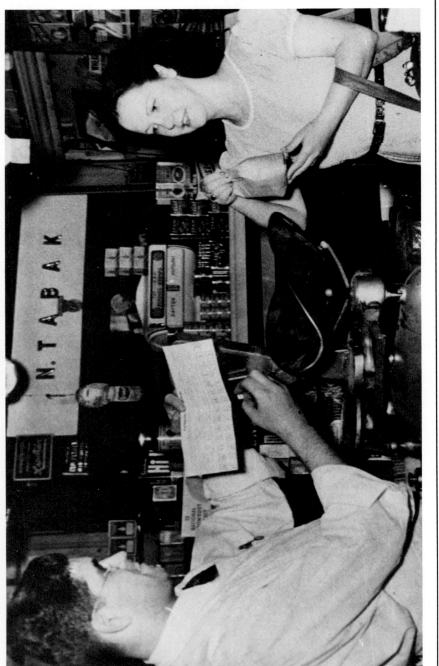

was the rise of a strong anti-Communist movement in this country. Just as the threat of a Bolshevik revolution had been exaggerated after World War I, the fear of Communist infiltration mushroomed following World War II. Several Baltimoreans figured prominently in the tragic circumstances.

A graduate of Johns Hopkins and former editor of the student *Newsletter*, Alger Hiss received an honorary LL.D. from his alma mater in the university's Commemoration Day ceremonies in February, 1947. He was honored for distinguished service in international relations. Less than three years later, Hiss was convicted of perjury for lying about his affiliations with the Communist Party.

Owen Lattimore, director of the Walter Hines Page School of International Relations at Johns Hopkins and an expert on the Far East, was accused by Senator Joseph McCarthy of being the top Communist agent in the United States. The university resisted pressure to fire Lattimore, and faculty members, including George Boas and Clarence Long, rallied to his support. Finally, Maryland Senator Millard E. Tydings cleared his name before McCarthy's committee. McCarthy then undertook to remove Tydings from the Senate, which he did in the scandalous campaign of 1950 when McCarthy supporters juxtaposed photographs of Tydings and a former head of the American Communist Party, Earl Browder, to give the impression that they worked together. Ugly incidents like these occurred all too widely in Baltimore and elsewhere until the frenzy subsided in the mid-1950s.

Baltimore's post-war history is a success story. Like much of the rest of the nation, the city in 1945 faced major problems of readjustment and rehabilitation which had been accumulating through the crises of the Great Depression and World War II. Baltimore's solutions stirred heavily.

enthusiasm both locally and throughout the nation. The involvement of many segments of the population and the broad cooperation between the public and private sectors in planning and executing rehabilitation projects have played a large part in the success of Baltimore's "renaissance."

The renewal program began under Mayor Thomas D'Alesandro, Jr. who was elected in 1947. He defeated Curran's candidate, Howard Crook, in the primary and Republican Deeley K. Nice in the general election. D'Alesandro had the support of a number of ward leaders including Ambrose Kennedy, Patrick O'Malley, Jack Pollack, and Joe Wyatt. D'Alesandro wanted to build, and he took office at the right time to do just that.

Blight had been spreading across downtown Baltimore through the poverty of the 1930s and the war years of the 1940s. A survey made in 1950 revealed the decay which was most extensive in a ring around the downtown area. Of Baltimore's two hundred fifty thousand homes, ninety-one thousand were in blighted areas. One-third of the city's people lived in those areas. Over forty-five thousand homes were classified as substandard and eighteen thousand as dilapidated. Between twenty thousand and thirty thousand homes lacked toilets, baths, hot water or all three. Most census tracts were either all black or all white.

Shortages of schools and recreation facilities had worsened during the war. Inner-city decay and post-war prosperity accelerated suburban growth. People who could afford to were abandoning the inner city to people whose needs for city services were greatest. The central business district suffered heavily as fewer people shopped downtown. Traffic congestion and lack of parking kept increasing numbers of Baltimoreans away. Its assessed value declined heavily.

Above:
V-J Day is hailed by this crowd at
Baltimore and Charles Streets.
Finally the long war had ended

Top:
News of the German surrender
brought crowds to the streets

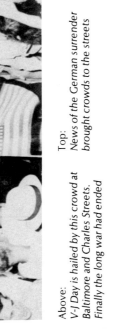

Above:
Peace brought happy reunions
on Pier 11 at Canton

Several programs were begun to ameliorate the decay. A comprehensive system of housing rehabilitation which became known as the Baltimore Plan resulted in the restoration of homes by the enforcement of sanitary and safety regulations. Despite a crash program, twenty-five thousand substandard homes still surrounded the downtown area in 1954. Mayor D'Alesandro's building program had given the city five hundred miles of new streets, 17 recreation centers and pools, 9 new schools, 7 off-street parking garages, 4 new firehouses, a new expressway and the lower deck of the new Memorial Stadium.

Big league teams came to Baltimore to play in the new stadium. The National Football League Colts began to play here in the fall of 1953 after Carroll Rosenbloom and other local investors purchased the team. Their first win of an NFL championship in January, 1959 gave Baltimore a bigger boost than all the building projects combined. Major league baseball came to the city when the season opened in the spring of 1954, after Clarence Miles headed a group of Baltimoreans who purchased the St. Louis Browns. Joseph Iglehard and then Jerold C. Hoffberger served as chairman of the board. In 1966, the year after Hoffberger took over, the Orioles won the American League pennant and the World Series.

More innovations appeared. Baltimore became the first American city to add fluorine to its water supply. D'Alesandro hired the nation's foremost traffic engineer, Henry Barnes, to straighten out the city's horrendous traffic problems. The new Friendship Airport begun under Theodore McKeldin's administration opened. Mayor D'Alesandro, Governor William Preston Lane, and President Harry Truman dedicated the facility in 1950.

The years 1954 and 1955 saw several key events that set the future course of Baltimore's development. By the end of that time, a pattern of cooperation of the city's residents, business leaders, and government officials was beginning to evolve. Several processes occurred simultaneously. Blacks, the one major group which had been excluded from power, began to integrate more fully than ever before into the life of the city. At the same time, businessmen and politicians joined in a venture to promote the city and improve the environment for both business and living.

The events of 1954, the year of the Supreme Court school integration decision, signalled a new beginning for Baltimore's black community. Just under a third of the total population at this time, Negroes had been without elected political representation since 1931 when the last black Republicans served on the City Council. A blacks moved into the Democratic party in increasing numbers during the 1930s, a small number of patronage jobs were distributed among them, but the policy-making positions were retained by whites. Then in 1954, a group of Negroes led by a Republican, Harry Cole, successfully challenged Jack Pollack's domination of the 4th District. Harry Cole won election to the State Senate. Emory Cole, also a Republican and no relation, and Truly Hatchett, a Democrat, gained seats in the House of Delegates.

The following year, Pollack included a black candidate, Walter Dixon, on his victorious City Council ticket. In 1958, Verda Welcome and Irma Dixon became the first black women ever elected to the Maryland State Legislature. Verda Welcome's supporters formed the nucleus of the Fourth District Democratic Organization. Dr. Carl Murphy and William "Little Willie" Adams were early contributors. Over the years warring factions splintered off and formed new groups. As the Negro population in Eas

Baltimore increased, they established a political power base there as well. By 1970, black political organizations were strong enough to elect Parren Mitchell to Congress.

As blacks were beginning to move into elective offices in Baltimore, where they would speak out in favor of rehabilitating the city's slum, some other people began to formulate a program to revitalize the downtown business district. They planned to rejuvenate the central area and make that a catalyst for future renewal programs throughout the city.

A group of businessmen formed the Greater Baltimore Committee in 1955. They chose Clarence Miles to be chairman, Thomas Butler vice-chairman, Jerold C. Hoffberger secretary, and Daniel Lindley, treasurer. James Rouse became chairman of the executive committee. William Boucher, III joined the group as executive director in 1956. Mayor D'Alesandro appointed municipal agencies to work with the G.B.C. Thus, from the start, the principle of partnership of public and private groups was established. They set out to define Baltimore's problems and then develop a concrete program to revive and promote the city.

The Greater Baltimore Committee, joined by the Committee for Downtown, presented the concept of the Charles Center to city government in 1958. The project was designed to halt the deterioration of the downtown business district and to rejuvenate the social, cultural and economic life of the city. The plan called for use of the resources at hand so development could take place in a relatively short time. Private business was to finance the major portion of the costs. The planners hoped that Charles Center would lead to improvements in the accessibility of downtown via mass transit. The city accepted the program and issued urban renewal bonds to help raise money. The Charles Center Management Office was

opened under the direction of J. Jefferso[n] Miller.

As the building began, a mayoral primar[y] election replaced D'Alesandro with machin[e] opponent J. Harold Grady as the Democrati[c] nominee. Despite Pollack's "vote you[r] conscience" support of Republican candidat[e] Theodore McKeldin, Grady won and held th[e] office during the initial construction stage[s]. When he resigned to accept a judgeship in 196[?] Philip Goodman, who was President of the Cit[y] Council, filled the vacancy. The following yea[r] McKeldin defeated Goodman and became no[t] only mayor, but the only Republican office[?] holder in the city. During this same period, th[e] city benefitted from the recently create[d] Maryland Port Authority which had bee[n] authorized by the state in 1956 when McKeldi[n] was governor and Marvin Mandel the chairma[n] of the city delegation in the House of Delegate[s].

Ground-breaking ceremonies for On[e] Charles Center in 1961 marked the beginning o[f] the renewal in new public and privat[e] investment in office buildings, apartments, hotel, a theater, commercial and specialty space[,] parks, overhead walkways and undergroun[d] garages. The Civic Center with its 10,000-sea[t] sports arena and 100,000 square-foot exhibitio[n] hall opened nearby in 1962.

Before Charles Center was completed, par[t] two of the dream started to materialize. Abe[l] Wolman joined others who viewed the inne[r] harbor as the perfect place to continue renewal. He urged McKeldin to set in motion plans fo[r] the neglected waterfront area. At the urging o[f] William Boucher III, the mayor reassembled th[e] winning partnership that had created Charle[s] Center. David Wallace and Thomas Todd dre[w] up the master plan in 1964. The following yea[r] the city signed a contract to allow Charle[s] Center Inner Harbor Management, Inc. to direc[t] the planning and operation of both projects. B[y]

Left:
James Rouse, who built Cross Keys, was chosen to develop a commercial complex at the Inner Harbor

Right:
Owner Jerry Hoffberger talks with three members of the winning team. Left to right: Hank Bauer, Andy Etchebarren, and Boog Powell.

Above:
Charles Center was the first stage in Baltimore's downtown renewal

Center Right:
Theodore McKeldin (center) won the mayoralty in 1963 and became the city's only Republican official. With him here (left to right) are: John Marshall Butler, J. Glenn Beall, Samuel Culotta, and James Devereaux

Right:
The Morris A. Mechanic Theatre in Charles Center began drawing crowds back to the downtown area in the evening hours

1967, with the full cooperation of the city's new mayor, Thomas D'Alesandro III, Project I which dealt with a one-block deep area along the harbor's edge was unveiled. With both public and private money, the actual development began in 1971. Inner Harbor investment to 1980 represents $775 million. Private investors have borne 80 percent of the costs. Real estate tax revenues have increased by an average of $5 million a year.

During the planning years of the Inner Harbor, Baltimore saw racial tensions culminate in riots that followed the assassination of Dr. Martin Luther King in 1968. Those riots expressed in a vivid way the frustrations of blacks with the continuing poverty and discrimination that they faced. Although National Guard commander General George Gelston minimized personal confrontation by issuing orders against shooting, six people died and property damage was assessed at over $14 million. The city that the planners were trying to solidify split wider apart. More suburbanites than ever declined to come downtown for any reason at all. In fact, census figures of 1960 and 1970 revealed that Baltimore had lost residents in both preceding decades. And, despite all the planning, the city's public image remained poor.

A major turnaround came with the election of Mayor William Donald Schaefer in 1971. His enthusiasm for his native city quickly communicated itself to city and suburban dwellers alike. He took Charles Center and the Inner Harbor and loved them out loud. With his support, the City Fair, begun in 1970, grew into the largest urban festival in the nation. Ten years later, as a firmly entrenched tradition, the fair draws millions to the Inner Harbor each September. Schaefer and his co-workers capitalized on success. To the fair they added ethnic festivals and "Sunny Sundays" in the Inner Harbor. To

the large urban renewal programs they added dollar houses, neighborhood revitalization programs like the ones in Washington Hill and Butcher's Hill, and blocks upon blocks of renovated houses that are bringing middle income taxpayers back to Baltimore as home owners. The new community called Coldspring planned by Moshe Safdie, on the site of a rock quarry, should house twelve thousand people when it is finished.

The real genius of Baltimore's renaissance has been its inclusiveness. All the city's neighborhoods, and most economic and ethnic groups have joined in the planning. Renewal has encompassed both buildings and living. In the decade of the 1970s, a cultural blossoming has drawn people back to downtown Baltimore. Crowds and facilities have grown together. Creations of the 1950s like Arena Players and of the 1960s like Center Stage perform to large audiences in modern theaters. The Morris Mechanic Theater in Charles Center draws more subscribers each year. The Baltimore Symphony, transformed under the direction of Sergiu Comissiona, soon will play in the new Maryland Concert Hall, sponsored jointly by the city, the state, and Joseph Meyerhoff. During the 1970s, a new wing at the Walters Gallery has allowed more complete exhibition of its treasures. Construction of an aquarium is underway on the north shore. The Science Center with its planetarium opened on the southwest corner of the Inner Harbor. The Art Museum has broken ground for a sculpture garden.

Baltimore's renaissance began, like most urban renewal projects, with businessmen planning buildings for the city's commercial district. The flowering, which has won Baltimore national acclaim, made people the center of the renewal. In the peaceful 1970s, Baltimoreans have had the opportunity to rediscover the joys of urban living.

Left:
Joseph Meyerhoff presents a model of the new Maryland Concert Hall

Above:
The Inner Harbor, Baltimore's showplace, contains office and residential buildings, green space and promenades, museums, and a marina

Left:
Joining in the 1973 groundbreaking of the IBM Building on Pratt Street are (left to right) Robert Hubner, Vice President of IBM, State Comptroller Louis Goldstein, Mayor William Donald Schaefer, and Baltimore Housing Commissioner, Robert Embry. Behind them, former mayors Theodore McKeldin and Thomas D'Alesandro, III look on

The Surviving Past

VI

Baltimore is a kaleidoscope. It has been known variously as northern or southern, elegant or slum-ridden, metropolitan or provincial. Like many other cities, it has suffered and it has prospered. It spawned a lively mercantilism along with a wide assortment of industries. Mainly because its harbor has been, from the beginning, the primary attraction for most of those who settled here, the popular image that emerges is that of Baltimore: port city on the Patapsco.

The growth of Baltimore involved a colorful cast. There were sturdy seamen, rough-and-tumble railroad workers, canny merchants, tough military types, and other nameless categories of folk. Later, a great number of these were, of course, immigrants. The plurality of the latter added to the general social ferment, and antagonisms mushroomed at alarming rates. Quite naturally, war played its role in shaping the mind and spirit of this fledgling town. In 1776, when Congress authorized the fitting out of "private armed vessels," enthusiastic Baltimoreans seized the opportunity to aggrandize themselves while

defending the port's commerce and protecting the citizens as well. Privateering, in the view of one cynical nineteenth-century observer, thus became not only an act of patriotism, but lucrative business in the bargain. In the larger historical perspective, though, Baltimore's Revolutionaries, with their ideals and fervor, have lingered as gallant heroes in the minds of those generations which were to follow. But in spite of the numerous wartime adventures that have enriched Baltimore's past, there is little doubt that the inspiration of Francis Scott Key's "Star Spangled Banner," during the War of 1812, remains the cynosure of its military history.

Whether Baltimore is known as Monumental City, or Mobtown (as it was called after the riots of the mid-nineteenth century), or the Charm City of today, it is indisputably a city whose past is more than prologue. What has gone before has a value of its own; preoccupations and focal points surface in the following color photographs, which is only a glimmering reflection of Baltimore's heritage.

Jean A. Wittich

All photographs here, aside from the antique lithographs, are by Alain Jaramillo.

An 1832 View of Baltimore

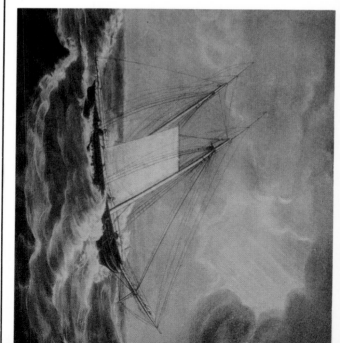

An 1840 lithograph of a Baltimore Clipper

Fort McHenry as it looked in 1865

One of the most dramatic and important changes in the last decade is the development and restoration of Baltimore's Inner Harbor. Above is an 1847 view of Baltimore painted by Robert Havell. Below is a photograph of today's harbor

City Hall was designed by George A. Frederick and is an example of post-Civil War popular Ecole des Beaux Arts Baroque style. Built in 1867, it was completely restored by 1976. Although some of the marble floors remain, much of the interior ornamentation has disappeared

Above:
The Engineering Society Building originally belonged to Mr. and Mrs. Robert Garrett, who commissioned Stanford White of New York to design the first part of the house in 1884. Because of its cost, size, and style, it became a controversial issue. Largely it was criticized for its "non-conservative" character. However, the carved wooden spiral staircase has long been one of the most distinctive showpieces of Mount Vernon Place

Right:
The Baltimore and Ohio Transportation Museum has its entrance through Mt. Clare Station (1830) the first railroad station to be built in the United States, and probably the first in the world. Adjoining the station is the annex which houses working models of the earliest locomotive, including the Tom Thumb

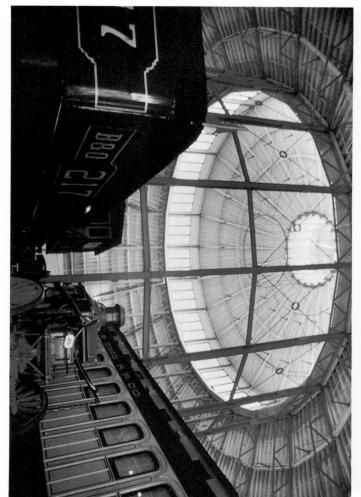

The Peabody Institute, built in
1861 by Edmund Lind, has a
formal Renaissance facade.
Although originally housed on
the second floor of the west
wing, the library now occupies
the spacious central hall. Stacks
of books rise six floors to the
ceiling in an impressive display of
cast-iron columns and railings

Above:
Federal Hill offers a magnificent view of the harbor and downtown Baltimore. Its name is thought to derive from a great parade celebrating Maryland's ratification of the Constitution. The procession terminated here in the year 1788. One of the floats carried a model of a fully rigged ship called the Federalist, commanded by Revolutionary hero, Joshua Barney

Right:
A Federal Hill house on Flag Day

The distinctive marble steps have for generations been a Baltimore symbol

The Basilica of the Assumption was the first Roman Catholic cathedral in the United States. The Basilica's architect was Benjamin Henry Latrobe, who also served as architect for the Capitol of the United States. The War of 1812 delayed construction and it was not dedicated until 1821, a year after Latrobe's death

*Henri Crenier's "Boy and Turtle"
is set on Mt. Vernon Place.
Originally purchased by the
Municipal Art Society, it was
given to the city in 1924*

Right:
"Naiad," by sculptress Grace
Turnbull

Bottom Right:
These stairs are an excellent
example of classic architectural
style in Baltimore

Early craftsmen were masters in design
Right:
Detailed brasswork such as this is still abundant throughout Baltimore

Left:
The Shot Tower, built in 1828 by an unknown architect, is a genuine relic among Baltimore landmarks. There were three such towers at one time and from these molten lead was poured from the top. As it fell it formed into balls, and when hitting the cold water at the bottom, became "shot." The cornerstone for this surviving tower was laid by Charles Carroll of Carrollton

Top:
The Baltimore City Fair is said by some to be the biggest urban festival in the world.

Above:
The preparation and eating of Chesapeake Bay crabs has become a fine art in Baltimore

Right:
This colorful costume gives accent to the city fair

In 1880 carriages such as these for sale on North Howard Street provided private transportation for the wealthier Baltimoreans

Partners in Progress

VII

Personal accounts of perseverance, ambition, sacrifice, survival, and success are an integral part of the history of Baltimore, "the Port." On the following pages are found the stories of those who envisioned a world port and worked for its reality. Here also are the personal histories of men and women who built Baltimore's factories, financial institutions, warehouses, and ships. Baltimore is the story of the men who determined the conformation of her streets, shipped her goods to foreign ports, and participated in revolutions in transportation and industry.

Intricately woven in the fabric of Baltimore City are the lives of individuals with vision and a special fascination for the future. When Baltimore was still a town, a handful of men saw and realized the capabilities of "the Basin," Baltimore's historical mudflat that was transformed into one of the world's most important and lively ports. As Baltimore's ship traffic increased, so evolved the many goods and services required to accommodate the international exchange of goods.

Many of those who committed their talents and energy to the growth of Baltimore's business community first sailed into the Chesapeake Bay making for the Port of Baltimore. They came from England, Ireland, Germany, France, Russia, Italy, and hundreds of other European countries in search of opportunity.

Many of the enterprises you will read about extended their roots into Baltimore soil when much of the land bordering the city consisted of rural estates and farms. At one time almost all important business and industry were within easy walking distance. The streets were cobblestone. Horse-drawn carriages were the major form of transportation.

The growth of Baltimore is also a story of humble beginnings. Time after time the same tale is told: "We began in a little basement room . . . one desk, one chair . . . ." Yet, massive buildings were erected along Baltimore's streets; factories rose in corn fields; impressive structures were built to evidence the strength of financial institutions; the city's skyline was transformed.

An early Baltimore retailer once wrote: "Baltimore and Progress are synonymous terms." Baltimore industries are proud of their reputation for progressiveness. Companies boast of their willingness to innovate, to modernize, to be the first: the first dental school in the world, the first branch bank, the first asphalt mixer, the first one-story warehouse, the first computer. The growth of Baltimore is founded on the stories of enterprising men and women who quietly and without fanfare revolutionized entire industries.

Baltimore firms are equally proud of the men and women who, through loyalty and hard work, helped the city grow and flourish. Baltimore business leaders rarely take personal credit for their firm's accomplishments. Rather, they cite good fortune in being associated with dedicated and inspired employees and take pride in providing a work environment which encourages, recognizes, and rewards individual achievement.

Many of the firms which first opened their doors of business in Baltimore now claim the city as headquarters for national and international trade. Other companies, realizing Baltimore's future was strong, opened plants or branch offices, bringing new and talented people to share in the city's growth and development.

With the success of enterprise in Baltimore came a commitment to the community that helped make it possible. Corporate contributions to Baltimore's charitable, cultural, civic, religious, and educational organizations have enabled the city's residents to realize multi-faceted and meaningful lives. Philanthropic endeavor continues to be an essential component of Baltimore's business community. Countless dollars are matched with long hours of volunteer effort.

There is a special feeling in Baltimore. The people who work there love their city. They've worked hard and have truly earned the right to boast: "Baltimore Is Best."

Alex Brown & Sons

More than 150 years ago, Alexander Brown advised his son, William, "Be satisfied with a reasonable return. Do not attempt too much. It is a mistake." Alexander Brown & Sons, the oldest name in American investment banking, has successfully weathered 180 years of national crises, including wars, financial panics, depressions, and the Great Baltimore Fire, so the advice has proven to be well founded.

The firm was established in 1800, when Alexander Brown, an immigrant from Northern Ireland, set up a shop in Baltimore to import fine Irish linens. He soon expanded the business to become a dealer in cotton, tobacco, and other commodities. Within a few years, he was joined in business by his four sons.

To make their commodity trading faster and more efficient, the firm operated an extensive fleet of sailing ships, the famed Baltimore Clippers. The company's exports and the imports of manufactured goods from Europe were financed by means of bills of exchange, which could be sold on the open market.

In 1810, the company undertook its first investment banking transaction by underwriting an equity issue for the Baltimore Water Company and distributing the stock to individuals, insurance companies, and other businesses.

A letter signed by Brown in 1824 created the first letters of credit, which were issued to travelers going abroad, enabling them to obtain money from overseas correspondents of the firm. This sideline of the banking business soon grew to a significant size, for it led ultimately to today's internationally used travelers' checks.

During the ensuing years, the firm introduced many other new ideas to the investment banking world. For example, in 1827, when the Supreme Court, in *Brown* vs. *Maryland*, ruled in favor of Alex Brown & Sons, the Maryland law requiring all importers and wholesalers of imported goods to buy a license was declared unconstitutional.

The Brown family was active in unifying Baltimore's mass transit system and in developing the Baltimore & Ohio Railroad. Alex's son, George, helped to convince a group of the city's leading merchants in 1827 that a railroad was the best way to regain Baltimore's declining trade with the West. Thus, the B&O was born. George Brown became the first treasurer of the railroad, and part of the early financing was raised by selling B&O bonds in England through Alex Brown & Sons' Liverpool house, the first step in the now accepted practice of placing American securities abroad.

Financial historians who study investment banking in the United States discover that Alex Brown & Sons was one of the first innovators in the principles of investment banking. For instance, four days after the Bank of Maryland closed in 1834, Alexander Brown declared that "no merchant in Baltimore who could show that he was solvent would be allowed to fail." His loans helped tide the business community over this financial crisis.

When Alex Brown died in 1834, he was one of the richest men in America. From the day he arrived on these shores, Alex Brown's heart was in Baltimore, despite the fact that the company subsequently opened offices in Philadelphia, New York, and Boston, as well as in Great Britain and Europe. Many Baltimore institutions, such as Hopkins, the Walters Art Gallery, and Brown Memorial Church, owe much to this merchant banking house.

In 1918, the firm organized a syndicate to market the first issue of the Federal Land Bank bonds. And in the 1930s, the company proposed an imaginative plan to the state of Maryland for the construction and financing of toll bridges. The senior partner at the time, B. Howell Griswold, suggested pooling revenues so that excess toll collection from the heavily traveled bridges would help support the bonds of the less traveled crossings. In this way, the bridges and highways became jointly self supporting. Today, the firm enjoys the largest municipal underwriting position outside of New York City and has become a recognized authority on revenue bond financing.

The Browns of Baltimore bear a remarkable resemblance to the Rothschilds of Europe. Like the Rothschilds, Alexander Brown sent his sons to other commercial centers to expand his business. One son, William, went to England to found what is now Brown, Shipley & Co., Ltd., of London, a major British investment banking house. Another son, John A., went to Philadelphia, and yet another, James, to New York to establish offices that eventually became Brown Brothers, Harriman & Co., a prestigious private banking house. A fourth son, George, remained in Baltimore to work with his father.

Today, Alexander Brown & Sons maintains a cordial relationship with its corporate "offspring," although there are no formal ties of ownership binding the companies and each is fiercely independent. The closest affiliation exists with Brown, Shipley & Co., which serves as Brown's London correspondent. Also like the Rothschilds, the Browns of Baltimore have an unbroken line of family leadership. Although F. Barton Harvey, Jr., is now managing partner, Benjamin H. Griswold III was the sixth genera

The distinguished headquarters of Alex Brown & Sons graces this corner of East Baltimore

tion of Browns to lead the company and his two sons, Ben and Jack, are also active in the company, assuring the involvement of the next generation.

The main banking house at Baltimore and Calvert Streets —the third building the company has occupied on the site since 1803 —was built in 1900 and was one of the few buildings to survive the Great Fire of 1904.

The old and the new live happily side by side at Alex Brown & Sons today, symbolized by the traditional 80-year-old headquarters in downtown Baltimore and the modern 12-year-old operations center in Towson. Contrasts are also evident inside the main building, with marbled columns, flags, and roll-top desks standing alongside Telequote machines and computers.

Today, Alexander Brown & Sons is involved in public and corporate finance as well as investment services. The total offerings of municipal and other tax-free bonds, managed or co-managed by the company since 1908, exceed $3 billion. And, as always, the distinguishing characteristic of the firm is its commitment to serving medium-sized growth companies, and to preserving the traditions that have given Alex Brown & Sons a special place in the world of investment banking.

Alexander & Alexander

In 1914, Alexander & Alexander landed their first major account, the B&O Railroad. William F. Alexander (upper left) and his brother Charles B. Alexander (upper right) soon opened an office on St. Paul Street, where this photo was taken around 1920

Alexander & Alexander is the second largest international insurance brokerage and financial services firm. As such, it provides a broad range of risk management services to clients of all sizes, representing a cross section of American business and industry.

Headquartered in New York City, it employs 7,500 employees at offices in eighty-three cities and forty-three foreign countries. In 1979, the company reported revenues in excess of $368 million. Its stock is traded on the over-the-counter market. Since going public in 1969, A&A has recorded increases in sales and revenues every quarter.

Founded by two brothers, Charles B. and William F. Alexander, in Clarksburg, West Virginia, in the 1890s, the company opened its first Baltimore office in 1914. It was located on St. Paul Street, across from A&A's first major account, the Baltimore & Ohio Railroad. Today, A&A still handles that client's successor, the Chessie System.

In 1923, A&A became a Maryland corporation. Since then, it has expanded its Baltimore operations to include corporate finance and administrative offices, a general insurance and actuarial office, and headquarters for the mid-Atlantic region. Baltimore also is home of two A&A subsidiaries, Benefacts and the premium finance division. A&A's Baltimore offices employ more than 660 people.

Since going public in 1969, Alexander & Alexander has experienced a growth record unparalleled in the insurance brokerage industry. The company has been involved in more than 150 mergers, including the largest single one in industry history. With this track record, it has developed creative approaches to risk management that have brought new products and services to its clients.

Working from the client's point of view, A&A people try to develop an understanding of the client's operations, objectives, and goals. From this, they plan and execute a comprehensive and cost-efficient insurance program to protect the client's assets.

In the future, A&A's growth will come not only in the insurance brokering arena but also in financial services. Already, the company offers a nationwide property tax consulting service and made its first move into investment counseling in early 1980. As they have for the past sixty-six years, the people of Baltimore will play a key role in A&A's growth through the 1980s.

Armco-Baltimore Works

Armco's Baltimore Works, with a force of 1,300 employees, evolved from the Hess Steel Company, built in 1912. The predecessor firm specialized in the manufacture of gun barrel steel. In 1924, the International Rustless Iron Company, financed by the Wild brothers, was organized, and the stainless steel process known then as the "rustless process") began in Baltimore.

The technical melting process for the conventional stainless steel known today took years to develop. Yet, by the 1930s, the Baltimore steel plant was furnishing a growing market for stainless steel. The first big market was the emerging automobile industry, which utilized steel for trim. In 1937, the Rustless Company formed a close relationship with Armco to resolve research and engineering problems.

In 1939, construction began on what is today the North Plant. These new facilities included a blooming mill (which is still used today), a rod mill, and a new wire-drawing department. By World War II, the new manufacturing facilities were playing an important role in producing materials crucial for the nation's war effort.

Late in 1945, the Rustless Iron and Steel Corporation merged with Armco through an exchange of stock. Since that time, as part of Armco, the Baltimore plant has played a vital role in the development of special stainless steels and processes.

Over the years, some of the most important patents in the history of stainless steel have resulted from research performed at Armco's Baltimore Works. In 1934, the rustless scrap process was developed, whereby the first use of stainless steel scrap and chromite ore in the melting process permitted economical production of stainless steel in the U.S. The plant has also been a leader in the production of auto exhaust valve steel and in the development of nitronic alloys, which include steel used for boat shafting, nuclear reactor control rods, hydraulic tubing, and for many products used in general industry. There have also been several patents resulting from the firm's efforts to improve stainless steel polishing and finishing.

In Baltimore, Armco has gained recognition for its role in the community. One of the more unique examples of Armco's commitment to the Baltimore community is Armco's annual Founders Day, usually held in April. Armco employees observe the birthday of Armco's founder, George M. Verity, by participating in community work projects. Directed toward helping local charitable and nonprofit organizations, projects range from painting old church buildings to clearing vacant lots.

Armco's Baltimore Works produces a complete range of quality stainless steels, including coiled wire, straight length wire, and stainless steel rods and bars in numerous shapes, sizes, finishes, and conditions. From large atomic reactors to small screws, nails, and springs, the applications of stainless bar and wire are infinite. Armco's Baltimore Works serves as an important part of the Armco network, as well as a good neighbor to Baltimore.

Armco's Baltimore Works grew from a Baltimore steelmaking facility built in 1912. Over the years, some of the most important patents in the history of stainless steel have resulted from research performed at Armco's Baltimore Works

Baltimore Works Allied Chemical Corporation

How did one of the world's largest chrome chemical companies come to be located in Baltimore? The story begins more than 150 years ago with a chance discovery. Chromite was found on the Bare Hills estate of Baltimore's Tyson family in 1810. Isaac Tyson, Jr., recognized the value of this discovery and started mining the ore for export to English paint and ceramic factories.

Since that time, Baltimore has been a world center for chromium. The business that Tyson established is now part of the Allied Chemical Corporation. It's a pillar of Baltimore industries and currently the only company producing a complete line of chromium chemicals.

A second chance discovery of chromite in 1828 enabled Tyson to turn his operation into an international success. This time, the setting was the Belair market. A farmer had used large blocks of chromite to hold a load of cinder barrels on his wagon. Tyson traced the rocks to a farm near Jarretsville and discovered the largest deposits of chrome ore known in the world at that time.

On the basis of observations made at Bare Hills and Jarretsville, Tyson prospected the entire mid-Atlantic region. Soon Tyson Mining held rights to all deposits of chromite

in the area. He established an ore-shipping and storage facility on the back basin of Baltimore's harbor in the late 1820s. And, in 1845, he opened his own plant, the Baltimore Chrome Works, for processing the chromite ore into chemical products. The company controlled the world market for chrome through the late 1850s.

In the mid-1800s, when the discovery of high-grade chrome ore in Turkey made local mining impractical, the Baltimore Chrome Works began importing ore from California and later from company-owned mines in New Caledonia. Until a rival plant was established in Philadelphia in 1882, the Tyson plant supplied all the chromium chemicals used in American industry, shipping its products to paint, dye, and tanning businesses throughout the nation.

The Great Baltimore Fire of 1904 destroyed businesses and homes within a block of the Works, but fireboats contained the fire before it could reach the plant and a neighboring lumber yard. Employees manned pumps and soaked company buildings to prevent damage from flying embers during the height of the blaze.

The Mutual Chemical Company of America was formed

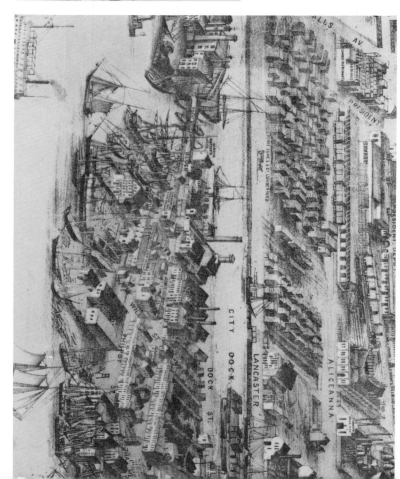

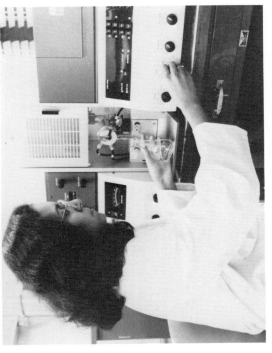

Top:
In the lower left foreground is the Allied Chemical Corporation's Baltimore Chrome Works today

Above:
Today, a complete line of chromium chemicals is produced at the Works' modern lab facilities

n 1908, combining the Baltimore Chrome Works with hose of the American Chrome Company of Philadelphia nd the Mutual Chemical Company of New Jersey. The ompany established its headquarters in New York and concentrated chrome production at Baltimore and Jersey City.

Mutual expanded its Baltimore facility just before World War I and again in the 1930s. Production of chromium chemicals for use in steel manufacturing was a priority activity during World War II, and the plant operated throughout the war years, modifying its process to accommodate material shortages.

After the war, Mutual began a multimillion dollar expansion of its Baltimore Works, and in 1950 work was completed on the world's then-largest chromium chemical plant. The Allied Chemical and Dye Corporation acquired Mutual Chemical in 1954. The company's chrome production was concentrated in Baltimore and was operated as a subsidiary until 1955, when Allied incorporated the Baltimore plant as the Mutual Chemicals Division. It is now part of the Chemicals Company, Allied Chemical Corporation.

Hygiene and environmental control systems at the plant were improved to keep pace with pollution laws passed during the 1960s, and in 1973 Allied was the first Maryland plant to receive both state and federal discharge permits. It continues to meet or exceed all state and federal requirements for air and water pollution and solid-waste control.

The Block Street facility, with 400 employees, is one of the largest plants of its kind in the world. The Baltimore Chrome Works was one of the city's first industries. Located at the edge of the Inner Harbor renewal area, the plant continues to be a part of the balance of commercial, industrial, and residential interests in one of the city's oldest and most historic neighborhoods.

A.S. Abell Company

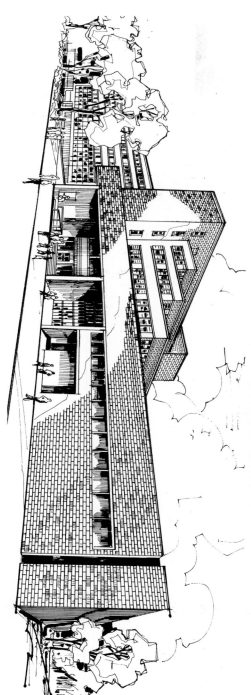

Arunah Shepherdson Abell published the first issue of *The Sun* in Baltimore on May 17, 1837. The paper was successful from the start; it was one of the first newspapers to develop and use every available means of communication, including its own pony express service, stagecoaches, steamboats, railroads, a flock of 400 carrier pigeons, and electric telegraph.

The Sun attained a national reputation by 1847, just ten years after it was founded, through its Mexican War coverage, which included informing the President of the United States that U.S. forces had won the decisive battle of Vera Cruz.

In 1851, *The Sun* moved into new quarters, the Sun Iron Building, which, because of new principles of construction, became a landmark in the history of commercial architecture in America and progenitor of the skyscraper. It was destroyed in the Great Fire of 1904.

The Sunday Sun was founded in 1901, *The Evening Sun* in 1910. Ten years later, the "Sunpapers" underwent a reorganization and rejuvenation under Van-Lear and Harry Black, who had become principals in the A.S. Abell Company, publishers of the paper. *The Sun* became even more influential and noted for its reporting on Washington and national politics. The Washington Bureau, established in 1837 and probably the oldest in Washington, is one of the largest of any non-Washington newspaper. The newspaper has also established a worldwide network of foreign bureaus: London, Moscow, Bonn, Paris, Tokyo, Cairo, Hong Kong, New Delhi, and Peking.

The Sunpapers have won ten Pulitzer Prizes, the most prestigious awards in journalism, for editorial cartooning, distinguished editorial writing, distinguished national and international reporting, and meritorious public service. The first was won in 1931; the most recent, by *The Evening Sun* in 1979, was the first ever awarded for feature reporting.

The Sunpapers were the first newspapers to introduce a three-paper electronic production system in the news and composing rooms. The firm also uses electronic capabilities to produce its classified advertising and in its circulation department to service subscribers.

The company, led by president and publisher Donald H. Patterson, is erecting a three-story press annex to its six-story building on North Calvert Street. It will contain two lines of Rockwell-Goss Metroliner offset presses of eighteen units each and will be able to accommodate a third line of presses. When the presses are rolling, scheduled for early 1982, the newspaper will have "the most cost-effective newspaper production facility available — the latest application of automated and electronic systems."

Left:
The founder of The Sun, Arunah S. Abell, believed in using every possible means of communication for gathering news, including stagecoaches, railroads, and carrier pigeons

Below:
The Sunpapers' building will have a three-story press annex when it is completed in 1982

Baker, Watts & Co.

illiam G. Baker, Jr., and Sewell S. Watts, graduates of the University of Maryland Law School, class of 1899, opened the doors of their office at Baltimore and South Streets on March 1, 1900, with total capital of $43,000. Four years later, following the Great Baltimore Fire, new and expanded quarters were occupied in the building of the recently formed United States Fidelity and Guaranty Co. at the corner of Calvert and German (now Redwood) Streets. The partnership remained there until 1974, when it moved into the new U.S.F.&G. Building at the Inner Harbor site. The cordial, relaxed nature of business affairs in earlier years is demonstrated by the fact that until its last move, Baker, Watts and the building owner had never executed a lease agreement.

The partnership soon achieved financial success and prominence in the business affairs of the community. In its early years, the firm was investment banker for the fledgling Black and Decker Co. and later to the founders of the Noxzema Chemical Co. (now Noxell) and Waverly Press, Inc. The company was fiscal agent for Commercial Credit Co. when it began operations in 1920. During the collapse of the real estate market in the late 1920s, Baker, Watts & Co. was prominent as one of four managers of the Refunding Plan backed by the Reconstruction Finance Corporation, which resulted in saving many surety companies, both local and throughout the country, from impending bankruptcy.

Most of the business done by the firm in its first quarter-century of existence was with bonds, and "country banks" were important customers. As commercial banking changed, leading to the establishment of larger entities throughout the state, the firm has assisted in the recapitalization and merger of many of the state's banking institutions.

Recently ranked among the nation's leading municipal bond underwriters, the firm has long been prominent in the underwriting and distribution of these issues, with particular expertise in the debt securities of the states of Maryland and West Virginia and their political subdivisions and agencies. It has also acted as financial advisor to many subdivisions in both states in connection with the issuance of new bonds.

Early in its history, the firm became a member of the New York Stock Exchange. As investment interest has broadened during its history, first to include then to emphasize equities, the firm's business has changed accordingly. In its role as investment brokers, Baker, Watts & Co. has arranged both public and private financing for start-up and emerging companies, with particular success in the communications field.

The wrought iron door, which has become the firm's trademark and which for three generations has admitted so many clients to Baker, Watts' services, is still the entry to the firm's offices. For many years, the company used "Counselors in investments" as its slogan, and this phrase was prominently displayed on placards appearing on streetcars throughout the city. Although this slogan is no longer used, the founders' concept of providing a full line of investment services of the highest quality has been carried on by succeeding partners, who have included both the son and the grandson of founder Sewell S. Watts.

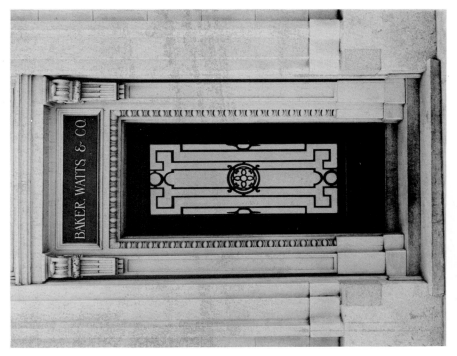

For more than three quarters of a century, this door has opened into the main offices of Baker, Watts & Co., first in the U.S.F.&G. Building on Redwood Street, and most recently in the new U.S.F.&G. Building at Pratt and Light Streets

The Baltimore Asphalt Paving Company

The Baltimore Asphalt Paving Company has played a major role in transforming the streets of Baltimore from cobblestone to the most modern type of pavement. In April 1913, when Robert J. Padgett took over the business of the F.E. Schneider Company and the Pen-Mar Construction Company, the new Baltimore Asphalt Block and Tile Company (as it was known before 1963) utilized teams of horses and wagons to lay the streets and sidewalks of a growing Baltimore.

In addition to serving as general contractors, the firm, as its name implies, was a major manufacturer of asphalt blocks and tiles, the first in Maryland to produce this new material. The firm had the first contract to lay the now famous "inch-inch" paving on St. Paul, Calvert, and Charles Streets, three of Baltimore's most heavily traveled arteries. This new method was executed while a continuous flow of traffic was maintained. The firm also became the first Baltimore contractor to lay rubberized asphalt on Baltimore streets.

With the success of motorized transportation, a need arose for a paving formula that could withstand increasingly heavy traffic. Company engineers developed a bituminous concrete formula, copyrighted with the United States Patent Office under the trade name BABCO, which proved so strong, flexible, and durable that many of Baltimore's largest industrial concerns found it the solution for their difficult paving problems.

A long-standing reputation for efficiency has earned this old Baltimore company numerous commendations. As early as 1921, the firm completed a seventy-day paving contract for the Maryland State Roads Commission in twenty-six days and received formal commendation from the Commission. In 1974, the company completed a 700-day project in 240 days. Mayor William Donald Schaefer dedicated the complete rehabilitation of Calvert Street from North Avenue to 33rd Street with this praise for the company: "We appreciate the extra effort Mr. Coblentz's firm displayed. Rehabilitating a major street causes much inconvenience to residents and motorists. This contractor reduced the anticipated inconvenience time by fully 427 days."

In addition to street paving, the company has surfaced airports, dock yards, and railroad yards. Acres of paving at the Dundalk Marine Terminal were constructed by this Baltimore firm. And the company was privileged to surface the first Chesapeake Bay Bridge in 1952. This surface carried traffic for more than twenty years before resurfacing was required. The company has also built numerous parks for Baltimore City's Department of Parks and Recreation, installing specialized surfaces for playgrounds, tennis courts, athletic fields, and even interior floors.

The Pen-Mar Company, a wholly owned subsidiary of the firm, has supplied building materials for area contractors for many years. Calvin H. Coblentz, owner of the firm, is only the third president in sixty-seven years. His predecessor, William R. Padgett, was president from 1932 until his death in 1968. Robert J. Padgett served as president from 1913 to 1932. In addition to Mr. Coblentz, officers of the Baltimore Asphalt Paving Company are Richard A. Sutton, vice president; Sophia T. Coblentz, secretary; Mary T. Kroen, treasurer; John R. Elliott, chief estimator; and Gary W. Rohrer, general superintendent.

Proud of its growth as a member of the Baltimore community, the Baltimore Asphalt Paving Company has consistently paved the way for the development of the area's industries, as well as Baltimore city, state, and federal governments.

Top:
In 1913, the Baltimore Asphalt Block and Tile Company, as it was then known, took over the business of F.E. Schneider and the Pen-Mar Construction Company and utilized teams of horses and wagons to lay asphalt block and tile in Baltimore

Above:
The firm continues a tradition of efficiency and excellence. This photo, taken from the identical point of view as the accompanying photograph, depicts the firm's modern-day equipment along Monroe Street in Baltimore

Baltimore Federal Savings and Loan Association

The year is 1884. Chester A. Arthur is president of the United States. The port of New York witnesses a constant tide of immigrants from southern and eastern Europe. In Chicago, the first modern skyscraper is built. In Baltimore, on May 5, Gustav Bueschal, a butcher, and John Gith, a produce merchant, meet with Louis Meyer in his tailor shop at 476 Pennsylvania Avenue. Together they hold the first directors' meeting of the Pennsylvania Avenue Permanent Building and Loan Association. Bueschal is elected president. Later that year Gith succeeds him, serving as president until 1906.

At that time, building and loan association members pooled their resources to allow individual members to build or buy homes that otherwise were beyond their available means. "Permanent" meant that the association would continue to exist after the needs of the original members had been met. During the first two years, five mortgages were transacted covering properties on Pennsylvania Avenue, Mosher Street, and Moore Alley, allowing the institution to commit itself to the community.

Edward F. Hoffman was elected president in 1906, and the association's offices were subsequently located at 2504 and 2404 Pennsylvania Avenue. In 1931, the young association reached $1 million in assets.

As Baltimore grew, it became apparent that the association would have to assume a broader role in helping the area and its citizens sustain necessary growth. So, in 1937, the name Baltimore Federal Savings and Loan Association was adopted, reflecting the association's desire to serve the growing community. The next year, the association's headquarters were moved from Pennsylvania Avenue to 19 East Fayette Street. Assets reached $10 million in 1941. Decisions to federalize the charter and to move to a location at the heart of Baltimore's financial district were made under the capable management of Henry P. Irr, who was elected president in 1944. In 1950, the building at 19 East

The Pennsylvania Avenue Permanent Building and Loan Association, known as Baltimore Federal Savings and Loan Association since 1937, was founded in Baltimore in 1884. Originally located in Louis Meyer's tailor shop at 476 Pennsylvania Avenue, the young association later moved to 1504 and then 2404 Pennsylvania Avenue

Fayette Street and three others were razed, and work began on what would become popularly known as "The Colonial Corner."

Baltimore Federal passed $100 million in assets in 1954 and became one of the first savings and loans in the country to install electronic accounting equipment. Assets doubled to over $200 million in 1958, and in 1961 Baltimore Federal opened its first branch offices in Eastpoint Mall and Westminster. Additional offices in Towson and Reisterstown quickly followed.

The 1960s and 1970s signaled a commitment to the Eastern Shore, Western Maryland, and the Washington suburbs. Mergers with Aurora Federal Savings and Loan in 1971 and Hearthstone Savings and Loan in 1975 and expansion into other market areas have produced twenty-five offices throughout Maryland.

Eugene K. Reilly became president in 1967, followed by Charles E. Williams and, since 1974, Robert E. Hecht, Sr. Baltimore Federal has expanded its services over the years to include statement, certificate, and passbook savings; mortgage, consumer, and commercial loans; and such conveniences as Cashflow telephone transfer, Transmatic savings, and tax-deferred retirement plans. Today, nearly a century after a tailor, a butcher, and a produce retailer organized the company between bolts of material in Louis Meyer's shop in northwest Baltimore, Baltimore Federal is a billion-dollar financial institution — and better equipped than ever before to serve its customers throughout Maryland.

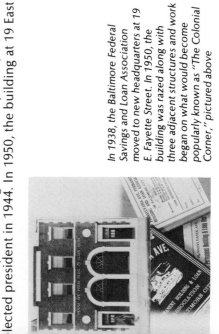

In 1938, the Baltimore Federal Savings and Loan Association moved to new headquarters at 19 E. Fayette Street. In 1950, the building was razed along with three adjacent structures and work began on what would become popularly known as "The Colonial Corner," pictured above

Bethlehem Steel Corporation

In 1887, much of the Sparrows Point area was farmland belonging to Captain and Mrs. William Fitzell. They enjoyed their farm and were reluctant to sell it until a representative from the Pennsylvania Steel Company played the hymn "Almost Persuaded" on their parlor organ and they changed their minds.

Shortly after the contract was signed, workmen arrived at the site to begin building the plant's first blast furnaces. By 1889, Sparrows Point was producing pig iron and growing. It built a reputation for producing high-quality rails, and growth of the plant was attributed, in part, to a unique advantage over inland plants in that it could import raw materials by ship. When the Panama Canal opened in 1914, this asset increased in value, as goods could be shipped by water to the growing West Coast market.

Bethlehem Steel acquired Sparrows Point in 1916 and began expanding the operation. Before long, the plant was producing important new products (tinplate, sheet steel, rod, wire, and pipe) and was becoming one of the largest, most diversified steel plants in the United States.

The town of Sparrows Point, which had sprung up around the plant, was also growing quickly. A railway service began in 1889; the trip to Baltimore's Penn Station took forty minutes with six stops en route. The company built a community center and dairy for its employees,

forming one of the nation's first shopping centers, a place where everything from food, clothing, and tobacco to housewares, furniture, and books could be purchased. The town also had its own volunteer fire and police department and, by 1925, its own country club and golf course.

The years 1916 to 1929 marked a period of constant growth and development both for the plant and the town. The plant installed the most up-to-date equipment. The town built new churches and schools, and the resident took great pride in their immaculately kept streets and gardens and their "Red Rocker" trolley car. But 1929 marked

Left:
The "L" furnace is one of the largest and most technically advanced blast furnaces in the Western Hemisphere

Below:
Steelmaking and shipbuilding operations are located side by side at Sparrows Point

Above:
The American Spirit is one of five 365,000 deadweight ton tankers built at the Sparrows Point Shipyard

Left:
The quality of coiled rod produced on the No. 3 rod mill is second to none in the industry. Coils weighing up to 3,000 pounds each are rolled in one continuous length

the start of the Great Depression, and although construction began on No. 3 open hearth that year, the continuing economic slump forced the shop to remain idle until the mid-1930s.

As the steel business began to pick up, the plant was soon confronted with new challenges — the greatest of which was World War II. More than any other past conflict, this one depended on all-out civilian involvement. Any plant exceeding its production goal was given the coveted Army/Navy "E" Award for exceptional performance on the industrial front. Sparrows Point earned this honor within a year of the attack on Pearl Harbor.

The years following the war were truly a golden era for the steel business. The United States accounted for more than half of the world's steel production. During this period, Bethlehem embarked on an expansion program that included construction of the Pennwood Power Plant, new cold sheet and hot strip mills, and No. 4 open hearth shop.

A record-breaking development program announced by Bethlehem in 1956 involved the investment of $300 million to expand its steelmaking capacity by 3 million tons or 15 percent over the next two years. Two-thirds of these funds were allocated to the Sparrows Point plant.

The summer of 1959 marked the beginning of a strike that lasted 116 days. By the time it was over, many contracts had gone overseas and foreign competition had become a reality. Yet Bethlehem couldn't afford to stand still. To remain competitive, Sparrows Point had to continue modernizing its production facilities.

New installations built during the sixties and seventies included a basic oxygen furnace shop, No. 3 rod mill, No. 2 sinter strand, and the Humphreys Creek waste water treatment plant. But the most ambitious undertaking of these two decades was the building of the giant "L" blast furnace. Since it began operation in November 1978, this

furnace has regularly set iron production records for a single unit. The "L" blast furnace was the largest of its kind in the Western Hemisphere at the time it was built and cost more than $200 million.

Located conveniently next to the steel plant is Bethlehem's Sparrows Point shipyard, which is managed separately. Established in 1891 and acquired by Bethlehem in 1916 along with the steel plant, the shipyard has consistently been a leader in the construction of all types of new ships. In 1969, for instance, the yard delivered a greater number of merchant ships (six) and more total tonnage than any other American yard. Sparrows Point shipyard, with a 1,200-foot-long shipbuilding basin completed in 1971, can construct large tankers up to 300,000 deadweight tons.

Bethlehem's ship repair facilities in the Port of Baltimore consist of the 35-acre Key Highway yard and the 14-acre Fort McHenry yard. Combined under one general manager and operated as a single yard, these plants represent the largest ship repairing facility in the United States.

The range of work offered by the Baltimore yards covers the entire spectrum of ship repair, reconditioning, and maintenance services, plus large-scale vessel conversion and jumboizing. The yards can handle thirty vessels simultaneously and, with mobile equipment, can service many more at pierside and anchorage.

Baltimore also hosts Bethlehem's Buffalo Tank Division, one of the nation's largest producers of all types of storage tanks, pressure vessels, and piping sub-assemblies. Near Buffalo Tank in south Baltimore is Bethlehem's reinforcing bar fabricating shop, which is capable of bending, shearing, and shaping reinforcing bars to virtually any configuration. The rebars fabricated at the shop are used for construction applications such as foundations, bridge piers, and highway pavement.

Bethlehem Steel is the largest private employer in Maryland with 24,000 employees and a yearly payroll of nearly $500 million. The company's support of the annual Central Maryland United Way campaigns (including employee contributions and the corporate gift) represents nearly one-tenth of all the money raised in the Baltimore area. In 1979, this pledge amounted to $2.7 million.

Black and Decker

In 1910, two young men in their mid-twenties who were both working for the Roland Telegraph Company decided to form a company of their own. Duncan Black sold his Maxwell automobile and Alonzo Decker borrowed from his uncle to raise the $600 they each needed to open their first office on Calvert Street in Baltimore.

For the first five years, Black & Decker produced tools from their own designs, including a milk bottle capping machine and a candy dipping machine. They soon realized that in order to be successful they had to design their own products. In 1916, the two introduced the first products to carry their own Black & Decker trademark. The following year, they were awarded a patent for a unique pistol grip and trigger switch drill design. These features set the standards for today's electric power tools. Another innovative idea was the Lectroflater, which electrically inflated tires by air compression, an enormously successful tool until it was superseded by service stations.

Black & Decker's first manufacturing plant — all of 1,200 square feet — was opened on the outskirts of Towson in 1917. Within a year, the company opened customer service centers in Boston and New York City and acquired representatives in England, Canada, Russia, Australia, and Japan. By 1919, Black & Decker passed the $1 million sales mark and built a 20,000-square-foot concrete and steel factory. A two-story administrative building for executive and sales offices was added in 1924. This building, though remodeled, still serves as the company's international headquarters.

The company's first attempt to popularize power tools came in 1923 with the introduction of the first low-cost, half-inch BB special drill.

During World War II, Black & Decker made fuses, gun shells, and other tools for the war effort, for which the company later received the Army/Navy "E" Award. It was during this time that a postwar planning committee decided to develop the do-it-yourself market for power tools. In 1946, the first line of home utility drills was introduced.

Above:
Founding partners S. Duncan Black and Alonzo G. Decker discussed plans to improve their business enterprise in this 1910 photograph

Right:
In 1917, Black & Decker patented the world's first portable power drill to offer a universal motor with pistol grip and trigger switch

Below:
The Black & Decker plant at Towson, Maryland, was built in 1917

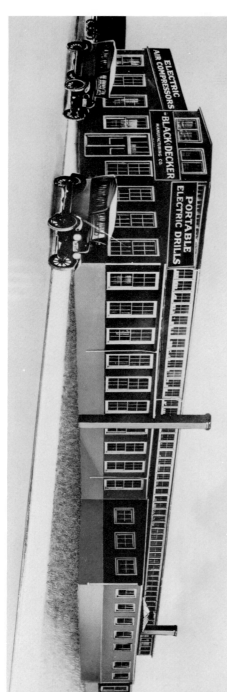

Top:
*This "schoolroom on wheels"
toured the United States
demonstrating products in 1925*
Above:
*In 1968, Black & Decker
developed the no-torque, cordless
power head drill used on the
Apollo 15 mission in 1971 and on
subsequent Apollo 16 and 17
missions*

Twenty years ago, Black & Decker's total manufacturing space covered one million square feet in five plants. Today the figure has risen to four million square feet in more than thirty plants around the world. The company employs more than 18,000 persons, half of whom live outside the United States. Sales have risen continuously, passing the $100 million mark in 1964, the $200 million mark just four years later. In 1979, sales were $1.2 billion, passing the billion dollar level for the first time. Yet, in terms of actual dollars, the price of the Black & Decker economy model one-quarter-inch drill is much lower today than it was thirty years ago. In this way, the company has managed to stay a step ahead of foreign competition.

More than forty-five branches or subsidiary companies have opened worldwide to help Black & Decker become an international leader in laborsaving devices. In most cases, the managers of these companies are nationals of the country in which they are located. This operating philosophy has helped Black & Decker grow rapidly in international markets.

Since 1910, the company has operated under the leadership of five chief executives officers. S. Duncan Black held the post from 1910 to 1951. Upon his death, Alonzo G. Decker took over until his demise in 1956. Black's brother, Robert D. Black, a marketing expert, was chief executive officer from 1956 to 1964, and was succeeded by Alonzo G. Decker, Jr., an electrical engineer. In 1975, Decker relinquished this post and Francis P. Lucier took over as chief executive officer.

Many innovative products have been developed by Black & Decker throughout its seventy years in business. More recent developments include the world's first cordless electric drill, powered by self-contained nickel-cadmium cells; the first all-insulated drill; a cordless minimum-torque reaction space tool used under weightless flight conditions by astronauts on Project Gemini; and the Apollo Lunar Surface Drill, used to remove core samples from the Moon. Closer to home has been the introduction of exciting products such as the Workmate work centers, the Dustbuster hand-held vacuum cleaner, and a wide range of tools for consumer and industrial use.

Throughout its history, Black & Decker has enjoyed increased sales, and its constant growth and product development assures that there will be many more milestones of success in the company's future.

Baltimore Gas and Electric Company

He was an accomplished artist, showman, and impetuous dreamer. Nevertheless, when Rembrandt Peale astounded the patrons of his Holliday Street museum with a burning-gas display that prophetic evening of June 11, 1816, he ushered in a new era. In less than a week, four prominent Baltimoreans — William Lorman, James Mosher, Robert Cary Long, and William Gwynn — joined Peale in a bold design to light the city's streets. Their enterprise, the Gas Light Company of Baltimore, was the first gas company in America and the direct predecessor of Baltimore Gas and Electric.

By September 1816, a gas house was under construction; a few months later a band of dazzled citizens watched as the first street lamp was ceremoniously lighted on Market (Baltimore) Street.

As the years passed, the small gas company grew along with its native city, already the third largest in America and a thriving shipping port. Over the next fifty years, a host of rival gaslight companies emerged in the wake of the city's prosperity, only to be eclipsed before the turn of the century by Edison's incandescent lamp, which heralded the rise of electric companies and diverted gas from lighting into ovens and water heating.

Many of the rival utilities, however, faced with inadequate resources, stiff competition, and poor management, failed. The survivors, perceiving the economic futility of multiple operating and supply systems, consolidated. Thus, in 1906, two years after the Great Baltimore Fire, United Electric Light and Power gathered the city's two remaining electric companies and merged with Consolidated Gas Company of Baltimore City, the descendant of the corporation inaugurated by Rembrandt Peale. This final merger gave the city its first fully integrated gas and electric service company — Consolidated Gas Electric Light and Power Company of Baltimore.

The new company prospered, extending its service boundaries and supplanting independently produced electric power with more economical and reliable energy and eventually adding steam to its public service supply. Then, in 1955, amid increasing demands for additional gas and electric service, Consolidated changed its name to Baltimore Gas and Electric Company.

During the fifties, demands for electricity mounted at an unprecedented rate. To keep pace, BG&E constructed two new electric generating plants, added additional turbines to three of its existing generating stations, and entered into a partnership with Safe Harbor Water Power Corporation for purchases of hydroelectric power. BG&E also became a vital link in the Pennsylvania-New Jersey-Mary-

Peale's ingenious application of gas lighting inaugurated the gas industry in America

land (PJM) Interconnection, the pioneer regional power pool in the United States. With electrical service permeating Baltimore and extending into outlying areas, a new 500,000-volt transmission system was constructed to transport additional electric power from electric generating plants in Pennsylvania, which are owned in common by a number of PJM companies, including BG&E.

In addition to other company improvements, BG&E has extended its gas distribution mains over 2,000 miles since 1950, constructed a fourth turbine-generator at its H.A. Wagner Station, acquired gas peaking turbines, established liquefied natural gas (LNG) facilities, erected a synthetic natural gas plant, and doubled the feedstock of its existing propane plant.

The highlight of these years, however, has been the building of the Calvert Cliffs Nuclear Power Plant which after intensive planning and environmental study, went into service in May 1975 when the first of two units was placed on-line. A second unit followed in 1977, so that approximately 57 percent of the electric consumption in BG&E's service territory is currently supplied by its nuclear plant.

Today BG&E supplies electric utility service to a territory of approximately 2,300 square miles, with a population of more than 2.3 million. Gas service extends to a 600-square-mile area and is utilized by an estimated 1.8 million people. Steam is also produced for sale to the downtown commercial area. In total, BG&E's service area includes Baltimore City and all or portions of nine Maryland counties.

As an investor-owned utility with wide distribution of ownership, 54 percent of BG&E's common stockholders own 100 shares or less, and 48 percent live in Maryland. Some 8,500 employees are presently on BG&E's active payroll and continue to be among the company's prime assets.

Blue Cross and Blue Shield of Maryland

The depression years were as difficult in Maryland as anywhere else. Hospitals were particularly affected by the financial problems of that period. People found it difficult enough to meet day-to-day expenses, much less the unexpected cost of a stay in the hospital.

It was not long before Maryland's community leaders and lawmakers recognized the need for a publicly accountable organization to help Marylanders prepay the cost of hospital care. Their action resulted in the Maryland General Assembly's creation of Blue Cross in 1937.

This special act of the legislature charged Blue Cross with meeting the health care needs of Maryland through a number of special arrangements. Blue Cross was to be nonprofit; it was not to be investor-owned, nor pay dividends to stockholders; and it was to be supervised by the State Insurance Division.

Under those unique arrangements, Blue Cross of Maryland opened its doors in November 1937. By the end of the year, 4,000 Marylanders had subscribed to this new program to protect themselves against the cost of hospital care. Each successive year saw more and more Marylanders covered by Blue Cross, and, by the end of the organization's first decade of service, more than 500,000 Marylanders were members.

The success of the Blue Cross concept of prepaying hospital costs soon led to considerations of a similar means to help Marylanders prepay the costs of physician services; thus, in 1950, Blue Shield of Maryland was founded. This program also gained immediate acceptance from the community. By 1958, more than 500,000 Marylanders were covered by Blue Shield.

The 1960s ushered in new community-service responsibilities for Maryland's Blue Cross and Blue Shield. First, a special health care protection program was created in 1960 for employees of the federal government. Under this program, federal employees were allowed to choose their protection from several health care companies, and nearly 80 percent of the eligible federal employees in Maryland elected Blue Cross and Blue Shield.

Six years later, the U.S. Congress created the Medicare program to provide health care protection for people sixty-five years of age and older. Blue Cross and Blue Shield were chosen to handle this new and extensive health care program for Maryland's senior citizens.

With each decade, these organizations have evidenced a capacity for versatility and change to meet the changing needs of the community. Increased consumer demand for specialized coverage has been met with the introduction of programs to help meet the cost of mental health care, prescription drugs, dental care, vision services, alcoholic rehabilitation, and major medical coverage to help meet the cost of catastrophic illness.

Additionally, Blue Cross and Blue Shield have accepted a responsibility on behalf of their members to work with hospitals, doctors, and others in the community to help bring about better control of the cost of health care. This diverse activity includes cooperative efforts with the state's regulatory agency, which approves hospital charges, health planning agencies, hospital utilization review committees, physician peer review groups, and others. At the same time, Blue Cross and Blue Shield have developed programs such as preadmission testing, home health care, same-day surgery, and second surgical opinion to allow members to obtain the health care they need in the most appropriate setting.

Today Blue Cross and Blue Shield are the largest health care protection companies in Maryland

Throughout the 43-year history of Blue Cross and the 30-year history of Blue Shield in Maryland, the organizations have been guided by boards of directors composed of members of the community. They have served their fellow Marylanders with distinction, voluntarily and without compensation.

Blue Cross and Blue Shield today are the largest health care protection companies in Maryland. More than 1.5 million Marylanders rely on Blue Cross and Blue Shield for dependable protection against the cost of health care. Each working day, Blue Cross and Blue Shield respond by processing more than 30,000 claims, representing $4 million in benefits. More than 90 percent of every dollar Blue Cross and Blue Shield receive is returned to members in benefits. For the majority of those 1.5 million Marylanders, their Blue Cross and Blue Shield cards have truly become the most important cards they carry.

The Canton Company

Before the Canton Company occupied the site 150 years ago, the land was part of several large estates formed during the late 1700s. One of these was owned by Captain John O'Donnell, a seafaring merchant who made his fortune in trade through China's port of Canton. When he left the sea in 1780 and settled in Baltimore (becoming a colonel in the Maryland Militia), he named his waterfront estate after his favorite Chinese port.

Forty-seven years later, Colonel O'Donnell's son, Columbus O'Donnell, was active in a group petitioning for an act to incorporate the Canton Company. This bill was passed in 1829.

It is virtually impossible to count the number of changes that have taken place in the Port of Baltimore since 1829. Yet one thing is certain: the Canton Company has played a major role in port activity in the years that have followed its incorporation. This growth and development was apparently anticipated by the charter of incorporation, which granted the right to own up to 10,000 acres (later increased) and "to improve it in such a manner as may be comfortable to the laws of the State, and lands which shall belong to said company, by laying out streets, etc., in the vicinity of Baltimore on or near navigable water, and erecting and constructing wharves, ships, workshops, factories, stores, dwellings, and such other buildings and improvements as may be deemed necessary, ornamental, and convenient."

Right:
The Canton Company works around the clock to load and unload ships as fast as possible.
Photo courtesy H.E. Davis

Far Right:
This illustration depicts the Port of Baltimore as it appeared in 1869

Real estate, Canton's earliest interest, guided the company's extraordinary diversification. Today Canton operates the largest privately owned marine terminal on the East Coast. The terminal encompasses 184 acres of land on which are situated open storage, a bulk materials crane pier, a fully integrated container-to-ship terminal, completely modern roll-on and roll-off facilities (truck-to-ship), 150,000 square feet of modern covered space, and a public warehouse facility of 750,000 square feet. All of the facilities are supported by the small but busy Canton Railroad. Also serviced by trucks, Canton boasts a banana operation that handles over 3 million boxes of bananas shipped annually for distribution in Maryland and its bordering states.

On a 22-acre site adjacent to the Dundalk Marine Terminal, Canton engages in the export packaging of large project shipments and warehousing. Shipments have included a fully equipped baby food plant destined for the Soviet Union, materials and construction equipment for an airport in Saudi Arabia, and a coal conversion plant for South Africa.

Canton also has subsidiary companies to provide stevedoring and commercial, contractors, and personal insurance.

As an independent, the Canton Company plays a vital role in the Port of Baltimore. Practically all tonnage shipped through Canton Marine Terminal are solicited by Canton employees, and their efforts bring much needed business to the city of Baltimore and the economy of Maryland.

If one were to travel in time, from the day Captain John O'Donnell arrived in Baltimore through the early years of the Canton Company to its present position in the port, one would review a kaleidoscope of successful industries, famous vessels, and marvelous memories: Thompson's Sea Girt House (50¢ fish and chicken dinners), the Canton Race Course (where a national Whig convention nominated William Henry Harrison for President and four years later nominated Henry Clay), Riverview Park ... and on and on. The list is long and the names are legend. Ahead lies the powerful potential of the Canton Companies and their future accomplishments for the Port of Baltimore.

Central Savings Bank

Even for a firm that has had 125 birthday celebrations, October 2, 1979, was a very special day for Central Savings Bank. Mayor Don Schaefer of Baltimore declared that day "Central Savings Bank Day," calling attention to two important milestones: first, the bank's 125th Birthday, and second, its merger with Arlington Federal Savings and Loan Association. Total assets climbed to $170 million, a sum that would tax the imagination of Central's founders.

After receiving its charter in 1854, the bank welcomed all depositors, including those who wanted to open an account with as little as ten cents. The new bank's official name was Dime Savings Bank, but just as often it was called the Quaker Bank, because so many of its founders and directors were Quakers.

Bank personnel celebrated 125 years of service to Baltimore in 1979

After the Civil War, the name seemed misleading. Dime Savings Bank suggested the bank was just for children, and people were surprised to learn that deposits for as much as a dollar were acceptable. So in 1866 the charter was amended, and the present name, Central Savings Bank, was adopted.

The first building occupied by the bank was at the corner of Calvert and Fayette Streets, a prime location directly opposite Barnum's, one of Baltimore's finest hotels. City Hall, then housed in the Peale Museum Building, was nearby. As the city was fairly small, almost all important business and industry were within easy walking distance.

The bank's first home was rented. When the owners decided to sell the building in 1869, the board of directors acquired a new building on Lexington Street just east of Charles. A third move was made three years later, when the old Lorman residence on Charles Street at Lexington was purchased and remodeled for the bank. By 1890, business was so good that the bank was "bursting at the seams." Management decided to design a building with every modern convenience. The present "brownstone" corner building, which rose on the site of the Lorman house, is said to be the city's first combination bank and office building.

The Great Baltimore Fire of 1904, which destroyed 140 acres of the city's business district, spared the new bank; it was the only building to remain standing in that block. More than likely its height helped check the fire's progress northward.

In 1931, the banking floor was remodeled; the front door was lowered to street level and the old iron teller cages were replaced with a counter. Following the "bank holiday" in March 1933, Central was one of the first banks to reopen, signifying its strength and stability.

The Hopkins Savings Bank and the Citizens Savings Bank merged into the Central Savings Bank in 1944 and 1953, respectively, as the bank's assets continued to grow and its services continued to expand. The merger with Arlington Savings and Loan Association in 1979 provided four additional banking locations for a total of twelve serving the Greater Baltimore area.

There have been only ten presidents in the bank's 125-year lifetime. The first president of Central Savings Bank, Francis T. King, held the office from 1854 to 1891. Other presidents include John Curlett, 1892 to 1896; Robert K. Waring, 1896 to 1913; Wilton Snowden, 1913 to 1926; Harry G. Evans, 1926 to 1930; James D. Garrett, 1930 to 1944; L. Alan Dill, 1944 to 1959; Jason W. Stockbridge, 1959 to 1973; and John W. Edelen, Jr., who served in 1973. The president today is C. Edgar Smith, Jr., who was elected in 1973. John W. Edelen, Jr., is chairman of the board and Harry E. Karr, Jr., is vice-chairman, as Central Savings Bank heads into the 1980s offering more banking services than ever before.

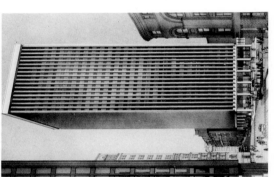

Central's additional banking quarters were acquired through its merger with Arlington Federal Savings and Loan Association on October 1, 1979

Chesapeake & Potomac Telephone Company

Young Harry Dunn probably didn't realize it at the time, but he was crucial to events in Baltimore 100 years ago; the lad was the city's first — and only — telephone operator. By 1879, only three years after Alexander Graham Bell invented that wondrous device called the telephone, Baltimore had its first switchboard. And 17-year-old Harry Dunn was its only master.

Dunn slept beneath the converted telegraph board at night so that he could handle calls at all hours. Because he was the city's only operator, when Harry got hungry, he closed the office to go out for meals. Still, the telephone industry had made great strides in Baltimore by the time Dunn plugged in his first cross-town call.

That ingenious mix of wires and circuitry that is part of nearly every household and business today first arrived in Baltimore in 1877, scarcely a year after Bell's monumental discovery changed the course of history. The first city residents to own the talking boxes, Augustus G. Davis and John Henry C. Watts (whose name was well-suited to his profession), were partners in an electrical firm. The men

began experimenting with a pair of telephones connected between two rooms. Initially, they had trouble hearing each other speak, which prompted a letter to Bell's company for advice: "Does it require practice," they asked, "or is the sound intended to be very low? How far from the mouth, when speaking, should the instrument be held?"

By and by, Davis and Watts got the hang of it. And in the following year, 1878, the two men were chartered by the state for the construction, ownership, and operation of telephone and telegraph lines in Maryland. The Maryland Telephone Company of Baltimore was born. With Davis as president, 4,990 shares of stock were issued at ten dollars a share and the beginnings of what is now the Chesapeake & Potomac Telephone Company of Maryland took root.

Before 1879, the few Baltimore residents who owned telephones had the thin, electrical line strung only be-

250

tween two places, usually from one home to another. But with the first switchboard in 1879, intercommunication was made possible and business began to boom. One Baltimore doctor sent his patients a postcard message, which read: "Dr. D.W. Cathell now has a telephone, and messages can be sent to him by anybody, free of cost, from any telephone in the city."

Telephone advertising began, and Davis soon came up with a novel idea — providing a circular listing of all the city's telephone subscribers. The first "phone book" was published in 1879. Davis took the opportunity to say that the telephone "has not only sprung into existence, but it has attained a simplicity — almost perfection — in a com-

paratively short time . . . and fully adapted to supply a long-felt want."

That first directory listed ninety telephone subscribers. At the top of the directory the company announced: "The following firms and individuals have already availed themselves of the advantages of the Speaking Telephone." Among these subscribers were the city police department, a distiller, an undertaker, several shipping and coal manufacturers, and fourteen persons with residential telephone service.

People were very interested in the relatively new invention. Business in general was on the upswing, and, technically speaking, the telephone industry was making great advances in the latter part of the nineteenth century. New operating stations opened in Baltimore and telephone service was rapidly making its way to the state's outlying areas. In the city, evidence of the telephone was everywhere. In 1889, the Baltimore City Council passed an ordinance allowing the telephone company to place its wires underground to alleviate overhead congestion on city streets.

In 1892, the Maryland General Assembly passed the first bill setting rates for telephone service, thus beginning regulatory action governing the telephone industry in Maryland. In 1910, the legislature created the Public Service Commission to set telephone rates.

By 1895, the Chesapeake and Potomac Telephone Company served 3,000 Maryland residents, all but 300 living within the Baltimore exchange. Long-distance cables were stretched across the state, and instead of sending messengers to collect for each long-distance call, as had been the case, the company began billing customers monthly in 1897.

Long-distance calling was becoming very popular. A slogan on the back of a telephone directory in 1899 read: "The mail is quick, the telegraph is quicker, but the long-distance telephone is instantaneous and you do not have to wait for an answer." It did not take much to sell the public on long distance, or telephones in general, for that matter. And C&P executives heartily undertook the company's expansion.

On February 6, 1904, two more Baltimore central offices were opened — the Mt. Vernon office on St. Paul Street and the Gilmor office on West Baltimore Street. None too soon, either, because on the next day, February 7, the Great Baltimore Fire consumed ninety-eight city blocks and completely destroyed the original St. Paul office, which served downtown businesses and housed the long-distance switchboard.

Operators remained at their posts until the heat from the blaze shattered the office windows. Telephones in service dropped from 14,000 to 9,000. But despite the fact that the Mt. Vernon and Gilmor offices were less than a day old, they were able to handle the bulk of the St. Paul subscribers.

Through the early 1900s, telephone cable was laid across the country, connecting Baltimore with New York, Delaware, and other urban centers on the East Coast. In 1915, regular telephone service opened between Baltimore and San Francisco, with a three-minute call costing about nineteen dollars. This was just four months after the first transcontinental call had been placed on a line from New York to San Francisco. Today, a Baltimore caller can dial San Francisco on a three-minute call for just a little over one dollar.

Both world wars hindered the commercial growth of the telephone industry, as the Bell System and C&P offered support to the war effort. During World War I, the government actually took control of several industries, including the Bell System. But by the 1920s, private ownership again prevailed and a new breakthrough was made — the "two-longs-and-a-short" method of calling a friend gave way to the first dial telephones in Baltimore. And at that time (and until 1952), a local coin telephone call cost only a nickel.

By 1938, one out of every six Marylanders had a telephone, which could be connected to 93 percent of the 40.6 million telephones in the world at that time. Today, there are more than 423 million telephones across the globe. The Chesapeake and Potomac Telephone Company offers telephone service to 1.6 million customers and there are 3.3 million telephones in Maryland. In 1978, more than 4.4 billion calls were put through C&P switchboards with the help of more than 14,000 employees. The company spent $206 million on construction projects alone that same year.

If they were alive today, no doubt the sophisticated electronic and computerized equipment used by the Bell System and C&P would have Harry Dunn and Alexander Graham Bell smiling, if only a bit confused.

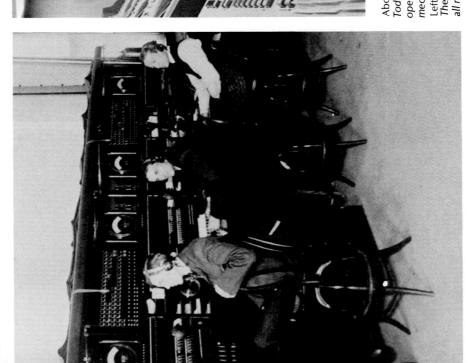

Above:
Today's telephone operators operate ultra-modern, highly mechanized switchboards
Left:
The first telephone operators were all male

Chessie System

The success of any city, and especially a port city like Baltimore, depends on the quality of its land transportation. For more than 150 years, the link between Maryland's premier port and its natural western and southern markets has been the Baltimore and Ohio Railroad. Now part of the Chessie System, it serves the region as the oldest operating railroad company in the world.

It was no accident that Baltimore should sire the country's first real railroad. By the end of the American Revolution, the city had matured as a rival of New York and Philadelphia for trade supremacy. Baltimore merchants imported vast tonnages of staples and commodities, which were shipped inland with manufactured goods from Europe and the East Coast. The completion of the National Road to Wheeling in 1818 enhanced Baltimore's status as the seaport closest to the West.

That prosperity, however, was short-lived. The opening of the Erie Canal in 1825 gave New York a tremendous advantage in the western trade. In response, Washington and Virginia planned canals from Tidewater to the Ohio River, Philadelphia devised an elaborate scheme of turnpikes, canals, and inclined-plane tramways to connect that city with Pittsburgh. As Baltimore's trade volume slipped, its need for a reliable tie to the West became much more acute.

The answer was to come from England, where the primitive coal mine tramways of the eighteenth century had evolved into a full-fledged railway. The technology was sufficiently advanced to interest the merchants and bankers of Baltimore. By late 1826, Philip E. Thomas was actively promoting the idea of a railroad, and as president of the Mechanic's Bank, his voice carried a great deal of weight in the business community.

The choice was not an easy one, for no real railroad had been built in the U.S. It worked in England, where there were short distances, high traffic volumes, and adequate capital sources, but could Baltimore construct a railway through 300 miles of wilderness to the Ohio River, cresting the Alleghenies in the process? Would there be enough traffic to support the road? And enough money to build it?

The twelve most influential citizens of Baltimore who met in George Brown's home on February 12, 1827, decided "yes" to all counts. A charter was quickly drawn, and on February 28, 1827, the state of Maryland authorized creation of the Baltimore and Ohio Railroad Company.

The following July 4 was chosen as a fitting time to begin construction, and on that day in 1828 most of the city turned out to watch. Besides parades and related festivities, tradition dictated other activities at the ceremony also. The Masons officiated, and a symbolic "first stone" was placed at the official start of construction. Ninety-one-year-old Charles Carroll of Carrollton turned the first spade of earth for the B&O Railroad at the same time that President John Quincy Adams was doing the same for the C&O Canal in Georgetown, D.C. As the only surviving signer of the Declaration of Independence, Carroll was the country's most venerated citizen. An ardent backer of the B&O, he lent a great deal of prestige to the fledgling company.

The story of the construction of the railroad to the Ohio River at Wheeling is one of hardship, innovation, delay, and, ultimately, triumph. It took twenty-five years to reach the river, and in that time the city grew as a commercial and industrial power. Centered around the port, that growth came about almost entirely as a result of the railroad to the West.

By 1842, the B&O had moved to the coal fields of Cumberland, Maryland. Possessing this direct route to vast, high-quality coal deposits, Baltimore quickly became one of the East's primary suppliers of fuel and an increasingly important bunkering port for the growing fleet of ocean-going steam vessels. As the B&O provided transportation for raw materials and finished goods, employment and economies of scale increased, which led to more work and a better standard of living.

The railroad's direct influence was itself staggering. Locally rolled iron wound its way to the Ohio; Baltimore-built locomotives pulled home-built cars full of Maryland citizens. Supplies for the entire system were purchased in Baltimore, and the Mt. Clare shops (now the site of the B&O Railroad Museum) employed over 1,000 men. Indeed, few Baltimore families cannot claim at least one relative who worked for "the railroad."

As the B&O's gateway to the world, Baltimore's activities grew with the traffic. The railroad opened Locust Point in 1849, and after the Civil War developed the peninsula into one of the world's finest facilities for coal, grain, and general cargo. Beginning in 1868, Locust Point also served as the point of disembarkation for hundreds of thousands of European immigrants sailing to America on the North German Lloyd line. Many continued westward in special B&O trains, while a large number settled in Baltimore, contributing to the city's ethnic diversity.

Even Locust Point ultimately proved inadequate. In the 1880s, the B&O expanded its port activities to Curtis Bay. Chosen as the site of the B&O's coal piers, Curtis Bay also provided a large tract of industrial development land especially suitable for chemical development concerns. Making land and transportation available for businesses to locate in Baltimore has always been important to the B&O, and in fact began in the 1830s, when many concerns established themselves adjacent to the tracks on Pratt Street. That practice continues to this day in such diverse areas as the Camden Station redevelopment plan and the MPA's Masonville Terminal.

The B&O and Baltimore never lacked for firsts. For example, when the B&O built its line to Philadelphia under Howard Street in 1895, it employed the first practical electric locomotives in the world to pull the trains between Camden Station and Waverly. The first telegraph message was received in the B&O's Pratt Street Station in 1844, over wires laid along the tracks to Washington. And, sadly, the first Maryland bloodshed of the Civil War resulted when Massachusetts troops attempted to march from President Street to Camden Station to board B&O trains to the South. Andrew Jackson became the first president to ride a railroad, between Baltimore and Ellicott's Mills. The country's first passenger trains had departed from Mt. Clare in 1830.

Throughout the twentieth century, the railroad has improved steadily, and the city and its people have been the beneficiaries. The tremendous line relocations undertaken all over the B&O in this period were designed in Baltimore. Many of the cars and locomotives that bettered freight and passenger service were built at Mt. Clare, and the entire region benefited from the huge investment made in the piers and warehouses that serve the harbor.

The B&O was perhaps the single most important project ever undertaken in the state of Maryland. Certainly, it was the foundation upon which most of Baltimore's commerce and industry was built. In essence an extension of

the Atlantic Ocean to the Midwest, the B&O was always much more than a transportation system. Conceived, financed, and built by local interests, it soon expanded into a national system connecting this seaport with virtually every major East Coast and Midwest city. But more than that, it has been an integral part of Baltimore's economic, social, and cultural fabric since 1827.

Today, as a part of the Chessie System, the Baltimore and Ohio Railroad is still a viable, contributing force to the nation's indispensable railroad network — and will continue to be so into the future.

Above:
A Chessie System merchandise train rumbles across B&O's historic Thomas Viaduct at Relay, Maryland; the bridge was constructed in 1835

Right:
Thousands of tons of West Virginia bituminous coal are transported by Modern Chessie System diesel-electrical locomotives eastbound across the Potomac River at B&O's Harpers Ferry, West Virginia, station

Below:
The B&O Railroad Museum in downtown Baltimore features an unexcelled collection of locomotives and cars from the heritage of American railroading

Commercial Credit Company

In the very early years of the century, many customers settled their accounts with a business only twice a year; a new company often waited months before receiving payment for the goods it sold. Thus, many enterprises lacked working capital for expansion, and financial institutions were reluctant to advance money to new accounts whose assets and net worth appeared unable to provide sufficient protection to the lender.

Alexander E. Duncan, founder of Commercial Credit Company, learned firsthand about the financial problems of growing businesses. While a special agent for a credit company in Cincinnati, he was asked to assess a new company which was buying accounts receivable from manufacturers and wholesalers. Mr. Duncan saw immediately that such a business had great potential, was financially sound, and should prove profitable.

A few years later Duncan was transferred to Baltimore. On May 29, 1912, with two associates and $300,000 in borrowed capital, he started Commercial Credit Company with the goal of providing accounts receivable financing for small businesses. The company occupied offices in the Keyser Building for a few months while awaiting office space in the newly erected Garrett Building, which housed the company until 1924.

By the end of 1912, Commercial Credit had provided accounts receivable financing for manufacturers in excess of $2 million. The following year the receivables outstanding grew to nearly $9.5 million. Behind this rapid growth lay the development of a positive working relationship between Commercial Credit and the banking industry, as bankers in Baltimore, Philadelphia, and Chicago found Mr. Duncan's innovative financial practices to be sound and provided lines of credit for the new company.

Almost at once Commercial Credit began to expand its services. In 1916, the Baltimore firm became one of the first companies in the nation to enter a controversial new field: helping automobile dealers finance the purchase of new cars for their showrooms — and then financing the installment sales of those automobiles to consumers. This installment plan was soon adopted by other financial institutions across the country and provided the foundation for Commercial Credit's entry into consumer financing.

Alexander E. Duncan, founder of the Commercial Credit Company, is pictured here in the firm's first offices in the newly constructed Garrett Building, which Commercial Credit occupied until 1924

Today, Commercial Credit Company, with its headquarters at 300 St. Paul Place, is one of the nation's leading diversified financial institutions, with assets of over $5.5 billion and approximately 9,000 employees

Combined with Henry Ford's mass production techniques, consumer financing through installment buying made the automobile truly available to the general public for the first time.

In fact, consumer acceptance of automobile financing led to the development of other installment buying plans for home appliances and consumer goods. The company became a leader in the field of sales finance and in 1939 began direct lending to consumers.

Insurance services became a natural adjunct to Commercial Credit's growing family of financial services during the 1930s and 1940s. In 1936, the firm acquired American Credit Indemnity Company, a major credit insurer and Mr. Duncan's former employer. A casualty insurance company became part of the Commercial Credit family in 1939, and the firm organized a company to offer life, hospitalization, and disability policies to individuals and large groups in 1944.

When World War II began, American industry switched from automobiles and household goods to munitions and military supplies. As the direction of national need changed, Commercial Credit also put its large financial resources into the war effort. It entered the field of manufacturing, producing items which ranged from gears, nuts, and bolts to munitions and canned rations for the armed forces.

During the 1960s, the firm began to divest itself of manufacturing firms in order to concentrate once again on its specialties — financing and insurance — and began to establish itself as a leader in vehicle and equipment leasing and other types of industrial financing.

Then, in 1968, Commercial Credit became a wholly owned subsidiary of Control Data Corporation, a worldwide corporation committed to a strategy of addressing society's major needs as profitable business opportunities. Headquartered in Minneapolis, Control Data has more than 58,000 employees and offices in forty-seven countries. Founded in 1957 by William C. Norris, the company has designed and built the world's most powerful computers. It is also a leader in data services and produces one of the computer industry's broadest lines of peripheral products.

During the 1970s, Commercial Credit's growth and diversification continued with the addition of thrift services, real estate and second mortgage loans, a regional property and casualty company in nine southwestern states, a mortgage insurance company, computer-based education for consumers and businesses, relocation services for transferred employees, credit cards, and direct lending by mail.

The company's leasing group currently ranks as one of the largest vehicle leasing companies in the country and one of the leading general aircraft financing and leasing companies in the world. The company also handles leasing and financing of capital equipment and provides third-party vendor financing and leasing. Tax-sheltered leasing and tax-exempt financing arrangements frequently involve participation with banks and other financial institutions. Today Commercial Credit is one of the nation's leading diversified financial institutions, with assets of more than $5.5 billion, approximately 9,000 employees, and nearly 1,000 offices in the U.S., Canada, Europe, Israel, Japan, and Brazil. The company provides financial, insurance, education, and techology services to more than a million businesses and consumers.

Crown Central
Petroleum Corporation

altimoreans come into daily contact with Crown Central Petroleum Corporation, whether through one of the company's distinctive service stations, its headquarters at One North Charles Street, or its involvement in and support of community activities. Many people are unaware of the company's wide-ranging activity within the oil industry, however. Although originally a refiner, Crown has evolved into a corporation whose operations encompass every aspect of the petroleum business — from exploring for and producing crude oil and natural gas to refining petroleum products, transporting the finished product to market, and delivering it to the customer. Crown ranks 345th in the Fortune 500 companies and is one of two that has its headquarters in Baltimore.

Crown Central Petroleum Corporation became a Baltimore-based company in the early 1930s because of the interest of two of the city's most fascinating citizens — Louis and Jacob Blaustein. The Blausteins had developed the original antiknock, water-white gasoline and sold it successfully under the American Oil brand. American agreed to buy Crown's high-antiknock-quality gasoline in 1928, and Crown's role in Baltimore and along the East Coast began. This arrangement paved the way for the Blausteins' entrance into Crown's management three years later through the election of Henry A. Rosenberg, Sr., as vice president.

Louis Blaustein was a salesman, and a very good one, too. Born in Russia, he and his son, Jacob, had built up Baltimore's vast American Oil Company. They began by selling oil products from a horse-drawn tank wagon along Baltimore streets. One of the sales ideas that Blaustein believed in most strongly was brand-consciousness. The company was one of the first to utilize the marketing concept that if a product's name was before the public

enough times and in enough places, people would ask for it regularly.

That principle seems obviously simple compared to today's modern advertising techniques, but the idea was still untested in the early 1930s. Part of the early marketing effort was to back up the company name with color. Thus, when Crown opened its first service stations in the Baltimore area in the late 1940s, Crown brand products were always sold in stations marked by the company's blue and red/orange colors.

Today, Crown Central Petroleum Corporation has a reputation as one of the great innovators in the area of gasoline marketing. The company's concept of a multipump station, offering service twenty-four hours a day, seven days a week, 365 days a year, while providing

Above:
Today's Baltimore Crown stations are noted for their fast, courteous service and clean, pleasant surroundings

Left:
Crown Central Petroleum Corporation became a Baltimore-based company in the early 1930s because of the interest of two of the city's most fascinating citizens, Louis and Jacob Blaustein. Pictured in this 1948 photograph is one of the first Baltimore Crown stations, located at Harford Road and Royston Avenue

quality products, efficient service, and aesthetically pleasing surroundings, proved to be a trend-setter in the industry.

Crown has earned and retained its reputation as a highly successful marketer of gasoline primarily because it remains sensitive to the needs of the community and the motoring public. Crown's landscaped and carefully designed stations continue to win community and property improvement awards in Baltimore and throughout Crown's marketing area.

Moving products from the refinery in Houston to markets on the East Coast of the United States has always been a part of Crown's operation. In 1942, the company became the first independent petroleum refiner and marketer to utilize a direct pipeline link between its refinery and its outlets. In 1945, Crown began using a terminal on Clinton Street in south Baltimore. Since that time, the company has been able to expand its market through the growth of a transportation system that includes pipelines, ships, and tank trucks.

Although exploration and production have not been a major area of concentration, the company has continued to expand its capital investment in domestic oil and gas leases. In addition, Crown is one of the few independent, integrated oil companies that have established and maintained direct relationships with foreign petroleum-exporting nations to ensure a continuous supply of raw material.

Above:
The tanker Crown Trader *out of Baltimore, moored in the Houston Ship Channel during the 1940s*
Left:
Crown's refinery on the Houston Ship Channel has continued to modernize and expand to better provide products for customers

The pivotal factor in Crown's growth and development has been the company's refinery, built in 1914 on the Houston Ship Channel. The first finished product of the refinery was 500-viscosity red oil, a heavy lubricating oil that is a long way from today's complex and highly refined Crown products. The Houston facility has continually provided high-quality products to customer outlets in the Southeast and on the East Coast, with Baltimore being historically one of the largest recipients. Today Baltimore ranks as the flagship market for all of Crown Central's marketing efforts.

The company established its original Baltimore headquarters in 1930 on one floor of the old American Building at the corner of Baltimore and South Streets. Longtime employees remember when fewer than twenty people comprised the entire headquarters there. Since 1963, Crown has resided in the Blaustein Building, located at One North Charles. The company and its operations, from Texas to New York and overseas, employs over 1,300 people and maintains exploration and production facilities across the continental United States.

As a corporate citizen, Crown is unique within the petroleum industry in its commitment to the community in which it is located. Nowhere is this commitment more firm than in Baltimore. Because the company established itself within the city, and because the corporate headquarters are also located in Baltimore, there is a special feeling of responsibility towards the citizens who have participated in and supported the growth of Crown. In deference to this, Crown has maintained an ongoing policy of contribution to the cultural and community life of Baltimore. Examples include sponsorship of public television programming, support of Baltimore's clipper ship goodwill ambassador, *Pride of Baltimore*, promotional activities each year for the Baltimore City Fair, and support of the Baltimore Symphony Orchestra.

Chas. H. Steffey, Inc.

In 1915, passers-by on Baltimore streets were urged by a cart merchant to attend Sunday land auctions. Those who attended and bought lots were promised a free set of silver in return. In those days, lots that sell now for many thousands of dollars sold for between $1,000 and $2,000. Sometimes the land was divided into 25-foot lots, and buyers would acquire two or three of them in order to build a house. Such opportunities encouraged the growth of Maryland's business and residential communities, aided by Charles H. Steffey, who became a giant in the state's realty history.

Steffey began his lifelong career in real estate before the turn of the century, when he joined the oldest real estate firm in Baltimore, Martein & Co., as an office boy. He was quick and eager to learn, and by 1904, at only twenty-one years of age, he joined Caughy, Hearn & Carter as a real estate salesman. Carter, the senior partner of the firm, was impressed by young Steffey's abilities. In 1914, they formed a new company called Carter & Steffey. Within a year, sudden illness forced Carter to retire, and Charles Steffey was left as sole owner. The firm flourished in the decades to come, growing from an initial staff of six to over one hundred employees and a real estate sales staff of more than four hundred associates in twelve branch offices.

Charles Steffey found time to hold office in many civic organizations, serving a term as president of the Baltimore Real Estate Board in 1919 and as a member of the Maryland Real Estate Commission from 1938 to 1956. He died in 1958, but he had contributed enormously to the real estate industry in Maryland.

In 1949 Charles Steffey brought his son, Jack, into the company. After a very successful start as a real estate salesman, he was transferred to the administrative side of the business. After his father's death in 1958, Jack Steffey was appointed president and carried on in his father's footsteps.

Under his guidance, the company expanded its areas of service beyond the original real estate brokerage activities so that it now provides additional full professional services in the fields of mortgage banking, commercial and investment real estate, construction, property management, land development, insurance, and joint venture investment.

Geographically, the company has grown to the extent that it serves the central Maryland area and has real estate financing activities in Delaware. It also is involved in the transfer of corporate employees between Baltimore and cities all over the nation.

Today, John W. Steffey is chairman of the board and Theodore M. Chandlee, Jr., who joined the company in 1962, is the president. The company is still owned by the family of the founder and Jack Steffey's two sons, John W. Steffey, Jr., and William C. Steffey, are active in the business, representing the third generation of this real estate oriented family.

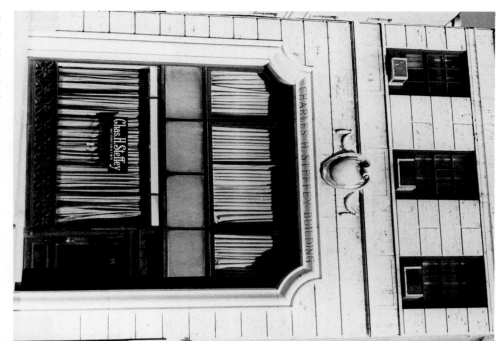

This building which once stood at 18 East Lexington Street was the headquarters of the Steffey Company for many years. At the time, this block of East Lexington Street was known as "Real Estate Row," as most of the major real estate companies had their offices there

E.J. Codd Company of Baltimore City

At the corner of Caroline and Aliceanna Streets in historic Fells Point stands a handsomely renovated brick building with the date 1881 on the iron supports of its large doors. At this location in 1860, Edward J. Codd, a lifelong resident of East Baltimore, founded a machine shop, iron foundry, and boilerworks. His business prospered, and by 1898 his plant on South Caroline Street employed over 100 men.

The E.J. Codd Company experienced remarkable growth during Mr. Codd's lifetime and had a well-earned reputation for high-quality workmanship and reliability. In 1891, the firm built and installed the coal-burning engines in Baltimore's first fireboat, the Cataract, a wooden-hulled vessel which served the harbor until 1914.

Following Mr. Codd's death, the business was sold in 1911 to Henry Hazlehurst Wiegand and Thomas Dobbin Penniman, both well-known Baltimoreans. Mr. Wiegand was an art lover, a longtime member of the Charcoal Club, and served many years on the commission that built the Baltimore Museum of Art. He invented and patented the Wiegand Chain Furnace Curtain which is still produced solely by the Codd Company. Mr. Wiegand's great-nephew, Ray Wiegand Kauffman, purchased the business in 1953.

The E.J. Codd Company has progressed with the times from riveting to welding, from steam power to electric power, and today uses some numerically controlled machinery. An apprenticeship with this firm has been recognized as a valuable background by generations of machinists, boilermakers, and welders.

Steam boilers built by Codd are still in service in some of Baltimore's older buildings. Over the years, the E.J. Codd Company engineered and built many innovative machines from early fish presses, ice cream cone machinery, and sewage treatment tanks to the working model for the diplomatic mail delivery system for the United Nations Building, the first atmospheric incore detector and cutter for a nuclear facility, as well as lead burning work for protective corrosion systems and precipitators.

The company has built and installed an entire distillery; machined the first and largest plastic insulators; produced tail fin assemblies for cannon-fired high altitude rocket missiles; engineered special machinery for in-place repair of railroad suspension bridges; worked on the Chesapeake Bay Bridge; designed, built, and installed an aluminum conveyor and storage rack system for a clothing manufacturer; and installed a protective lead lining for the roof garden of the new Walter Reed Hospital in Washington, D.C.

Today Mr. Kauffman owns and operates E.J. Codd Company of Baltimore City, Codd Fabricators & Boiler Co., Inc., and the Baltimore Lead Burning Corporation at Codd's original location. His plant on Caroline Street has modern equipment for and specializes in contract machining, steel fabricating, lead burning, and the repair of industrial equipment for many local businesses, including oil and sugar refineries, steel manufacturers, and chemical plants. This unique combination of industrial skills — fabricating, machining, and lead burning — is finding increased applications in the high technology fields of nuclear energy, medicine, environmental protection, and public utility.

In its 120th year, this old family-owned firm still operates under the personal supervision of experienced, practical personnel; and in the words of E.J. Codd in 1898: *"thus insures to the trade only such production as will withstand the most critical tests, both in regard to the material used in their construction and workmanship employed .... The business of the concern has had a remarkable growth and bids fair to still further increase and multiply, owing to the exceedingly high character and repute which it has always sustained, and the high favor in which it is held by all who have ever sustained business relations therewith."*

The E.J. Codd Company plant specializes in contract machining, steel fabrication, lead burning, and the repair of industrial equipment

Established 1860, incorporated 1888

Eastmet Corporation

The Eastmet family of firms combines the production know-how of the steel mill, the distribution experience of the service center, the casting of metals and plastic parts, the production of engineered metal products, and the worldwide contacts in overseas markets.

Although the corporation was formed in 1972, the story of Eastmet actually begins in 1918, when ground was broken in Baltimore County for a new steel mill. By 1920, the Eastern Rolling Mill Company was rolling carbon steel sheets on newly installed hand mill equipment. With the development of continuous rolling mills by the carbon steel industry in the 1930s, Eastern could no longer compete and, therefore, turned to the new stainless steel field, limiting production to rerolling stainless steel sheets on hand mills until the mid-1940s.

John M. Curley, Sr., founder of Industrial Steels, Inc., of Massachusetts in 1924, used the Eastern Rolling Mill Company as a source of sheet and plate. Industrial had become the first exclusive distributor of stainless steel in 1933. In 1945, the two firms combined to form Eastern Stainless Steel Corporation, with Industrial Stainless Steels, Inc., as a wholly owned subsidiary.

During the next decade, the Eastern Stainless Steel Corporation continued to renovate and expand facilities and to install the most modern equipment available in the industry. With the installation of a "Z" mill in 1957, Eastern became a complete supplier of sheet, strip, and plate for the stainless steel market.

Eastern began to emerge as a diversified metals company in 1968. With the acquisition of several metals-related industries, the name "Easco" was adopted to signify the expansion from its long association solely with the steel industry. Eastern Stainless Steel became the name of the Mill Division. A year later, John M. Curley, Sr., died, ending his 60-year association with the steel industry.

In 1972, shareholders of Easco Corporation approved a plan of reorganization which resulted in the formation of Eastmet and a spinoff of the assets and liabilities of three operating companies — Eastern Stainless Steel Company, Industrial Service Centers, Inc., and Philipp Overseas, Inc.

Eastern Stainless Steel Company remains the largest operating unit of Eastmet, with manufacturing facilities and headquarters located in Baltimore.

In 1970, Eastern led the U.S. stainless steel industry by installing the first commercial-size argon-oxygen decarburization furnace, more commonly known as an AOD vessel, which brought the newest process in steel refining to Eastmet. In 1974, Eastern again led the industry by in-

stalling a continuous casting furnace for the exclusive production of stainless steels. By late 1980, Eastern will have completed a multimillion-dollar expansion program which will increase its production of cold rolled flat rolled stainless steels by 45 percent. These continuing changes in plant modernization and increasing capacities have placed Eastern among the nation's foremost producers of stainless steel plate and cold rolled stainless steel sheet.

Industrial Service Centers, Inc., with branch warehouses in Massachusetts and Buffalo, performs the service function between the mill and the fabricator, selling and processing stainless steel and aluminum.

Philipp Overseas, Inc., the international trading and marketing subsidiary of Eastmet, is an established exporter and trader of stainless steel and other metals and metal products. All of the Philipp Overseas' warehousing functions are now located in Baltimore and Warren, Ohio.

UIP Corporation is a recently acquired company specializing in the fabrication of heavy structural and plate steel products, the casting of high ductile iron and stainless steel parts, and the production of engineered metal products such as specialized machinery used in building construction and specialized parts for the energy and pollution control markets.

The utilization of specialty steels in our modern way of life is wide and growing. Eastmet's combination of production, marketing, and international expertise will surely enable this young Baltimore corporation to remain a viable force in the ever-growing metals industry.

Ellicott Machine Corporation

Charles Ellis Ellicott was only twenty-four years old when he founded the Ellicott Machine Corporation in 1885. He had a degree in mechanical engineering and $10,000. "After five years," he wrote, "everything was the same, except I did not have the ten thousand."

The site of the original company (a general engineering and machinery manufacturing firm) was on Smith's Wharf (Pier 3) at the end of Gay Street, today the site of the city's World Trade Center.

Soon after its founding, the company designed a new pump and gear box for a dredge operating on the Potomac River near Washington, D.C., and the success of this project encouraged the company to become builders of dredges. In fact, the firm's maritime history had begun a hundred years earlier, when Ellicott's ancestors had built a wharf at Pratt and Light Streets to facilitate the shipment of flour ground at their mills in Ellicott City. Because of shallow water at this location, the Ellicott brothers, John and Andrew, attempted to dredge the inner harbor by dragging the bottom with iron scoops drawn and raised with the help of a windlass and a team of horses.

The company, however, did not achieve success immediately. By 1894, the young founder was earning an annual income of only $1,800. The company moved from the Smith Wharf location to another on Holabird Avenue. After a fire destroyed that plant in 1900, the company started again near Carroll Park on Bush Street, their present location.

The first big jobs came from the U.S. Army Corps of Engineers, which commissioned the company to build a steam-powered dredge to be used in deepening the harbor in San Pedro, California. To cut transportation costs,

half the company moved to California to build the dredge's wooden hull right in the harbor, shipping only the machinery across country. The project lasted twelve months, but the dredge lasted more than fifty years. The company was later contracted by the corps to design and construct the machinery for a series of large, hydraulic pipeline, cutterhead dredges for the Panama Canal, and over the years has built more dredges to maintain the canal.

By 1912, Ellicott's son, C. Ellis Ellicott, Jr., had started working in his father's shop while still in college. Trained as a naval architect, his active service with the company spanned fifty-three years, interrupted only by service as an army officer overseas during World War I.

During both world wars, the company built triple expansion steam engines for transports taking supplies to the war zones. In addition, a very large dredge, the "MINDI," was built during World War II for the Panama Canal and is still in operation there today.

Although Ellicott started exporting dredges as early as 1922, its overseas sales became the predominant part of its business following World War II. Today 70 to 80 percent of dredge production is shipped abroad, and Ellicott dredges are now located in more than sixty countries with more than one thousand produced since 1904. Through licensee arrangements, many more dredges have been built to Ellicott designs in such countries as Argentina, India, Japan, and Spain.

In 1957, Ellicott acquired the McConway & Torley Corporation in Pittsburgh, which today is a major supplier of steel couplers and yokes to the railroad industry.

Ellicott technological innovations lead the dredging industry, and its products can be found deepening channels, reclaiming land, digging sand and gravel, mining ores, and creating food-growing areas in such countries as Argentina, Brazil, Egypt, Indonesia, Mexico, the People's Republic of China, and many others.

Equitable Trust Bank

In 1913, Baltimore was awakening to its future. The city's population of 600,000 ranked it as the eighth largest city in the United States, and its growing trade and industrial centers contributed to its importance as a major East Coast port. Baltimore was keenly interested in expansion, new capital, new business, and new ideas. In this atmosphere of optimism and growth, Baltimore welcomed the Munsey Trust Company. Named after Frank A. Munsey, one of its principal founders, the new bank soon changed its name to the Equitable Trust Company.

Today, Equitable Trust is one of the largest banks in Maryland. The story of Equitable's growth, from its $2 million assets in 1913 to today's assets of nearly $2 billion, is the history of an institution served by singularly creative and imaginative leaders.

Frank Munsey believed that a bank must do more than accept deposits and make loans; it must also be part of the community. These were new thoughts in 1913, but they endured and set the tone for Equitable's future.

The first local bank to install open-counter windows, a decision that has also proven symbolic, Equitable Trust became the first bank in the Baltimore area to respond to other customer needs by offering special checking accounts, drive-in facilities, electronic bookkeeping equipment and computerized checking accounts, an overdraft system (Check Command), and the automatic teller machine now known as Harvey Wallbanker®.

Increasingly responsive to the interests of the Baltimore business community, the Equitable Trust Company created Freight Command, a service designed to assist financial activities of shippers and receivers, and it remains the only bank in Maryland to offer this unique service.

During the 1960s and 1970s, Equitable expanded well beyond the Baltimore area to serve the entire state of Maryland from Elkton to southern Maryland, from Gaithersburg to the Eastern Shore. To provide for the orderly development and marketing of a broad range of related financial services to retail and corporate customers throughout Maryland, the Equitable Bancorporation was organized in 1972. This holding company is presently composed of three banks (Columbia Bank and Trust Company, Farmers and Merchants Bank of Hagerstown, and the Equitable Trust Company) which have broadened representation to include eleven Maryland counties as well as the city of Baltimore. The Equitable Trust Company remains the leading bank in the holding company and accounts for more than 85 percent of the total assets of the affiliate group.

Related financial services are provided through Bancorporation's nonbanking affiliates: Investment Counselors of Maryland, founded in 1972; Equitable Financial Corporation, established in 1975 to provide residential second mortgage loans; Equiban Life Insurance Company, and Equitable Bank Realty Corporation.

Since its founding, the Equitable Trust Company has evidenced a strong commitment to the community. More than 90 percent of deposits originate in Maryland, and these deposits are converted into loans and investments that are returned to Maryland residents, communities, and local businesses. The new Equitable Bank Center, bounded by S. Charles, S. Hanover, W. Pratt, and W. Lombard Streets in the heart of Baltimore's Inner Harbor redevelopment area, is a visible sign of Equitable's continuing belief in the economic strength of the Port of Baltimore and the vitality of the Chesapeake Bay Region.

Fidelity and Deposit Company of Maryland

In 1890, while surveyor of the Port of Baltimore, lawyer, businessman, and politician, Edwin Warfield conceived the idea of forming a company which would write fidelity and surety bonds. He found it difficult, however, to convince state legislators to grant him a charter. Traditionally, friends and family were asked to sign a pledge guaranteeing an employee's honesty and promising to reimburse any loss that a company or employer might incur as a result of misappropriation.

The legislators remained unimpressed by this innovative idea until some months later, when the state treasurer disappeared with about $200,000 of public funds. His family and friends lost everything they owned in trying to cover the loss. Shocked legislators hurriedly changed their opinion of Mr. Warfield's idea and granted him a charter.

And so, the Fidelity & Deposit Company was born in June 1890, in a modest office at 7 North Calvert Street with a staff of six and capital of only $200,000. It took just four years for the business to expand into an eight-story building at the corner of Charles and Lexington Streets, and by 1913, fifteen floors were needed to house the growing company. As Mr. Warfield proudly stated in the 1898 Company Report, "The history of Fidelity and Deposit is the history of corporate suretyship." The company's and industry's progress was helped by a bill passed by Congress in 1894 authorizing acceptance of corporate sureties in federal projects and employees. The bill was Mr. Warfield's brainchild and F&D was the first company to be approved under this act.

The company's first president was General Clinton P. Paine. He was succeeded by Lloyd L. Jackson. Edwin Warfield became president in 1893 and held the office until the end of 1919. During the years from 1903 to 1908, Warfield was also governor of Maryland, but he did not sever his connections with F&D. Years later, as he considered the words for his own epitaph, he looked with such pride of the Fidelity and Deposit Company and Governor of Maryland" — in that order!

Over the years, the F&D has headed groups of companies that provided bonding for the construction of the Chesapeake Bay Bridge; the Baltimore Harbor Tunnel; the Golden Gate Bridge; Hoover Dam; the San Francisco-Oakland Bay Bridge; the Coolidge Dam; the N.S. Savannah, the first nuclear-powered passenger and cargo ship; the nation's first underground missile sites; and the Moon Rocket Vehicle Assembly Building at Cape Kennedy.

Well-known people have worked for Fidelity and Deposit. Franklin D. Roosevelt, for example, was vice president of F&D's New York City branch from 1920 to 1928, when he resigned to become governor of New York; Theodore Roosevelt McKeldon, who spent five years with Fidelity and Deposit in the treasury and contract bond departments, was mayor of Baltimore from 1943 to 1947 and governor of Maryland from 1951 to 1959.

In 1969, the F&D joined the American General Group of insurance and financial service companies, one of the largest such groups in the country. Today F&D's bonds and policies are available throughout the nation from thousands of independent insurance agents and brokers, and the company maintains expertly staffed underwriting and claims offices in many cities to deal promptly and efficiently with all its clients.

This photograph of the Fidelity Building, home office of Fidelity and Deposit Company, was taken in the early 1970s

The First National Bank of Maryland

When the forerunner to The First National Bank of Maryland, the Mechanics Bank of Baltimore, opened its doors to customers in 1806, there were only twenty-eight banking institutions in the entire United States. Chartered by the Maryland General Assembly in 1806, ten years to the day after the city of Baltimore was incorporated, Mechanics Bank began with paid-in capital of $640,000. The bank was originated to serve small businesses and enhance the growing industrial life of the Baltimore community. In fact, a provision in the bank's constitution stipulated that nine of the twelve members of the board of directors should be practical mechanics or manufacturers and, furthermore, that the directors should "actually wrought at some mechanical or manufacturing trade for the term of three years at least."

The First National Bank of Maryland was formed from the merger of Mechanics and other Baltimore banking institutions: in 1913 Merchants Bank and Mechanics Bank merged; and in 1928 Merchants National Bank and Citizens National Bank merged to become The First National Bank of Baltimore. That institution became The First National Bank of Maryland in 1962. But before the mergers, there was much history to be made in Baltimore and the forerunners of The First National Bank of Maryland played an integral part in making that history.

Baltimore's most distinguished residents and businessmen were instrumental in the railroad's, as well as the bank's, formation. Mechanics Bank President Philip E. Thomas, along with George Brown, a bank board member and partner in the Baltimore investment house of Alexander Brown & Sons, organized a meeting in 1827 that ultimately led to the formation of the Baltimore & Ohio Railroad. Thomas and Brown presented their idea for a railroad linking Baltimore with midwestern trade routes to the General Assembly in early 1827. The state's legislators approved the plan in February.

Thomas was named president of the new B&O Railroad and Brown was the company's secretary. Brown, along with Johns Hopkins, was also among the founders of Merchants Bank of Baltimore, chartered by the state in 1835 and eventually merged with Mechanics Bank in 1913.

The banking institutions that finally formed First National Bank of Maryland all managed to weather Baltimore's bad times, including the bank panics during the Civil War (which prompted the federal government to pass the National Bank Act of 1863), the Great Depression, and the two world wars. Even the Great Fire of Baltimore in 1904 did not damage

The First National Bank of Maryland evolved from an institution chartered in 1806. Its vault has been equally durable, having survived the disastrous Baltimore fire of 1904

depositors' holdings at Mechanics Bank, despite the fact that the bank building, along with 1,500 others in downtown Baltimore, was destroyed. The bank vault, according to board meeting minutes was "found in absolutely perfect condition . . . containing cash and securities." And the minutes add, "The building alone, [was]lost, and that well insured."

In 1974, the bank formed a holding company, First Maryland Bancorp, another step in the history of a bank which has uniquely displayed its strength and integrity for almost 175 years.

Following its philosophy of balance and discretion, The First National Bank of Maryland has charted a plan of strategic growth. With headquarters at 25 South Charles Street and over 100 facilities in Maryland, First National has assets in excess of $2 billion.

264

General Motors Assembly Division

Assembling automobiles and trucks is not new to the Baltimore area. On October 16, 1934, Baltimore's Mayor Jackson and Chevrolet representative E.A. Nimnicht broke ground for a new Chevrolet and Fisher Body Assembly Plant on Broening Highway in the southeast section of Baltimore. The plant was designed to produce 80,000 cars and trucks a year.

This enormous undertaking was completed in record time. On March 11, 1935, the first day of truck production, three trucks were built. On March 26, 1935, twelve passenger cars were built. The new plant produced a total of 24,885 passenger cars and 6,627 trucks during its first model year. About 2,500 people, many of whom had worked on the construction of the plant, were employed during the first year of operation.

The original plant site covered 45.7 acres and consisted of five buildings, six railroad sidings, driveways, walks, test roads, and a parking lot for employees' cars. The principal unit was the assembly building, which covered 13.5 acres of floor space. Chevrolet occupied two-thirds of the building, and Fisher Body one-third.

Car and truck production was interrupted early in 1942, when the plant was converted to wartime activities. The Chevrolet portion of the plant was operated as a military parts depot where parts were received, processed, and packaged for shipment around the world. The Fisher Body plant became a part of the Eastern Aircraft Division of General Motors Corporation and was assigned the task of assembling fuselages for Grumman carrier-based aircraft.

In August 1945, immediately following the end of the war, the plant was reconverted to automobile and truck production. By 1949, after eleven years of car and truck production, one million units had been assembled at the Baltimore plant.

Although Chevrolet cars and trucks have represented the largest portion of the Baltimore plant's production, other car lines have also been manufactured. The versatility of the plant was tested in 1964 when Buicks, Chevrolets, Oldsmobiles, and Pontiacs were assembled one after another on the same passenger car line. In the ensuing years, the number of car lines produced has changed several times. GMC Truck and Coach Division shared Baltimore's truck production as early as the 1947 model year.

A major change occurred on November 4, 1968, when the Baltimore plant's two separate General Motors units, Fisher Body Division and Chevrolet Motor Division, were unified under the administration of General Motors Assembly Division.

Above:
In 1935, the original Baltimore General Motors plant occupied 45.7 acres on Broening Highway
Top:
Today the Baltimore General Motors Plant covers more than 160 acres with 2.5 million square feet of building floor space

On May 24, 1978, with many of Baltimore's business and civic leaders present, Robert K. Bates, plant manager, and Baltimore Mayor William Donald Schaefer drove the plant's eight-millionth vehicle off the assembly line.

By 1979, the Baltimore General Motors Assembly Division plant site had increased to more than 160 acres with nearly 2.5 million square feet of building floor space. Its 7,000 employees are proud of the cars and trucks produced in Baltimore.

Glauber's Fine Candies

John H. Glauber began a small candy manufacturing and retail operation in Baltimore at 1037 South Hanover Street in 1876. More than a century later, the third generation of the Glauber family participates in the manufacture and sale of fine candies. Modern technology has altered many of the methods utilized by John H. Glauber, but time has failed to change the family tradition of excellence and personal service. The Glauber family operates the second oldest retail candy manufacturing business in the country.

By the time the accompanying photograph of Mr. Glauber's first candy store was taken in 1912, two sons had joined the family enterprise and the business became known as John H. Glauber & Sons. Howard A. Glauber, Sr., and J. Milton Glauber soon helped their father expand his manufacturing and retail operations. Early marketing efforts included family stalls at the Cross Street and Hollins Street markets in Baltimore. The Glaubers also manufactured fine candies for well-known Baltimore department

This photograph of John H. Glauber's first candy store was taken about 1912. Pictured left to right are J. Milton Glauber, John H. Glauber (founder), and Howard A. Glauber, Sr.

stores, neighborhood groceries and bakeries, and other market stalls.

By 1935, the Hanover Street establishment proved inadequate for the growing business. Howard purchased a property at 1020 Regester Avenue in North Baltimore where he could both live and work. Additions to the house accommodated the manufacturing portion of the operation, and a small retail shop was also started. By this time the firm had changed its name to the H.A. Glauber Candy Company.

Upon the death of Howard A. Glauber, Sr., in 1939, his wife, Miriam, and eldest son, Howard A. Glauber, Jr., took over the family business. The third eldest son, Kenneth, joined the firm upon graduation from college.

Under the leadership of this third generation, the Baltimore market operations were continued and expanded. After Baltimore's famed Lexington Market was rebuilt in the early fifties, a new addition was a Glauber's candy stall. Change came in 1963 when Glauber's Fine Candies, Inc., opened its first modern retail establishment at the Yorkridge Shopping Center in Lutherville, Maryland. The shop featured traditional candies manufactured by the Glauber family as well as cards and gifts. By 1965, when Glauber's Fine Candies opened a second retail store in the Perring Plaza Shopping Center, the market operations had become a closed chapter. The success of the modern retail concept was quite evident by 1971, when a third store opened at the Eastpoint Mall.

The Glauber family's modern candy-making operations bear little resemblance to John H. Glauber's original efforts. In fact, much of the early machinery utilized by the founder is on display at the Maryland Academy of Science Industrial Museum, a gift from the company. Yet basic ingredients and recipes remain the same, and there are a few tasks that seem unaltered by time. Howard and Kenneth Glauber still make caramel, fudge, and nougat products through an open-kettle cooking process. Howard Glauber, Jr., still roasts fresh nuts and crushes them with a large old-fashioned rolling pin. All Glauber candies continue to be hand-packaged. The old-time hollow chocolate metal molds have been replaced by today's modern fiberglass. But the end product — the Chris Kringle, Easter Bunnies and Chicks, and the toy shapes — are as tasty and pretty as 100 years ago.

Saturdays and holidays find a fourth generation of Glauber family members at work in the candy kitchen and retail establishments. Residents of Baltimore and the surrounding metropolitan area will enjoy Glauber's fine candies for many years to come.

The Greater Baltimore Committee

Twenty-five years ago, downtown Baltimore was not a city that appeared on a list of "Places to Visit." Urban decay was rampant, affecting not only housing and community development but also the city's commerce, industry, transportation, cultural life, and support services. A single, unified approach to solving Baltimore's problems was sorely lacking.

James Rouse, a young mortgage banker and member of the Citizens Housing and Planning Association, called a meeting to discuss the problems facing the port city's business community. Joining him were his brother, Willard; Robert H. Levi, executive vice president of the Hecht Company; Louis B. Kohn II, vice president and treasurer of Hochschild, Kohn & Co.; and Guy T.O. Hollyday, chairman of the Title Guaranty Company.

The participants at the meeting agreed that worthy projects were failing because they lacked general support. The business community was not providing impetus for change. Realizing that the private sector had to work together with relevant public agencies to reverse the downward trends in Baltimore, the men decided to organize. They modeled their group after the Allegheny Conference of Pittsburgh, Pennsylvania, adopting similar guidelines: cohesive planning, practical goals, and united action to spur renewal efforts. Membership would be limited to the city's top 100 corporate executives, who would focus attention on individual projects designated by the majority of members.

James Rouse outlined the plans and purposes of the proposed Greater Baltimore Committee (GBC) at a meeting chaired by Clarence Miles at the Belvedere Hotel in November 1954. Twenty-five businessmen discussed the potential strength of the private sector and evaluated the goals and plans of the GBC. The majority of those present agreed to the proposed organization, and on January 5, 1955, eighty-three business leaders convened to adopt a charter and elect officers.

The first officers of the Greater Baltimore Committee were chairman, Clarence W. Miles, partner, Miles & Stockbridge; vice-chairman, Thomas B. Butler, president, Mercantile-Safe Deposit and Trust Company; treasurer, Jerald C. Hoffberger, president, the National Brewing Company; and secretary, Daniel A. Lindley, president, the Canton Company.

Today the Greater Baltimore Committee continues the aggressive plan of action established in 1955. Using a catalytic approach in addressing the city's urban revitalization, the GBC has achieved numerous successes, among them the Civic Center, the Charles Center, the In-

ner Harbor, continued efforts to secure dredging of the harbor, and support for improving public education through the innovative Adopt-A-School Program. The group also encourages the building and maintenance of transportation facilities in the area, be they highways, rapid transit systems, or air service terminals.

In January 1978, the Chamber of Commerce of Metropolitan Baltimore merged with the Greater Baltimore Committee to become Baltimore's cohesive business voice in community affairs. While many of the GBC's original members remain, the organization is now supported by hundreds of business leaders who volunteer both time and energy. A paid professional staff keeps the GBC focused on its principal aims. Financed by the membership dues of area businesses, GBC develops and promotes programs that directly affect the economic and social vitality of the region.

The GBC's strength derives from its ability to represent a consensus of a diverse array of interests on issues of importance. Marked by its willingness to tackle tough public policy issues confronting metropolitan Baltimore, the GBC remains an influential voice on matters ranging from the future of Baltimore's port to that of public education.

The key to the organization's vitality is the dedication and commitment of Baltimore's top business leaders and the ongoing support of a broad base of the region's businesses.

Parts excerpted from Opening Days: Memoirs of Clarence Miles

Greiner Engineering Sciences, Inc.

I n 1908, John E. Greiner left his position as assistant chief engineer of the Baltimore and Ohio Railroad and began a new career in private practice. Since that time, the organization which he founded has been continuously engaged in providing professional engineering services to public and private clients.

Many of Mr. Greiner's early clients were railroad companies whose operations crisscrossed the eastern United States. His services included the design and construction engineering of fixed and movable bridges, ore docks, and coal piers.

With the development of the country's highway system, Mr. Greiner adapted his focus to include highway bridges. Rail and highway bridges engineered by Greiner spanned the Ohio, Allegheny, Monongahela, James, Rappahannock, Potomac, and Susquehanna, providing major crossings for both modes of transportation.

By the late 1930s, J.E. Greiner Company had begun to serve as consulting engineer for the planning, financing, design, and construction of revenue bond transportation projects financed by toll highway users. The original Pennsylvania Turnpike, the first modern major toll highway in the nation, was a Greiner project. The Baltimore-based firm also provided similar services during the development of the Ohio Turnpike, the Indiana Toll Road, and all of Maryland's toll facilities. Additionally, Greiner provided continuing services for their operation and maintenance.

With the advent of World War II, Greiner provided services for the design and construction of numerous military bases and installations. The firm grew in size and extended the scope of its activities. Today, Greiner Engineering Sciences encompasses such diverse fields as highways and expressways, railroads, bridges, tunnels, buildings, airports, mass transportation, marine terminals and related facilities, land use, flood control, sewer and water, highway and airfield lighting, housing, and commercial and industrial development.

The firm has also developed a reputation for leadership in the area of environmental studies and assessments. Greiner engineers wrote the Federal Aviation Administration's guidelines for preparation of environmental impact statements, and their expertise in the field is widely known and respected.

For almost seventy-five years, Greiner has participated in the development of Baltimore area transportation facilities, including the Potomac and Susquehanna River Bridges, Chesapeake Bay Bridges, the Baltimore Harbor Tunnel, the John F. Kennedy Memorial Highway, the Fran-

cis Scott Key Bridge, and many others.

Responsive to growth in the southeastern United States, Greiner established a second principal office in Tampa, Florida, in 1957. Since that time, such notable projects as the Tampa International Airport, the Orlando International Airport, the Space Shuttle Landing Facility at the Kennedy Space Center, and the fishing port at Vacamonte, Panama, have been added to the impressive list of Greiner accomplishments.

The firm became a subsidiary of Easco Corporation of Baltimore when it joined that company in 1969. The present permanent staff of about 350 employees includes approximately 280 professional and technical personnel. Since its founding in Baltimore in 1908, Greiner engineers have performed services in thirty-eight states and territories of the United States and in twenty-nine other nations.

The Greiner organization looks forward to a continued role in Baltimore's development and future.

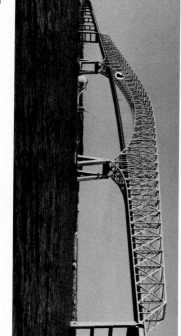

Top:
Although Greiner's early clients were railroad companies, the firm adapted with the advent of the modern highway system. Pictured here is the Howard Street Bridge in Baltimore, completed in 1939

Above:
For almost seventy-five years, Greiner Engineering Sciences has grown with and participated in the development of Baltimore's transportation facilities. One of the company's recent projects is the Francis Scott Key Bridge, which crosses Baltimore's Outer Harbor and closes the Beltway

Hamburger's

When 20-year-old Isaac Hamburger moved to Baltimore from Niedenberg, Germany, he became a clerk in a clothing store owned by Philip Herzberg. In 1849, at age twenty-four, Isaac married Bertha Hamburger and, a year later, left Mr. Herzberg to open his own small shop on Harrison Street. Though it began as little more than an eight-by-eight-foot wooden shanty abutting the office of the Justice of the Peace, the fledgling store brought its customers back year after year.

By 1855, Hamburger's had grown so much that it was moved to a larger building on West Pratt Street, where Isaac began a wholesale trade, as well as maintained his retail business. In the years that followed, the company had to move nearly a dozen times as it continued to flourish and expand.

In 1869, Isaac's first son, Samuel, entered the business at age fifteen. A year later, his 13-year-old brother, Manes, joined the firm. At that time, the starting salary for Hamburger's employees was one dollar for a 10-hour day. During the slow season, salesmen were sent "on the road" to generate the wholesale business.

For many years, "Ike," as Isaac was affectionately known to his employees, allowed only handmade clothing to be produced in his shop, resisting the use of a mechanical sewing machine. It wasn't until son Henry became a member of the firm in 1885 that the first sewing machine was purchased for $185. Just three years later, the company started the manufacture of ready-to-wear clothes and began to operate a nationwide mail-order business.

By the 1890s, the firm had added branch stores in Washington, D.C., and Wilmington, Delaware. Hamburger's became widely known for its "selection of the finest foreign and American woolens and suitings, made up in the most fashionable styles, and finished in the most elaborate manner." The company opened a large department store on Howard Street in 1894. With more than 100 employees in the main store and 300 others in branch stores, Hamburger's still continues to grow.

The Great Baltimore Fire of 1904 crept to within one block of the Howard Street location. Soon after, the store was sold and a handsome, eight-story building was erected at the corner of Baltimore and Hanover Streets. Its upper floors were devoted to manufacturing and custom tailoring, while on the first three floors, clothing, general haberdashery, and men's accessories were sold.

After Isaac's death in 1909, Samuel became president and remained in this post until his death in 1918.

Today, after more than 125 years of continuous service, Hamburger's is Baltimore's oldest clothing retailer with

over thirteen stores and a distribution center. Customer care is still of paramount importance, and Hamburger's employees make sure they still retain Isaac's high standards of fine apparel with an emphasis on personal service.

Isaac Hamburger and Sons, Inc., as it was known at the turn of the century, moved to the corner of Baltimore and Hanover Streets in 1905 and then to Charles Center in 1963

Hartman, McLean & Schmidt, Inc.

Hartman, McLean & Schmidt, Inc., demonstrated a commitment to Baltimore with the total rehabilitation of the Canton House, located at 300 Water Street. In 1978, the structure was designated for inclusion in the National Historic Register (Photo circa 1925)

Since its inception in 1943, Hartman, McLean & Schmidt, Inc. (HMS), a large multiline insurance agency, has pledged its commitment to the growth of Baltimore City.

As part of this commitment, the agency purchased Canton House, an impressive colonial structure located at 300 Water Street overlooking the Inner Harbor. Since the early 1920s, this building has been a well-known Baltimore landmark and has played an integral role in the growth of the Port of Baltimore. In September 1978, HMS was honored to accept designation of their headquarters for inclusion in the National Historic Register.

Indeed, HMS's growth and development have paralleled the Inner Harbor's expansion and the city's quest for greater national recognition. The port city's continuing progress is reflected in the agency's expanding services to the business community of Baltimore. As these businesses have grown, so has HMS through its modern technology and addition of office facilities in the Washington area. Although HMS has been a leader in future planning, it has never relinquished identity with its historic heritage.

Throughout its history, Hartman, McLean & Schmidt, Inc., has specialized in construction bonding and is recognized as the leading contract bond agency in this region. This achievement, coupled with its evolution as a primary commercial and personal lines market, enables the agency to occupy a place of leadership among independent insurance agencies.

In addition to its capabilities in the property, casualty, and surety fields, HMS has become literally a full-service market for financial protection services. The agency now houses a subsidiary, HMS Financial Services, Inc., devoted exclusively to the protection of life, health, hospitalization, and estate planning.

HMS has the flexibility to operate broadly within its field through its association with every major carrier and organization in the insurance and bonding industry. Employing the team approach to client services, HMS encourages direct contact between its professional staff and their clients. Knowledge of insurance regulations and requirements is routinely coupled with a working knowledge of the client's business; extensive research and on-site familiarization form the basis of insurance recommendations. HMS's personnel are given every advantage in upgrading their knowledge through educational programs and the utilization of the agency's complete up-to-date library.

Almost anything of value comes within the range of HMS expertise. The firm insures general contractors and subcontractors, individuals and institutions. This range extends from buildings under construction and completed buildings to manufacturers, retailers, shopping centers, and apartment houses, in addition to homes, boats, and cars.

Although services are provided mainly in the mid-Atlantic region, the firm is active along the entire length of the Eastern Seaboard and abroad.

Hochschild, Kohn and Company

The Reconstruction era following the Civil War was a difficult and stimulating period for American business. When Bernhard Kohn, a German immigrant, came to Baltimore and established B. Kohn and Brother, a wholesale dry goods and notion business, he began a Kohn family tradition of high standards that has been carried on by Hochschild, Kohn and Company, one of Baltimore's finest department stores.

Upon the death of Bernhard Kohn in 1891, his eldest son, Louis B. Kohn, became head of B. Kohn and Brother. The dry goods business had prospered in the late nineteenth century, and while Louis managed the business, his younger brother, Benno, traveled for a time purchasing merchandise. But Benno Kohn was a retailer at heart and soon began looking for an opportunity and a location.

When he approached his brother with a plan to open a retail store at the corner of Howard and Lexington Streets in Baltimore, he discovered that Louis had been discussing the same possibility with Max Hochschild, a family friend and local retail merchant. Louis and Benno Kohn and Max Hochschild each contributed an equal amount of capital for the initial investment, and on November 15, 1897, Hochschild, Kohn and Company opened for business amid great fanfare. An opening advertisement stated: "Baltimore and Progression are synonymous terms and our progression will be based on your patronage . . . ."

The store promised its new patrons "good honest values and honest prices." The first building was a four-story, 6,000-square-foot structure. The store introduced a one-price policy, an innovation when bargaining was an accepted practice, as well as generous credit and monthly statements.

Through the purchase and lease of properties adjacent to the original location, the store was enlarged, and by 1912, the retail establishment had grown to six stories, occupying an area bound by Howard, Lexington, and Clay Streets and Kimmel Alley. A nine-story service building, which connected to the main store, was soon constructed on Clay Street.

By 1922, the firm included Walter and Irving Kohn, sons of Louis. When Max Hochschild sold his interest in 1926, Walter Sondheim, an expert in personnel and management from the store's beginning, and Walter and Irving Kohn assumed management responsibilities.

When the Great Depression hit, sales dropped almost 50 percent. It was a difficult time for Hochschild, Kohn and Company, but by 1935, when Benno's son, Martin B. Kohn, joined the management, the store began a period of gradual recovery and improvement. Howard Street store

Above:
When Baltimore streets were paved with cobblestones, Kohn yellow and black horse-drawn wagons lined Lexington Street twice each day until 1917
Left:
The main store at Howard and Lexington Streets is shown here during World War II. Following the War, Hochschild's was ready for expansion, and branches replaced this structure by 1977

windows were rebuilt, air conditioning was installed, and Hochschild's introduced new concepts in merchandising that were soon followed by competitors. The 5-day, 38-hour work week and evening openings to accommodate working women were novel ideas in the 1940s.

After World War II, the store was ready for expansion. Under the leadership of Martin B. Kohn, who served as president from 1945 to 1965, and Louis B. Kohn II, the company opened its first major branch in the Baltimore area in Edmondson Village in 1946. The Belvedere branch opened in 1948, and by the late 1950s, the branch system included stores at Eastpoint and Harundale. In 1959, the Brager building was acquired and connected to the main store via a bridge over Clay Street.

The store was sold to an investment company, Diversified Retailing in 1966, continuing operations under the same executive management. Three years later, it was purchased by its present owners, Supermarkets General Corporation, and currently operates as a division of this retail concern. Although the original downtown establishment closed its doors in 1977, expansion efforts continued. Today Hochschild, Kohn and Company includes eight branch department stores in the Greater Baltimore area.

Hutzler's

In 1858, Abram Hutzler was just a boy when he took over a retail dry goods business from his brother-in-law, Elkan Bamberger, on the first floor of the Bamberger residence at Howard Street and Clay Street. The "M. Hutzler" over the door actually referred to Abram's father, Moses, because Abram was too young to obtain credit in his own name. After establishing the Howard Street store, Abram and his brother Charles opened a wholesale business on Baltimore Street, leaving the youngest brother, David, a boy just out of school, in charge of the retail store. Both enterprises were owned jointly by all three brothers. Following the Civil War, the retail trade grew to such proportions that the brothers discontinued the wholesale business to concentrate all their efforts on the Howard Street store.

In 1868, when bargaining was the rule, the Hutzler brothers pioneered the one-price policy, which was to revolutionize retailing in the nation. An employee fringe benefit program was started in 1870, when dimes were given to women clerks to buy apples. This concern for the employees' health eventually developed into other employee benefit features.

Hutzler's started a customer delivery service in 1874, the first in Baltimore. With the growth of business in the late 1880s the Hutzler store at Howard and Clay Streets gave way to the majestic new "Palace Building." Designed by Baldwin and Pennington, leading Baltimore architects, this imposing stone structure with a handsomely carved facade rose to a height of five floors.

Hutzler's was one of 100 stores across the country to be chosen by *Harper's Bazaar* as a "Fashion Store of the Century." Although merchandising is Hutzler's principal function, members of the firm have always recognized their responsibility to the community in civic affairs and cultural activities. During World War II, Hutzler's entered enthusiastically into the bond-selling campaign. It was the first store in the country to install a bond window conveniently located to attract purchasers. Hutzler's numerous community interests have endeared the company to all Baltimoreans.

As Baltimore has grown in population, Hutzler's has also grown, in the city as well as the suburbs, to meet the demands of its customers. In the 1970s, changing with the times, Hutzler's joined the revitalization of the Inner Harbor with a new store in the Equitable Building, and additional stores are planned. W. Austin Kenly, the first nonfamily president, continues to manage Hutzler's with the same enthusiasm, imagination, and concern of his predecessors — the five generations of Hutzler's.

Far Left:
The original Hutzler Brothers (Abram, David, and Charles) were teenagers when they started to manage their first retail store

Left:
If the ghosts of nineteenth century Baltimoreans returned today, they would have no trouble recognizing the Palace Building of Hutzler's — it looks much the same as when it was built in 1888

Industrial Realty Company, Inc.

The Industrial Realty Company has been helping businesses and industries select their locations in the Greater Baltimore Metropolitan Area since 1947. Maintaining an up-to-date inventory of available sites and buildings, the company is expert in marketing industrial property. Currently serving as president is J. Carey Martien, the fourth generation of the Martien family to pursue a real estate career. The story of the Industrial Realty Company, however, is the story of his father, William Martien.

While serving as a naval flight instructor in Florida during World War II, William Martien learned that his father had sold the family business, William Martien and Company, begun by his grandfather in the 1880s. William had worked for the firm and fully intended to return to it after the war. A.J. Harris, a Baltimore pioneer in the one-story building concept, convinced him to return to Baltimore anyway and gave him the confidence to begin his own business.

Lawrence Chambers, a fraternity brother and close friend, rented him a small room in the 3600 block of Roland Avenue, which he furnished with a card table, chair, and telephone. The rent was ten dollars a month, when he could afford it. Here, Martien decided to study what he most enjoyed: "warehouses, factories, and industrial real estate." Martien named his new enterprise the Industrial Realty Company.

In the same year, William Martien began a task that was

William Martien, after serving as a naval aviator during World War II, returned to his native city and established the Industrial Realty Company. Long before computer technology had reached the small businessman, Martien had surveyed and manually catalogued every industrial site location within twenty miles of downtown Baltimore

to assure his future success: "I began to conduct a complete site survey of every industrial property within twenty miles of Baltimore." By the time data processing became available to the small business, he was able to provide clients with complete site information (including plats, topography, utilities, transportation, and zoning) within five minutes.

William Martien became a member of the Society of Industrial Realtors in 1948 and served both as a board member and a regional vice president. In 1961 he became the founding president of the Maryland-Washington chapter of this national professional organization. (J. Carey Martien served as president of the chapter from 1977 to 1978.) It was during a Chicago meeting of the Society of Industrial Realtors that William Martien "decided to invest in what I knew best." The year was 1957, and the Industrial Realty Company was considered expert in its field. Gradually acquiring interest in many Baltimore area industrial properties, often in return for developing the land to its best advantage, William Martien developed the future of the Industrial Realty Company, which today participates in a number of joint ventures involving Maryland's future as a commercial center.

The firm, now located at the Village of Cross Keys, was once located in a basement office at 13 West 25th Street. When Coleman Hedley, one of the company's most colorful salesmen, was asked if he worked for a Martien at a prestigious downtown location, he replied: "No, I work for the Martien in the basement on 25th Street."

"The backbone and the mainstay of the firm for twenty years, however, was the late Bayard H. Waterbury," notes Martien. "He was a first class appraiser."

In 1972, William Martien transferred the management of the Industrial Realty Company to J. Carey Martien, who continues the work begun by his father. "Land is an irreplaceable commodity," explains William Martien, currently serving as chairman of the board. "We all have a responsibility to utilize this resource to its best advantage."

J. J. Haines & Co., Inc.

Captain John J. Haines served in the Confederate Army under the command of General Stonewall Jackson until he was taken prisoner of war in the spring of 1862. Despite deplorable prison conditions, Haines was not idle during his two years of captivity. He occupied himself with thoughts of the future, for he had seen the devastation caused by the Civil War. He knew that his family in Virginia had suffered tremendous losses and that life at home would not be as it was. Much strength and work would be needed to return home and help with the restoration of the South, so he took immediate action on his plans to start anew and establish his own business. He began to accumulate the necessary capital through the only means available to prisoners of war: he played poker with the Union guards who were well-supplied with cash!

Haines left prison on foot with $800 sewn into his belt. When he arrived in Virginia, he invested the money in a general store near Upperville and set to work learning all he could about store management. As time passed and his store prospered, Haines recognized the lucrative possibilities of becoming a wholesaler of woodenware, a rapidly growing area of business.

Traveling to Baltimore many times on buying trips for his general store, Haines had the opportunity to study its business climate. He saw that the city was the prime supplier for the ravaged South, and that it welcomed the Southerners who flocked there in search of a new beginning. He decided to sell the store in Upperville and secure a building at 27 South Howard Street in Baltimore.

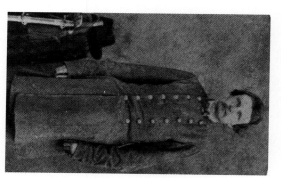

John J. Haines proudly wore the Confederate uniform sneaked to him through Union lines under the skirts of his mother and sisters

The move was a good one; his business was an instant success. Haines quickly learned the ins and outs of sole proprietorship — he met demands, ran his store efficiently, and treated his customers well. Only a few years later he was ready to expand. He moved into adjoining buildings at 29 and 31 South Howard Street and began to manufacture as well as sell wholesale goods.

The J.J. Haines, Company employed thirty-five people, including eight salesmen who covered southern territories with the company's diversified line: brushes, twine, matches, buckets, paper, pipes, and other dry goods. The company continued to prosper, and by 1893 the staff had increased dramatically, both in Baltimore and with traveling salesmen in the field. The founder's son, Harvey Lee Haines, soon joined the firm, as did Casper T. Marston, Haines' son-in-law, who had been serving an apprenticeship with the company. Thus began the line of a succession of family members who still manage the Haines Company today.

As the company grew, one of the most important developments came with the addition of the floor covering department under the direction of Marston. Inexpensive grass matting from the Orient was introduced to replace the fine carpets that were cut up by Union soldiers to use as saddle blankets or that were fashioned into trousers for men returning from the war in rags. To get the jump on competing East Coast importers who shipped by stream, each spring Haines leased a fleet of fast clipper ships to bring rolls of matting "around the Horn" to Baltimore. Haines also carried a rag carpet known as "Hit and Miss." The rugs were made from strips of cloth sewn together and rolled into large balls for dyeing (hence, the hit and miss effect). Enterprising Southerners tacked the rugs over evenly spread straw to achieve a softness reminiscent of fine Brussels carpets.

In 1900, after twenty-six years of leading his company, John J. Haines retired and Casper Marston took over the helm. The floor covering department began to dominate the business as the demand for woodenware gave way to public demand for galvanized iron articles. By 1909 the company had become the largest wholesaler of floor coverings in the East and moved to larger headquarters at 31 Hopkins Place. In order to continue the company's expansion, Marston added a variety of new floor coverings to their stock: oil cloth, wool carpeting, and linoleum. This successful growth did not go unnoticed in the world of commerce, and the Haines Company was chosen by the Armstrong Cork Company to be one of their original distributors.

World War I brought an end to Haines' matting business, but the company continued to thrive with domestic
floor coverings and some of the household items that the
company had always carried. The Great Depression,
however, brought changes in the company's sales policy.
Because salesmen were often unable to travel to distant
customers, many sales were lost. John Haines Marston, the
third-generation president, met the challenge of sales
difficulties by introducing branch warehouses to bring
merchandise closer to his customers. The first opened in
Richmond in 1935, followed closely by Roanoke, Bristol,
and Norfolk. The company's reputation, established since
1874, for quality merchandise, sound business practices,
and cooperation with customers carried Haines through
the long depression years. By the outbreak of World War
II, all Haines warehouses, now including Goldsboro,
North Carolina, soon to be joined by Florence, South
Carolina, were fully stocked with floor coverings, and
business was booming once again.

In the early years of World War II, Haines was able to
keep its customers supplied only by liquidating all stock.
As goods became more and more scarce, Haines assured
each customer that he would get his fair share of available
merchandise based upon past purchase volume, and this
policy was adhered to throughout the war.

At the end of the war there began another period of expansion, enlargement, and innovation that would affect
the future of the entire wholesale operation. In 1950,
under the guidance of another grandson of J.J. Haines,
treasurer Jack Marston, the company moved its home office and warehouse to 4800 East Monument Street in
Baltimore. This gave the firm access to major highway arteries as more and more goods were transported by truck
rather than by ship or rail. The warehouse was the first
single-story warehouse in Baltimore with a palletization
and forklift system to facilitate easy storage and retrieval of
floor tile.

John Marston always kept an eye open for new trends
that would increase efficiency. He and executive vice
president Linwood Tunnell introduced specialized selling
in the carpet and resilient flooring divisions of the company. Salesmen were given a broad education in the flooring field and were then trained to become specialists in
either the carpeting or the hard surface flooring area. Innovations in marketing included the "Mobile Showcase"

program produced in conjunction with Armstrong. These
shows, pioneered by Armstrong, proved so successful
when introduced in the Baltimore area that they were
taken on a tour of over 125 cities in the South. For the
company's 100th anniversary extravaganza, the show
featured John Marston, chairman of the board; Lee
Marston, president; Mort Creech, vice president of the
carpet division (also a great-grandson of J.J. Haines); Newt
Krabbe, vice president of the resilient division; and starred
the Armstrong Players. (Additional officers now include T.
Nelson Gilbert, financial vice president; James L. Rupert,
vice president, operations; and James F. Bancroft, con-
troller.)

The company has always maintained that a wholesaler's
key responsibility is to help the retailer make bigger prof-

Left:
Militia guards patrolled the
Baltimore business district in the
aftermath of the Great Fire of 1904.
J.J. Haines and Company
(background) escaped the flames
as the fire, which had started
across the street, spread in the
opposite direction
Below:
This building at 33-35 Hopkins
Place served as J.J. Haines &
Company's third home in its first
seventy-five years

its. One method of achieving this goal is to employ financial experts to provide advice and consultation for the retailers. Another method emphasizes the training of sales representatives in areas of retail selling so they can offer help to retailers on promotional campaigns, department layout, and floor displays. In the 1960s and 1970s, this training expanded to include special workshops in sales training and credit management which were offered to retailers themselves.

These practices point to the basic business policy of the Haines Company: the sale is not complete until the merchandise is profitably moved from the retailer's store to a satisfied customer. The company continues to maintain this policy through innovative systems and market research and, as a result, in 1979 added Bruce Hardwood Floors to supplement the Armstrong resilient flooring and carpet lines. Haines believes that a close bond between wholesaler and retailers is a sound business practice. Haines looks forward with great confidence and optimism to the completion of its second century of service.

Right:
Lee Marston is president of J.J. Haines and Company and great-grandson of the founder

Bottom Right:
Mort Creech is executive vice president and great-grandson of the founder

Below:
John Marston, grandson of the founder, was active in the management of Haines for over fifty years until his death late in 1979

The Kirk Stieff Company

In 1815, Samuel Kirk, a young silversmith, opened a small shop in Baltimore, thus giving birth to Samuel Kirk & Son, Incorporated, the oldest makers of silverware in the United States. Recently, Samuel Kirk & Son joined forces with another fine, well-established Baltimore firm to become the Kirk Stieff Company. Though new in name, the company continues to assure the country's fine quality sterling heritage.

Born in 1793 in Doylestown, Pennsylvania, Samuel Kirk was a direct descendant of Jonah Kirke whose mark is registered in Cripps' *Old English Plate* in Goldsmith's Hall, England. At the age of seventeen, young Kirk was apprenticed to James Howell, a silversmith in Philadelphia. From the beginning, Samuel Kirk brought to America the tradition of fine silver artistry which his ancestors had practiced in England. A distinctive, imaginative flair characterized many Kirk pieces. Some of his earliest work bears the stamp K&S, evidence of his short partnership with a man named Smith.

Only five years after he opened his shop, Samuel Kirk introduced a form of silver decoration practiced by the Romans on their shields, now known as Kirk's Repoussé. The name was derived from a French term meaning "raised from beneath." After rough outlines are sketched on the outside of the piece, the design is raised from the reverse side by means of a foot-powered "snarling iron" which transfers hammer blows to a long steel rod capable of reaching the inside surfaces of such items as goblets and cups. The piece is then filled with hot tar and pitch which, when cool, provide resiliency for the succeeding hammer blows on the decorated surface. Small tools, tapped by a hammer, deftly provide the flower and foliage designs in sharp relief. Repoussé is often now referred to as "Baltimore Silver." Hand chasing, for which Kirk is famous, is one of the oldest and most exacting art forms still in practice today.

In 1846, Samuel Kirk's son, Henry Childe Kirk, joined the firm as a partner, and the house name changed to Samuel Kirk & Son.

Kirk silverware creations have always been among the proud possessions of illustrious personages, including Jerome Bonaparte, Charles Carroll, Robert E. Lee, and Jefferson Davis. When Lafayette visited Baltimore in 1824, he ordered two neo-classic Kirk goblets which he presented to his Maryland host, David Williamson.

In 1906, the citizens of Maryland raised funds to buy a silver service from Samuel Kirk & Son for presentation to the U.S.S. *Maryland*. Composed of forty-eight pieces, the set displays more than 200 Maryland scenes and is

regarded as one of the most distinctive masterpieces of silversmithing in existence.

During its growth through generations of American history, the Kirk Company has survived fires, wars, panics, and major depressions. Today, S. Kirk Millspaugh represents the generations that have given direct and personal supervision to the creation of fine silverware and follows a heritage of developing new products and designs to keep pace with modern tastes.

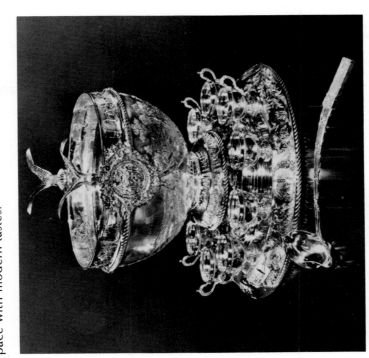

Above:
In 1906, the citizens of Maryland raised funds to buy a silver service for the U.S.S. Maryland
Left:
Joseph S. Student demonstrates the Repousse technique for decorating Silver. Courtesy James Karmrodt Lightner

Koppers Company, Inc.

S ailor and Canton, the cast-iron dogs which flank the entrance of Koppers Engineered Metal Products Group and its subsidiary, Environmental Elements Corporation, are talismans of the firm's prosperity. When, some years ago, these Newfoundland forerunners of the Chesapeake Bay retrievers were removed during the redesign of the office building on Scott Street, the hard times that followed were directly credited by some to the absence of the dogs. They were immediately re-enshrined and prosperity reigned once again. When the new office building was completed in 1975, Canton and Sailor were placed at the entrance to welcome visitors.

In the 1830s, the firm (known then as Bartlett-Hayward, after Edward S. Bartlett and Jonas and George M. Hayward) introduced the Latrobe Stove, sometimes called the Baltimore Heater, from which was developed the conventional hot-air system we use to heat our homes today. The company was to grow and become America's largest builder of gas holders and gas plant equipment. The firm's architectural iron business mushroomed into nationwide prominence in 1853. The Peabody Library in Baltimore displays the designs and castings of the Bartlett-Hayward Company, some of the finest examples of the cast-iron architectural era.

The company was also instrumental in developing and manufacturing munitions, which were essential to Ameri-

can armies during World War I. Following the war, the company's munitions plant was closed, and the Bartlett-Hayward Company, under the direction of Howard Bruce, successfully entered into new manufacturing fields. One acquisition was the American Hammered Piston Ring Company. With the aid of other acquisitions, the company continued to expand.

The Bartlett-Hayward Company was purchased by Kop-

pers Company, Inc., in 1927 and is presently part of its Engineered Metal Products Group. A member of *Fortune Magazine's* 500, Koppers is a diversified manufacturing concern headquartered in Pittsburgh. It has 249 manufacturing facilities selling more than 100 industrial products in thirteen primary markets.

Koppers Engineered Metal Products Group designs and manufactures such products as processing machinery and power transmission products, piston rings and seals, machinery for making corrugated containers, and systems for air-cleaning, air-handling, sound control, water treatment, and solid-waste handling and disposal. The combined activities employ approximately 6,000 people in thirty-nine locations around the world. There are five

manufacturing plants in the Baltimore metropolitan area. Thomas M. St. Clair, president, directs Koppers Engineered Metal Products Group. Donald L. DeVries is senior vice president of Koppers Company and is headquartered in Baltimore. His participation in Baltimore civic activities personifies the spirit of the firm — community interests and concerns as diversified as those of the company's founders and pioneers.

Lacy Foundries, Inc.

In the aftermath of the Civil War, 1865, five men formed an iron foundry on Block Street near Fells Point. The business did not prosper. James J. Lacy, the businessman of the group, bought out the others and retained a molder, Robert Beatty. The business soon blossomed. The foundry is now entering its fifth generation of Lacy management and descendants of Beatty have continued at Lacy as molders for over a century.

The foundry originally supplied household metal products, machinery cylinders for steam engines, ornamental iron fronts for buildings, and water pipe for the growing needs of Baltimore. It also provided cast kettles and separation pans to the Shot Tower. In time, the number of molders grew to eighteen. Their efforts included protecting the foundry roofs against airborne burning debris during the Great Baltimore Fire of 1904.

The son of James Lacy, Joseph, managed the business from 1906 to 1924. He was followed by his son, James, who presided over the firm from 1924 to 1950. Baltimore

Following the war, water and gas utility covers were major products and most are still in place along many Baltimore streets. Third generation James Lacy also found time for Maryland politics. He was elected comptroller of the state of Maryland in 1948.

Joseph, the son of James, assumed control of the foundry in 1956. During his stewardship the foundry has been modernized, a complete pattern shop capability added, new casting processes perfected, and a broader customer base established, one that reaches out beyond the limits of Baltimore. To serve this expanded market, Joseph purchased the Pennsylvania Bronze Foundry of Harrisburg, Pennsylvania, in 1973. The Lacy Foundries family has grown to fifty employees. They are providing castings for heavy-duty machinery manufacturers and buoy castings. The financial base and casting capabilities of the firm are, thus, stronger and broader than they have ever been in contrast to the general decline of privately owned foundries throughout the United States.

Above:
President Joseph J. Lacy and his son, Joseph J. Lacy, Jr., represent the fourth and fifth generation of Lacy's at the foundry
Left:
Molders and other company personnel pose in front of the Lacy foundry in the late 1800s

shipyards were major customers during these periods. As the Baltimore shipyard industry grew, the Lacy foundry grew. A brass foundry was added in 1925 and the plant enlarged to a triangle encompassed by Wills, Block, and Philpot Streets.

The growth culminated in a seven-day, 24-hour operation during World War II, when the foundry was casting large cylinders, columns, and pistons for Liberty ships.

Joseph, Jr., the fifth generation Lacy member, is now serving his apprenticeship. He recently assisted in the installation of a sophisticated air pollution control system. While aware of stringent government regulations affecting the operation of the foundry, he nonetheless is eagerly anticipating continued growth. He intends to build on the foundry's 115 years of customer service, a Lacy family tradition perfected over five generations.

The Legal Profession of Baltimore

In this volume on the two-and-one-half centuries of Baltimore history, the large numbers of people and the role of economics justify the emphasis given to commerce and industry. Yet, just as important to the fabric of life in Baltimore have been the fundamental threads of the professions: religion, medicine, education, arts, and the law. Weinberg and Green is one of many law firms that has made substantial civic, professional, and governmental contributions nurturing and sustaining Baltimore's impact on America over the years.

Baltimore history abounds with the names of explorers and soldiers, shipowners and ship captains, engineers and builders, merchants and financiers, but every generation also featured lawyers who furthered Baltimore's growth from village to town to city to today's vast metropolis.

The Criminal Courts building was constructed in 1896 to 1900; at the laying of its cornerstone on June 25, 1896, Senator William Pinkney Whyte declared his hopes that the building would be used in memory of such noted lawyers and judges in Baltimore history as Dulany, Pinkney, Martin, Wirt, Johnson, Steele, and Wallis, men whose accomplishments in government, war, and politics added distinguished merit to the profession of law.

On January 8, 1900, John Prentiss Poe dedicated the courthouse in a speech containing this passage about Baltimore's legal profession:

We cherish with just pride the great work of our past judges and constantly go to their weighty judgments for strength and inspiration. We exult in the memory of the illustrious leaders of our Bar of the generations that are gone. We treasure the records and traditions of their commanding eloquence and preserve with care the proofs of their high moral and intellectual endowments as amongst the best of our possessions.

In the succeeding generations of the twentieth century, Baltimore lawyers and judges have carried forward these same traditions.

Since 1900, the distinguished names of Latrobe, Ritchie, Soper, Gorter, Dennis, O'Dunne, Straus, Rayner, Gans, Machen, France, Sobeloff, Niles, Curran, Nice, Perlman, McKeldin, and dozens of other noted lawyers have graced Baltimore's Bench and Bar; many law firms of today count these names amongst their forebears and founders.

The partners and associates of Weinberg and Green are proud to belong to the Bar of Baltimore, distinguished by past and present lawyers who have contributed to the profession's continued impact upon the life of their community.

Governor Albert C. Ritchie, Leonard Weinberg, and Attorney General (and later U.S. Solicitor General) Philip B. Perlman planned strategy on the floor of the 1932 Democratic National Convention, in an effort to have Ritchie nominated as Presidential candidate. Photo courtesy the Baltimore Sun and Washington Star

Legg Mason Wood Walker, Incorporated

At the determined young age of twenty-five, George Mackubin decided he knew enough about the stock and investment business in Baltimore to start his own company. In 1899, he borrowed $300 to buy a seat on the Baltimore Stock Exchange and rented a single desk in the stock exchange building. His firm was appropriately called George Mackubin & Company. Although his name is no longer reflected in the title, Mackubin started what is today one of Baltimore's oldest and largest investment houses, Legg Mason Wood Walker, Incorporated.

It was at the turn of the century, only a year after its founding, that Mackubin took on G. Clem Goodrich as a partner and the firm of Mackubin, Goodrich & Company installed a stock board for its customers. Board boys were hired to chalk up the latest prices, but the job was subject to frequent fluctuations, and board boys didn't last long.

Young John C. Legg, Jr., however, not only lasted, but went on to become a partner and driving force in the firm until his retirement in 1960. He was employed in 1900 and was almost immediately taken off the stock board and given more responsibilities as a bookkeeper. He was made a partner in 1905, a year after the firm's first substantial setback. That setback was the Great Fire of Baltimore, which destroyed nearly all of the downtown area in February 1904. The firm lost all its books and records with the exception of one ledger.

After the fire, the determined young company rented the second and third floors over a florist shop at 318 North Charles Street until 1917, when it moved to 111 East Redwood Street. Today, offices are nearby at 7 East Redwood

Street in a 20-story building owned by the firm and several associates.

The road to success was a bit slow after the fire, with a money panic in 1907 and later two world wars, but the firm persevered and expanded. By 1916, with a total of thirty-two employees, a seat on the New York Stock Exchange was acquired at a cost of $65,000. Only two other Baltimore firms were members at that time and both are no longer in business. This gives Legg Mason Wood Walker the distinction of being a member longer than any other house with headquarters in Baltimore.

Throughout the 1930s, the firm specialized in refinancing insurance companies and today it offers an insurance stocks service which analyzes the entire spectrum of insurance and makes investment recommendations to many major institutional investors. It also provides a Washington service which monitors the investment implications of

the myriad of activities undertaken by the Congress and various government agencies.

Mr. Legg's name was placed in the firm title in 1933. Mason and Company, with offices in Washington, D.C., and Virginia, was merged in 1970, and Wood Walker & Co., a New York firm, was added in 1973. The company now has over 350 employees in eighteen offices. While eleven of the offices are located in the Maryland-D.C.-Virginia area, the others extend from New York to Los Angeles. For the past twenty years Legg Mason Wood Walker has continued to follow a pattern of profitable growth based on a dedication to providing superior service to individual investors.

Far Left:
George Mackubin was a founding partner from 1899 to 1941
Center:
G. Clem Goodrich served as a partner from 1900 to 1932
Left:
John C. Legg's partnership spanned fifty-eight years from 1905 to 1963

Leonard Jed Company

Left:
Leonard Jed, founder and president of the Leonard Jed Company, is responsible for many of the "nuts and bolts" required to transform the skyline of a progressive America

Far Left:
The Leonard Jed Company, founded in 1946, moved to this site at 1301 Covington Street in South Baltimore in 1962

When the John G. Maiers Company was founded on Gay Street in Baltimore in 1870, the firm manufactured and sold only paint. Today, the Leonard Jed Company, which evolved from the Maiers operation, has over $5 million worth of finished hardware goods available for immediate delivery.

By the early 1900s, Maiers' firm included his children and was known as John G. Maiers Sons' Company. He had also added the distribution of glass to the product line. The company continued to operate as a family enterprise on Gay Street until 1925, when Morris Zweigel purchased the firm. Mr. Zweigel expanded operations to include retail hardware supplies.

In 1946, Morris Zweigel's stepsons, Leonard and David Jed, began an industrial supply business to support the increasing demands of the growing Baltimore manufacturing and building industries. By 1952, the Jeds acquired Coggins and Owens, an old-line Baltimore wholesaler of nuts and bolts established on Pratt Street in the late 1800s. The company acquired the Commercial Hardware Company, suppliers of builders' hardware and doors, in 1974.

The Coggins and Owens Pratt Street facility proved inadequate for the growing firm by 1966, so Jed purchased a property on Covington Street, just south of Baltimore's historic Federal Hill. The new firm, known as the Leonard Jed Company, incorporated Coggins and Owens and the John G. Maiers and Sons' Company, moving both enterprises to the Covington Street facility.

The Leonard Jed Company entered the manufacturing

business in 1972, when the firm purchased the Maryland Bolt and Nut Company, producers of ferrous products. The firm acquired a manufacturer of nonferrous nuts and bolts, the William H. Haskell Company of Pawtucket, Rhode Island, in 1976.

During this period of growth and diversification, the firm established warehousing operations in Bladensburg, Maryland, in York and Philadelphia, Pennsylvania, and in Richmond, Virginia. Not only did the Leonard Jed Company become a significant factor in the eastern industrial and construction community, but the firm simultaneously developed a reputation as a resource for industries nationwide.

Although not apparent to the casual observer, the Leonard Jed Company is directly responsible for much of the hardware required to transform the skyline of a progressive city. Numerous structures and industrial products incorporate materials manufactured or distributed by this Baltimore-based firm.

Leonard Jed, president of the firm, his brother, David Jed, vice president, and Cecil Ashley, vice president, describe the Leonard Jed Company of today as "just a bigger hardware store." More than 14.5 acres of enclosed facilities are evidence of the firm's growth and success. Yet Leonard Jed points with obvious pride to the firm's 300-plus employees, whose average length of service is twenty years, many having served forty years. Personal dedication to providing service and products to the industrial user is a continuing heritage of the Leonard Jed Company.

Lever Brothers Company

For the many passersby on Holabird Avenue, the main artery through the Canton section of Baltimore, the Lever Brothers Company plant is a landmark. And for the multitude of people who travel Interstate 95 on trips north or south, the sprawling structure is a familiar reminder that they are passing through East Baltimore's industrial section — just an exit away from the Harbor Tunnel.

Located on the site of an old dairy farm, the 54-year-old plant opened as the Gold Dust Corporation, later to become Hecker Products, and finally a part of Lever Brothers Company when the well-known maker of soaps, detergents, foods, dentifrices, and toiletries acquired the five-story building and surrounding property in 1939.

Today, Lever Brothers employs over 1,000 residents of surrounding Baltimore communities like Dundalk, Highland Town, and nearby Canton. For most of those Baltimoreans, Lever has been synonymous with steady employment. In fact, over 90 percent have more than ten years of service and better than 15 percent have more than twenty-five years with the company. In addition, some 300 retired employees still make their homes in the Baltimore area.

Elmer Curl of Dundalk, a painter at the plant, started in 1938, a year before Lever acquired Hecker Products. He remembers those days well. "I joined Hecker as a press operator in the bar soap department, making Fairy Soap, White Floating, and Sunny Monday," he said. Of course, those products no longer exist, but they were popular items at that time.

Recently retired Lena Hammer of Sykesville spent forty-one years with Lever — first as a payroll clerk and then as a cashier. "When I came to Lever, there was just a small, old office where we all worked together," she said. Ms. Hammer also remembers the "major" brands, most of which were introduced to the plant in 1940. The "majors" were

the first Lever brands — Lux Toilet Bar, Lifebuoy, Lux Flakes, and Rinso soap powder.

Another retiree, Tony Velivlis of Dundalk, also spent forty-one years at the plant, finishing his career as a sanitation supervisor. "My first job with Hecker was shoveling soap powder into bins for use as Silver Dust," said Velivlis. Silver Dust, a Hecker mainstay, was continued by Lever for many years after the acquisition.

Much of the history of modern soap-making is contained within the walls of Lever's Baltimore facility. However, in recent years there's been modernization in some areas, with high-speed automated equipment replacing outdated machinery. And products have changed to keep up with the changing household needs of the homemaker. Brands like Wisk liquid detergent, Dove beauty bar, and Concentrated All powdered detergent have become the mainstays of the Baltimore plant.

Lever's facility also includes a mammoth warehouse and distribution center — large enough to fit five football fields. Opened in 1966, the center accommodates customers in an 11-state area along the East Coast. And in 1976, Lever's confidence in Baltimore's economic growth and progress was again in evidence when the company added a major liquid detergent operation.

Since 1939, the Baltimore plant has played a significant role for Lever Brothers, an 85-year-old company and a leading member of the worldwide Unilever organization which operates more than 500 companies around the world.

A plaque at the plant entrance greets visitors with this message of the company's mission: "To make cleanliness commonplace, to lessen work for women, to foster health and contribute to personal attractiveness, that life may be more enjoyable and rewarding for the people who use our products."

Left:
Lever manufactures a variety of popular household products, including Caress, a body bar, and Dove, a beauty bar
Far Left:
Lever Brothers Company's Baltimore plant and East Coast warehouse and distribution center are located on Holabird Avenue

Loyola Federal Savings and Loan Association

Loyola Perpetual Building Association was born in Baltimore in 1879, a time when the city had just begun to flex its muscles after the Civil War. The late 1870s must have seemed a less than propitious time for establishing a savings and loan association, for Maryland had also experienced the nation's depression of 1873.

In the nineteenth century, Baltimore was a city without suburbs, though streets were being paved and newly installed "horseless trolleys" were extending the city limits. It was in this climate of early resurgence of business and industrial activities that five businessmen, all members of St. Ignatius parish, saw the need for a building and loan association from which fellow Baltimoreans could obtain money to purchase houses. Loyola's five founders first met in a basement room of the St. Ignatius Loyola College building on Calvert Street (a building whose southern wing now houses Center Stage) in 1878, and on February 19, 1879, the new association was incorporated.

In those early years, funds were funneled to hundreds of city residents wishing to buy homes in Baltimore, and as the new association's first decade drew to a close, it listed assets of $374,000. Two years later, in 1891, Loyola Perpetual moved from its cramped, one-room, basement quarters to property it had purchased across the street at 713 North Calvert. Baltimore's population approached 435,000, and Loyola's assets stood at $400,000. By the time the growing association moved to its third home at the southeast corner of Charles and Preston Streets in 1914, assets had exceeded $1 million and Baltimore's population had expanded to 580,000.

During the depression years of the 1930s, the association continued to pay regular dividends. In 1934, Loyola Perpetual joined the Federal Home Loan Bank System, and a year later became known as Loyola Federal Savings and Loan Association.

World War II tolled the end of the depression, but it did not end the slump in homebuilding that had characterized the 1930s. Loyola Federal responded by encouraging new accounts and investing in war bonds and government securities, causing deposits to soar. By the end of the war, Loyola Federal was in an excellent position to participate in the "housing boom of the century."

Through a 1945 merger with Acadia Federal Savings and Loan Association, Loyola Federal acquired its first branch office and began a period of expansion. Much of the credit for laying the early foundations of Loyola's expansion throughout the state of Maryland is given to Sam Wheatley Borden, who had joined the association in 1939 as executive vice president. (At his death in 1974, he was the chair-

man and chief executive officer of Loyola Federal.)

In 1952, with assets of $23 million, Loyola Federal moved to its present-day main office at Charles and Preston Streets. In the intervening years, the association has grown into an "ocean-to-mountain" savings network, yet it has maintained a firm commitment to Baltimore. With the addition of a new Charles Center branch in 1972 and a new renovation of its main office, Loyola stands firmly in the city of its birth.

The association has also taken an active role in redevelopment, participating in the rehabilitation of North Charles Street and the neighboring Lyric Theatre. Loyola Federal also participates in Baltimore Neighborhood Housing, Inc., one of the most successful renovation projects in the nation.

Loyola Federal celebrated its 100th anniversary year with assets exceeding $1 billion and is today the largest savings and loan association in Maryland. Yet the fundamental purpose propounded in 1879 remains the same — to encourage thrift and home ownership.

Loyola's five founders first met in a basement room of the St. Ignatius Loyola College building on Calvert Street. Here on December 30, 1878, they proposed to form an association from which fellow Baltimoreans could obtain money to purchase houses. On February 19, 1879, the new association was incorporated

Martin Gillet & Co., Inc.

Established in Baltimore in 1811, Martin Gillet & Co., Inc., was once known as the oldest tea importer in the nation. Today the firm manufactures quality mayonnaise and salad dressing products

One of Baltimore's oldest and most venerable firms is Martin Gillet & Co., Inc. Established in Baltimore in 1811 by Martin Gillet, the company recently announced the purchase of Baltimore's Cross and Blackwell plant; the seven-acre site on Eastern Avenue not only affords the firm ample room for continued growth and expansion, but the landmark status of the firm's newest facility also provides a fitting location for one of Baltimore's oldest industries.

Prior to 1931, Martin Gillet & Co., Inc., was exclusively an importer and distributor of fine teas. When Martin Gillet first imported this "fragrant herb," the port and the city of Baltimore had just begun to acquire an international reputation as a business center. The War of 1812 provided Martin Gillet with his earliest opportunity. Through the sale of tea to the United States government, the young firm experienced early prosperity.

Martin Gillet brought his son-in-law, Owen A. Gill, into the firm as a partner. Following the death of his father, Owen A. Gill, Jr., joined the firm in 1874 and developed major innovations in the tea industry.

Prior to this time, tea had been sold in chests of forty pounds or more. Martin Gillet & Co. was the first to market tea in convenient one-, half-, and quarter-pound packages. These novel paper packages of tea were put up by then became synonymous with the fine products of Martin Gillet & Co. In 1955, Eric Jacobsen, a fifth generation descendant of Martin Gillet, sold the company to its present management.

Joseph J. Katz, now president, soon began an ambitious program of expansion and growth. Modern mayonnaise and salad dressing production was begun in 1957. New product distribution, primarily Private Label, was sold in New York, New England, the Midwest, and the South. The brand name "House of Lords" was retained, but label design, advertising, and promotional campaigns were updated to reflect the company's modern outlook.

packages. These novel paper packages of tea were put up in Japan and were called "He-No." For a short time other importers and traders considered the strange packages a topic of merriment and referred to "He-No" as "Gill's Sausages." (Some of the original packages are on display in the offices of the company.) The fame of Martin Gillet & Co. and the "He-No" brand soon spread throughout the country, earning the firm a sound reputation for the consistent quality of its products.

Reputed to be the oldest tea importer in the nation, Martin Gillet & Co. began to diversify in 1931 with its initial production of mayonnaise and salad dressings. The new products bore the label "House of Lords," which had

Martin Gillet and Co. sold the tea business in the early 1970s, but kept the House of Lords brand. The original tea merchant's sign still hangs above the entrance to the main office.

In 1975, Martin Gillet & Co., Inc., through a wholly owned subsidiary, United Food Industries, developed and patented a new cholesterol-free dressing which it markets under the trademark "Bright Day." The company continued to diversify in 1977 by entering the food service business — with a full line of pourable dressings.

Management looks forward to the challenges and opportunities of a new decade, as Martin Gillet & Co. has for over a century and a half in Baltimore.

Maryland Port Administration

The Baltimore port area began operations in 1706, twenty-three years before official establishment of the city of Baltimore. By 1812, the city had risen from absolute insignificance to a degree of commercial importance which has brought down upon it the envy and jealousy of all the great cities of the Union," according to the *Niles Weekly Register*, one of the most influential trade journals of its day.

In 1814, when the British made a determined but unsuccessful attack on the city's defenses, the land and naval strikes culminated in the bombardment of Fort McHenry, an event which moved a young Maryland lawyer named Francis Scott Key to write the poem, "The Star Spangled Banner," which later became the national anthem of the United States of America.

The introduction of steam power to vessels in the years of the War of 1812 led to the organization of the Baltimore and Ohio Railroad in 1827, making it possible for the Port of Baltimore to compete with New York for the Midwest trade, even though New York had the advantage of the Erie Canal.

The Civil War had a devastating effect on Baltimore's ship and commercial traffic, as the city's industries were forced to produce mostly military supplies, which were carried on the tactically vulnerable B&O Railroad. Yet, it did not take local businessmen long to start rebuilding the port's trade after the end of the war.

The real rehabilitation of the port as a center of maritime commerce depended on the efforts of the railroads to recapture their once lucrative inland traffic. As a result, many railroads expanded, playing major roles in the construction of individual ocean terminals at the harbor's edge.

Huge by the standards of their day, the railroad companies turned Baltimore into a "railroad port," with the port's policies and growth determined in large measure by the owners of these facilities.

Business was brisk in the early part of the twentieth century, spurred by the opening of the Panama Canal which enhanced rapid shipping of west-bound tonnage from Baltimore. Additionally, the two world wars permitted Baltimore's port and industrial concerns to operate at a high-efficiency level.

But the wars revealed weaknesses in existing port facilities that required swift correction. By 1950, it became clear that a controlling authority would have to be established to coordinate the growing number of agencies, groups, and businesses engaged in port operations and trade development. As a result, in 1956, the Maryland Port

Authority was created by the Maryland General Assembly. The Authority became the Maryland Port Administration, part of the then newly created Maryland Department of Transportation, in 1971.

Nearly three centuries after its establishment, the Port of Baltimore has achieved a preeminence in world trade far surpassing what its founding fathers would have dreamt possible. But the maritime community is not resting on its achievements. It is looking to the future, confidently geared to continue offering customers the high standards of service they have come to expect when shipping through the Port of Baltimore.

Left:
The World Trade Center Baltimore, focal point of international trade in the mid-Atlantic region, stands at harborside in downtown Baltimore. Courtesy Jerry Wachter

Below:
Offering twelve berths and 550 acres of space, the Dundalk Marine Terminal is the largest cargo-handling facility in the Port of Baltimore

Maryland Specialty Wire, Inc.

Maryland Specialty Wire, the leading producer of stainless steel wire in the United States today, was founded in 1945 as the Brooklandville Wire Mill. Organized by Leonard (Red) C. Crewe, Jr., the operation was started in a rented barn about ten miles north of Baltimore in response to the increasing market need for fine and specialty steel wire.

Operated by just two employees during its first year, the company's only product was green, enameled, florist wire for the wholesale florist market. Innovation in production methods provided the basis for success then, as it has ever since. For example, while the rest of the industry was manufacturing wires one at a time, the Brooklandville Wire Mill was drawing and enameling the wire 100 pieces at a time in two operations.

Within two years, business had outgrown the barn, and in 1946, the first new building was erected on the company's present nine-acre site in Cockeysville. Despite devastating fires which destroyed the plant in 1948 and again in 1949 after rebuilding, the company continued to prosper as it improved both production methods and equipment and upgraded product lines to meet changing market requirements. Progressively, the company moved from low-carbon to high-carbon wire, and in response to the needs of the U.S. Army Signal Corps during the Korean War, production of stainless steel wire began. While more exotic alloys are playing an increasingly important role today, stainless steel wire remains the firm's principal product.

Strong growth continued throughout the 1950s and the 1960s, both internally with the development of new products and externally through acquisition and joint ven-

tures. In 1963, Hi-Alloys, Inc., was started at the Maryland location with a Swedish partner as a producer of high-speed steels; in the same year, Rigby-Maryland, Ltd., was started in England in association with an English partner, John Rigby and Sons, Ltd.

In 1967, Maryland Specialty Wire entered a new era with its acquisition by Handy & Harman, a leading U.S. fabricator and refiner of precious metals. Mr. Crewe became a member of its board of directors and was succeeded by Richard Nash, Jr., a Maryland native, as president in 1972. Under Mr. Nash's leadership, Maryland Specialty Wire has continued its impressive record of growth. Operating as a member of the Specialty Metals Group of Handy & Harman, the future of Maryland Specialty Wire is bright.

The production of fine wire requires precision equipment, as well as skilled employees. Most of the equipment in the Maryland mill has been designed and built by the firm's own engineers in order to manufacture specialized products. Even purchased machinery is subject to the design innovation of Maryland Specialty Wire.

In ancient civilizations, wire was used solely for decoration and had few practical uses. Today, applications for specialty wire number in the hundreds of thousands and can be found in industries vital to our nation's economy. Throughout its history, Maryland Specialty Wire has anticipated and responded to these ever-changing market needs, as it will in the future. Active research and development of both new wire products and new production methods, and the unrelenting search for high-strength corrosion resistant alloys of the future assure that the company will remain a dynamic force in the Greater Baltimore business community.

Left:
This recent photograph shows the wire rod storage area and the latest building addition to Maryland Specialty Wire
Below:
The Brooklandville Wire Mill was the genesis of Maryland Specialty Wire, Inc., in 1945

Misty Harbor, Inc.

"Wear It In Good Health," the woven inscription on each Misty Harbor raincoat, is just one of the many personal details one may expect from this company, a division of Jonathan Logan, founded by Ed Kraus and Lou Rothstein just a scant fifteen years ago. The name Misty Harbor was inspired by a foggy harbor scene painted by Mr. Kraus, who, along with Mr. Rothstein, had the vision to design quality rainwear for women.

Richard Schwartz, president, and David Schwartz, chairman of the Jonathan Logan firm, were well aware that the Kraus-Rothstein team was a knowledgeable combination when they hired the two men away from top positions at a rival company. With a staff of only thirty-five, these energetic and talented men were able to sell 25,000 coats in a few short months without even a sample to show. Their idea of tailored rainwear had impressed retailers.

Today Misty Harbor rainwear is manufactured in Baltimore, Arbutus, and Essex, making it one of the area's largest manufacturers of rainwear. The staff now numbers more than 1,000, and the company has an annual payroll of $10 million.

Kraus and Rothstein make sure that the design and craftsmanship of Misty Harbor rainwear improve every year. The spirit of "nothing is impossible for us" is per-

vasive among employees. Given a difficult design, they take pride in proving their competence.

After only one year, Misty Harbor had annual sales close to $5 million, and then the Harbor Master rainwear for men was launched. A harbor master had always appeared in the background of Misty national ads, and now it was time to provide him with his own raincoat. (Appropriately enough, the company presented the first Harbor Master coat to the Baltimore harbor master.)

In 1978, the famous designer Halston, a perfectionist himself, created a small collection of raincoats to be mass-marketed. The label read "Halston for Misty Harbor," one of the few times Halston allowed a manufacturer's name to share equal billing with his own.

Today Kraus and Rothstein believe, as they did when the company was first incorporated in 1964, that integrity, honesty, and the continual improvement of their product are the reasons for Misty Harbor's success. Despite a battle with rising costs, the company maintains its high standards of quality. Although many manufacturers are fleeing the cities in search of lower operating costs, Misty Harbor continues to grow in Baltimore. Integrity and fine craftsmanship may sound old-fashioned, but this relatively new company has thrived on these ideals.

The main office of Misty Harbor in Baltimore is one of four plants in the greater Baltimore area

Monumental Life Insurance Company

The first president of Monumental Life Insurance Company turned out to be a good risk, despite the fact that he was, for a short time, imprisoned at Fort McHenry.

By the early 1860s, the Civil War had the nation in panic and fury. Colonel George P. Kane, the insurance company's first president, was also Baltimore's police marshal. Along with Baltimore mayor George W. Brown, Kane tried to restrain an angry crowd that ambushed troops marching through the city after the famous attack on Fort Sumter in 1861. Both men were arrested as Confederate sympathizers. However, they were soon released, and Kane later went on to become the mayor of Baltimore.

Kane also navigated a young insurance company on a course to great success. What is now Monumental Life started out in 1858 as the Maryland Mutual Life and Fire Insurance Company under a charter from the Maryland General Assembly. After ceasing operations for a time during the Civil War, the company re-entered the insurance business in 1870 with a new name — the Mutual Life Insurance Company of Baltimore. In 1935, the company adopted its present name, Monumental Life, to share an identity with Baltimore, which is known as the "Monumental City."

Like most businesses, Monumental Life sprang from humble beginnings. The firm's first organizational meeting was held in 1860 at 91 Second Street, today the 300 block of Water Street. The first premium rates adopted by the board of directors were those of a Newark, New Jersey, insurance company, which had been operating since 1845. The first policies written by Monumental Life were ordinary life insurance policies.

Monumental's first agent was employed in Texas, Maryland, a small community about twelve miles north of downtown Baltimore. In the post-Civil War era, the company initiated a unique program to serve the city's large German population. A German-speaking department was set up to offer life insurance to German residents not only in Maryland, but in adjoining states as well.

The company issued its first weekly premium life insurance policy to Baltimore resident Valentin Bauscher in 1873. It was one of the first — if not *the* first — weekly premium policy issued by an insurance company in the United States. Weekly premium policies sold in specific geographical territories constituted the majority of Monumental's operation until the early 1950s, when ordinary insurance-in-force exceeded weekly premium for the first time. The company discontinued writing weekly premium insurance in the 1970s.

By 1883, just a quarter-century after its founding, the company attained its first million dollars of insurance. By the turn of the century, insurance-in-force had grown to $2.6 million and the company's assets totaled $241,000. In 1928, two years after relocating its offices to the corner of Charles and Chase Streets, the company was converted from a mutual to a stock operation; its assets then were $11 million and insurance-in-force was $147 million. Monumental Life reached insurance-in-force of $1 billion by 1957 and attained its second billion of insurance-in-force in 1967.

Today, as part of a national corporation, Monumental Life has offices in more than forty American cities and is licensed in forty-four states and the District of Columbia. Total assets amount to $654 million and insurance-in-force exceeds $4 billion. Monumental Life markets its life and health insurance products through home-service district agents, general agents, and a new mass marketing division.

Monumental Life Insurance Company of Baltimore has been located on the corner of Charles and Chase Streets since 1926

P. Flanigan & Sons, Inc.

Young Patrick Flanigan, native of County Armaugh, Ireland, arrived in Baltimore in 1880. His life's work and that of his descendants is intricately bound to the history of an expanding port city. It is also the story of a man with vision and a fascination with the future. Today that heritage has become an essential part of the philosophy of P. Flanigan & Sons, Incorporated, where Patrick's great-grandson, Pierce J. Flanigan III, serves as president of one of the most venerable firms in the construction industry.

Five years after his arrival, Patrick Flanigan founded the Maryland Paving Company, which paved many of Baltimore's cobblestone streets. Soon after, he started his "great venture" — constructing a private sewer line beneath Charles Street. Soon, businesses were paying to hook into "Patrick Flanigan's Sewer," which, now owned by the city, remains in operable condition.

Patrick, who was skilled with explosives, assisted the city fire marshal during the Great Baltimore Fire of 1904 by demolishing buildings to create a fire break. The Baltimore Courthouse was to be the keystone of the project, and Flanigan prepared the building for demolition. However, a Supreme Court judge ordered the dynamite removed, and the courthouse escaped demolition, and later, through extraordinary efforts, the fire.

During the rebuilding and expansion of Baltimore following the fire, Patrick was among an influential group that installed a two-pipe system beneath city streets: one for storm water, another for sanitary drainage. (Baltimore was one of the first cities in the nation to put this novel concept into practice.) The present configuration of Baltimore's streets was also established during this period. The Maryland Paving Company, which now included Patrick's three sons, Edward, Pierce, and Leo, changed its name to P. Flanigan & Sons.

Bituminous paving was introduced in 1910, and Flanigan was one of its early proponents. The mayor and city council were persuaded to try this "new-fangled" asphalt paving, and once again P. Flanigan & Sons returned to the task of paving Baltimore's streets.

During World War I, P. Flanigan & Sons entered into joint construction projects to build training camps for soldiers. The firm provided the labor for the excavation work, the laying of pipe, and the paving of the roads at Aberdeen Proving Ground and Fort Meade.

In the early 1920s, the firm returned to work in Baltimore once again, this time with a novel steam-driven concrete mixer. Patrick had purchased his first truck in 1914, and by 1917 the Packard and Mack trucks had made Flanigan's 200 mules and horses obsolete. The firm's present office on Loch Raven Road was once the site of the company stable.

The Great Depression almost destroyed the construction business, but with the advent of World War II, military construction activity resumed. Patrick and his son Pierce had died and the firm, now including a grandson, Pierce J. Flanigan, Jr., helped build Bethlehem Steel's Fairfield Shipyard and the Bainbridge Naval Training Center. The company also manufactured and installed asphalt armor plate to protect the bridge and gun mounts of Liberty ships against bomb attacks.

After the war, P. Flanigan & Sons introduced the first asphalt placing machine in the area and participated in the novel inch-to-inch paving method in Baltimore. During the 1950s, this consistently innovative company, now including Patrick's grandson, William, expanded operations through the use of portable asphalt plants and laid the paving for many of Maryland's rural roads, as well as the Garden State Parkway. In the 1960s, the firm pioneered the use of slip-form concrete paving methods in conjunction with two major projects, the Jones Falls Expressway and the East-West Expressway.

Today, P. Flanigan & Sons is actively recycling asphalt and is researching new materials to alleviate reliance on petroleum products. The spirit of one of Baltimore's most inventive Irish immigrants continues to guide the firm.

Above:
Patrick Flanigan (front row, third from right) stands beside his two sons during this early company celebration

Right:
With the introduction of bituminous paving in 1910, P. Flanigan & Sons set about paving Baltimore's streets. The firm used the then-most modern asphalt, an asphalt kettle built on wheels, and the most up-to-date steam rollers available

Procter & Gamble Manufacturing Company

Left:
Today over 500 men and women are employed at the Baltimore plant of Procter & Gamble. Since 1930, twelve additional buildings have been erected and seventeen acres of land added to the original Locust Point acreage

Below:
Although the nation was undergoing the torments of the Great Depression, 225 Baltimoreans found work in P&G's fifteen newly constructed buildings on the seven-acre Locust Point site

Excellent port facilities, the availability of an able work force, and an expanding market for consumer products were important factors in Procter & Gamble's decision to choose Baltimore as the site for the company's second East Coast operation. Ground was broken on Locust Point in January 1929, and Procter & Gamble's major Baltimore plant began full production in 1930.

The Procter & Gamble story actually began in 1837 in Cincinnati, however, when James Gamble, soapmaker, and William Procter, candlemaker, combined their talents and interests for mutual benefit. Standing just a few feet from the site of their first plant in Cincinnati is the headquarters of an international company bearing their names — a business with more than $9 billion in annual sales.

Of the products manufactured in Baltimore in 1930, only Ivory Soap is still being produced there. P&G's policy of improving established brands and introducing new products as they become available, as well as the firm's commitment to research and development, have resulted in new and improved products. Among the familiar products currently manufactured in Baltimore are Ivory, Camay, Tide, Cheer, Oxydol, Bold, Gain, Ivory Liquid, Joy, Downy, and Cascade. Soaps and synthetic detergents for export and glycerine for industrial use are also made at the Baltimore plant.

The plant has been modernized throughout its history, enabling facilities to keep pace with developments in manufacturing, safety, and packaging techniques. In 1947, P&G's newly developed hydrolyzer process, a continuous soapmaking process, made possible the production of high-quality soap in hours. The national introduction of the synthetic detergent in the same year was the culmination of more than twenty years of research into laundry products. In 1950, the Baltimore plant expanded its production to make synthetic detergents, which revolutionized the laundry products industry.

In 1962, equipment was added for producing liquid detergents, which have become a mainstay of household cleaning supplies. Facilities for producing Cascade, an automatic dishwashing detergent, were installed in 1967. Today, more than seventeen production departments turn out products for distribution throughout the Eastern seaboard. The Baltimore plant employs more than 500 men and women. Twelve additional buildings have been erected, and seventeen acres of land have been added to the early location. The plant also serves as a warehousing and distribution center for P&G's soap and detergent products that are manufactured at other plants.

The importance of Procter & Gamble employees is perhaps best expressed by Neil H. McElroy, chief executive officer from 1948 to 1957: "We believe that the management of Procter and Gamble has no more important responsibility than that of seeing that employees at all levels and in all parts of the business are provided the kind of environment which encourages, recognizes, and rewards achievement." In 1877, the company established a profit-sharing program, now the oldest such plan in continuous existence in the nation. A comprehensive sickness-disability-life insurance plan to protect workers and their families was introduced in 1915.

The familiar "moon and stars" trademark, indicative of Procter and Gamble's high standards of craftsmanship and quality, is visible on products manufactured in Baltimore and throughout the world. Yet to Baltimoreans this symbol also signifies a corporate commitment to the city and its residents. Contributions by the plant and its employees to local charitable, educational, and civic organizations approach $75,000 annually.

Provident Savings Bank

The Provident Savings Bank, a Baltimore institution since the late 1800s, is the father of branch banking among the mutual savings banks of the United States. In fact, Provident began as a branch system. Not until six branch offices were in operation throughout Baltimore did the new bank open a main office.

In 1884, John Marshall, a former sailor working as a janitor at the Friends Gospel Mission on Light Street, began to hold small sums of money for men who frequented the Mission's free reading room. As John Marshall's informal banking system gained in popularity, he suggested to the reading room managers that some repository be started to deposit the money. For about two years, the managers took turns collecting the money on Saturday evenings; on the following Monday, the funds were deposited in a local bank. In 1886, this operation evolved into the Provident Savings Bank, and John Marshall's dream of a convenient savings system became a reality.

During its early months, Provident established six branch offices. At that time, Baltimore workers were usually paid on Saturdays, a day they could also visit the city's markets; so many of Provident's original branches were opened at convenient market locations: the Northeast Market, Belair Market, Northwestern Market, and Cross Street Market.

Not only were Provident's branches located strategically, but the bank's novel banking hours provided convenience as well. Because savings banks' hours (10 a.m. to 1 p.m.) were inconvenient for Baltimore's working populace, Provident conducted banking hours during the evenings and on Saturdays, with branch hours established according to the needs of the community being served.

Provident's first central office was established in 1887 at 407 East Baltimore Street, and a year later it was relocated to a new building on the corner of Howard and Franklin. This office, too, soon became inadequate for the growing savings bank. In 1901, Provident purchased the former Saratoga Hotel lot on the corner of Howard and Saratoga Streets, and in 1903 construction began. The new building, occupied in 1904, was designed to look like an old treasure chest. Throughout the 1900s, Provident Savings Bank has continued to "take the bank to the people," supporting the financial needs of the communities it serves by providing convenient branch locations and a full range of modern banking services, including mortgage and consumer loans. (Provident now limits its lending activities to the state of Maryland, a policy which reflects its commitment to its depositors.)

Today, the Provident Savings Bank remains firmly committed to the ideas that seemed so novel in 1884: to provide for "the gathering up and care of sums of money which would be subject to call in times of need" and to open branches in different sections of the city (now the state) during hours when wage earners can visit them. Baltimore's Provident Savings Bank not only originated branch banking for savings institutions in the nation, but today, with over thirty offices, it is the largest savings bank branch system in Maryland.

Upper Left:
Provident Savings Bank began at the Friends Gospel Mission on Light Street, where visitors to the free reading room on Saturday evenings would leave small sums of money with John Marshall, the Mission's janitor

Bottom Left:
The Provident Savings Bank is the largest savings bank branch system in Maryland and remains firmly committed to its founders' goal of "taking the bank to the people"

RPS Products, Inc.

In 1928, with only $2,000, Max Furman and his wife, Ruth, launched their first automotive parts store on Oliver Street in Baltimore. While his wife managed the store, M.B, as he is fondly known, was the company salesman, purchasing agent, and often delivery man — usually fifty-cent runs that he was glad to get.

The business of selling wholesale automotive parts was a new enterprise in the early 1900s and the Furmans recognized the importance of fast, reliable service — getting parts to the customer would be the key to success. Because RPS could carry only a limited stock in the beginning, when a manufacturer notified the Furmans of a shipment, M.B. would go out and sell the product before it was actually on the shelves.

During the depression, the auto industry suffered, but RPS prospered in response to the need to repair aging vehicles. By 1948, the flourishing company began to expand. Within a decade it was firmly entrenched in the Baltimore Metropolitan area and then embarked on a Middle Atlantic expansion that brought the number of stores to sixty-two in 1969. The Furman's sons, M. William and Edward F., joined the company during this growth period and now serve as chairman of the board and vice chairman, respectively.

Brand Products, Inc., was formed in 1956 to act as a warehousing operation for the company. In 1968, RPS Products, Inc., went public and by 1971 RPS common stock was listed on the American Stock Exchange.

The company made its first major move beyond its Middle Atlantic concentration with the acquisition of Jobbers Warehouse, Inc., and fourteen stores in Arizona in 1970. There are now one hundred stores and seven warehouses throughout nine states. The growth has been further strengthened by the addition of a line of staples under the RPS label, including batteries, antifreeze, etc. To manage its growing inventory, in 1970 RPS implemented what is believed to be the first computerized inventory in the industry. Presently RPS Products purchases and distributes more than 100,000 different automotive parts, accessories, and equipment for domestic and foreign cars every year. Its principal customers are garages, service stations, auto and truck dealers, fleet operators, leasing companies, bus and truck operators, and governmental organizations, but individual do-it-yourselfers account for 25 percent of the firm's business.

Although M.B. and Ruth Furman are retired, they still serve on RPS's board of directors. The spirit of family togetherness, hard work, and imagination that was the trademark of the firm's early success continues. In the entrance of the general office at 1700 Caton Street, there is a bronze plaque of tribute to M.B. Furman from his extended family — the employees.

Bottom Left:
RPS Products now has 100 automotive parts stores in nine states

Bottom Right:
Max Furman and his wife, Ruth, launched their first RPS automotive parts store in 1928

Robert C. Herd & Co., Inc.

Robert C. Herd's love for the sea began very early in his life. When he was twelve years old, he worked in a ship broker's office in Glasgow, Scotland, the great shipbuilding city on the River Clyde. At the age of fourteen, following "Clydeside" tradition, he signed aboard a square-rigger as a cadet apprentice; the ship was bound for Australia.

Herd's second voyage took the young sailor to the East Coast ports of South America, then north through the Caribbean. Finally, after three years at sea, Robert C. Herd was aboard a ship that sailed into the Chesapeake Bay, heading for the Port of Baltimore.

A stubborn eye problem forced Mr. Herd to seek medical care and employment on shore. Though his health was soon restored, he chose not to return to sea. Instead he remained in Baltimore, where he met and married Miss Lillian C. George and began what was to be a long and successful career in shipping. In 1910, he went to work for Furness, Withy & Company as a clerk; he worked diligently, and by World War I, he was managing the Green Star Liner, one of the largest operators in Baltimore. Later, employment with the W.F. Spice and Company gave Mr. Herd management of the Texas, Transport and Terminal Company's activity at the Port of Baltimore. After Mr. Spice died, Mr. Herd went to New York to serve as general traffic manager for Simpson, Spence & Young, but he soon decided to go into business for himself.

With the aid of two close friends, H.R. Buttner and William Schuyler, Mr. Herd established Robert C. Herd & Co. in 1927 and began to provide shipping lines with the vital services of a steamship agency. At the time of his death in 1952, the firm was handling five of the largest scheduled services in Baltimore.

Robert C. Herd was known as an executive sincerely dedicated to aiding the development of the Baltimore Port. As president of the Steamship Trade Association in 1941, he fought for the widening of the main ship channel leading into Baltimore. Anxious to ensure that the port's history be preserved, he served for many years on the board of the Maritime Committee of the Maryland Historical Society, a commitment carried on by his company today.

During World War II, Robert C. Herd received the King's Medal for services rendered to the British Empire's war effort. As a board member of the Merchant's and Miner's Steam Navigation Company, he was instrumental in converting the Baltimore cruiseship line into a cargo operation that carried foodstuffs and other vital supplies to the allies overseas. (The Dorchester, the Merchant's and

Robert C. Herd, founder of Robert C. Herd & Company, Inc., arrived in Baltimore at the turn of the century

Miner's ship that was sunk by a German U-Boat in February 1943, is remembered in history for the four chaplains who gave their lifejackets to others and went down with the ship.)

Today, Robert C. Herd & Co., Inc., represents shipping lines that carry cargo worldwide, including the Chilean Line (serving the Canal Zone and South America's West Coast); the Norwegian America Line (serving the continent of Europe); and the Columbus Line (Australia and New Zealand). The French Line, Mr. Herd's first account, continues to benefit from the firm's services. The firm also continues to operate the Western Maryland Railway's Bulk Facility at Baltimore.

For many years, Mr. Herd's two sons, Arthur C. and Robert E. Herd, and his son-in-law, Donald W. Carroll, carried on his maritime activities. Today Mr Carroll serves as vice president, while his son, Donald W. Carroll, Jr., has become the third generation of the Herd family to serve the company.

Operating from new offices at 32 South Street in Baltimore, the firm continues to be an integral part of Baltimore's thriving port commerce.

Rukert Terminals Corporation

The year was 1921. A man with a dream and an unsecured loan of $800 purchased a secondhand truck and rented a garage on George Street. It marked the beginning of Rukert Terminals Corporation, today one of the largest private terminal operators in the Port of Baltimore.

Captain W.G.N. Rukert started his career as a stock clerk for a local warehouse company. During World War I, he served in the U.S. Army Quartermaster Corps and managed the storage facilities at Camp Holabird. Deciding within a few months of his discharge that his future was tied to the future of Baltimore, he rented a large warehouse at the foot of Block Street and handled the first cargo of French potash to arrive in Baltimore after the war.

In 1930, Rukert discovered that docks along Thames Street were available for $135,000. Because he had only $3,000 as a down payment, he convinced Willoughly McCormick, founder of McCormick & Co., to let him pay the remainder out of profits. The next year, his son, Norman, entered the business after graduating from high school, and they acted as terminal operators for the Southern Pacific Steamship Line during the next twelve years.

Before long, the Rukerts realized that the piers along Thames Street were too small to handle the new larger deepwater vessels. So in 1937, they leased Pier 5 Clinton Street from the Pennsylvania Railroad and developed it into a modern terminal. This property was finally purchased from the railroad in 1966.

In the mid-1940s, two valuable waterfront properties were acquired. Historic Brown's Wharf in Fells Point was purchased from Western Maryland Railway, to be used as a dry storage warehouse, and Lazaretto Point was acquired

from the Pennsylvania Railroad and developed into a modern deepwater terminal. Two marginal piers with transit sheds were constructed, making the terminal one of the most efficient operations in the Port of Baltimore.

"Cap" Rukert relinquished the presidency of Rukert Terminals Corporation to his son in 1961. A grandson, Norman G. Rukert, Jr., joined the organization that same year. The company's growth and reputation for service con-

tinued, and twelve years later, George F. Nixon, Jr., another grandson of the founder, entered the firm. By then, it had truly become a family organization. Captain Rukert died in 1974, but his innovative spirit and determination have continued to guide the company, which today enjoys a worldwide reputation as the "Can Do" terminal.

Despite its expansion, Rukert Terminals has not lost sight of its community responsibilities. In 1976, Mayor Schaefer dedicated the Brown's Wharf Maritime Museum, established by the company to preserve the historical artifacts of a great port. The museum is operated on a non-profit basis and gives free guided tours with an audiovisual introduction. Significant exhibits include a 10-by-12-foot model of Fells Point as it was at the turn of the nineteenth century, many original documents of the Bond and Fell families dating from 1752, a collection of more than 450 coffee cups representing steamship lines whose vessels have called at Baltimore, a replica of an 1870 shipping office, and work exhibits demonstrating the early methods of stevedoring and handling commodities. The museum has received numerous awards from governmental and private agencies.

In addition to a very busy schedule as chief executive of the company, Mr. Rukert has found time to publish two successful books, *The Fells Point Story* and *Historic Canton*, recounting the histories of two communities that played a vital role in the development of the Port of Baltimore.

Right:
Captain W.G.N. Rukert, founder of Rukert Terminals, stands next to a cannon used in the defense of Fort McHenry in Baltimore Harbor in 1814. Captain Rukert had the cannon restored, authenticated, and installed

Far Right:
Rukert Terminal Corporation operates two deep-sea piers at Lazaretto Point, across from famous Fort McHenry in Baltimore Harbor. The firm also operates several other major warehousing and bagging facilities for bulk cargoes, making it the second largest private terminal operator in the Port of Baltimore

Russell T. Baker and Company, Inc., Realtors

When Russell T. Baker first walked into his modest downtown office at 2118 North Charles Street, a second-floor walk-up over a flower shop and beauty parlor, he had no idea what his future influence would be on Maryland real estate. World War II had just ended and the real estate market was booming. The first sale was a small bungalow on Sollers Point Road, which sold for $5,500. "That same property today would probably sell for $45,000 to $50,000," says Mr. Baker.

From this "rather inauspicious start," Mr. Baker reminisces, "our young company began to grow and wonderful things started to occur. New staff and salespeople were attracted to the firm and additional space in the building was leased. One of our top salesmen, Robert N. Schmidt, now president, was appointed general sales manager in 1960. Three years later, we moved our headquarters to 6229 North Charles Street and bought a building in Baltimore County, which is now the site of the Greater Towson Gallery. At that time, we had about forty-eight salespersons."

The big turning point for the Baker organization, however, came in 1966 with the introduction of a new concept called "Gallery of Homes." Until then, buyers selected homes on the basis of statistical data and routine site visits, but with this new innovation they were able to save time, money, and gasoline by conveniently viewing high-quality, illuminated, color photographs of homes at any of the eight Baker Galleries in Baltimore and five surrounding counties, with some 235 sales associates.

Today, Russell T. Baker & Company is probably the only real estate company in the area that limits its sales personnel to full-time career people. One can sense this concern for professionalism when visiting any of the Baker Galleries. Services offered include guaranteed sales plans, equity financing, nationwide relocation referrals, full computerization, total exposure, screening, consistent advertising, pricing assistance, third-party negotiating, financing, full-time personal service, extra-value selling, and a trained staff.

"During the eighties," Mr. Baker says, "we expect to add another five galleries. We were one of the first to serve the central city, and now, to participate in the rejuvenation of downtown Baltimore, we are planning to open a new office somewhere in the new Inner Harbor."

The future of real estate has probably never been brighter in Baltimore. In 1979, Russell T. Baker & Company reported over $170 million in settled sales. For the city's 250th anniversary year (and Baker's 32nd), the firm will top $215 million.

Upper Left:
A pioneer in real estate television advertising, Russell T. Baker (left) is shown here with WMAR-TV announcer, George Rogers, in the early 1950s

Above:
Robert N. Schmidt (left), president, and Russell T. Baker, founder and chairman of the board, examine some properties in one of the eight Baker Galleries

Schenuit Industries, Inc.

In 1912, when Frank G. Schenuit opened his modest Baltimore shop for business, it was the dawn of a transportation revolution. Mr. Schenuit was initially a distributor and soon a small manufacturer of the "novel" pneumatic tire. Soon he was able to open a larger plant in northwest Baltimore, where the firm manufactured auto and truck tires during the 1920s, supplying the needs for a fast-growing industry.

With the advent of World War II, the Frank G. Schenuit Rubber Company was among six United States tire manufacturers producing airplane tires for the war effort. The years following the war were difficult and crucial times for the Baltimore tire manufacturer, as the market for military aircraft tires virtually disappeared overnight.

Frank G. Schenuit died in 1948, leaving control of the company to his three daughters, Mrs. Elizabeth Schenuit Spilman, Mrs. Nancy Lee Schenuit Thompson, and Mrs. Mary Jean Schenuit Travers. Roy C. Neely was named president of the firm in 1948 and served in that capacity until 1963.

Schenuit made its first public stock offering in 1962, paving the way for future growth. During the 1950s, Oliver S. Travers, husband of Mary Jean Schenuit Travers, had joined the firm, initially working in the tire plant and later as manager of the sales force. In 1963, he was named president of Schenuit Industries, Inc. Under Mr. Travers' leadership the firm began a period of growth and change.

The Jackson Manufacturing Company, located in Harrisburg, Pennsylvania, was a leading manufacturer of wheelbarrows and a leading customer of Schenuit tires. In 1964, Schenuit acquired this firm, which now produces a variety of lawn care products (including Cyclone seeders and lawn spreaders) and contractor's equipment.

Schenuit added the Nelson Company, a manufacturer of industrial wood products, in 1966. With plants in Baltimore and Kentucky, this company's major products are pallets and wooden reels.

In 1967, Schenuit Industries, Inc., was listed on the American Stock Exchange. The firm also acquired the Perfection Manufacturing Company at this time. For many years, Perfection, located in St. Louis, has been recognized as a leading manufacturer of grass catchers. In 1975, Perfection acquired Innovex, Inc., a manufacturer of exercise cycles, providing another product line for Perfection and extending Schenuit's interest into the exercise equipment industry.

Three years later, Almet, Inc., a producer of aluminum tubing lawn and patio furniture, joined the Schenuit family of firms, which further expanded the company's in-

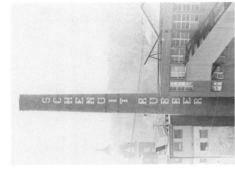

Left:
During the 1920s, the Frank G. Schenuit Rubber Company moved to this manufacturing facility in northwest Baltimore.
Bottom Left:
When Frank G. Schenuit opened his doors for business in 1912, it was the dawn of a transportation revolution.
Bottom Right:
In 1963, Oliver S. Travers became the third president in the history of Schenuit Industries, Inc.

terest in its primary lines of business of home, lawn, and garden products.

Schenuit's Tire Division gradually became incompatible with the firm's long-range objectives. In 1972, after fifty years in the tire manufacturing business, Schenuit sold its Baltimore tire plant. By 1978, Schenuit's tire distribution facilities were sold, and the transition to totally new product lines was complete.

Baltimore-based Schenuit Industries completed the last fiscal year with new records in sales and earnings. New corporate headquarters were occupied at the prestigious Green Spring Station in northwest Baltimore, and another new firm, Vitamaster Industries of New York, joined the Schenuit industrial family. Vitamaster is the leading manufacturer of exercise equipment and further expanded the corporation's interest in this field.

Schenuit Industries, Inc., having experienced a complete restructuring of its operations from tire manufacturer to its present position as a diversified manufacturer of consumer products, looks forward to continued growth and prosperity.

The Savings Bank of Baltimore

Although most of the city's 60,000 residents doubtless stayed home on New Year's Day, 1818, a group of Baltimore's leading citizens were at work planning The Savings Bank of Baltimore. They met at the Indian Queen Hotel on Baltimore and Hanover Streets, then the best lodging in town (and where Francis Scott Key four years earlier composed the poem that became the "Star Spangled Banner"). Born of that meeting was a mutual savings bank, a concept new to Baltimore and most other parts of the country in that its motive was philanthropic rather than profit-oriented.

The founders' purpose was to establish a safe depository for the humble savings of the city's "worthy poor," a place where prudent investment and honest savings could earn interest for old age or ill health. The bank would be run by a board of directors comprised of Baltimore's most distinguished citizens, but there would be no stockholders to share in the profits. All interest and profit would be divided among the depositors, after setting aside a reserve for their protection.

Such banking institutions already existed in Boston and Philadelphia and now it was Baltimore's turn to start a "provident bank." A month after the New Year's meeting, a board of twenty-five directors was elected. On March 16, 1818, The Savings Bank of Baltimore opened its doors for business.

Pioneered and navigated by the city's leading men, whose names and legends live today, during its 161 years of operation the bank survived fire, the Civil War, two world wars, and the Great Depression.

Recognizing their responsibility to less fortunate members of the community, the founding bank directors built the institution on pillars of "sobriety, industry, and economy," encouraging depositors to save for the future. The first advertisements for the bank read, in part, "He that gets all he can honestly and saves all he gets . . . expenses excepted, will certainly become rich."

The original founders of the bank included Moses Sheppard, founder of Sheppard-Pratt Hospital; Gerald T. Hopkins, uncle and business sponsor of Johns Hopkins; Alexander Brown, founder of America's oldest investment banking house; Fielding Lucas, founder of Lucas Brothers; Jesse Hunt and Jacob Small, both Baltimore mayors; Isaac McKim of clipper ship fame; and several members of the Carroll and Ellicott families.

Robert Garrett, who helped start the Baltimore and Ohio Railroad, was a director of The Savings Bank of Baltimore from 1836 to 1847. Johns Hopkins, who founded the university and hospital bearing his name,

Four of the bank's original corporators were Alex Brown, Johns Hopkins, William Patterson, and Enoch Pratt

became a bank corporator in 1865. Enoch Pratt, whose name is associated with two world-famous institutions, the Enoch Pratt Free Library and the Sheppard-Pratt Hospital, was director of the bank from 1871 until his death in 1896.

Baltimore's new bank opened with little fanfare in 1818 in a single room donated by the Phoenix Fire Insurance Company at 100 Market Street (now Baltimore Street). Banking hours were on Mondays only, from 11 a.m. to 2 p.m. The only salaried employee was a secretary who earned an annual stipend of $150. Two years later, the bank's offices were moved to Gay and Water Streets, where business was conducted until 1904, when the building was destroyed by fire.

The bank's original strongbox, twenty-one inches long, fourteen inches wide and thirteen inches deep, provided more than enough space to house the first day's take: $170 deposited by nine persons — a carter, a tavern keeper, two tailors, a barber, a clerk, a baker, a schoolmaster, and a housewife.

By today's standards, the bank did not have a very good first year. By the end of 1818, there was only $12,000 in deposits. But growth was steady; deposits hit the $100,000 mark in 1825 and $1 million by 1838. As of 1979, with twenty-two branch offices, the bank's assets are in excess of $961 million.

Actually, the bank's growth has been almost continuous except for eleven of its 161 years. Deposits dwindled in the wake of war, bank panics during the Great Depression, and other crises of both local and national proportion. Still, not one depositor in the bank's history ever lost one penny of savings during the lean years.

And there were lean years. The first serious dilemma came in 1834, when the failure of two leading Baltimore banks caused runs on all other city savings and lending in-

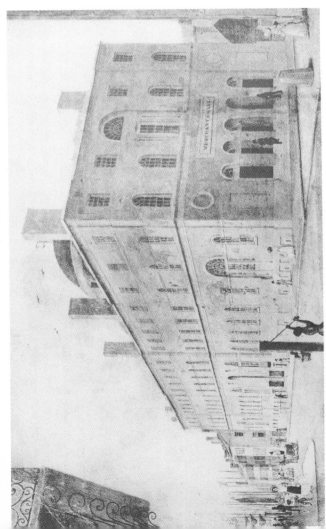

Left:
The Savings Bank of Baltimore transacted business from a room at the city courthouse until December 1907, when it moved into new offices on Charles Street

Center:
The interior of the main office was photographed prior to its renovation in 1954

Below:
Having survived numerous fires, the Civil War, two world wars, and the Great Depression, The Savings Bank of Baltimore is celebrating 161 years of operation

The banking industry's worst period occurred during the Great Depression of the early 1930s. A nationwide banking crisis had developed by 1933; banks were eventually closed by national proclamation between February 25 and March 14 of that year. Although the bank lost more than $5 million during that year, it is interesting to note that in the four depression years (1931 to 1934), the number of regular savings accounts increased by nearly 30,000. And during the entire depression era, when fifteen Baltimore banks either closed or operated on a limited-withdrawal basis, The Savings Bank of Baltimore met all of its depositors' demands — as in the Civil War — without having to borrow a penny from other sources.

From its first year of operation, The Savings Bank of Baltimore has grown from 200 depositors to more than 190,000. Today, in keeping with the founders' original intentions, loans are made primarily to individuals and homeowners rather than to private businesses. The first interest credits to depositors' accounts in 1819 totaled $165. In 1979, the interest credit climbed to over $44 million, with interest rates varying from 5.5 to 11.5 percent, depending on the type of account.

The idea behind the creation of The Savings Bank of Baltimore — a savings bank "to operate solely in the interest and for the profit of its depositors" — remains its guiding light.

stitutions. The crisis was met head-on by The Savings Bank of Baltimore. The bank waived its usual mandatory week's notice for withdrawals and opened daily, thereby restoring public confidence.

The Civil War created the greatest test of the bank's strength. In the early 1860s, both Union and Confederate sympathies were apparent in the port town. Caught in the uncertain atmosphere of war, depositors were withdrawing their savings. In 1861, deposits fell more than 30 percent, from almost $6 million to about $4 million. But thanks to the foresight of bank president Archibald Stirling, the bank was never forced to borrow money to meet its depositors' demands, for Stirling had retained close to $667,000 in cash accumulated from the sales of securities and maturing loans — money that was used by the bank to meet the crisis.

Almost fifty years after the Civil War, another catastrophe rocked the bank and the city, but the depositors' valuables were not harmed. The Great Baltimore Fire destroyed most of the downtown area in February 1904. The bank's offices were completely gutted except for the four walls and the vault. The steel vault took five days just to cool off, but when it was opened $25 million in cash and securities were found intact. The Savings Bank of Baltimore transacted business from a room at the city courthouse until December 1907, when it moved into new offices on Charles Street.

Stewart & Company

Eli and Samuel Posner established their first neighborhood notion and dry goods store in a three-story building on the south side of Lexington Street in 1875. Known then as Posner Brothers, the business prospered and was soon moved to a more advantageous location on West Lexington Street; after the move, Eli Posner died, and Samuel purchased his interest.

In 1891, once again due to expanding business, Samuel Posner erected a new building on the northeast corner of Howard and Lexington Streets. The gala opening was held on April 15, 1899. Full-page newspaper ads thanked the community for their support: "We are, have always been, and shall always abide, the devoted servers of your interests. Hence, we deem it a duty to confer with you, since your best good is interwoven with our own far more inseparably than the vine is wound about the oak."

The principle of "service to the customer," established by the founders, was perpetuated by Louis Stewart when he purchased and incorporated the business in 1901. The following year, the name Stewart & Company was adopted. During this early period of the twentieth century, Stewart & Company was growing and changing as rapidly as Baltimore. Within a year after Stewart acquired the business, the store became a subsidiary of the Associated Merchants Company and continued as such until procured by Associated Dry Goods Corporation in 1916. Today ADG is recognized as one of the nation's largest retailing organizations with sixteen locations in major cities throughout the United States. William Arnold is president and chief executive officer of the corporation, with headquarters in New York City.

Situated in the heart of Baltimore's shopping district, Stewart's earned customer confidence through quality merchandise, thoughtful service, and dependability. Elegant apparel and a wide selection of products at reasonable prices assured Stewart's growing success.

As the Baltimore area expanded, Stewart's stepped up its efforts to more conveniently meet the needs of its customers. In 1955, Stewart's York Road store was the second suburban store to be constructed in Baltimore, and in the years that followed, Stewart's suburban stores circled the city. Changing customer demands and shopping habits prompted the closing of Stewart's downtown store (at Howard and Lexington Streets) in January 1979. Under the management of Edward M. Condon, chairman and chief executive officer, the company's energies and concentration are being directed toward the five suburban stores in Reisterstown, Westview, Timonium, Golden Ring, and York Road.

Suburban Trust Bank

On the morning of August 30, 1972, the U.S.F. *Constellation*, the first commissioned man-of-war ship of the U.S. Navy and showpiece of Baltimore's Inner Harbor, fired a three-gun salute to Suburban Trust Bank. Baltimore City was honoring a bank that originated fifty-seven years earlier in Hyattsville, Maryland. The ceremony was the city's way of recognizing that Suburban Trust had indeed become a "Baltimore bank."

Suburban Trust's history began in 1915 at a meeting in Riverdale, Maryland, where a group of businessmen gathered to discuss the founding of a new bank, the Prince Georges Bank. They did not know then that the new bank (sixteen stockholders, $20,000 in capital, $5,000 in surplus) would, as Suburban Trust, expand into five counties and into the major metropolitan area of Baltimore itself. That growth, which in 1978 put the bank into the billion-dollar class, would be the result of imaginative management that would lead the institution through wars and depressions.

A spectacular leap forward in the history of Suburban Trust Bank (and the reason the bank is so named) was the merger in 1951 of the Prince Georges bank (assets of $29 million) with the Suburban National Bank of Silver Spring ($32 million). The new bank had ten offices in Montgomery and Prince Georges counties and, by 1960, assets in excess of $160 million.

The stage was set for further growth; Suburban Trust management looked to Baltimore, at that time a city with a rich past looking to the future. That future, forged of the blueprints and dreams of 1960, was the deciding factor. On September 13, 1970, Suburban Trust acquired the four-office, $23 million National City Bank of Baltimore, entering the Baltimore market formally and becoming an important part of the community.

National City Bank of Baltimore had opened on June 5, 1963, the first new national bank to be chartered in Baltimore in more than fifty years. Mayor Theodore R. McKeldin had been its first depositor.

On December 2, 1970, the Baltimore business community, through the Advertising Club of Baltimore, gave Suburban Trust an unprecedented welcome to the city. Suburban Trust management accepted the welcome and promised: "Baltimore will know we're here."

Suburban Trust has made good on that promise. The bank today has sixty-five offices statewide, ten of them in Baltimore and three in nearby Annapolis. It serves the banking needs of thousands of Baltimoreans and takes an active role in helping to sustain the quality of life in

Baltimore. All of this is why, on the morning of August 30, 1972, the U.S.S. *Constellation*, moored in Baltimore's historic Inner Harbor, fired a three-gun salute to Suburban Trust Bank — the bank that traces its past to Prince Georges County, but counts the city and the people of Baltimore in its future.

Above:
The U.S.F. Constellation fires a three-gun salute honoring Suburban Trust Bank
Left:
The Prince Georges Bank, founded in 1915 in Hyattsville, Maryland, merged with the Suburban National Bank of Silver Spring in 1951 to become Suburban Trust Bank

Tate Industries

William Tate, a marine engineer from Belfast, Ireland, came to Baltimore, where, in 1924, he founded the Tate Engineering and Marine Supply Company. Mr. Tate focused his business on supplying boiler replacement parts for merchant ships calling at the Port of Baltimore. From this inauspicious beginning, Tate Industries has grown to include three diverse companies: Tate Engineering, Inc.; Tate Temco, Inc.; and Tate Architectural Products, Inc.

Tate Engineering's main office and plant at 601 West Street in Baltimore was built for the firm and occupied in 1967. The firm also has service centers in Roanoke and Richmond, Virginia; Salisbury and Hagerstown, Maryland; Philadelphia, Pennsylvania; and Washington, D.C. Today, Tate Engineering sells, assembles, installs, and services systems and products in a broad range of industrial and commercial applications. Just a few of the design and installation services include steam and hot water boiler installations, large gas and oil conversion systems, and compressed air and vacuum units. Pumps, power transmission products, industrial rubber products, valves, and mechanical instruments are typical of product inventory. Tate Engineering's regional operations serve the entire mid-Atlantic area. Operations have been enhanced by the recent expansion of the Baltimore service facility which includes extensive material handling equipment.

Tate Temco was created in 1958 with the acquisition of the marine products line of Zurn Industries. A manufacturing facility was initially established on South Carey Street and subsequently moved to an expanded facility at 1941 Lansdowne Road in 1975. All phases of Tate Temco's international market for pipeline strainers, air dryers, and specialty valves continue to show a consistent and substantial rate of growth.

Created in 1964, Tate Architectural Products maintains the world's largest, most complete facilities for the manufacture, installation, and service of raised access flooring systems. For over two decades, access flooring was utilized primarily in data processing centers and computer rooms. Today, however, it is used in the general office environment, a result of the introduction of sophisticated communications networks, word processing systems, remote computer terminals, and the "open office" concept.

In 1966, Tate Architectural Products moved to 7510 Montevideo Road in Jessup, Maryland, where a substantial expansion of office and manufacturing facilities is currently under way. Manufacturing facilities are also located in Great Britain and the Netherlands, and a sales office in London serves Tate Architectural Product's European Markets.

William Tate's sons, Robert and Donald, have been instrumental in the growth of Tate Industries, which remains privately held. Robert Tate has been chairman of the board and chief executive officer of Tate Industries since 1948 and has established a high level of professional management to guide the companies successfully into the future. Donald Tate, as the president of Tate Architectural Products, has been instrumental in the development of this company and the growth of the access floor industry. A son, daughter, and a son-in-law of Robert Tate are also executives in the Tate Industries companies, insuring a continuity of family involvement in the enterprises through the third generation.

From 1951 through 1966, Tate Engineering and its divisions operated from this 501 South Eutaw Street location which was substantially damaged by fire in 1965

302

Tongue, Brooks & Company, Inc.

The firm of Tongue, Brooks & Company, Inc., has satisfied the insurance needs of Maryland business, industry, and individuals for more than three-quarters of a century. The firm is an outgrowth of two well-established Baltimore insurance agencies, T.T. Tongue & Company and Jos. W. Brooks & Company.

The insurance industry was in its infancy in the 1880s when Thomas T. Tongue established a new casualty insurance agency in Baltimore. In fact, T.T. Tongue & Company became the second general agency in the nation to be personally appointed by the Maryland Casualty Company's new president, John T. Stone.

Jos. W. Brooks & Company began in 1910 when Joseph W. Brooks, a steamship agent and customs house broker, began writing marine and fire insurance. Rodney J. Brooks, Sr., a young World War I veteran, joined his father's firm in 1918. Upon the death of Joseph less than a year later, Rodney assumed full control of the company.

Also in 1918, T.T. Tongue's son, Benjamin S. Tongue, joined his father's firm and was admitted to partnership two years later. In the late 1920s T.T. Tongue sought a merger for his firm and contacted Rodney J. Brooks. An agreement was reached between the two firms on December 16, 1929. Three days later, T.T. Tongue died.

The new firm, Tongue, Brooks & Zimmerman, was established under the leadership of Rodney J. Brooks, Sr., with Benjamin S. Tongue and Edgar R. Zimmerman serving as vice presidents. The merger proved advantageous; the company recorded an annual volume of $900,000 in premiums during its first year. The agency grew until it became one of the largest brokerage and agency firms south of New York City.

During the 1930s, the firm added a life insurance department. Now referred to as the Financial Planning Department, its services have expanded to include all types of pension trusts and group plans. A bond department was added in 1946. Today the company arranges fidelity, fiduciary, construction, and supply bonds, including guarantees on exotic and complex contracts involving the country's space program.

For convenience of operation, the firm became a partnership in 1937, with Rodney J. Brooks, Sr., as senior partner and general manager. Upon the death of Mr. Zimmerman in 1948, the firm's name was changed to Tongue, Brooks & Company, and soon after many of the present senior officers became associated with the company.

Rodney J. Brooks, Sr., headed the agency until his death in 1952. His commitment to the growth of the firm was surpassed only by his devotion to the Baltimore community. For twenty-five years he served as president of the St. Vincent de Paul Society of the Baltimore Archdiocese. He was a trustee for Johns Hopkins University and served as treasurer of the Maryland Historical Society. Today five of his sons are associated with the firm.

The philosophy of Tongue, Brooks & Company has always been based on personal attention to clients by full-time, qualified professionals. Representing only first-line stock companies, the firm remains one of the oldest, most respected, Baltimore organizations. Business is conducted at 213 St. Paul Place, the same address it had fifty years ago.

At the time of its second incorporation in 1974, the partnership was made up of the following principals: Rodney J. Brooks, Jr., Frank C. Brooks, John H. Brooks, F. Rodgers Brooks, Vandervoort Rand, William P. Beatson, Harvey S. Brooks, and Theodore W. vonEiff. Specializing in risk analysis and operating as a general agent and broker, the firm serves as an invaluable intermediary between the consumer and today's complex national and international insurance markets.

Far Left:
The insurance industry was in its infancy in the 1890s when Thomas T. Tongue established a new casualty insurance agency in Baltimore

Left:
Jos. W. Brooks & Company was begun in 1910 when J.W. Brooks, a steamship agent and customs house broker, began writing marine and fire insurance. Jos. W. Brooks & Company merged with T.T. Tongue & Company in 1929

Union Trust Company of Maryland

Union Trust Company of Maryland has seen more than 184 years of American history pass by its doors. The oldest bank in Maryland and the seventh oldest bank in the United States, Union Trust is the result of the acquisition or merger of twenty-four financial institutions over a period of sixty years. One predecessor company, the Bank of Baltimore, received its charter from the Maryland state legislature in December 1795 and began business in 1797 with capital of $1.2 million.

Some of the original stockholders of the Bank of Baltimore were Thorogood Smith, second mayor of Baltimore; Charles Carroll, a signer of the Declaration of Independence; William Patterson, whose daughter, Betsy, married Jerome Bonaparte, brother of Napoleon; and David Stewart, a dry goods provisioner who helped to equip George Washington's fledgling army.

In the early days, it took just five people to run a bank — a president, cashier, bookkeeper, document clerk, and runner — with a total annual payroll of less than $5,000. As Baltimore grew from 20,000 people in 1796 to 300,000 in 1870, the fortunes of its citizens fluctuated with the times. The early 1800s were years of great financial instability throughout the young country, but the Bank of Baltimore persevered.

The turmoil of the Civil War pointed out the need for a strong central banking system in the United States. The Bank of Baltimore converted to a national charter in 1865 and became known as the National Bank of Baltimore.

In 1898, the Realty Trust Company was incorporated by the Maryland General Assembly and two years later changed its name to the Union Trust Company of Maryland. The first president of Union Trust, George Blakiston, helped to develop the first commercial electric streetcar line in the United States.

The Great Baltimore Fire of 1904 gutted the heart of the city and destroyed both the National Bank of Baltimore and Union Trust buildings. The new National Bank of Baltimore office, occupying its original site, was completed in 1906, enlarged in 1924, and renovated once again in 1930 when the National Bank of Baltimore and Union Trust Company of Maryland merged. The emblem of the older bank, which shows a sailing ship and plow, symbols of commerce and agriculture, was retained. The merger brought together $65 million in deposits and over $75 million in resources. Fifteen years later, Union Trust's deposits had grown to $201 million and its assets amounted to $211 million.

By the end of 1979, the Union Trust Company of Maryland, with deposits of $906 million, eighty-two branches, and a staff of 1,500 was the largest subsidiary of Union Trust Bancorp, a $1.3 billion financial services organization with three nonbank lending and leasing subsidiaries operating at eighty-one locations in ten states.

Union Trust Company of Maryland headquarters at Baltimore and St. Paul Streets stands on the same site as the original building of its 1795 predecessor

University of Maryland at Baltimore

The Baltimore campus, birthplace of the University of Maryland, is unique. Its professional schools and university hospital were among the first in their fields, and its dental school was the first in the world. Today's 36-acre campus comprises seven schools — dental, law, medicine, nursing, pharmacy, social work and community planning, and graduate — and the University of Maryland Hospital, and each is proud of its distinguished heritage.

The growth of the Baltimore campus is a multifaceted story of pioneering efforts. From the founding of the medical college in 1807 to the establishment of the School of Social Work in 1961, the campus has been the site of many historical firsts.

The College of Medicine was originally established as a private institution in 1807, though the Medical College building was not erected until 1812. Renamed "Davidge Hall," in honor of John Beale Davidge, first dean of medicine, the building remains today the oldest medical school building in the country used continuously for medical education. The university's medical school is also the first in the country to build its own hospital for clinical instruction. The Baltimore Infirmary, forerunner of The University of Maryland Hospital, was founded in 1823. Excellence in teaching and research today forms the basis of the hospital's patient care program. Licensed now for 864 beds, the hospital is also the site of the internationally celebrated Shock Trauma Center of the Maryland Institute for Emergency Medical Services Systems, the Intensive Care NeoNatal Center, the Baltimore Cancer Research Program, and the National Institute for Sudden Infant Death Syndrome.

The curriculum at the University of Maryland School of Law includes many subjects covered by David Hoffman, Maryland's first professor of law. In 1812, a law faculty was added to the College of Medicine, though the Maryland Law Institute did not begin classes until 1824. Interestingly, the School of Law's emphasis on moot court has not changed since Hoffman established this technique. Today, the School of Law is stronger and more active than at any time in its history.

The first American lectures on dentistry were delivered at the School of Medicine by Dr. Horace Hayden. When the College of Dental Surgery opened in 1840, institutional dental education was offered for the first time in history. Baltimore is also the site of the first dental infirmary for clinical practice.

The School of Pharmacy is the oldest pharmacy school in the South. Incorporated in 1841 as the Maryland Col-

lege of Pharmacy, lectures were first given in a small office behind a drugstore. Pharmacy lectures were held in Davidge Hall as early as 1844, though the college was not directly affiliated with the university until 1924. In 1920, the University of Maryland (Baltimore) merged with the Maryland State College (College Park), and the combined institutions became the University of Maryland and the Department of Pharmacy became the School of Pharmacy.

The School of Nursing became an autonomous unit in 1952. Originally known as the Maryland Training School, it was established in 1889 under the direction of Louisa Parsons. Miss Parsons was a graduate of the first "modern" school of nursing founded by Florence Nightingale. She brought with her the pattern for the Nightingale cap (a white-fluted cap made of point d'esprit lace), which remains the Maryland School of Nursing cap today.

Currently recognized as one of the largest in the world, the School of Social Work and Community Planning is the youngest of the professional schools, established at the university in 1961. Today the faculty of this school is the largest, full-time, social work faculty in the world, and Maryland is considered an innovator in social work education.

The building of the University of Maryland at Baltimore is a multifaceted story of pioneering efforts. Currently undergoing architectural renovation is Davidge Hall, which remains today the oldest medical school building in the country used continuously for medical teaching purposes

United States
Fidelity & Guaranty Company

Left:
John R. Bland was the president and prophetic founder of USF&G in 1896

Far Left:
This building at Calvert and Redwood Streets served as USF&G's home office between 1906 and 1974

I t all began in a five-story warehouse building in Baltimore in 1896. A persistent and daring man had an idea for proper credit and collection facilities. The man, John R. Bland, founded the United States Fidelity and Guaranty Company, the largest and third oldest insurance company in Maryland. His idea seemed simple: to provide mercantile houses with a list of attorneys who were bonded by a surety company. For the next twenty-seven years, until his death in 1923, Mr. Bland's idea formed a vast network across the country.

John R. Bland was a keen judge of manpower. He personally surveyed the appointment of agents, for he knew their professionalism would be a worthy credit to USF&G's reputation. The first critical agency appointments initiated a tradition of personal concern and attention that has continued to strengthen and support the company's structure. Many of the agencies have long-standing, continuous relationships with the company amounting to seventy-five or more years.

John R. Bland believed in growth, and it came faster than he expected. From one humble office in Baltimore, the company was already feeling the pinch of tight quarters by the time of the Great Baltimore Fire in 1904. After temporary residence in an old church, the firm was ready to occupy its new home office in 1906 on the same site as the former office at Calvert and Redwood Streets. Several years later it was necessary to build again. The need for

more efficient space would continue well into the century.

The outward signs of growth were a clue of what was going on inside the company. From surety, its original business, to writing burglary insurance in 1900 and casualty in 1910, the business mushroomed. By 1919, the casualty business was easily double that of the bonding lines.

The company's financial base continued to solidify also. When the Great Depression struck, most companies had to rely on something even more scarce than money: a combination of financial and business wizardry. Fortunately, E. Asbury Davis, an outstanding Baltimore businessman serving on the company's board of directors, filled the order precisely, and together with the company's internal structure, assured the company's survival. Elected chief executive officer in 1932, Davis saw USF&G through the country's greatest economic disaster and into more prosperous times.

Once the company was safely through the depression years, it could think about growth with profit once again. But it was not until after World War II that the company would return to complete normalcy. One of the most significant events for the company occurred with the acquisition of Fidelity and Guaranty Fire Insurance Company in 1952. Prior to this time, federal law did not permit the writing of all lines of insurance by a single company. The legislation changed, however, and with the merger USF&G was now classified as a multiple-lines company. And just as USF&G lost no time in gaining recognition as a leader in the surety business, it quickly became a leader among multiple-lines companies.

After Mr. Davis retired in 1955, leaving USF&G in its strongest financial position up to that time, Charles L. Phillips guided the company for the next four years. Upon

Williford Gragg is USF&G's chairman of the board and chief executive officer

Jack Moseley is president and chief administrative officer of USF&G

Right:
The spectacular USF&G skyscraper towers over Baltimore's Inner Harbor at 100 Light Street

his retirement in 1959, USF&G continued its long history of emphasizing strong agency development by electing William E. Pullen as chief executive officer. Mr. Pullen established new branches in strategic locations across the country. Under his leadership, USF&G gained recognition as the leading agency company and supporter of the American Agency System of marketing insurance, a reputation it actively maintains today. With his emphasis on continued quality growth, 6,200 independent agents in the United States and Canada now represent USF&G. Sixty-one branch offices, 150 claim and subclaim offices, five subsidiaries, and one managing general agent make USF&G the largest insurance company in Maryland as well as the largest domiciled Maryland corporation in terms of assets.

Before the 1950s were history, USF&G recorded another milestone in its record of growth: the formation of Fidelity and Guaranty Life Insurance Company in December 1959. And in 1962, the company would acquire the New York-based Merchants Fire Assurance Corporation and the Merchants Indemnity Corporation. In January 1966, a complete merger of the companies into USF&G was approved.

Perhaps the most dramatic events in USF&G's history have occurred in the late 1960s and 1970s. Under the leadership of Walter J. Jeffery, then chief executive officer, growth was continued to the point that construction of a new home office building, which would centralize operations and make for more efficient utilization of space and energy requirements, became necessary. The company at that time owned and occupied a total of eight buildings, including the original 1906 home office. USF&G was the first company to affirm its faith in the ultimate success of the Inner Harbor Project. USF&G is credited for anchoring the project and insuring that there would be more than theory and blueprints to Baltimore's future. Yet, as the spectacular new Inner Harbor building reached for new heights, the insurance industry sank to new depths. At least one major and many smaller insurance companies were experiencing the threat of bankruptcy when USF&G completed its move to the 40-story tower in 1974.

Property and casualty insurance experienced a devastating combination of very large underwriting losses at exactly the same time that a major recession was gripping the country. Along with the normal recessionary problems

faced by all businesses, the insurance industry was buffeted by extraordinarily large reductions in capital funds as a result of sharp declines in stock market investments. In fact, the company's surplus declined over a 21-month period by an average of $1 million per day.

Fortunately, again, the company had a strong leader at the helm. Williford Gragg, elected chief executive officer in 1972, provided the responsive leadership required by the conditions. That leadership, combined with a sound and capable organization of employees and agents, brought the company through a crisis of the same magnitude as the Great Depression.

More significantly, the company was soon to experience unprecedented years of growth and profit. For 1978, Mr. Gragg reported that USF&G had the highest underwriting profits of any stock insurance company. And, as of June 1979, total assets stood at $3,399,576,000, the highest ever.

As the company nears its 100th anniversary, it faces a legion of complex and formidable challenges from both inside and outside of the industry. As federal and state regulatory pressures intensify, unpredictable economic vicissitudes hover on the horizon, demands of the technological age grow more acute, and litigation increases, John R. Bland's philosophies have never been more applicable, nor more requisite. His blend of courage, drive, and uncompromising standards of performance made his business career something of a legend, especially in Baltimore's business circle.

The Vinegar Works

Left:
The Vinegar Works began production as the old Melvale Distillery in the 1860s. This early advertisement illustrates the plant as it appeared at the turn of the century. From the collection of the Enoch Pratt Free Library

F ort McHenry . . . America's first Washington Monument . . . the famous marble stoops . . . the Battle Monument . . . all are universally known landmarks of Baltimore.

But what about the Vinegar Works?

It, too, is a part of Baltimore history. What's more, it fulfills its historic role today while actively serving a function it has performed for more than half of its more than 100 years of existence.

The Vinegar Works — officially the Baltimore Vinegar Plant of Standard Brands Incorporated — stands on Cold Spring Lane near Falls Road. It began life in the 1860s as the old Melvale Distillery and has been owned and carefully maintained by Standard Brands since 1956.

Originally used for distilling Maryland rye whiskey, the building today houses a modern vinegar manufacturing operation, supplying makers of mayonnaise, salad dressing, ketchup, mustard, and pickles throughout the eastern United States. Most of our pantry shelves are stocked with condiments made from this Baltimore vinegar. The change from making whiskey to making vinegar occurred during Prohibition, but the Vinegar Works had an interesting past even before then. Built as part of the Rural Merchant Mill complex, it was begun, records indicate, between 1862 and 1872. Architecturally, the stone structure recalls the time when the Italian influence was strong in the Jones Falls Valley. Other buildings of similar style are still standing farther south along the Falls. Their wide roof projections with bracketing, arched windows, and square cupolas mark them as typical rural industrial structures and tell us much about the tastes of the period.

John Gambrill was an early owner of this property. His family, long associated with milling, was also prominent in the cotton industry in Hampden and Woodberry. During Gambrill's ownership, the Northern Central Railroad tracks were laid across part of the property, running along the west bank of the Jones Falls and crossing a bridge just north of the mill. This bridge assumed strategic importance during the Civil War when Union Troops and sup-

plies were transported along the line into Baltimore. On April 20, 1861, a group of Southern sympathizers set the bridge afire, leading the Union Army to station a company of troops on the site to guard against further sabotage.

The Gambrills later sold the mill to William Denmead, who established the Melvale Distillery Company. He and subsequent owners operated a commercial rye whiskey plant which produced "a manufactured whiskey distilled from the highest grade rye . . . its pronounced high flavor, character, and bouquet mak(ing) it most desirable for medicinal and other purposes," according to a 1914 advertisement.

Prohibition brought about the change of the plant to a United States government-bonded warehouse manufacturing and distributing spirits under strict federal supervision. In 1928, William A. Boykin, Jr., acquired the distillery and converted it to the production of vinegar. Standard Brands purchased this business from Boykin in 1956.

Although modern manufacturing methods have done away with the pungent odor which neighbors used to associate with The Vinegar Works, it is still very much a going business and a living part of the history of Baltimore.

Left:
Vinegar from this storage and process area is used in the preparation of many of the condiments which complement meals throughout the eastern United States

Below:
Once a part of the Rural Merchant Mill complex, this historic stone structure on Cold Spring Lane today houses the Baltimore Vinegar Plant of Standard Brands Incorporated

Von Paris
Moving and Storage

When Eligius von Paris emigrated to the United States from Germany in the late 1870s, he did not know that his family's progress would one day "read like the pages of a fine historical novel." Yet a grandson of the firm's founder, on the seventy-fifth anniversary year of von Paris Moving & Storage, would write a company history that related a classic example of the "American Dream."

When Eligius von Paris settled in east Baltimore, he worked for the brewing industry and was a member and organizer of the Brewery Workers Guild, once serving as president. Because his fellow workers moved frequently from one brewery to another and moved their families with them, Eligius decided to start a small moving business for household goods and local contractors.

He purchased a team of horses, two dump carts, and a double team wagon and located the new business at 3325 Foster Avenue, which was also his home. Moving household goods was, at first, an infrequent occurrence. Von Paris derived most of his income from his "cart contracting" business, moving clay, building materials, and ice.

At age twelve, Eligius's eldest son, Bonaventure, went to work for his father, and, by 1904, von Paris and Son had become movers of household goods exclusively. Bonaventure, eager to explore "up-to-date methods of moving and storage," spent 1904 and 1905 in New York City, where he learned the latest techniques in moving, rigging, and storage; he returned to his father's business to apply his newly acquired skills.

In 1907, von Paris & Son conducted their first "long-distance" household move. Two wagon loads with double teams traversed the distance from Baltimore to Washington, D.C., in just two days. When Eligius's health failed, Bonaventure purchased wagons and horses and continued business at Foster Avenue until 1909. Then, with his new bride, Theresa, he moved to a newly purchased three-story building at 400 First Street (later Highland Avenue).

The company acquired its first motor van by early 1915. Referred to as the "house on wheels" by the community, it was featured in the 1915 Baltimore Auto Show. The von Paris operation became completely motorized by 1919, as Bonaventure pioneered long-distance moving in the Middle Atlantic states.

Through the family's determined efforts, the company survived the Great Depression. Four of five von Paris sons

joined the firm during the 1930s and 1940s. The youngest member followed in the capacity of legal advisor in 1959. Daughters participated also, following the tradition established by Theresa von Paris, who had managed the office as well as nine children.

B. von Paris and Sons was incorporated in Maryland in 1947, with the senior Bonaventure serving as chairman and the junior Bonaventure elected as president. The firm continued an impressive record of growth, and in 1954 a new terminal was established at Erdman Avenue.

The 1960s was a decade of expansion for von Paris operations. In 1961, the firm acquired an established local competitor, Hampden Moving and Storage, and also became an affiliate of North American Van Lines. By 1962, a new warehouse and office facility opened at Erdman Avenue to meet the development of container operations. B. von Paris and Sons, Inc., received certification for moving household goods by air, domestically and internationally in 1964, and in 1965, von Paris established corporate headquarters and new warehouse facilities in Timonium, Maryland. These facilities were later expanded and are among the finest in the country.

The year 1976 saw continued expansion with the acquisition of Potomac North American, a Washington, D.C., moving and storage business. Today, fourth and fifth generations of the von Paris family and nonfamily members whose long association with the firm has earned them family status, continue the tradition of "movers with the gentle touch," the company's motto since 1892.

W.C. Pinkard & Co., Inc.

Left:
Walter Clyde Pinkard opened the
real estate company which bears
his name in 1922
Right:
Walter D. Pinkard, Sr., currently
serving as chairman of the board
and chief executive officer of W.C.
Pinkard & Co., Inc., joined his
father's firm in 1945

In 1922, Walter Clyde Pinkard opened a small real estate office in Baltimore at 12 East Lexington Street, concentrating on rural and residential real estate. In those days Baltimore did not include extensive suburbs, and much of the land bordering the city consisted of rural estates.

During the difficult depression years, Pinkard served as agent for Penn Mutual Life Insurance Co. and in this capacity was responsible for running "Kernan's $1,000,-000 Enterprise" — the Maryland Theater, the Auditorium Theater, and Kernan's Hotel. He eventually negotiated the sale of these properties, which had fallen victim to the demise of vaudeville. The Auditorium Theater is now the Mayfair, and the Congress Hotel was once part of the Kernan theatrical empire.

Pinkard is remembered for assisting with the formation of the Governmental Efficiency and Economic Commission, which flourished under Baltimore's Mayor Jackson. Highly regarded by the professional real estate community, Pinkard served as president of the Real Estate Board of Baltimore (now the Greater Baltimore Board of Realtors) in 1940 and 1941. Through his association with this active group, he was instrumental in originating the first multiple-listing service in the area.

Walter D. Pinkard joined his father's firm in 1945, after graduating from Princeton and serving in the army during

World War II as a commissioned major in field artillery. Walter D. Pinkard soon became quite active in the Baltimore business community, serving the Junior Association of Commerce, the Mortgage Bankers Association, and the Citizen's Planning and Housing Association. In 1946, he was named a member of the board of directors of the Real Estate Board of Baltimore. He is past president and national director of the Society of Industrial Realtors, Baltimore-Washington Chapter, and currently he is chairman of the board and chief executive officer of W.C. Pinkard & Co., Inc.

With the Baltimore office under the capable management of his son, who was instrumental in focusing the firm's activities on the areas of commercial and industrial real estate, Walter C. Pinkard was able to pursue his greatest interest, rural real estate. He opened a branch office in Easton, Maryland, which was active during the 1950s and 1960s.

In 1959, Philip C. Iglehart became associated with the company and played a major role in its evolution into one of the state's leading commercial and industrial realty concerns. Mr. Iglehart was elected president of the company in 1975 and became the first non-family stockholder in the firm's history.

The present activities of W.C. Pinkard & Co., Inc., center around three areas of real estate — office buildings, shopping centers, and industrial land and buildings. The firm is also active in leasing, marketing, sales, property management, and development in each of the three areas.

Pinkard is now the largest manager of downtown office buildings, including the IBM Building, Arlington Federal Building, Sun Life Building, and the First National Bank Building (where the firm has been located since 1926). The company is also responsible for the project marketing of the new Equitable Bank Center.

In regard to shopping centers, the firm's most recent project was the development and leasing of the North Plaza Mall, one of Baltimore's ten largest shopping centers. Industrial activities include the marketing of the Baltimore-Washington Industrial Park for the Arundel Corporation and the marketing and management of more than 500,000 square feet of buildings in the Baltimore-Washington Industrial Park owned by Prudential.

In 1974, after graduating from Yale and Harvard Business School, Walter D. Pinkard, Jr., became the third generation of the Pinkard family to become associated with this well-known Baltimore real estate firm. He has been very instrumental in the company's present-day positioning as a primary force in the real estate marketplace.

The Ward Machinery Company

What happens when an enterprising gentleman builds a machine that operates three times as fast yet sells for two-thirds less than the then-best machine on the market? If he understands how to sell his machine and can locate a skilled and capable labor force to meet consumer demand, he can revolutionize an entire industry.

Today, The Ward Machinery Company in Cockeysville, Maryland, is one of the world's leading manufacturers of corrugated box machines. Leaders in the paper industry throughout the United States, Canada, South America, and Australasia use machines manufactured by The Ward Machinery Company. Licensees in Germany and Japan manufacture for the European, African, Middle East, and Far East markets, and the firm supplies more rotary die cutters to the industry than all its competitors combined.

William F. Ward, a 1940 graduate of Johns Hopkins University, worked for others for twenty years before starting his own company. He virtually grew up in the box-making machine industry in Maryland. When this talented engineer became the victim of a corporate merger in 1962, he found the time to work on his invention.

In the basement of his home in Lutherville, with just one assistant, Ward assembled his first rotary die cutter, a machine that punched out a variety of shapes in flat sheets of corrugated board. Work expanded to the carport and then to the garage behind the famed Lutherville Octagonal House next door. There, with two helpers, the first 50-by-80-inch rotary die cutter was assembled. Ward's idea had become a reality in just one year; his first industrial machine was sold to St. Regis Paper Company, and the revolution in the corrugated box industry had begun.

The Ward Die-Vise Company, as it was first known, grew to three employees and moved to a larger garage on Falls Road. A second location in Texas, Maryland, was soon acquired, and by 1964, the entire operation moved to a 13,000-square-foot building specifically designed for the manufacture of rotary die cutters. Here the first 66-by-80-inch machine was assembled. By that time, several of these novel machines were in use, and the firm's reputation had grown to international proportions.

By 1965, in addition to producing machines capable of handling larger sheets of corrugated paper, the firm introduced the first full-width, flexo-printer/die cutter. Plant expansion the following year increased floor space to 22,000 square feet. Employees now numbered sixty-five. In March 1966, The Ward Die-Vise Company acquired a portion of Flynn & Emrich engaged in the design and

manufacture of printer-slotters, and the name was changed to The Ward-Turner Machinery Company. Accompanying this acquisition was yet another plant expansion and an increase in the number of employees to ninety-five.

During this period of growth, other Ward family members joined the firm. Ward's two brothers, John and Dave, serve as vice presidents in charge of production and engineering, respectively. Virginia P. Ward, Bill's wife and business associate, initially managed all office functions single-handedly. She is now vice president and secretary of the firm and a member of the board of directors.

During the next few years, the firm introduced the most advanced in-line system of box-making machinery available in the world. Throughout the 1970s, the firm has led the industry in the transition to computer-controlled machines and has continued to expand its product lines. The firm moved to its present-day location in Cockeysville in 1969, occupying a 120,000-square-foot facility. In 1970, the company name was changed to The Ward Machinery Company. A recent $2-million expansion accommodates the firm's 360 employees. William F. Ward, Jr., who holds degrees in electrical engineering and computer science from Johns Hopkins University, was named president and chief operating officer in 1979.

Western Electric

The year was 1929. America was still in the "flapper era," as across the nation business and industry expanded, pushing the economy upward. Herbert Hoover had become the thirty-first President. In Baltimore, H.L. Mencken was writing about his town, which was celebrating its 200th birthday.

In the late 1920s, the increasing need for telephone systems necessitated a third manufacturing unit for Western Electric, the Bell System's manufacturing arm. Baltimore was selected as the site for the first Western Electric plant below the Mason-Dixon line, largely due to its status as one of the largest seaports in America.

For thirty years, Riverview Amusement Park, nestled in the southeast Baltimore area of Point Breeze, had offered city dwellers a pleasant retreat, and the razing of the park to make way for Baltimore's newest manufacturing facility marked the end of an era. Ground was broken for Western Electric's Baltimore Works in January 1929; by the following October, America and the world were rocked by the stock market crash, and the difficult years of the Great Depression followed. Yet, at a time when jobs were becoming scarce, Western Electric's new plant provided work for thousands of Baltimoreans.

Twenty million telephones were in use in 1929, and the demand for new lines and new equipment was increasing. Today the Baltimore Works is one of the largest industrial employers in the Baltimore area, with over 6,500 employees. The present plant site encompasses 168 acres

and occupies more than 2.5 million square feet of floor space. Appropriately, Western Electric adopted the name "Point Breeze" for its new Baltimore plant. In 1960, the Point Breeze Works officially changed its name to the Baltimore Works.

The first reel of telephone cable (6.4 million conductor feet) came off the Baltimore Works' production line in December 1929. Today, over 60 billion conductor feet of cable are produced at Baltimore annually. Plastic insulated cable is the prime cable product at the Works. Baltimore's Cable shop is also the only Western Electric manufacturing location making coaxial cable, wire and tape armored cable, and "squirrel-protected" cable. During the 1960s, the Baltimore plant was the sole Bell System supplier of ocean cable; more than 14,000 nautical miles of that cable were manufactured in Baltimore.

The Baltimore Works added insulated wire to its manufacturing line, and by October 1930, 30,000 pounds of wire were shipped from the plant's new Insulated Wire building. Presently, 7.9 million conductor feet of wire are produced annually. Baltimore houses the only Station and Outside Plant Wire shop within the Bell System. Here, drop wire, service wire, station wire, and armored wire, equipped with a special sheath, are manufactured.

The Baltimore Cord shop is responsible for nearly all telephone cords manufactured within the Bell System, designs, manufacturing techniques, and even new cord colors are first tested and manufactured at the Baltimore

Works. The plant manufactures cords in thirty colors, as well as clear plastic, and ships 44 million cords each year.

Millions of intricate parts are produced for the Bell System telecommunications equipment at the Baltimore Works' Loop Transmission Apparatus shop. In 1929, the apparatus organization was proudly producing between 900 and 1,000 cable terminals each day. By 1978, 660,000 cable terminals were produced in one year. Cable terminals, however, represent only one aspect of the shop's production. Approximately 2,500 different codes or pieces of apparatus are manufactured in Baltimore. These devices range in size from the miniscule to the massive and are used to terminate, splice, cross-connect, and electrically protect the cable and wire that extend from the Bell System to millions of individual homes.

The Baltimore Works was the only Western Electric location in Maryland until 1965, when the Regional Service Division Headquarters opened in Cockeysville. At this location, engineers plan new telephone systems and additions for Bell Telephone Companies in a six-state area.

Baltimore's Western Electric employees continue a long record of community service activities. In 1931, during the depths of the depression, employees pledged over $10,000 to the Community Fund. More recently, Western Electric employees pledged more than $335,000 to the United Way.

The Pioneers, telephone employees with eighteen or more years service, are also strong community assets. The Point Breeze Chapter, organized in 1963, is responsible for the Teletypewriter Program for the Deaf in Baltimore. Volunteers repair and recondition units, which are then donated to deaf citizens and institutions working with the hearing-impaired. The Pioneers also run an answering service, where teletypewriter messages are received from deaf persons transacting business. Many other community services are rendered by both the active Pioneers and the life member (retired) Pioneers.

Certainly there have been awesome changes in telecommunications since the first reel of telephone cable

was manufactured and shipped from the Baltimore facility in 1929. Today the Apparatus shop's new products make use of electronic components. In addition, modular cords now come fitted with plug-in jacks, enabling the customer to easily detach the cord from the telephone. Waterproof cable is being produced in larger sizes than ever before. Baltimore Works Wire shop engineers are designing and adding new products to the industry each year.

During World War II, in addition to the production of radar components and pilot simulators, Western Electric's Baltimore employees supported the war effort through the purchase of war bonds, with 95 percent of the work force investing more than 10 percent of their pay. Employees continue to invest in U.S. Savings Bonds through payroll deductions.

Throughout the years, the Baltimore Works has also provided financial support and assistance to many Baltimore area institutions for educational, scientific, cultural, and charitable purposes. The Baltimore Works sponsors employee memberships in civic, professional, and service organizations and is proud of its employees who are officers in leading professional and technical organizations.

The Baltimore Works has been actively associated with the Red Cross Blood Bank drives since 1958, and employee response during seasonal crises has merited Red Cross awards for the company during each year of program participation.

Concern for future leaders is best illustrated through Western Electric's involvement in the Adopt-a-School Program, sponsored by the Greater Baltimore Committee. College/Industry Cluster Program, Project GO, Junior Achievement, Project Business, IAESTE, and Operation Native Sons and Daughters are among many of Western Electric's educational involvements.

The speed of new developments in the communications industry is just beginning to gather momentum, and Western Electric's Baltimore Works looks forward to new challenges in the future.

Wm. E. Hooper & Sons Co.

When William Hooper arrived in Baltimore from Londonderry in 1800 at the age of twelve, he apprenticed for a sailmaker named Hardester and soon became his partner. This partnership was the beginning of Wm. E. Hooper & Sons, a textile company operated by six generations of the same family for 156 years.

In the early nineteenth century, Baltimore Clippers brought Baltimore worldwide fame as a shipping center. Equipping these and other vessels with sails created a large and specialized industry. After buying out his former partner in 1823, William Hooper displayed energy and determination. Arising long before daybreak, he would row out to the mouth of the Patapsco River to meet incoming ships and be the first on board to secure orders for new sails. He also became one of the city's largest purchasers of cotton, supplying the local cotton duck manufacturers and selling their product as well. His son, William E. Hooper, became president of the company in 1848, and the firm began purchasing mills in the Woodberry area of Baltimore for the manufacture of cotton duck to compete with English imports. James E. Hooper, the third generation of the family, had much to do with eliminating the evils of child labor in Baltimore, where industries commonly hired young boys and girls to work from sunrise to sunset for meager pay. Hooper was one of the first Maryland advocates of a child labor law and, in 1873, he ran for the state legislature in order to further this cause.

The company has supplied material for every American war cause since the Revolution. During World War II, the firm operated around the clock manufacturing and treating canvas for the military. One of the company's most notable achievements was the development of the first permanent outdoor canvas finish called Fire Chief, which protects fabrics against fire, water, weather, and mildew. The patent rights were given royalty-free to the U.S. government during the war years, and the Fire Chief formulas were used for all major military procurement.

In the 1960s and 1970s, with the market for wide, heavy canvas diminishing, Lawrence L. and James E. Hooper, Jr., the sixth generation of Hoopers to run the company, concentrated on the manufacture of narrow fabrics and textile specialties.

Wm. E. Hooper & Sons is the nation's largest manufacturer of wicks, which range from kerosene lamp and torch wicks to journal-box lubricator pads for railroad freight cars. The webbing and narrow fabrics supply many different markets: automotive, industrial, retail, and sport-

Top:
William Hooper, founder of the company, was a Baltimore sailmaker's apprentice in his youth

Above:
William E. Hooper, son of the founder, became president of the company in 1848. Photos courtesy the Kenneth M. Brooks Studios, Inc.

ing goods. In the early 1960s, the company purchased Massasoit Company, the oldest U.S. manufacturer of cotton waste products, including floor mops, wicking specialties, and marine caulking cotton. With a number of new products about to be launched, the Wm. E. Hooper & Sons Company faces the challenges of the future with confidence.

Wm. H. Cole & Sons, Inc.

Enoch Pratt came to Baltimore in 1831 and opened a small warehouse stocked with nails, horseshoes, and iron implements. Known as E. Pratt and Brother, this small enterprise was located at 23-25 South Charles Street.

By the early 1850s, when Maryland coal mines began producing on a commercial scale and furnaces were built to produce hardware locally, Enoch Pratt decided to concentrate his efforts in the area of wholesale iron.

Meanwhile, William Howard Cole, a 23-year-old entrepreneur, formed a partnership with James Hiss, who was associated with E. Pratt and Brother. In 1851, the two gentlemen opened a new firm "for the purpose of carrying on the American Hardware Commission business in Baltimore," which Pratt had begun.

The firm's first location was at 27-29 South Charles Street, adjacent to Pratt's new wholesale iron business. Under the leadership and guidance of William H. Cole and his descendants, the new enterprise prospered and, with the exception of a brief period following the Great Baltimore Fire of 1904, remained located within a single block of South Charles Street for the next 106 years.

In October 1957, after fire once again destroyed the place of business, the Wm. H. Cole & Sons firm, still under the direct ownership and management of family members, opened for business at 1110 Batavia Farm Road. In its newly constructed plant, it became the only wholesale hardware business in the area to operate from a one-story building. The new structure included over 40,000 square feet of warehouse space stocked with thousands of items, as well as modern air-conditioned offices.

"Since its founding the company has weathered the dislocations caused by four wars, the fire of 1904, and a half-dozen nationwide or worldwide panics and depressions." This was noted by descendants of William H. Cole in celebration of the firm's 100th anniversary in 1951. Family members expressed pride in the company's "demonstration of essential vitality as well as fitness to survive."

By the time Wm. H. Cole & Sons celebrated its 125th anniversary in 1976, the company had become a member of PRO Hardware, the largest, independently owned, voluntary chain of wholesale hardware firms in the nation.

Although modern computer technology has totally altered the operational process at Wm. H. Cole & Sons, the firm continues to work with manufacturers who have been suppliers since William H. Cole and James Hiss established their hardware commission business in 1851. Today Wm. H. Cole & Sons stocks thousands of hardware items and serves customers in Pennsylvania, Delaware, Virginia, and West Virginia, as well as Maryland.

Two years after the Great Baltimore Fire of 1904 destroyed Wm. H. Cole & Sons' place of business on South Charles Street, the firm moved to 40-44 South Charles Street, where it remained until 1956

For the first 111 years of its existence, Wm. H. Cole & Sons functioned as a partnership. Family members are justifiably proud of the fact that this long-lived company remained a functioning and viable entity for these many years on the basis of a series of gentlemen's agreements among family members. This held true with the Cole family in the nineteenth century and also with the Vander Horst family in the twentieth century. In 1962, the firm became incorporated and still remains family-owned and operated. Members of the third and fourth generations of the Cole family continue to lead the firm with a strong commitment to the values of loyalty and progressiveness that were begun in Baltimore in 1851.

Bibliography

Andrews, Matthew Page. *The Fountain Inn.* New York, Rich R. Smith, 1948.

Baker, Jean H. *Ambivalent Americans: The Know Nothing Party in Maryland.* Baltimore, The Johns Hopkins University Press, 1977.

Baker, Jean H. *The Politics of Continuity.* Baltimore, The Johns Hopkins University Press, 1973.

Barker, Charles Albro. *The Background of the Revolution in Maryland.* New Haven: Yale University Press, 1940.

Beirne, Francis F. *The Amiable Baltimoreans.* New York, Dutton, 1951.

Beirne, Francis F. *St. Paul's Parish Baltimore.* Baltimore, St. Paul's Parish, 1967.

Blum, Isidor. *The Jews of Baltimore.* Historical Review Publishing Company, Baltimore, 1910.

Bready, James H. *The Home Team.* Baltimore: Baltimore Baseball Club, 1979 (3rd ed.).

Brown, George William. *Baltimore and the Nineteenth of April, 1861.* Baltimore: N. Murray, 1887.

Browne, Gary L. *Baltimore in the Nation, 1789-1861.* Chapel Hill: University of North Carolina Press, 1980.

Bullock, James G., Jr. *A Brief History of Textile Manufacturing Along the Jones Falls.*

Coyle, Wilbur F. *The Mayors of Baltimore.* Baltimore: The Baltimore Municipal Journal, 1919.

Crooks, James B. *Politics and Progress: The Rise of Urban Progressivism in Baltimore, 1895 to 1911.* Baton Rouge: Louisiana State University Press, 1968.

Cunz, Dieter. *The Maryland Germans.* Princeton: Princeton University Press, 1948.

Dehler, Katharine B. *The Thomas-Jencks-Gladding House.* Baltimore: Bodine and Associates, 1968.

Dorsey, John, and Dilts, James D. *A Guide to Baltimore Architecture.* Cambridge, Md.: Tidewater Publishers, 1973.

Eddis, William. *Letters from America.* Ed. Aubrey C. Land. Cambridge: Harvard University Press, 1969.

Fein, Isaac M. *The Making of an American Jewish Community.* Philadelphia: The Jewish Publication Society of America, 1971.

First Records of Baltimore Town and Jones Town, 1729-1797. Mayor and City Council of Baltimore, 1905.

Griffith, Thomas W. *Annals of Baltimore.* Baltimore, 1824 (printed by William Wooddy).

Gurn, Joseph. *Charles Carroll of Carrollton, 1737-1832.* New York: P.J. Kenedy and Sons, 1932.

Hall, Clayton Colman. *Baltimore: Its History and Its People.* New York: Lewis Historical Publishing Co., 1912.

Hirschfeld, Charles. *Baltimore, 1870-1900.* Baltimore: The Johns Hopkins University Press, 1941.

Hoffman, Ronald. *A Spirit of Dissension: Economics, Politics, and The Revolution in Maryland.* Baltimore: The Johns Hopkins University Press, 1973.

Janvier, Meredith. *Baltimore in the Eighties and Nineties.* Baltimore: H.G. Roebuck and Son, 1933.

Kelly, Jacques. *Peabody Heights to Charles Village.* Baltimore: The Equitable Trust Co., 1976.

Kenny, Hamill. *The Origin and Meaning of the Indian Place Names of Maryland.* Baltimore: Waverly Press, 1961.

King, Thomson. *Consolidated of Baltimore.* Baltimore, 1950 (published by the Consolidated Gas Electric Light and Power Company of Baltimore).

Lucas, Fielding. *Picture of Baltimore.* Baltimore: A.T. Francis, printer, 1832.

Manakee, Harold R. *Indians of Early Maryland.* Baltimore: Maryland Historical Society, 1959.

—————. *Maryland in the Civil War.* Baltimore: Maryland Historical Society, 1961.

Maryland Gazette. Annapolis, 1745-   passim.

Maryland Journal and Baltimore Advertiser. Baltimore, 1773-   passim.

May, Alonzo. *May's Dramatic Encyclopedia.* Baltimore, 1904.

Owens, Hamilton. *Baltimore on the Chesapeake.* Garden City: Doubleday, Doran and Co., 1941.

Papenfuse, Edward C., et al. *Maryland: A New Guide to the Old Line State*. Baltimore: The Johns Hopkins University Press, 1976.

Quarles, Benjamin. *The Negro in the American Revolution*. New York: Norton, 1961.

Renzulli, L. Marx, Jr. *Maryland: The Federalist Years*. Rutherford, New Jersey: Fairleigh Dickinson University Press, 1972.

Scharf, J. Thomas. *The Chronicles of Baltimore*. Baltimore: Turnbull Brothers, 1874.

_____. *History of Baltimore City and County*. Philadelphia: Louis H. Everts, 1881.

Semmes, Raphael. *Captains and Mariners of Early Maryland*. Baltimore: Johns Hopkins University Press, 1931.

Shivers, Frank. *Bolton Hill*. Baltimore: The Equitable Trust Co., 1978.

Sioussat, Annie Leakin. *Old Baltimore*. New York: MacMillan, 1931.

Skaggs, David Curtis. *Roots of Maryland Democracy 1753-1776*. Westport, Conn.: Greenwood Press, 1973.

Skidmore, Howard. *The Story So Far, Sesquicentennial of the Baltimore and Ohio Railroad, 1827-1977*. Baltimore, 1977.

Smith, Ellen Hart. *Charles Carroll of Carrollton*. New York: Russell and Russell, 1942.

Stevens, Barbara M. *Homeland: History and Heritage*. Baltimore, 1976.

Sunpapers. Baltimore, passim.

Thom, Helen Hopkins. *Johns Hopkins: A Silhouette*. Baltimore: Johns Hopkins University Press, 1929.

Wagandt, Charles Lewis. *The Mighty Revolution: Negro Emancipation in Maryland, 1862-1864*. Baltimore: The Johns Hopkins University Press, 1964.

Walsh, Richard, and Lloyd Fox, William. *Maryland: A History, 1632-1974*. Baltimore: Maryland Historical Society, 1974.

Williams, Harold A. *History of the Hibernian Society of Baltimore, 1803-1957*. Baltimore: Hibernian Society of Baltimore, 1957.

Wright, James M. *The Free Negro in Maryland, 1634-1860*. New York: Octagon Books, 1971 (1st ed., 1921).

The following articles from the *Maryland Historical Magazine* were especially helpful:

Arnold, Joseph L. "The Last of the Good Old Days: Politics in Baltimore, 1920-1950." Fall, 1976, pp. 443-448.

Arnold, Joseph L. "Suburban Growth and Municipal Annexation in Baltimore, 1745-1918." June, 1978, pp. 109-128.

Bridner, Elwood L., Jr. "The Fugitive Slaves of Maryland." Spring, 1971, pp. 33-50.

Bruns, Roger and William Fraley. "'Old Gunny': Abolitionist in a Slave City." Winter, 1973, pp. 369-382.

Curl, Donald Walter. "The Baltimore Convention of The Constitutional Union Party." Fall, 1972, pp. 254-277.

Della, M. Ray, Jr. "The Problems of Negro Labor in the 1850s." Spring, 1971, pp. 14-32.

Gardner, Bettye. "Ante-Bellum Black Education in Baltimore." Fall, 1976, pp. 360-366.

Gardner, John H., Jr. "Presbyterians of Old Baltimore." September, 1940, pp. 244-255.

Garonzik, Joseph. "The Racial and Ethnic Make-Up of Baltimore Neighborhoods, 1850-70." Fall, 1976, pp. 392-402.

Greeman, Betty Dix. "The Democratic Convention of 1860: Prelude to Secession." Fall, 1972, pp. 225-253.

Hoyt, William D., Jr. "Logs and Papers of Baltimore Privateers, 1812-1815." June, 1939, p. 165ff.

Kimberly, Charles M. "The Depression in Maryland: The Failure of Voluntarism." Summer, 1975, pp. 189-202.

Muller, Edward K., and Groves, Paul A. "The Changing Location of the Clothing Industry: A Link to the Social Geography of Baltimore in the 19th Century." Fall, 1976, pp. 403-427.

Norfleet, Fillmore (ed.). "Baltimore As Seen By Moreau de Saint-Méry in 1794." September, 1940, pp. 221-240.

Pancake, John S. "Baltimore and the Embargo: 1807-1809." Fall, 1952, pp. 173-187.

Putney, Martha. "The Baltimore Normal School for the Education of Colored Teachers: Its Founders and Its Founding." Summer, 1977, pp. 238-252.

Ridgway, Whitman H. "McCulloch vs. the Jacksonians: Patronage and Politics in Maryland." Winter, 1975, pp. 350-362.

Ritchey, David. "The Baltimore Theater and the Yellow Fever Epidemic." Fall, 1972, pp. 298-301.

Roseboom, Eugene H. "Baltimore As a National Nominating Convention City." Fall, 1972, pp. 215-224.

Stopak, Aaron. "The Maryland State Colonization Society: Independent State Action in the Colonization Movement." September, 1968, pp. 275-298.

Sullivan, David K. "William Lloyd Garrison in Baltimore, 1829-1830." Spring, 1973, pp. 64-79.

Thomas, Bettye C. "Public Education and Black Protest in Baltimore, 1865-1900." Fall, 1976, pp. 381-391.

Wheeler, William Bruce. "The Baltimore Jeffersonians, 1788-1800: A Profile of Intra-Factional Conflict." Summer, 1971, pp. 153-168.

Index

Illustration Credits

Baltimore Afro-American: 183 top left, 195 center, 195 bottom, 201 top, 207 top, 209 bottom

Baltimore and Ohio Railroad Museum: 82 left, 82 right, 83 right, 83 bottom, 118, 119, 147 bottom, 151, 155, 157 bottom, 159 top, 175 center, 205 bottom

Baltimore Hebrew Congregation: 187 bottom right

Baltimore Neighborhood Heritage Project: 153 bottom, 183 bottom, 189 bottom left

Baltimore News American: 183 top left, 207 bottom left, 209 bottom

Baltimore Orioles: 209 top

Baltimore Public Schools: 165 left, 177 bottom right

Baltimore Sunpapers: 87 bottom left, 159 bottom, 161 left, 167 top right, 177 left, 187 bottom left, 195 top left, 197 top, 197 left, 199, 201 bottom, 205 top, 207 top, 207 bottom right, 210, 211 top left, 211 top right, 211 center, 213 top, 213 bottom

Blackstone Studios, Inc.: 189 top

Bragg, Arthur: 166

Bryn Mawr School: 141 top

Cummings, Harry Jr. and Louise Dorcas, daughter of Harry Cummings: 167 top left, 167 top center, 169 top left, 169 top right

Ehlers, Brenda: 187 center

Enoch Pratt Free Library: 9, 21 top, 21 bottom, 37 right, 41 left, 41 right, 55 bottom right, 61 top right, 61 bottom right, 71 bottom, 83 left, 91 bottom, 109, 111, 121 top, 121 center, 125 top, 133 bottom, 135 top right, 137 top right, 165 right, 191 bottom left, 191 bottom right

Goucher College: 183 top right

Hughes Company: 133 top left

Jaramillo, Alain: 187 top, 211 bottom, 213 center, Chapter 6 color photos

Johns Hopkins University Archives: 139 top, 139 center, 139 bottom

Lemon, Jessie Fitzgerald: 200

Library Company of the Baltimore Bar: 87 bottom right

Maryland Historical Society: Frontispiece vi, 3 top, 3 center, 3 bottom, 5 top right, 5 top left, 5 bottom right, 5 bottom left, 7 top, 7 center, 7 bottom, 11 top, 11 bottom left, 11 bottom right, 13, 14, 15, 17, 19 left, 19 center, 19 right, 23 top left, 23 top right, 23 bottom, 25 top, 25 bottom left, 25 bottom right, 26 top, 26 bottom, 27, 29, 30, 33 top, 33 bottom, 35, 37 left, 41 bottom, 41 right, 43 top left, 43 center left, 43 bottom left, 43 right, 45 left, 45 top right, 45 bottom right, 47 top, 47 bottom, 49 top, 53 left, 53 right, 55 top, 57 top, 57 bottom left, 59 bottom, 59 top right, 59 center, 67 top right, 70 bottom, 71 top, 71 center, 72, 75 top, 75 bottom, 77 left, 79 bottom, 81, 85, 87 top, 89, 91 top, 93 bottom, 95 top, 95 bottom left, 95 bottom right, 97, 99 top, 99 bottom, 101, 102, 103, 107, 115 top, 121 bottom, 125 bottom, 126, 128, 129 top, 129 bottom, 130, 131 top, 131 center, 131 bottom, 133 top right, 135 bottom, 137 top left, 137 bottom, 141 bottom left, 141 bottom right, 143 top, 143 bottom, 145 top, 147 top left, 147 top right, 149 top, 150 top, 152 top, 154, 161 right, 175 top, 175 bottom, 178, 180, 185, 189 center, 191 top, 193, 203 top, 203 bottom right, 203 bottom left

Merricken, Leroy: 197 right

Peale Museum: 21 center, 115 bottom, 123 bottom, 157 top

University of Maryland, Baltimore County: 149 bottom right, 150 bottom, 163, 179 top, 179 center

University of Maryland Medical School: 55 bottom left

Waldek, Alfred: 153, 189 bottom right

Young, Raymond: 61 left, 63 top, 167 bottom